INTERPERSONAL COMMUNICATION

SARAH TRENHOLM
Ithaca College
ARTHUR JENSEN
Fairfield University

WADSWORTH PUBLISHING COMPANY
Belmont, California
A Division of Wadsworth, Inc.

COMMUNICATION EDITOR: Kristine M. Clerkin
PRODUCTION EDITOR: Leland Moss
DESIGNER: MaryEllen Podgorski
PRINT BUYER: Barbara Britton
ART EDITOR: Toni Haskell
COPY EDITOR: Anne Montague
TECHNICAL ILLUSTRATOR: Valerie Felts
COMPOSITOR: Thompson Type
COVER PHOTOGRAPH: Don Ivers/Jeroboam, Inc.
SIGNING REPRESENTATIVE: Dawn Beke

Printed in the United States of America   34

1 2 3 4 5 6 7 8 9 10—92 91 90 89 88

Library of Congress Cataloging-in-Publication Data
Trenholm, Sarah, 1944–
 Interpersonal communication.

 Bibliography: p.
 Includes index.
 1. Interpersonal communication.   I. Jensen, Arthur, 1954–   . II. Title.
 BF637.C45T72   1988   158'.2   87-10630
 ISBN 0-534-08268-8

CONTENTS
IN BRIEF

CONTENTS

CHAPTER EIGHT

AFFECTING OTHERS: SENDING RELATIONAL MESSAGES 178

CHAPTER NINE

AFFECTING OTHERS: INTERPERSONAL INFLUENCE 202

PART III

RELATIONAL CONTEXTS 231

CHAPTER TEN

FAMILY INTERACTION PATTERNS 232

REPAIRING RELATIONSHIPS: CONFLICT MANAGEMENT AND LISTENING 322

PREFACE

LFRED NORTH WHITEHEAD once said, "It requires a very unusual mind to undertake the analysis of the obvious." Interpersonal communication *is* obvious—we do it every day and we take the process for granted. Our goal in writing this book was to encourage you to see through the obvious, to question "common sense," and to think more critically about the way we communicate.

We ask you to keep two themes in mind as you read this text. First, we want you to remember that interpersonal communication involves a genuine two-way process—conversations and relationships are always the products of two people, simultaneously sending and receiving messages. For stylistic and organizational purposes, we will sometimes discuss message making as if the sender had more or less complete control of the process. Of course, it is not that simple. Communication is *transactional*—that is, the effects of messages depend on the action of one party and the reaction of the other. We can never fully predict the outcome of communication, because we don't always know how parties will interpret and react to each other's messages.

Second, we want you to make yourself an "active" reader rather than a "passive" one. Read this text critically, keeping in mind that

even scholars don't always agree with each other's theories. We honestly believe that the more you "talk back to the text," the more you will learn.

The text is divided into three parts. Part One introduces you to the field of speech communication. In Chapter 1, we define communication, discuss its importance, and talk about some of the things we think it takes to be a competent communicator. In Chapter 2, we focus more specifically on interpersonal communication, explaining what it means to form interpersonal bonds.

Part Two looks at the basic processes behind communication competence. In Chapter 3, we discuss the relationship between perception and successful communication. Chapters 4 and 5 focus on how our social and individual identities are formed and how they affect interactions. Nonverbal and verbal codes are the topics of Chapters 6 and 7, while Chapter 8 looks at the way we use these codes to send relational messages. Finally, Chapter 9 covers interpersonal influence processes.

In Part Three, we show how communication principles are manifested in various contexts. Chapter 10 discusses interpersonal communication in the family. Chapter 11 looks at the way intimate relationships work, while Chapter 12 examines professional relationships.

Finally, we end with a discussion of some of the skills needed to become more competent in all contexts.

Throughout the text you will find boxed materials. These contain interesting and unusual applications of communication principles. Drawn from the fields of anthropology, ethology, history, psychology, philosophy, education, linguistics, popular culture, and the like, they demonstrate that communication occurs in many different contexts. We've included them not only because we think they're interesting, but because they give you sources for additional reading and study.

At the end of each chapter, you'll find a section called "Process to Performance." This section is full of suggestions about how to improve your communication skills. Your instructor may ask you to do some of the exercises or may assign papers based on the observation guides. Even if they are not required, you may want to read through this section. It can guide you in becoming more sensitive to the interaction around you.

We hope that reading this book will open your eyes to a whole new world of interaction. While you've communicated your entire life, you've probably never really seen communication. Most people don't take time to observe and analyze familiar, everyday activities. When they do, they are often amazed at their richness and complexity. We believe that after reading this book, you will never again dismiss communication as uninteresting or commonplace. You'll have the tools to observe context and increase competence.

Finally, we want to thank all of the people who contributed insights, examples, and constructive comments about the earlier drafts of this text. Our initial thanks goes to Kristine

Clerkin, our editor at Wadsworth Publishing Company, for giving us free rein to develop the text in ways that were important to us, while still providing considerable options and valuable feedback. She was also responsible for choosing a group of very hard-working reviewers, whose detailed comments and suggested revisions helped shape the text in immeasurable ways. Our thanks to Kenneth Cissna, University of South Florida; Lawrence W. Hugenberg, Youngstown State University; Sandra Metts, Illinois State University; Martha W. Moore, Murray State University; Charles Petrie, SUNY-Buffalo; Karyn Rybacki, Northern Michigan University; and Ralph Smith, Southwest Missouri State University. In some cases, we plodded on in spite of reviewers' suggestions and for that, and any other shortcomings of the text, the authors are fully responsible. In addition, we'd like to thank all of our students and colleagues at Ithaca College. Our students were the first sources of feedback on many of the ideas presented here. The faculty and staff of the Department of Speech Communication helped produce this text in ways that even they will not recognize. Their comments in the hallways, responses to our idea-testing, and examples they have shared were fertile ground for exploring interpersonal communication. Our thanks to Laurie Arliss, Jane Banks, Richard Buttny, Rosemary Deusser-Jensen, Michelle Egan, Paul Frye, John Gunning, Tom Isbell, Gus Perialas, Irene Scott, and Frank Sharp. There are many others to thank—our families, our mentors and favorite authors, and our friends, who have contributed so much to our thinking. We are grateful to each of you.

SARAH TRENHOLM
ARTHUR JENSEN

PART I   **INTRODUCTORY
                              PERSPECTIVES**

CHAPTER ONE

In attempting to understand our world, we often look outward toward the remote and the exotic. Everyday processes, however, are equally fascinating and complex. We can discover worlds in our own behavior.

INTRODUCTION: COMMUNICATION AND COMPETENCE

Now, I do not deny, nor do I doubt, that should communication be opened, the reaction among mankind would be very strong—not because of the content of the message but simply from the fact that a message could in fact be received. Such an experience would say to us human beings, "We are not alone in the universe," And this, I think . . . might by itself quite justify any expenditures made in the search for extraterrestrial intelligence.[1]

—W. H. McNeill

Only a few years ago, the idea that people might one day communicate with extraterrestrials seemed ridiculous. Those who believed it possible were considered to be, at best, misguided, and, at worst, lunatics. Nowadays, however, some very high-powered astrophysicists are taking the idea seriously. They are convinced that communication with alien intelligence may one day be possible.[2]

Think about it for a minute. Try to put yourself in the place of these scientists. Imagine that you are trying to make contact with alien beings. Remember that the beings you're trying to reach—if they exist at all—have given you no address. All you know is that they live somewhere in the vast stretches of the universe, hundreds or thousands of light years away. And even if you succeed in making contact, you still have to design an intelligible message. Despite movies like *ET* and *Close Encounters of the Third*

Kind, extraterrestrials are unlikely to respond (or even look) like any organism you have ever seen. The chances of their being able to understand human language, let alone English, are infinitesimally small. How can you be sure that aliens will recognize your communications? How will you be able to recognize theirs? What if you have already come in contact with their messages without realizing it?

In the face of all these problems, your only choice would be to do exactly what all of us do when we communicate: Rely on guesswork and faith. You would begin by assuming a desire for cooperative communication. You would then try to guess what extraterrestrials are like and how they see the world, searching for a point of similarity that would allow connection. After that, you would simply wait and hope.

Of course, the subject of this book is not interstellar communication, but a more mundane one: the way normal human beings communicate as they go about their everyday lives. We believe, though, that unusual examples help us see the commonplace in new ways.[3]

If you think about it, there are some interesting similarities between earthbound and intergalactic communication. First of all, in both cases we must resist "communicative chauvinism," the belief that everyone else thinks and acts as we do. Communication depends on

The need to overcome isolation—to make contact with others—is a fundamental reason we communicate.

sensitivity to differences and on a real desire to establish common ground. Second, people who wish to communicate must learn to "speak the same language"; they must take the time and trouble to adjust to one another. Cooperation and coordination are necessary for any kind of communication, whether it's with neighbors in the next street or in the next galaxy.

We often take interpersonal communication for granted, overlooking what an amazing process it really is. The purpose of this book is to help you see interpersonal communication in a new light. While it may not be as exotic as interstellar communication, interpersonal interaction is still a complex and fascinating process. We hope that by the time you finish this book, you'll have a better understanding of how it works.

WHAT IS COMMUNICATION?

Although communication has been written about for over 25 centuries,[4] there is still disagreement about its definition. In this section we'll look at a number of definitions of communication, offer our own, and then explore its implications.

Definitions of Communication

In 1973 Frank Dance and Carl Larson surveyed our field for definitions of communication. They found 126.[5] Even more have been formulated since then. Obviously, a process as complex as communication is hard to sum up. Each person who thinks seriously about it brings a different perspective to the task. There are many valid ways to view a process, each providing a different insight.

Before we give you a number of definitions to consider, stop and jot down your own ideas about communication. Then compare your definition with those below. Ask yourself which comes closest to your understanding of what communication is. More important, ask yourself why.

Communication is the discriminatory response of an organism to a stimulus.[6]

Communication . . . is an "effort after meaning," a creative act initiated by man in which he seeks to discriminate and organize cues so as to orient himself in his environment and satisfy his changing needs.[7]

Speech communication is a human process through which we make sense out of the world and share that sense with others.[8]

Communication: the transmission of information, ideas, emotions, skills, etc., by the use of symbols . . . .[9]

Each of these definitions attempts to explain a different part of communication. Below we offer yet another definition, not because we feel that our definition is closer to what communication *really* is, but because it helps us make some points about interpersonal interaction.

Characteristics of Communication

For us, **communication** is *the process whereby people collectively create and regulate social reality.* Let's try to understand what this definition has to say about communication by looking at each of its parts.

Communication as Process

Any object or activity can be viewed either as a thing or a process. Things are static, bound in time, and unchanging. **Processes** are moving, have no beginning and no end, and constantly change. Our first point is that communication is a process, not a thing.

The communication process is like a river: active, continuous, and flowing, never the same from one minute to the next. If we try to understand a river by analyzing a bucket of water drawn from it, we are not studying the river as a whole. The same is true of communication. Individual sentences, words, or gestures make sense only when we see them as part of an ongoing stream of events. To understand communication, we have to look at how what we do and say is connected to what others do and say. We have to view communication as an ongoing process.

Communication as Uniquely Human

The term *communication* has been used to describe the behavior of many organisms. Geneticists, for example, describe the instructions for development and growth in the DNA of cells as a kind of communication. Physiologists use the term to describe how the body maintains and regulates itself. Biologists see all kinds of animal behavior as communication, including the distress signals of birds, the courtship ritual of jumping spiders, the use of threat displays by Siamese fighting fish, and the play of gorillas and baboons.[10]

The kind of communication we are interested in, however, is *human* communication.

Bonzo Goes to College: Attempts to Teach Language to Primates

Part of what we are, part of how we communicate and behave, has been inherited from our animal ancestors. But how much? What is the difference between animal and human behavior and what difference does it make? Studies of animal behavior can help answer these questions.

A number of studies have focused on whether primates other than human beings can be taught to use "language." Since the 1950s, when an infant chimpanzee named Vicki was adopted by a human family and taught four human words, a number of chimps have been given language lessons. Four of the most famous of these "students" were Washoe and Nim Chimsky (who were instructed in the use of American sign language); Sarah (who was taught to manipulate magnetized plastic tokens); and Lana (a computer-trained chimp). The results of these experiments have led most people to revise their ideas about the nature of the boundaries between human and animal thought.

All of the chimps learned to associate arbitrary signs with physical referents. They could recognize symbols for such objects as bananas, monkey chow, and cola. They could also use symbols to ask for rewards from their keepers. Washoe, for example, could ask her trainer to tickle her, and Lana could type on her console, "Start pour coke stop" to activate a soft-drink dispenser.

The chimps were also capable of more abstract tasks. Sarah, for example, learned to use the tokens symbolizing *same* and *different* in very sophisticated ways. She was able to solve simple visual analogies. For example, if asked whether an apple and a knife were the same as a piece of paper and scissors, she would indicate that they were. When the scissors was replaced with a bowl of water, she would indicate that the sets were now different. She also seemed able to recognize the class to which tokens belonged. Thus when given the token "banana" and asked whether it was a name or a color, she would correctly identify it as a name. Similarly she would label the "yellow" token as a color.

Just what can we make of these achievements? The chimps were able to recognize the communicative function of symbols and make simple associations between these symbols and objects

---

We believe that people communicate in unique and powerful ways, quite different from those used by other animals. Although there have been several recent attempts to teach higher primates to use human communication codes, results of these studies are inconclusive. Box 1.1 summarizes some of the research on this subject.

Most everyone will agree that only people use language naturally and spontaneously, giving us a flexibility and creativity denied to all other creatures. Of course, as Aldous Huxley pointed out, this power is not always to our advantage.

For evil, then, as well as for good, words make us the human beings we actually are. Deprived of language, we should be as dogs or monkeys. Possessing language, we are men and women able to persevere in crime no less than in heroic virtue, capable of intellectual achievements beyond the scope of any animal, but at the same time capable of systematic silliness and stupidity such as no dumb beast could ever dream of.[11]

Communication as Collective Activity

All languages depend on social agreement for their meaning. This brings us to the next part

in much the same way young human children do when they begin to learn language. However, the chimps never learned to link symbols together into complex "sentences." Although they used language to gain immediate goals, they showed no interest in using it to comment on the world. The ability to make up stories, which develops very early in human children, was absent.

Chimps also did not exhibit linguistic creativity, nor did they use language to direct their activities, as human children do when they guide themselves through a task by talking out loud. Finally, they never spontaneously developed a language of their own. As Stephen Walker points out, "In a state of nature, we expect humans to talk, and, by comparison, the most unrelenting efforts to induce our closest living relatives to reveal hidden linguistic potential have left the discontinuities [between human speech and animal communication] bloodied but unbowed."

Source: *Stephen Walker,* Animal Thought *(London: Routledge & Kegan Paul, 1983).*

ADDITIONAL READINGS

Gardner, Beatrice T., and R. Allen Gardner. "Two-Way Communication with an Infant Chimpanzee." In *Behavior of Nonhuman Primates*, Vol. 4, edited by Allan Martin Scheier and Fred Stollnitz, pp. 117–83. New York: Academic Press, 1971. (Washoe.)

Hayes, Keith J., and Catharine Hayes. "The Intellectual Development of a Home-Raised Chimpanzee." *Proceedings of the American Philosophical Society* 95 (1951): 105–9. (Vicki.)

Premack, David. *Intelligence in Ape and Man.* Hillsdale, N.J.: Lawrence Erlbaum, 1976. (Sarah.)

Rumbaugh, Duane M., ed. *Language Learning by a Chimpanzee: The LANA Project.* New York: Academic Press, 1977. (Lana.)

of our definition: Communication is *collective*. The relationship between human society and human communication is circular; one could not exist without the other. On the one hand, what holds a society together is the ability of its members to act as a coordinated whole, which would be impossible without communication. On the other hand, communication presupposes social cooperation; interpersonal communication cannot occur unless at least two people mutually engage in creating meaning.

Joost Meerloo tells us that the word *communication* comes from the Latin word *munia*, meaning service and connoting "mutual help, exchange, and interaction of those belonging to the same community."[12] In ancient times, members of the community who were exempt from public service were referred to as having *immunity*. If an individual committed a crime so terrible that he or she was deemed no longer fit to experience things in common with the rest of society, the criminal was *excommunicated*. Meerloo explains, "Wherever the concept of communication comes into play, the emphasis is on the common sharing of material and ideological wealth, on social intercourse, mutual exchange and 'the bestowing of feelings and thoughts onto each other."[13]

We live in a world of constructed realities. Consider this ferocious warrior guardian: To us the image may seem nothing but a curious artifact, but to the people of 13th-century Japan, its significance was quite different.

Communication as Creative Endeavor

A direct result of communication is *creativity*. When we agree with others that something can be talked about, we create that thing: We cause it to exist. While some things we agree to talk about (such as books or telephones) already exist in the physical world, others (like truth or justice) exist only in the shared symbolic world created by language. This doesn't mean, however, that symbolic things don't have powerful effects on us.

Let's take the word *demon*. For most of us, this word has little reality. For many people in other parts of the world, however, demons have a real and objective existence. In Bali, for example, demons can cause illness; they can make crops fail, pigs die, and volcanoes erupt. In order to survive, the Balinese must pacify and cajole them. On the Day of Silence, for example, everyone must sit "silent and immobile all day long in order to avoid contact with a sudden influx of demons chased momentarily out of hell."[14] The Balinese live in a symbolic world that is inhabited by—among other things—demons.

Are we superior to the Balinese? Is our world any less symbolic and more real than theirs? Think for a minute about how much of what you know and believe comes to you from direct experience and how much is a product of talk. You may be surprised to find that most of your reality is created and sustained through communication.

Communication as Regulatory

Communication allows us not only to create the world around us, but to take possession of it as well. Through communication we can act on our world. In this sense, communication is *regulatory*. If you have ever come down with a bad case of laryngitis, you know how helpless you feel when you can't speak. Such a loss illustrates the connection between communication and power.

Communication allows the formation of close personal ties and a coordination of activity. (Paul Gauguin, *Breton Girls Dancing, Pont Aven*, 1888)

This connection is as old as civilization. Even today, words are associated with magic. By reciting incantations or writing an enemy's name on a piece of paper and then burning it, primitive people try to control others.[15] Even sophisticated moderns retain some superstitions about communication. One of the most common is reluctance to speak about good or bad fortune. If two friends are studying for an exam and the first asks, "What if we fail?" the other is likely to respond, "Don't even talk about something like that." We still retain vestiges of the belief that talking about something can either make it come true or jinx it.

Superstitions aside, communication is a powerful regulator of action. Through communication we can persuade, dissuade, anger, hurt, soothe, entertain, or bore one another.

We can even use communication to control our own actions, talking ourselves into taking risks or comforting ourselves when we are afraid. Communication is a powerful way of regulating and controlling our world.

Summary and Implications

All definitions have implications. What are the implications of our definition of communication? Although we see at least four, perhaps you will be able to think of more.

1.   Much of what we think of as real is actually the product of communication. This implies that there is no single reality. Instead, *through communication, we each create our own reality*. People with different communication experiences will see the world in different ways. We can never be totally sure that others see the world as we do. If we stop from time to time to check our perceptions, if we try to see things from others' perspectives, we may be surprised at how different the world looks.

2.   The fact that reality is a product of communication also has another implication. *Too often we allow what we have created through communication to control us*. When the Balinese created demons as an explanation for natural events, they put themselves in the position of spending the rest of their lives placating a concept. We too create our own kinds of demons. The expectations we have for ourselves, things like "success," "perfection," and "reputation," are examples of concepts that can control our lives and relationships.

3.   Of course, individuals are not totally free to create any reality they want. Most of us are strongly influenced by the cultures we live in. *Communication always takes place in a cultural context*. To forget this fact is to become a prisoner of culture. Erving Goffman has analyzed the powerful but unstated social rules that govern interaction.[16] Although we will have much more to say about Goffman's work

throughout this book, it might be useful to introduce you to one of his concepts now, the concept of **face**.

Goffman defines *face* as an approved social identity, what we present to others for their approval. He believes that we spend a great deal of our time trying to fit face both to situation and to self-image. Communication that is incongruent with face will be judged as socially unacceptable. For Goffman, although face may be an individual's most cherished possession, "it is only on loan to him from society; it will be withdrawn unless he conducts himself in a way that is worthy of it. Approved attributes and their relation to face make of each man his own jailer; this is a fundamental social constraint even though each man may like his cell."[17]

It is clear that many of our most personal behaviors are culturally derived. One tension we all experience is that between independence and conformity. To communicate successfully, we must conform to social rules; to act creatively, we must often oppose them. This tension will be discussed in more detail in Chapter 2.

4.   Finally, communication requires cooperation. We are influenced not only by our cultures, but by every individual we communicate with. This means that *what is important in interpersonal communication is what people do when they are together, not what each does separately*. Throughout this text we will stress the idea that interpersonal communication is mutual. In order to understand relationships, we must look at the relationship itself, not at each individual member. Most of the time we don't do this. For example, when a relationship fails, most of us try to figure out who to blame. We may blame the other person, feeling he or she is insensitive or egocentric; or we may blame ourselves, wishing we had taken more time or been less selfish. The truth is that communication is never the product of only one person. In order for relationships to work,

both parties have to take responsibility to strive to be competent communicators.

THE NATURE OF COMMUNICATIVE COMPETENCE

Communication doesn't always run smoothly. This may be one of the reasons you've decided to study interpersonal communication. If you're like most people, at some time in your life you've run into communication problems. You've probably been in situations where you couldn't think of what to say next. Or you may have been unable to express yourself clearly. Perhaps you insulted someone unintentionally or blurted out something thoughtlessly. If you've experienced any of these situations, you know how important it is to be able to communicate competently.

What, exactly, does it mean to communicate competently? We believe that **communicative competence** is *the ability to communicate in a personally effective and socially appropriate manner*. Although this definition appears simple, competence is a complex subject that has generated a lot of research and discussion. One reason is that competent communication involves two separate levels: a surface level, consisting of the part of competence that can be seen—the actual performance of day-to-day behaviors—and a deeper level, consisting of everything we have to know in order to perform. Although the surface level has many different names, we will call it **performative competence**. It is demonstrated every time someone produces effective and appropriate communication behaviors. The second, underlying level we will call **process competence**. It consists of all the cognitive activity and knowledge necessary to generate adequate performance.

For example, when you hear someone give a particularly gracious and sensitive compli-

Through competent communication we create lasting bonds. Who we become is often a function of early communicative experience. (Jean-François Millet, *The Knitting Lesson*, 1869)

ment, what you observe is only the surface level. What you cannot see is the mental activity that led up to it. Giving a compliment involves a lot of thought. It entails knowing when a compliment is appropriate and when it isn't; predicting whether the recipient will be pleased or embarrassed; choosing content that sounds sincere but not ingratiating; and knowing how to phrase the compliment in a graceful and pleasing style. All of this is part of process competence.

A Model of Communicative Competence

There are many different models of communicative competence. Some focus on performative

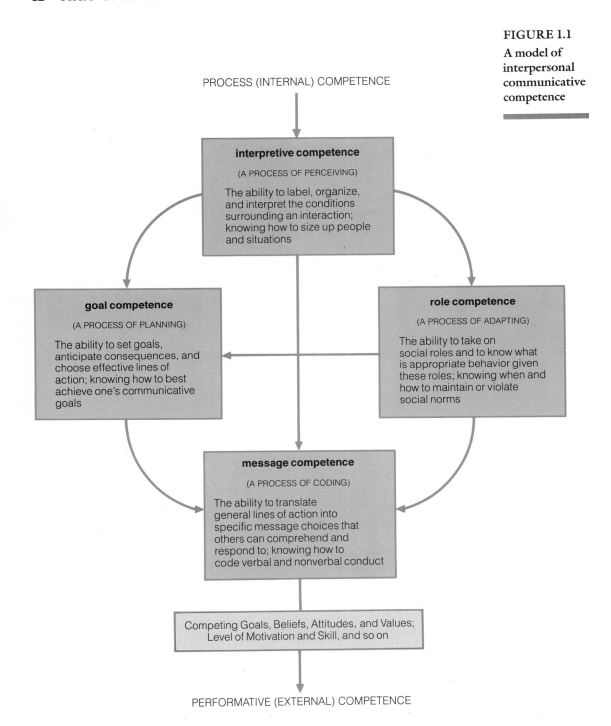

FIGURE 1.1

A model of
interpersonal
communicative
competence

PROCESS (INTERNAL) COMPETENCE

interpretive competence

(A PROCESS OF PERCEIVING)

The ability to label, organize, and interpret the conditions surrounding an interaction; knowing how to size up people and situations

goal competence

(A PROCESS OF PLANNING)

The ability to set goals, anticipate consequences, and choose effective lines of action; knowing how to best achieve one's communicative goals

role competence

(A PROCESS OF ADAPTING)

The ability to take on social roles and to know what is appropriate behavior given these roles; knowing when and how to maintain or violate social norms

message competence

(A PROCESS OF CODING)

The ability to translate general lines of action into specific message choices that others can comprehend and respond to; knowing how to code verbal and nonverbal conduct

Competing Goals, Beliefs, Attitudes, and Values; Level of Motivation and Skill, and so on

PERFORMATIVE (EXTERNAL) COMPETENCE

aspects,[18] some on process,[19] and some do a little of both.[20] The model presented in Figure 1.1 is primarily a process model. It is our way of answering the question *What does a person have to know or be able to do in order to communicate in a personally effective and socially appropriate manner?* Figure 1.1 is a representation of four of the processes we think are involved.

We believe that people who wish to be competent communicators must know how to do four things well: (1) assign meanings to the world around them; (2) set goals strategically; (3) take on social roles appropriately; and (4) generate intelligible messages. These four abilities correspond to the four types of process competence outlined in our model: interpretive competence, goal competence, role competence, and message competence.

When we say that people who wish to be competent must "know" how to do the things listed above, we're talking about implicit rather than explicit knowledge. **Implicit knowledge** is knowledge we don't stop to think about, that we use unconsciously to guide our behavior. Grammatical knowledge is a good example. From the time we are quite young we can say things in well-structured and meaningful ways. We can even recognize and correct errors when we make them. However, most children (and indeed most adults) would be hard pressed to recite the rules of grammar. The formal grammatical rules we learn in English class are attempts to express explicitly the implicit rules we follow when speaking.

The first kind of implicit knowledge we need about the world is perceptual. In order to communicate, we must be able to assign meaning to the world; we must know how to "see" it. This kind of competence we call interpretive competence. We must also be able to set communicative goals, to foresee the results of communication and make adequate plans. This we refer to as goal competence.

Next, we must adapt to the needs and expectations of others. We must know what behaviors are appropriate and expected and what are prohibited. Doing this involves us in role competence. Finally, we must be able to use all of this knowledge in actual speech situations. To do this we need message competence, the competence that allows us to express our ideas in ways other people can understand. Lack of process knowledge in any of these areas will result in poor performance at the surface level. Although we will discuss each of these types of competence separately, remember that all are interconnected and dependent on one another. And all involve us with others in the mutual activity of creating meaning.

Interpretive Competence
The first process in our model of communicative competence is perceptual. It involves **interpretive competence**: *the ability to label, organize, and interpret the conditions surrounding an interaction.* We live and communicate in a world full of diverse stimuli. Perception is more than a simple matter of recording everything that is "out there"; it is a matter of choice and interpretation. Because we would experience overload if we tried to pay attention to all of it, we must figure out what information is important.

If you have ever been in a completely unfamiliar situation, you know how difficult it can be to sort out sense impressions. First-time campers lying alone in a tent in the dead of night hear all kinds of inexplicable sounds. An experienced camper could easily classify and dismiss these stimuli. Novice campers, however, have difficulty perceiving and labeling objects; they have problems recognizing the nature of impending situations; and they often don't know how to organize their behavior. What they lack is interpretive competence.

The need to assign meanings is especially important during interpersonal interactions. In order to communicate effectively, we must reach agreement about the nature of the context in which we find ourselves as well as the kind of people we are dealing with. We also have to be able to identify our own feelings and needs. If we misinterpret our surroundings or misjudge our partners or overlook our own feelings, we may find ourselves saying things that get us into trouble.

Interpretive competence may be difficult to achieve. Through insensitivity, or lack of effort, or a desire to see only what we want to see, key information can be overlooked or underestimated. Perceptual competence helps us size up situations and people, name them, identify their outstanding characteristics, and, inevitably, decide on an attitude toward them. If we succeed at this, our transactions will have a strong base; if not, they will result in confusions and misunderstandings.

Goal Competence

A second process necessary for communicative competence is planning. This process involves **goal competence**: *the ability to set goals, anticipate probable consequences, and choose effective lines of action.* Although not all communication is intentional, a great deal involves "strategic verbal choice-making." In order to make adequate choices, a communicator must know what he or she is trying to achieve, determine the obstacles in the path of goal attainment, and find a line of action to overcome those obstacles.[21] This sequence is well known to salespeople. One of our students once worked for a large company that sold encyclopedias. During training he was given a long list of objections a prospective buyer might have. Next to each was a persuasive argument designed to overcome that objection.

If, for example, the prospect couldn't afford a set of encyclopedias, the seller was supposed to say, "Money spent on a child's education is an investment in the future." If the prospect wanted to discuss the decision with a spouse, the seller asked, "But doesn't your husband (or wife) trust you to make decisions for the children's welfare?" If the prospect pointed out that the library had plenty of books, the recommended response was, "Well, there are telephone booths on the corner, but when you want to make a call, you want to use a phone that's quick and convenient, don't you? In fact, if you had to go out every time you wanted to call, there are probably a lot of important calls you wouldn't make."

Nothing was left to chance; the company made all strategic decisions. All the trainee had to do was recite a "canned" sales presentation. Planning in real life takes a great deal more creativity and imagination. Seldom are our objectives so clear and our lines of argument so explicitly laid out; we must be able to think on our feet.

Goal competence doesn't come easily. If we can't imagine the world as others see it, if we lack empathy, we may find ourselves in trouble. We may also experience problems if our range of behaviors is limited. Some people lack alternatives. They realize that bullying or whining will only turn people against them, but these are the only tactics they know. Goal competence allows us to set goals, imagine how others will react to us, and choose messages most likely to be personally effective.

Role Competence

Because communication is a transaction, people who cannot adapt to others will not be effective communicators. Not only must individuals learn to articulate personal goals, they must learn how to achieve them in culturally approved ways. This brings us to a kind of competence we call **role competence**: *the ability to engage in appropriate role behavior.*

People who demonstrate role competence know for any given situation who it is safe for them and others to be, which constellations of behaviors are appropriate and which are off limits. When conflicting social demands arise, they know how to choose. Role-competent individuals manage to maintain a desired identity. They also know how to protect the identities of others by acting with care and consideration.

Role-competent individuals must be aware of the subtle rules governing interaction, rules that are seldom spelled out explicitly. They must be able to sense when an unstated social rule is being violated. Those who wish to navigate uncharted social waters must be sensitive to subtle danger signals.

Awareness of social rules is especially necessary when we leave the safety of our own cultures. While most of us manage to learn the norms of our own groups, we're often at a loss when we have to interact with people not brought up as we were. The individual who is snatched from his or her own environment and put down in a very different one has always been a rich source of comedy—the "fish-out-of-water" genre. Movies and plays are full of characters who are amusing because they lack role competence. The working-class heroine who suddenly finds herself in high society (*My Fair Lady*) or the time traveller who somehow ends up in a different era (*Back to the Future, The Time Machine*) are examples of characters who must somehow learn new ways of behaving. We empathize with these characters because all of us have to be able to "fit in."

It is easy to forget that norms of communication are socially controlled. Often we feel that our way of doing things is the only possible way. Throughout this book we'll try to give you examples of ways other cultures define communication competence. As an introduction, consider the description of communicative behavior given in Box 1.2. We think it will point up the fact that different cultures solve interpersonal problems in different ways.

Message Competence

No matter how sensitive and empathic we are, no matter how socially aware, if we can't code messages effectively, we won't be competent communicators. The word *code* may suggest images of spies sending secret messages, or the tapped-out dots and dashes of Morse code. These are certainly examples of codes, but so are everyday verbal and nonverbal behaviors. A **code** is any system of signs designed to allow people familiar with the system to exchange meaningful messages. **Message competence** is *the ability to translate general lines of action into specific message choices that others can comprehend and respond to.*

All of us have at least two kinds of codes at our disposal: verbal and nonverbal. In order to communicate effectively and appropriately, we must master both. We must know how to say the right thing at the right time in the right way, and we must know how to accompany what we say with appropriate behavior.

Knowing the meanings of words and how to combine them is obviously necessary for message competence, for without this knowledge, performances would be unintelligible. Schizophrenics who use language and gestures in a bizarre and individualistic way cut themselves off from normal discourse and create an impenetrable private world. Foreigners who lack vocabulary and grammar must rely on rudimentary sign language; they will be unable to convey complex ideas or desires. But knowing meanings of words and gestures isn't enough. To be truly competent, we must know how others will react to our words and gestures. We must be able to use a code to accomplish our ends.

The Link between Process and Performance

The four processes we have discussed are all necessary for good performance. Unfortunately, knowing how to communicate doesn't guarantee we will say or do the right thing.[22] A person can know perfectly well what is required in a given situation and still not perform

BOX 1.2

Insulting the Meat: An Interpersonal Communication Ritual

Cultural understandings guide virtually every aspect of our lives. They show us how to dress and move and speak. They tell us how to make friends, how to make enemies, and how to make love. They indicate what objects to hoard, what people to value, and what gods to worship. But precisely *because* they tell us so much, we often fail to realize their influence. Studying the customs of different cultures can remind us that the way we do things is not the only natural and proper way.

One example of how another culture communicates is described by Richard Lee, who studied the Dobe !Kung, the so-called Bushmen of the Kalahari. The !Kung are nomadic foragers who survive in a harsh environment by hunting and gathering. They have developed a number of rituals that have helped them adapt to this way of life. One of the most interesting is known as "insulting the meat."

In !Kung society, the wild game and edible plants gathered by members of the group are normally shared with the entire tribe. A lot of time and attention are devoted to the fair distribution of goods, particularly of meat. One way of ensuring fair distribution is demonstrated by the following communication pattern.

Strict norms govern the way a hunter announces his results when he returns from a successful hunt. He must sit in silence until someone asks him how the hunt went. He must then say that he found nothing of any worth. On the following day, when his companions go out with him to collect the kill, they are expected to do so with a minimum of enthusiasm, complaining loudly about the distance and wretchedness of the game. Instead of being offended, the hunter agrees, apologizing for his lack of skill.

What can we make of this behavior? Wouldn't it be more "natural" for a hunter to boast of a good kill? Lee tells us that the "heavy joking and derision are directed toward one goal: the leveling of potentially arrogant behavior in a successful hunter." Lee believes that "insulting the

adequately. A number of factors can cause communication to fail: individual physical states such as fatigue or anxiety; contradictory attitudes, beliefs, and values; poor motivation; or sheer stubbornness. Finally, lack of practice can cause a performance to come off as stilted and artificial.

This last point is an important one. If you want to improve your competence, you must practice communication skills until you can perform with ease. In this book, we will provide you with some of the theoretical knowledge necessary to understand the four basic processes we have discussed. Through classroom activities and by completing some of the assignments in the "Process to Performance" sections that follow each chapter, you can gain the practice necessary to put knowledge into action.

IMPROVING COMMUNICATIVE COMPETENCE: TAKING A PROCESS PERSPECTIVE

In addition to mastering knowledge and practicing skills, you can learn to take what we call a **process perspective**. This means becoming aware of what's going on when you communicate; beginning to recognize how the underlying processes involved in communication manifest themselves in everyday performance.

"meat" is a way of maintaining a sense of equality. Because the !Kung depend on sharing for survival, generosity is something that should not be praised but simply expected. Praise might lead to pride and arrogance, potential threats to the !Kung way of life. As Tomazho, one of the !Kung, expressed it:

When a young man kills much meat, he comes to think of himself as a chief or a big man, and he thinks of us as his servants or inferiors. We can't accept this. We refuse one who boasts, for someday his pride will make him kill somebody. So we always speak of his meat as worthless. In this way we cool his heart and make him gentle.

For most of us, this is a peculiar way of doing things. We believe that people should take pride in their accomplishments and show gratitude for generosity. But stop for a moment and think about the social results of concepts such as "gratitude" and "accomplishment" and "generosity." How do they affect our relationships with others? The answer to this question may make you see more clearly how seemingly innocent and trivial patterns of communication are tied to larger social issues.

Source: *Richard B. Lee,* The Dobe !Kung *(New York: Holt, Rinehart and Winston, 1984).*

ADDITIONAL READINGS

Geertz, Clifford, *The Interpretation of Cultures.* New York: Basic Books, 1973.

Spradley, James P., and David W. McCurdy, eds. *Conformity and Conflict: Readings in Cultural Anthropology,* 5th ed. Boston: Little, Brown, 1984.

Too often people communicate in a mindless kind of way. They are so busy thinking about what they're saying or doing (the content of communication) that they fail to consider how they're going about it (the form communication takes). Taking a process perspective means concentrating on form in addition to content. It means sitting back and watching yourself as you communicate.

At first this isn't easy, for it involves a kind of "double consciousness." The competent communicator must be able to act naturally and spontaneously and at the same time observe and analyze communication patterns. This is somewhat like being a good actor. On one hand, actors exist within that imaginary world of the play, reacting as their characters would. On the other hand, they remain aloof and in control, watching for the cues that signal exits and entrances, remembering their blocking and lines, and adjusting to audience reaction. Beginning actors often have a hard time finding just the right mixture of involvement and distance.

The beginning speech communication student must also find the right balance between performing and analyzing. At first, students have problems removing themselves from the content level. They have not as yet learned to see process. Later on, as they learn more about communication, they may become too analytical, annoying their friends by giving instant analyses of every interaction. But with practice it is possible to learn when to act and when to analyze. The transitions become easy and automatic.

We cannot stress strongly enough how important it is to begin to start analyzing interactions. For one thing, it will make learning theory more interesting and enjoyable. You will begin to see connections between what you read about and what you and those around you actually do. Even more important, developing the ability to observe behavior will allow you to diagnose and improve your own performance.

REVIEW TERMS

The following is a list of major concepts introduced in this chapter. The page number where the concept is defined is listed in parentheses.

communication (5)
process (5)
face (10)
communicative competence (11)
performative competence (11)
process competence (11)
implicit knowledge (13)
interpretive competence (13)
goal competence (14)
role competence (14)
code (15)
message competence (15)
process perspective (16)

SUGGESTED READINGS

Budd, Richard W., and Brent D. Ruben, eds. *Interdisciplinary Approaches to Human Communication*. Rochelle Park, N.J.: Hayden, 1979. An interesting collection of essays on communication written by scholars from many disciplines. The essays are well chosen and should provide you with new ideas and insights.

Civikly, Jean M. *Contexts of Communication*. New York: Holt, Rinehart and Winston, 1981. Essays that give an overview of the field of speech communication by examining the forms communication takes in a variety of contexts. Easy reading and useful if you want to get a feel for what is studied in speech communication.

Matson, Floyd W., and Ashley Montagu. *The Human Dialogue: Perspectives on Human Communication*. New York: The Free Press, 1967. A compilation of essays from a variety of fields, including works by mathematicians, physicists, psychoanalysts, philosophers, theologians, sociologists, psychologists, novelists, and essayists. Hannah Arendt, Jacques Barzun, Martin Buber, Albert Camus, Erich Fromm, Oliver Wendell Holmes, and E. B. White are just a few of the contributors.

Walker, Stephen. *Animal Thought*. London: Routledge & Kegan Paul, 1983. If you are at all intrigued by animal communication, you will find this book fascinating. It is clear and easy to read, but it also does a thorough job of evaluating the scientific literature.

PROCESS TO PERFORMANCE

TOPICS FOR DISCUSSION

1. In the introduction to this chapter, we tried to draw a parallel between extraterrestrial and interpersonal communication. Think of at least five additional ways that the process of communicating across cultures is like the process of communicating interpersonally. (We consider communication with extraterrestrials to be the ultimate in cross-cultural communication.)

2. Define communication. What kinds of behaviors are included and excluded in your definition? According to your definition, would a person sitting alone in a room thinking about a friend be communicating? Would a blush of embarrassment be communication? If you became tongue-tied, so that the message you were trying to get across became distorted, would communication have taken place? For a behavior to qualify as communication, does it have to involve two people? be intentional? be successful?

3. In this chapter we suggested that the realities people create through communication often control them. We used the example of Balinese demon worship. Can you think of words or concepts that control the lives of people in our culture? Discuss.

4. Goffman argues that much of what we do, including our communication, we do because society says we must. To what extent do you believe you are controlled by social rules and roles? How much freedom do you have?

5. Perception is a complex process involving the ability to interpret situations and episodes, what other people are like, and what we ourselves are thinking and feeling. Think of at least three examples of how problems in perception could lead to failures in communication.

6. Discuss the relationship between role competence and goal competence. Is it possible to have one without the other? What would a person who was role competent but had no goal competence be like? Is it possible to be goal competent without being role competent?

7. Assume that a visitor from another planet asked you to give it some advice on how to get along at your college or university. Pick a simple activity, say, attending a one-hour class, working out at the gym, or going out for pizza. Perceptually, what would the alien have to be able to do to handle this situation? What social roles would it have to master? What kinds of plans and strategies would it need? What verbal and nonverbal rules would it have to follow to be communicatively competent?

8. Have you ever been in a situation where your inability to handle language effectively caused an interpersonal problem? Have you ever committed a nonverbal faux pas? If they aren't too personal, share these experiences. What do they tell you about message competence?

9. In this chapter we argued that mastering process doesn't always lead to perfect performance. What factors can intervene between process and performance? What can be done about them?

10. Discuss the ritual of insulting the meat (Box 1.2). Can you think of other rituals in our culture that have a social-control function?

OBSERVATION GUIDE

1. Analyze a recent conversation by applying the model of communication competence presented in this chapter. Identify the level of interpretive, goal, role, and message competence you and your partner achieved. For instance, how successful were you in sizing up the situation? Did you accurately perceive your partner's intentions? How many message strategies did you consider? Did you have a clear understanding of the social roles called for? Were there any verbal or nonverbal misunderstandings? Judge your performance. How well did you do what you wanted to?

2. Take a look at the other courses you're enrolled in this semester. How can these courses give you an understanding of communication? Make a list of at least 15 topics from other courses that are related to interpersonal communication. Take one and describe what it taught you about the communication process. For example, you may have read a short story in a literature class that described interpersonal relationships. You may have come across a theory in psychology that explains some aspect of communication. Describe in detail what you learned.

EXERCISES

1. Work in pairs. Begin by individually thinking of the best and worst communicator you ever knew. Describe them to your partner. Working together, come up with a list of at least ten attributes that differentiate your good and bad communicators. Now ask your partner to describe his or her best and worst and repeat the process. How did your ideas differ? How do you stack up on both your own and your partner's list? What is your strongest point? What areas need more work? Discuss.

2. Taking a process perspective means becoming aware of how people communicate with one another. It means looking for cues that signal what's going on between people. Choose a partner and go to a public area on campus. Find a group of people who look interesting and observe them for 10 or 15 minutes. As you observe, make notes on what's going on in their interaction. Share your notes with your partner. From your combined observations, make a list of all of the things you were able to tell about interpersonal relationships just by observing. At the next class, share your list with others. Together come up with an observation guide, a list of things to look for in interaction. Use this observation guide to observe another group. You should begin to see more and more happening as you gain experience in observing others.

3. A model is a simplified explanation of a process. Models can help us understand the characteristics of a process, the factors that affect it, the way it operates, and so on. There are many ways of describing any process; consequently there are many models of it.

a. To get some practice in model making, think of a fairly complex process or object that you're familiar with (a football game, eating at a restaurant, graduating from high school, a first date). Working in groups, construct a model of that process. Pretend that you are preparing materials for people from a vastly different culture who will be visiting your college. Your model will help these people learn how things are done in your culture. You can create a verbal description, a flow chart, a diagram, a rule book. Share your model with the class.

b. Now try constructing your own model of communication.

CHAPTER TWO

Interpersonal relationships are varied—some fleeting and public, others long-lasting and intimate. Each relationship will follow its own unique trajectory. (Pierre-Auguste Renoir, *The Luncheon of the Boating Party*, 1881)

INTERPERSONAL COMMUNICATION: BUILDING RELATIONSHIPS

OMMUNICATION TAKES MANY forms. It can be as simple and direct as a smile or as complex and eloquent as a novel. It can occur between two people or among thousands, with a small group of friends or in an impersonal bureaucracy. Because communication has so many forms, it's easy to forget that all are part of the same process: the act of creating and sharing meaning. No matter how technologically sophisticated the channels or how vast the audience, communicators must share meaning with one another. It is for this reason that communication is, at heart, an interpersonal process.

One of the authors of this text was once asked at a party what he taught. When he answered, "Interpersonal communication," he was asked, "But isn't all communication interpersonal? Doesn't it always occur between people?" The question isn't a bad one. Although it is common to reserve the label *interpersonal* for intimate communication between two people in face-to-face interaction, there is clearly a sense in which all communication is interpersonal.

In this chapter we explore the relationship between interpersonal and other forms of communication. We begin by looking at tradi-

tional approaches to interpersonal communication and by offering our own definition. We then describe what happens to people when they form interpersonal bonds, and we consider how interpersonal communication and intimacy are related. Finally, we look at the special kind of competence it takes to build relationships.

WHAT IS INTERPERSONAL COMMUNICATION?

There are several ways to distinguish interpersonal from other forms of communication. In this section we will discuss and criticize two of the most popular, the situational and developmental approaches.

The Situational Approach

This approach holds that the situation in which communication occurs determines what kind of communication is going on: Different situations result in different forms of communication.[1]

When we're alone, for example, our communication is often quite different from when we are with others. First of all, it is silent,

Interpersonal communication fulfills many functions. World leaders can discuss policy, teachers can pass on knowledge, or two old friends can simply share their delight in each other's company: Mohandas Gandhi talks with Jawaharlal Nehru at the All-India Congress, July 6, 1946.

taking place inside our heads. Most people believe that this kind of communication, called **intrapersonal communication**, is also more disconnected and repetitive and less logical than other kinds.[2] Whenever you daydream or fantasize, consider a difficult personal problem, or try to make sense of the world around you, you're engaging in intrapersonal communica-

tion. You are both sender and receiver of your own message.

According to the situational approach, intrapersonal communication can be distinguished from **interpersonal communication**, communication between two people, generally in face-to-face interaction. Another name for this form of communication is *dyadic*. Dyadic

communication is generally spontaneous and informal; the participants receive maximum feedback from each other. Roles are relatively flexible, as partners alternately act as senders and receivers. When you sit down with a friend to recall old times, when you ask a professor what will be on the test, or when you have a serious discussion with someone you love, you are engaging in interpersonal communication.

When a third person joins an interaction, it ceases to be interpersonal and becomes **small-group communication**. While the size of a small group may vary, it must be small enough so that everyone can interact freely. In a dyad, the participants are connected directly; if the link between them is severed, communication stops. In a small group, communication is not destroyed when the link between two of the members is cut. Members can communicate with one another in a variety of ways.

Coordinating group interaction is relatively complex. For most of us, groups are psychologically more difficult to handle than dyads. One of the reasons formalized roles like that of leader emerge is to allow groups to handle the difficult problem of coordinating activity.[3] Students working on a class project together, cabinet members setting government policy, sports teams, and social clubs all engage in small group communication.

The next situational level involves **organizational communication**. This form of communication occurs in complex organizations such as large businesses, industries, and government institutions. Here communication takes place within a strongly defined hierarchy. Organization members experience, in addition to interpersonal and group relationships with coworkers, a relationship to the organization itself and to the bureaucracy that runs it. Roles tend to be more specialized and differentiated than at other levels, and rules for behavior more formalized. Successful communication requires

a knowledge of these roles and rules, often referred to as "organizational culture."[4]

When a single speaker addresses a large group of individuals simultaneously, he or she engages in **face-to-face public communication**. The speaker doesn't know audience members on a personal basis and must therefore compose the message for a hypothetical receiver. Because of the size of the audience, mutual interaction is also impossible. The speaker therefore acts as sender, while the audience takes on a passive receiver role. Clear organization, careful preplanning, and a fairly formal, nonconversational style are hallmarks of public communications. A political candidate on a whistle-stop tour, an evangelist exhorting a congregation, even a lecturer in a mass-enrollment course are examples of people communicating on the public level.

Finally, when speaker and audience become separated in both space and time, indirect ways of sending and receiving messages are used. Messages must be stored until they can be received by their intended audience. When the audience is large but the transmission is indirect, **mediated public (or mass) communication** occurs. Whenever "a medium replicates, duplicates, and disseminates identical content to a geographically widespread population," mass communication is taking place.[5] Radio and TV broadcasts, newspaper and magazine articles, and recorded music are examples.

According to the situational view, as we move from intrapersonal to mass communication, the following change: (1) number of interactants; (2) their physical proximity; (3) their ability to deliver and receive feedback immediately; (4) formality of communication roles; (5) their ability to adapt messages to others' specific needs; and (6) the degree to which communicative goals and purposes are preplanned and structured.[6] Of all of these variables, size probably has the biggest effect,

FIGURE 2.1

Characteristics of Interaction		
number of persons	few	many
proximity of interactants	close	far
nature of feedback	immediate	delayed
communication roles	informal	formal
adaptation of message	specific	general
goals and purpose	unstructured	structured
Situational Levels:	Intrapersonal Small Group Public	
	Interpersonal Organizational Mass	

since a change in size leads to all other changes.[7] Figure 2.1 shows how these factors affect communication.

According to the situational view, whenever two people interact in direct proximity, interpersonal communication is taking place. Before we decide whether this is a useful approach, let's look at a second way to define *interpersonal*.

The Developmental Approach

Under the situational approach, the interchange between a customer buying a new pair of shoes and the clerk who hurriedly waits on him is just as interpersonal as the interaction between lovers trying to work out problems in their relationship. The **developmental approach** rejects this view, holding that interpersonal communication has a quality dimension. Under this approach, only long-lasting, reciprocal relationships in which members respond selectively and specifically to each other can be

classed as interpersonal.[8] Thus interactions between lovers would be interpersonal, but brief commercial interactions would not.

The most detailed explanation of the developmental approach is given by Gerald Miller and Mark Steinberg.[9] They argue that all dyadic relationships start by being impersonal. Only if certain changes occur do they become interpersonal. First of all, the rules governing the interaction must move from the cultural to the psychological level. Miller and Steinberg believe there are three levels of rules that guide our actions. **Cultural-level rules** are those common to all members of a culture. For example, most Americans share rules for greetings and farewells. We know that it is appropriate to acknowledge another's presence when we meet, and we generally do it in similar ways, by smiling, nodding, or saying hello. **Sociological-level rules** are rules shared by members of specific groups within a culture. Soldiers, for example, have a unique greeting ritual, the salute. Lodge members may follow a

People have always tried to control external forces through ritual use of symbols.
(Fred Kabotie, *Pueblo Green Corn Dance*)

sociological-level rule that tells them to greet their compatriots with a secret handshake. Finally, **psychological-level rules** are worked out by individuals. Some friends greet each other by slapping each other on the shoulder; others by hugging. Some use joking insults; others always begin an interaction with a compliment. There are no general cultural or group rules governing this practice.

Miller and Steinberg believe that communication becomes interpersonal only when the psychological level is reached. They also believe that other changes occur as relationships become interpersonal: the kind of information people have about each other becomes increasingly unique; as a result, the level of knowledge they have about each other deepens. Interpersonal relationships are no longer based on stereotypes: Partners can predict each other's behaviors and motivations.

When we interact with a strange clerk in a shoe store, we have no background knowledge. We cannot treat him individually. Instead, we treat him according to the role he is fulfilling for us. Our relationship occurs at the surface level. It is *impersonal*, not interpersonal. When we interact with a friend, however, we have a shared background of experiences; we can sense his or her moods before anything is said; we know the person as an individual. Our relationship is *interpersonal* rather than impersonal.

Criticizing the Situational and Developmental Views

There are obviously advantages to both views. By focusing on *external* factors, the situational approach draws attention to the conditions surrounding communication. It tells us that context is important, and it allows us to divide communication into separate levels. The developmental approach, by focusing on aspects *internal* to relationships, reminds us that relationships vary in quality, evolving and changing over time. It emphasizes not just external variables but how interactants actually feel and act toward one another.

Are there any disadvantages to these views? We would like to suggest that they may oversimplify the problem of defining communication contexts, either by overlooking significant kinds of communication or by ignoring interactions between contexts. Let's look at each of these disadvantages in turn.

We believe the developmental view tends to restrict unnecessarily the meaning of interpersonal communication. Under the developmental view, only intimate relationships are of interest. While intimate relationships are extremely important, they are comparatively infrequent. Let's consider a typical day. Perhaps you decide to go to your favorite coffee shop for breakfast before having your license renewed at the department of motor vehicles and then heading to school. To get appropriate service you must communicate effectively with the waiter who serves you and with the motor vehicles clerk who goes over your paperwork. Once at school you must manage a variety of dyadic situations: with the person who steals the parking space you were patiently waiting for, the professor who wants to know why you're late, the clerk in the bursar's office who insists the school never received your check, and the fellow student who lost the notes she borrowed from you. While these interactions are not intimate or ultimately vital, they must be managed effectively and skillfully if you are to make it through the day. In each case, you and another person are briefly connected by your mutual efforts to make sense of the world and of each other. Under the developmental view, these kinds of relationships would not be given serious attention.

A disadvantage of the situational approach is that it ignores the complex relationships between different levels of communication. Under the situational view, you are either communicating interpersonally or you are communicating in some other way. No allowance is made for situations involving several levels simultaneously, nor is much said about the reciprocal effects of different levels on one another. In actuality, we often switch back and forth between levels rapidly. In talking to your boss, you may be operating in an organizational context, but you are also having a direct face-to-face interaction, as well as thinking to yourself about the topic you're discussing. You are therefore engaged in organizational, interpersonal, and intrapersonal communication.

When you stop to think about it, determining what level of communication you are involved in at any given moment is surprisingly hard. Levels blend and interact in interesting ways. Box 2.1 (pp. 30–31) discusses some of

Are you the same person when you are alone as when you are with others? (If a tree falls in a forest but no one is there, does it make a sound?) Is the person alone more "real" than the person interacting with others?

the ways different levels of communication can become intertwined.

Instead of thinking of interpersonal communication as separate from other forms of communication, we prefer to think of all communication as having an interpersonal element. While we believe that the clearest instance of interpersonal communication takes place when two people interact directly and personally, we also believe that many other interactions are partially interpersonal in nature. It may be useful to think of interpersonal communication as what philosophers and psychologists refer to as a "fuzzy set," a class that lacks clearly defined boundaries. We believe that *interpersonal communication takes place whenever two individuals, sharing the roles of sender and receiver, become connected through the mutual activity of creating meaning.* We also feel that an interpersonal exchange may be brief or long-lasting; its content may be private or public; it may take place when the two are alone with each other or when there are others around; it may be mediated or direct. What is important is that two people have formed a bond and that their interaction is mutual.

FORMING INTERPERSONAL BONDS

What does it mean to form an interpersonal bond? What happens to people when they share meaning? Perhaps the best way to answer

BOX 2.1

Is It Live or Is It Memorex? Forms of Mediated Interpersonal Communication

I t's not always easy to tell the difference between communication situations. Sometimes they overlap. In this box we'll look at three combinations of interpersonal and mass communication.

1. *Interpersonal mediated communication* is interpersonal communication in which some medium has been interposed between interactants. Conversations over telephone or citizens' band (CB) radio, messages sent by letter or electronic mail, and communication by audio- or videocassettes

are included. Telephone conversations are an interesting example because they call for suspension of the normal rules governing distance and intimacy. When we talk on the phone, our partner's voice is literally in our ear. Such vocal closeness normally occurs only in the most intimate of face-to-face interactions. Yet at the same time we are physically separated; other sensory channels usually found in interpersonal interaction (sight, touch, smell, sense of warmth and closeness) are absent. Robert Cathcart and Gary Gumpert suggest, "Perhaps this is why, at times, the telephone can be so threatening. It invades

intimate space, but denies us most of the sensory means of communication control and verification present in intimate situations."

CB communication, while generally private and conversational in tone, is public because anyone can listen in. The sender therefore becomes a kind of performer. If you have ever listened to the CB, you may have noticed the emphasis on either general information (weather conditions, presence of police) or on entertainment (singing, joke-telling, or humorous comments on the four-wheelers passing by.) The effective communicator in this medium must be a kind of interpersonal DJ.

2. *Media-simulated interpersonal communication* is public communication masquerading as interpersonal. In the TV talk show, for example, the audience listens to a conversation that has all the hallmarks of a typical interpersonal interaction. Listeners invite

these questions is to ask you to do a bit of imagining. Think about the last time you were completely alone. Try to picture yourself as clearly as you can. What do you look like? What are you doing? What's going on in your mind? Now imagine another person suddenly entering the scene and sitting or standing nearby. Picture your reaction. How does your relationship with yourself and with your surroundings change? What happens to you as a result of the mere presence of another?

Creating Interpersonal Relationships

We believe that whenever two people become aware of each other (and awareness is the point at which interpersonal communication begins), at least two fundamental changes occur. First, they reorient. Second, their behavior becomes constrained. To get a clearer picture of what it means to form an interpersonal relationship, we'll discuss each of these changes.

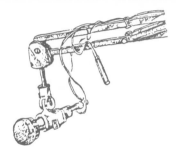

the host and celebrity guests into their living rooms, where they are exposed to personal disclosures. Audience members often know more about the lives of celebrities than they do about "real people." In fact, "it is less demanding for some people to work out a close relationship with Johnny Carson than with their next-door neighbor," Cathcart and Gumpert observe. Yet this sense of closeness is only illusory, since sender and receiver roles never change.

Radio call-in shows are another example of illusory intimacy. The format is that of a private telephone conversation. However, the host produces a cleverly orchestrated public performance. In return for their

collaboration, those who call in are allowed to set up a quasi-interpersonal relationship with a well-known public personality. For many, this form of interaction may supplement or substitute for "real life" intimacy.

3. *Uni-communication* is another mediated form of interpersonal communication. It involves messages "mediated by objects of clothing, adornment, and personal possessions . . . which people select and display to communicate to others their status, affiliation, and self-esteem." Wearing a "Save the Whales" T-shirt or a pair of expensive designer jeans allows an individual to announce priorities and commitments to the world without direct effort. In uni-comm, the individual is a kind of walking billboard. Because receivers are bombarded with these messages many times a day, uni-comm "creates a kind of national interpersonal dialogue about values, roles and status."

Cathcart and Gumpert believe "that the traditional division of communication study into interpersonal, group and public, and mass communication is inadequate because it ignores the pervasiveness of media."

Source: *Robert Cathcart and Gary Gumpert, "Mediated Interpersonal Communication: Toward a New Typology,"* Quarterly Journal of Speech *69 (1983): 267–77.*

ADDITIONAL READINGS

Gumpert, Gary, and Robert Cathcart. *Inter/Media: Interpersonal Communication in a Media World.* New York: Oxford University Press, 1979.

Novack, Michael. "Television Shapes the Soul." In *Mass Media Issues,* edited by L. L. Sellars and W. C. Rivers. Englewood Cliffs, N.J.: Prentice-Hall, 1977.

Toffler, Alvin. *The Third Wave.* New York: William Morrow, 1980.

Reorientation

To orient is to locate oneself in time and space. To reorient means to change one's sense of location. People who are entirely alone often slip into a world of fantasy and daydreams. The mere presence of another person acts to bring them back to a more objective state. One of the first things that happens is a "rude awakening." Perhaps this is a survival mechanism, allowing the organism to sense danger. Regardless of why it occurs, one of the consequences of the presence of others is a heightened awareness of the world and of the self.

People who suddenly realize they are being observed exhibit other interesting changes. They sit up straighter, tense relaxed muscles, automatically rearrange their hair and clothing, and cease doing things that would reflect badly on them. Being observed seems to remind them of their physical appearance and behaviors. Psychologists refer to this as a state of **objective self-awareness**.[10]

The presence of others serves as a kind of mirror, reflecting back an image of self. If that image is less than satisfactory, we correct our behaviors so as to present a more flattering one. This awareness of self is a salient characteristic of interpersonal bonds. This is a topic we shall discuss in much more detail later in this book. For now, what is important to remember is that interpersonal relationships show us who we are.

Behavioral Constraint

The presence of another not only gives us identity, it serves to constrain our actions. When we interact with a stranger, we immediately try to predict what he or she is likely to do. This prediction tells us what is possible within the interaction. It constrains our actions.

Behavioral constraint occurs in all relationships, even the most momentary. Have you ever seen a crowd crossing the street of a large city? Although hundreds of people pass each other in only a few seconds, they seldom collide. Seen in slow motion, their interaction is like an intricate dance. The "relationship" among them may last only a few seconds, but while it does their actions are coordinated.

William Wilmot gives an interesting illustration of the ways we are bound to others through communication.[11] The scene opens when Wilmot, sitting in a coffee shop, notices a young man staring intently at him. In order to avoid the stranger's stare, Wilmot turns away. When he glances nervously around, he sees that he is still the object of observation. Finally he rises and leaves, glaring at the young man as he exits. What is interesting is Wilmot's interpretation of this incident. Wilmot believes that an interpersonal interaction begins when there is a "perception of being perceived." As soon as two people become aware of one another, a relationship is formed, and as soon as that happens there is a corresponding loss of freedom. Wilmot believed that by staring at

him, the stranger was pulling him into a relationship he did not want. He resented the fact that his behavior was being constrained by a stranger.

Of course, behavioral constraint is much more important in long-lasting relationships. When we form a relationship, we enter into an implicit contract, agreeing to abide by the rules we create together. Perhaps this is why so many people see commitment as a loss of freedom.

A Systems View of Interpersonal Communication

So far we have argued that whenever two people become aware of each other, an interpersonal bond is created. Another way to express this idea is to say that when people communicate, they form an interpersonal system. To explore what it means to be part of a system, we will turn to a theory called **general systems theory**.

This theory arose when scientists working in many fields became aware that the same basic principles could be used to explain very different processes. Atomic structures, biological forms, and social patterns had one thing in common: They could be described as systems.[12]

In simple terms, a **system** is an organized collection of interdependent parts. Not every collection of parts is a system. The piles of rusted auto parts we see in a salvage yard are neither organized or interdependent. They are a heap, not a system. The chemicals on the shelf of a chemist's laboratory are not a system. They are isolated from one another. The people sitting in the sun in a public park are not a system because they are acting independently. Of course, all of the parts that make up these collections could become systems. If the auto parts were put back together into a functioning machine, they would form a mechanical system. If the chemist selected compatible chemicals and experimentally combined them in a test

How do the four characteristics of human systems apply to a typical moment at the New York Stock Exchange?

tube, a chemical system could be formed. And if the people in the park decided to get together to play a game of softball, a human system would be created.

Characteristics of Human Systems

There are a number of systems characteristics that can help us understand how relationships operate. The four most relevant to interpersonal communication are: wholeness, interdependence, nonsummativity, and equifinality.

Wholeness. One of the things separating a system from a heap is that it operates as a whole, taking on unique properties and char-

acteristics. Systems act coherently. Although a car is made up of many parts, it isn't the parts that we drive, it's the car. Although a team is made up of individual players, it isn't a single player who wins or loses, but the team. If we want to understand a system, we need to look at the unique ways the parts organize themselves and work together. What is important is the fact that the parts of a system are bound together into an entity that can be identified and observed in its own right.

Interdependence. When we say that the parts of a system act as a whole, we also imply the parts are interdependent. Each part affects and

Communication combines individual efforts in a unique whole. This friendship quilt, itself a product of interpersonal communication, is a perfect example of the blending of individual and group, private and public, efforts. (Baltimore, 1848)

is affected by every other part. A change in any part will be felt by all parts and by the system as a whole. Ecological systems are a good example. We know that the physical environment is delicately balanced. To destroy or change one part is to make far-reaching changes in the nature of the whole.

Nonsummativity.   Simply put, nonsummativity means that a whole is always more than the sum of its parts. Something emerges from a system that is much more complex than the individual parts. Water may be a combination of oxygen and hydrogen, but as an entity it is very different from each element by itself.

Similarly, when people join forces, they transform themselves into something more than what they were individually.

Equifinality. A final implication of wholeness is that we cannot predict what will happen in a system by looking at how it began. Human systems are capable of self-regulation. They can meet the changing demands of the environment by reorganizing themselves. Equifinality means that a system isn't bound by historical conditions: Two systems that start out at the same point may turn out very differently, while two systems that start out very differently may end up at similar points. The only way we can predict systems operation is to examine the way it organizes itself and responds to its environment. The system is its own best explanation.

Wholeness in Interpersonal Systems

What has all of this to do with interpersonal relationships? Systems theorists argue that when people engage in interpersonal communication, they create a system. This means their relationship manifests wholeness, interdependence, nonsummativity, and equifinality.

When two people communicate, the relationship they create is a unique whole. Each relationship develops its own characteristics; each is governed by a unique set of roles, norms, and rituals. This is why every dyad you form works in a slightly different way. Each relationship allows you to reveal a different aspect of your personality because you are part of a different whole.

When two people communicate interpersonally, they also become interdependent: Each affects the other. We often believe that we can enter a relationship without being touched by it. According to the systems view, this is impossible. We are always changed by our relationships with others, as they are changed by their relationships with us. Relationships

are mutual creations. If they go smoothly, it's because both parties coordinate their efforts effectively; similarly, if problems arise, both members are responsible.

The fact that a whole is always greater than the sum of its parts means that if we want to understand a dyad, we shouldn't try to analyze what the members do when they are apart, but rather how they operate when they're together. Strict systems theorists believe that it is counterproductive to analyze individual personalities in order to understand interpersonal communication. Since individuals are constantly changing in response to one another, the best way to understand their relationship is to look at their behaviors when they are together. Relationships are defined by what people do, not who they are.

Finally, the fact that relationships are equifinal means it is difficult to predict what will occur in a relationship without looking at the way the system organizes itself and adapts to environmental pressures. Two couples, similar in background and education—with, as far as anyone can tell, a similar potential for happiness—marry at the same time. One stays together forever, building a strong, secure relationship, while the other undergoes a bitter divorce within five years. And a third couple—who, in everyone's mind, is doomed to failure—survives, managing to create a lasting relationship.

Feedback in Human Systems

A system regulates itself in order to adapt to its environment by using **feedback**, the process of comparing its performance to a preset standard and using this comparison to control its output. The standard example of a feedback mechanism is the household thermostat, which takes periodic readings of room temperature and compares these to an initial setting.[13] If the room temperature rises above the setting, the furnace is turned off, and heat is reduced. If the temperature falls below the set point, the furnace is turned back on. In this way a steady state is maintained. Information about the system's operation is fed back into the system and used as a control mechanism.

This kind of feedback is called *negative feedback*. It is designed to discourage system deviation; it is meant to keep the system from changing. When you check your weight daily to keep from gaining or losing too much, you are engaged in a negative-feedback process. You are using information about your own behavior to control that behavior.

Of course, there are times when we don't want a system to stay where it is. Rather, we want it to increase or decrease its output. Feedback that encourages deviations is called *positive feedback*. A coach trying to encourage an athlete to outdo her previous record is using positive feedback. Information about performance is given to the athlete so that she can increase her speed rather than maintain it at a steady state. A person who wanted to get into *The Guinness Book of World Records* as the fattest man in the world would use positive feedback. Every day he would try to outdo his previous weight.

You may be used to thinking about negative feedback as unpleasant or punishing and positive feedback as pleasant or rewarding. Don't let this everyday usage confuse you. We're using the terms in a more technical sense. Just remember that negative feedback discourages deviation from a standard, while positive feedback encourages change.

Both feedback processes are found in relationships. If a relationship is going well, the partners will try to protect it from change through negative feedback. They may know, for example, how much argument they can tolerate. When conflict escalates, negative feedback will keep it from getting out of control. At other times, however, positive feedback may encourage change. Trust, for example, often leads to more trust.

A relationship runs on information about itself. If that information is cut off, the relationship can no longer regulate itself and is in danger of becoming obsolete or running out of control. Thus the ability to give and receive feedback is an essential part of communicative competence.

RELATIONAL PATHS: INTIMACY AND DISTANCE

Systems rarely stay at the same point. As the parts of the system respond to each other and to outside pressures, the system evolves and changes. Much of a system's energy goes toward defining the nature of that change. When you and I form interpersonal relationships, we too are concerned with the path our relationship is taking. Some relationships will become long-lasting and intimate, characterized by mutual trust and dependence. Other relationships will exhibit a maximum amount of distance; members will remain courteous but aloof. Most relationships will exist on some kind of middle ground. The path a relationship takes is often referred to as its **relational trajectory**.[14] In this section, we consider how communication determines trajectory.

Interpersonal Trajectories: Private and Public Paths

In his excellent review of interpersonal bonding, Arthur Bochner tells us that there are two general relational trajectories. "On the one hand there is the type of social bond that gains 'coherence from a sentimental bond between persons who are essentially homogeneous'; on

TABLE 2.1

A relational dichotomy: private and public bonds

Private	Public
In which we respond to the other in a personal and private manner.	In which we respond to the other in an impersonal and public manner.
Members are IRREPLACEABLE. It makes a difference who the other is.	Members are SUBSTITUTABLE. It makes no difference who the other is.
Members are INTERDEPENDENT.	Members are AUTONOMOUS.
Their way of knowing the other is PARTICULAR.	Their way of knowing the other is UNIVERSAL.
The rules governing behavior are INDIVIDUALISTIC.	The rules governing behavior are NORMATIVE.
The tone of the relationship is SENTIMENTAL.	The tone of the relationship is PRACTICAL.
Rewards are primarily INTRINSIC.	Rewards are primarily EXTRINSIC.
Examples: sexual pairs, kinship pairs, marital partners, best friends	Examples: strangers, acquaintances, colleagues, work partners

the other hand there is the type that integrates complementary differences into 'a practical organization in which mutual sentiments are unnecessary.'"[15] One way to label these two relational paths is to call the first private and the second public.

Private relationships are much like the kind of relationship described in the developmental view. Over time they become more and more personal and special. In a private relationship, who our partner is makes a great deal of difference. If we lose a friend or lover, we do not substitute someone else easily, for we are closely and interdependently connected. We are affected by each other in important ways, and our tie is very strong. In private relationships, we make sense of each other by using unique, particular information about each other. In general, the rules of behavior we follow are individualistic, the product of negotiation. On the whole, a good deal of sentiment is involved in private relationships. These relationships are

considered to be rewarding for their own intrinsic worth.

Public relationships are very different. The members of a **public relationship** are related in impersonal ways, and very little change occurs over time. Members are substitutable. If the clerk who waits on us is replaced by someone else, it will probably make very little difference to us. Instead of being interdependent, we are relatively autonomous. Our connections are slight and easily broken off. In public relationships, we have little particular information about one another; instead, we attend to general class memberships to make sense of one another. The rules governing behavior are socially rather than individually determined: We are courteous and polite. Often the reason for the bond is practical rather than sentimental, and its rewards are extrinsic rather than intrinsic. Table 2.1 presents a model of differences between public and private relationships.

We would like to make four points about this relational model.

1. *The two types of relationships are extremes; many possible variations exist.* As you can see in Table 2.1, we have listed six dimensions that distinguish private and public relationships. Individuals working out a relationship must find a position on each dimension, deciding, for example, the degree of importance and uniqueness of their partner as well as the amount of dependence that should characterize their bond. They must also determine how information should be exchanged and the kind of rules to be followed during interaction. Finally, they must know how much emotional energy to invest, and whether the relationship itself is of primary concern or whether it is simply a means to an end.

In a given culture, some kinds of relationships will occur more often than others. For example, people in our culture expect honesty and openness in private relationships and guardedness in public relationships. Couples are expected to tell each other everything, while strangers are to be told very little. Each of us, however, decides how far to go in following cultural norms. This means that although the culture may define only a few basic ways of relating, in reality there are as many kinds of relational paths as there are dyads.

2. *Over time, relationships will fluctuate and change.* Relationships are dynamic, constantly moving and adjusting along each of the dimensions we have described. While marriage partners are generally dependent on one another, the degree of autonomy and interdependence they require will vary through their married life. Constant readjustment of their position will be necessary. Friends too must continually monitor their behavior, deciding how much dependence and how much freedom should characterize their relationship.[16]

3. *Different skills and sensitivities are needed for different relationships.* Because we form many kinds of bonds, we must learn a variety of skills. We need to know how to build private bonds through self-disclosure, but we need equally to know how to maintain a distance from others. In the workplace, for example, we may want to discourage intimacy. Interpersonal competence is often a matter of knowing whether to employ public or private rules of behavior.

4. *Relational trajectories are defined through communication.* How do we settle on the path our relationship will follow? We constantly send each other messages (both verbal and nonverbal) about our relational expectations. Through a process of negotiation, we sift through these messages, deciding on a mutually satisfactory outcome. Sometimes this process is relatively easy, as when two people in love follow the intimacy path. At other times it can be extremely painful—for example, when one partner wants the relationship to deepen while the other wants to maintain it at a more public level.

Independence versus Conformity: A Basic Interpersonal Dilemma

One way to sum up the difference between private and public relationships is to say that private relationships allow us to exhibit uniqueness and independence, while public relationships stress conformity and social solidarity. While people need to feel connected to social groups, they also need to feel separateness.

We live in a society that tends to value the expression of personal individuality. Americans generally dislike dealing with people in terms of social roles. The idea of strangers bothers us; when we meet people, we try almost immediately to "get to know them." We want to interact on a friendly, informal, first-name basis right from the start.[17]

BOX 2.2

Mind Your Manners: Some Social Functions of Etiquette

What do you think of the rules of etiquette? Are they relics of an outmoded way of life? Ways of putting on a false front and deceiving people about your true feelings? Or do they serve any useful social purpose? Judith Martin, who makes her living as Miss Manners, author of advice columns and books on etiquette, believes that manners serve a useful function and that without social codes of behavior, people cannot live a civilized life.

Martin recognizes that today most people distrust the idea of good manners. She traces this belief to the 18th-century philosopher Jean Jacques Rousseau, who felt that civilization destroys everything that is natural and good in people. She also finds this idea in the human-potential movement's glorification of openness and authenticity as ways of life.

Martin believes codes of etiquette can also be destructive. They can, for example, be used as one weapon in class warfare. But she maintains that manners are necessary for smooth social interaction. By heading off conflict, social codes allow people with irreconcilable differences to coexist. For Martin, individual freedom has to be tempered by the needs of society. This means

that people cannot be free to do whatever they wish. Freedom and equality do not mean that everyone can be completely honest and exactly the same. To Martin, "a complete disregard of any distinctions, a total leveling of all hierarchies results in a kind of universal kindergarten where everyone wears the same play-clothes all the time for all occasions and is expected to participate in show and tell all the time."

Martin recognizes that many people today believe in being totally open and honest and establishing first-name relationships with as many people as possible. No longer is any distinction made between how we treat strangers and intimates. She feels there are dangers in this, one being that the techniques which work in the boardroom are being used in the bedroom. Everything is for sale. If you want to fall in love, she asks, what do you do? "You run a classified advertisement announcing a vacancy and you include a job description with the most detailed skill requirements." Friends and lovers are hired and fired with the same lack of emotion as employees.

While intimates are being treated like employees, strangers are treated as intimates. Nowadays being on a first-name basis with your waitress ("Hi, I'm Cherry, and I'll be your server tonight.") and your bank ("You've got a friend at Chase Manhattan.") is unavoidable. We no longer make any distinctions between the world of work (the public realm) and the world of home and family (the private realm). Martin points out a fundamental error in this kind of reasoning: While it may be the goal of business to move along and get things done, the goals of friendship and romance are to "repeat doing the same things and to like being where you are."

Martin believes people are confused about their obligations. She argues that we have to reestablish the dualism of the personal and professional realms so that everyone can have a reasonable portion of each. What do you think?

Source: *Judith Martin,* Common Courtesy *(New York: Atheneum, 1985). The text was originally delivered as an address at Harvard University under the title "The Question That Baffled Jefferson." An audiotape is available from the Harvard Forum.*

ADDITIONAL READINGS

Martin, Judith. *Miss Manners' Guide to Excruciatingly Correct Behavior*. New York: Atheneum, 1982.

Vanderbilt, Amy. *The Amy Vanderbilt Complete Book of Etiquette*. Garden City, N.Y.: Doubleday, 1978.

We carry this expectation into our long-lasting relationships, believing that over time relationships should increase in "personalness." We expect the same degree of "progress" in our personal lives that we do in the business world. Occasionally this means that we try too hard too soon, not allowing relationships to grow at their own pace.

As a culture, we tend to deemphasize public relationships, often losing sight of the fact that people have a need for distance as well as closeness. Public relationships are designed to give us that distance. They are meant to control and pace intimacy, keeping others from making personal demands on us or knowing us too well. Indeed, in public it is our place in the social structure rather than our individuality that defines us. We are identified by formal roles, and we are expected to act formally, following rules of courtesy.

While public relationships may seem undemocratic to some people, they have some advantages. First of all, they affirm the social order. They remind us of social expectations and duties, making it clear to us that we are part of a group. Second, they actually allow us to develop a sense of separateness. Psychologists tell us that without the ability to create boundaries between self and others, we would have great difficulty in developing a stable identity. Public relationships also save us a great deal of psychological investment. Think what your life would be like if you were expected to "share thoughts and feelings, reveal intimate information and secrets, extend emotional support, and seek advice"[18] with everyone you encountered. On a purely practical level, it would be impossible. Box 2.2 gives one author's view of the importance of maintaining politeness in public and of the problems that can occur when we rush into intimacy.

The tension between closeness and distance, the need to be recognized as a unique individual and the need to be part of a social collective are fundamental. When we work out the nature of our relationships, we are working out our answer to this dilemma. Because we believe this is a very important interpersonal tension, we shall return to it a number of times.

BUILDING RELATIONSHIPS: LEVELS OF RELATIONAL COMPETENCE

Our model of communicative competence in Chapter 1 suggested that in order to be a competent communicator, you must be able to perceive the world accurately and sensitively, to set realistic and practical goals, to know when and how to follow social norms, and to use message codes effectively. When individuals form interpersonal bonds, a new level of complexity is added. Not only must communicators be individually competent, they must be mutually competent. They must be able to adapt to one another in order to create a coordinated interpersonal system.

As Linda Harris points out, this isn't always an easy matter.[20] Some people hold inflexible views of how relationships should operate. Although they can handle simple and familiar situations, they're unable to adapt to unusual episodes or unanticipated demands from their partners. Their solution to the problem of coordination is to force their partner to adapt or to **altercast** (to choose a partner who agrees to play the "correct" interpersonal role). If two such inflexible individuals try to interact, and if their models of interpersonal relationships differ, the result is likely to be disastrous. Harris labels these people as having **minimal competence**.

People who have been exposed to a wider variety of situations have a more flexible relational model. Recognizing the value of adaptability, they are willing to change in order to fit

in if they sense that this willingness is reciprocal. Harris labels such people **satisfactorily
competent**. A bit conservative, their preferred
manner of coordination is compromise: Each
partner gives up a little in order to get
something in return. Harris believes that these
people are most comfortable in familiar situations; they lack the ability to work out problems
in new and creative ways.

People who are **optimally competent**
know when to adapt and when not to. They are
aware of the way their interpersonal systems
operate, and they can evaluate them objectively.
These people are not afraid of change; they
can handle relational problems creatively and
effectively.

What does it take to be optimally rather
than minimally competent? First, it takes experience and flexibility. A person who knows only
one way to do things will have trouble confronting new approaches; the more we learn
about alternative ways of organizing relationships, the more flexible we can become. Second,
relational competence involves the ability to
use feedback effectively. We said earlier that
interpersonal systems run on information. If
you're unwilling to give or receive feedback,
you're effectively restricting your ability to
control the relationship. Talking about your
place in the system and the system as a whole is
absolutely necessary for optimal competence.

REVIEW TERMS

The following is a list of major concepts
introduced in this chapter. The page number
where the concept is first mentioned is listed in
parentheses.

situational approach (23)
intrapersonal communication (24)
interpersonal communication (24)

small-group communication (25)
organizational communication (25)
face-to-face public communication (25)
mediated public communication (25)
developmental approach (26)
cultural-level rules (26)
sociological-level rules (26)
psychological-level rules (27)
objective self-awareness (31)
general systems theory (32)
system (32)
wholeness (33)
interdependence (33)
nonsummativity (34)
equifinality (35)
feedback (35)
relational trajectory (36)
private relationship (37)
public relationship (37)
altercast (40)
minimal competence (40)
satisfactory competence (41)
optimal competence (41)

SUGGESTED READINGS

Borden, George A. *Human Communication
Systems*. Boston: American Press, 1985. If you want
to know more about systems theory, this is one place
to start. In Chapters 2, 3, and 4 Borden offers a nice
introduction to systems concepts. His endnotes also
provide useful sources for further reading.

Miller, Gerald R., and Mark Steinberg. *Between
People: A New Analysis of Interpersonal Communication*. Palo Alto, Calif.: Science Research Associates,
1975. Miller and Steinberg introduced the developmental approach in a basic interpersonal text, which
has become a classic.

Sennett, Richard. *The Fall of Public Man*. New
York: Random House, Vintage Books, 1974. If you
are at all interested in history, this book will prove
fascinating. Sennett traces some of the ways interpersonal relationships have changed since the 18th

century. He provides an interesting comparison between the private and public spheres of interpersonal life.

Swanson, David L., and Jesse G. Delia. "The Nature of Human Communication," *Modules in Speech Communication*. Chicago: Science Research Associates, 1976. This well-written monograph is a good all-around introduction to the field of human communication. In addition, it gives a very sensible description of each of the situational levels and their relationship to one another.

PROCESS TO PERFORMANCE

TOPICS FOR DISCUSSION

1.   Think of a topic; say, a current event. How will communication about it change as communicators move from interpersonal to group, organizational, public, and mass communication contexts? Discuss changes in both the content and form of communication. Do you think there will also be changes in the reason the topic is discussed? Discuss the functions of communication at each level.

2.   Think about a close personal relationship you have now. How did your communication change as you got to know your partner? Are there any times when you move back to the impersonal level? Do you believe couples shift between being impersonal and interpersonal, or do you believe that once a relationship is interpersonal, it stays that way until it dissolves?

3.   Evaluate the advantages and disadvantages of the situational and developmental approaches. Which do you believe is the best way to think about interpersonal communication? Can you offer a third approach to the problem?

4.   Think about the ways interpersonal bonds change self-awareness. List five people you encountered today. Did they make you aware of any aspects of yourself or your surroundings? What kinds of self-evaluations did you make on meeting them?

5.   In what ways do others constrain the ways we behave? Think about the five people you listed in question number 4. Did you act the same way in front of each? Is this how you act when alone?

6.   Think of an interpersonal system—for example, a sports team, a group of close friends, a family, or an interpersonal dyad you are now involved in. Apply the concepts of wholeness, interdependence, nonsummativity, and equifinality to these systems. What understanding do you gain by thinking of these collections of people as systems?

7.   During a typical day, how much do you rely on feedback? Beginning from the moment you wake up and continuing through the day, list ways you seek feedback (for example, looking in the mirror as you brush your teeth, looking at the nonverbal responses others give you when you greet them). Discuss what it might be like if you received no feedback cues from others in your environment. Is it possible for a system to exist without feedback?

8. Discuss some of the subtle ways others control us through feedback. Focus on nonverbal aspects. How influential is nonverbal feedback from others in controlling your behavior?

9. Many social critics have suggested that our culture places undue emphasis on private relationships. Americans, they argue, are overly familiar. Discuss ways our culture encourages rapid development of private bonds (for example, the norm for clerks to tell strangers to "have a nice day"). Discuss advantages and disadvantages of this push toward "instant intimacy."

10. Think of people you have known who fall into Harris's competence categories. Describe their behaviors.

OBSERVATION GUIDE

1. Observe a couple you know for about half an hour. Watch carefully for all of the ways, both verbal and nonverbal, they give and seek feedback from one another. Describe these feedback attempts as well as the kind of control each exercises on the other. How do they differ from one another in control? How do they seek feedback, and how do they react to it once they have received it? What inferences can you make about their relationship?

2. Think of an interpersonal relationship that is important to you and has lasted for some time. Graph it on the following chart developed from our model of private–public relationships:

Other is:
irreplaceable   *substitutable*
            1 . . . 2 . . . 3 . . . 4 . . . 5 . . . 6 . . . 7
We are:
interdependent   *autonomous*
            1 . . . 2 . . . 3 . . . 4 . . . 5 . . . 6 . . . 7
The information we use is:
particular   *universal*
            1 . . . 2 . . . 3 . . . 4 . . . 5 . . . 6 . . . 7
The rules we follow are:
individualistic   *normative*
            1 . . . 2 . . . 3 . . . 4 . . . 5 . . . 6 . . . 7
The emotional tone is:
sentimental   *practical*
            1 . . . 2 . . . 3 . . . 4 . . . 5 . . . 6 . . . 7
The rewards I get are:
intrinsic   *extrinsic*
            1 . . . 2 . . . 3 . . . 4 . . . 5 . . . 6 . . . 7

Has the relationship always had this profile, or has it changed over time? Were there key incidents that caused the profile of your relationship to change? Is it at the point you want it to be right now?

EXERCISES

1. As a class, discuss metaphors for interpersonal relationships. Fill in the following sentence: Interpersonal relationships are like _____. Try to think of as many comparisons as possible, then look at what they tell you about the nature of relational bonds. What common themes can you uncover? Open the discussion by considering metaphors that are embedded in our language. For example, consider the following metaphors used in the context of love: prisoner of love, bound together, tie the knot, get hitched. What is the central message behind these metaphors? What others can you come up with?

2. Choose a partner and decide who is to be sender and who is to be receiver. The sender should think of a recent personal experience involving a problem in communication and recount that experience to the receiver. The receiver is to listen without giving any verbal or nonverbal feedback. If the receiver slips and gives feedback, start again. Once you have finished, reverse roles. Then discuss in a normal manner your experiences during this exercise. How easy or difficult was it to avoid giving feedback? How did you feel talking to someone who was not responding? In general, how important is feedback to interpersonal communication?

PART II

INTERPERSONAL
PROCESSES

CHAPTER THREE

This 19th-century engraving, entitled *Puzzle-Brain Mountain*, demonstrates the eternal interest that people have in perceptual puzzles and multiple interpretations of the same object or event. If you look at the drawing in a straightforward fashion, you probably perceive a mountain landscape; turning the picture on its side will reveal the outline and features of a man's face.

SOCIAL COGNITION: PERCEIVING CONTEXTS AND INDIVIDUALS

A FRIEND OF YOURS has arranged for you to be interviewed for an important position with the company she works for. In fact, she will be one of the interviewers. She has, of course, informed you that she cannot show any favoritism and will conduct the interview in a rather formal, businesslike manner. You are told that the interview will be held over coffee at a local restaurant and that two or three of the company's representatives, including your friend, will be there. You are to arrive promptly at 3 P.M., your friend says, and you may as well wait in the lobby until she gets there. Naturally, you are more than prompt, you're 15 minutes early. You hang around the lobby, feeling more nervous as each minute passes.

Finally, as 3 o'clock comes and goes, you sneak a peak inside the restaurant. Here is what you see: your friend is already seated at a table with two other people, a male and a female. All three are dressed in business suits. The two women are having wine, the young man is sipping a cup of coffee. Your friend is talking quite seriously with the young man who, quite frankly, looks a little nervous. The other woman is looking around the place, as if expecting someone. You begin to worry. Maybe you misunderstood your friend's instructions. She glances away from the man but doesn't see you. At last you decide that they must be waiting for you. So you check yourself in the mirror and

start walking toward their table. As you approach, you hear your friend say to the other woman, "Chris, do you have anything else you'd like to ask Mr. Gannon?" Suddenly, your friend notices you. She looks a little surprised, then acts very coolly toward you, and hesitates as if not sure what to do next.

Before you read on, take a few minutes to answer the following questions. (1) How would you define the situation described above? Which behaviors are most important in helping you define it? (2) What kind of people are involved? What impressions do you have of each one? (3) How are the participants related to one another? (4) How can you explain their behavior? Write down anything else you perceive to be important in this situation.

The four questions you have just considered are all concerned with **social cognition**, the study of the cognitive processes that enable us to categorize and explain people and the social events and relationships they produce. Investigators of these processes use a variety of terms to describe what they study: person perception, impression formation, self-monitoring, and attribution theory, just to mention a few. When you see these terms, you should recognize that we're talking about one of the ways people categorize social life in order to make sense of it.

At the end of this chapter we'll return to this scene and compare the perceptions you

---

The Four Social Cognition Questions

1. What is the definition of the situation?

2. What impressions do the participants have of each other?

3. What kind of relationship have the participants enacted? Do they both define the relationship in the same way?

4. What attributions do the participants make to account for their own and each other's behavior?

FIGURE 3.1

The four social cognition questions

---

have now with what you see after reading the chapter. But before you delve in, there is another way to test your social cognition skills and the value of what you are about to read. Take a short break and go someplace where you can observe people talking (for example, a coffee shop, cafeteria, bus stop). Write down what you see and hear, verbally and nonverbally, and then answer the four questions we posed above. When you have finished, come back and read about social cognition.

Before discussing specific social cognition factors, we'd like to talk briefly about why we think social-cognitive processes are an important part of communication. Then we'll look at the process of perception that underlies all of the cognitive processes. We'll detail the four major social cognition processes: (1) sizing up the situation; (2) sizing up people; (3) sizing up relationships; and (4) explaining interpersonal behavior. The chapter will conclude with some suggestions for improving our awareness of these four cognitive processes.

WHY IS SOCIAL COGNITION IMPORTANT IN INTERPERSONAL COMMUNICATION?

It may seem strange to spend an entire chapter on social cognition in a book about interpersonal communication. After all, cognition seems to be an internal process, more in the domain of psychology than communication. This distinction, while important, is also misleading. Each of the social sciences contributes significantly to the understanding of the others. In our case, the knowledge of how we categorize social phenomena helps us understand and, ideally, improve how we communicate. There are at least four ways that social cognition and interpersonal communication relate to each other. The way we categorize our social world affects how we receive messages; what actions we will think are appropriate; and how much control we have in that social world. Finally, our social categories can change as a result of communication with others.

Social Cognition and the Reception of Messages

Our observations are always influenced by our frame of reference (mental state, past experience, bias, and so on). This frame of reference then affects which of the many messages in our environment we pay attention to. If you are hungry and thinking about food, your frame of reference will predispose you to notice the smell of onions on a friend's breath, the picture of a hot dog on a billboard, and the familiar jingle of a fast-food restaurant on the car radio. If you expect to meet someone described to you as a "comedian," you will probably focus more on the funny things he says and either forget or be surprised by the serious remarks you hear. Since we cannot possibly pay attention to every message sent our way, the ones we do receive are greatly affected by our cognitive frame of reference. Listening, for instance, is a communication skill that can be greatly improved by recognizing some common cognitive biases that block or distort our reception of messages.

Social Cognition and Action

The ability to act in an appropriate or effective manner also rests on the frame of reference we have in any given situation. In every situation, we have to orient ourselves, to figure out where we are and what's going on. Too many people limit their message-sending options because they miss the relevant cues in their environment. Although we can never attend to or understand all of the cues, we can try to know as much as possible. As we see it, to create appropriate messages requires that you know (cognitively) *where* you are, *who* you are interacting with, *what* the two of you are doing together, what *relationship* you should assume exists between you, and finally, *why* you each say and do the things you say and do. As a result of these cognitive decisions, message options should become clearer.

Social Cognition and Control

Awareness of social cognition processes gives us back some of the control we lose when we take the process for granted. Most of the time we perceive things around us unconsciously, leading us to engage in sequences of behavior that Ellen Langer describes as "mindless interaction."[1] We zoom along on automatic pilot, following socially standardized patterns of interaction that require little or no mental effort. Greetings are a common form of mindless interaction. How many times have you communicated as automatically as Pat does in this

passing conversation in a crowded, noisy hallway:

PAT: Good morning, Chris. How's it going?

CHRIS: Not good. You want to make something of it?

PAT: Fine, thanks.

CHRIS: Good. Why don't we step outside?

PAT: Yeah, good to see you, too. Take care.

We tend to interact unthinkingly in many situations. The reason for the frequency of mindless interaction is that we overlearn situations so well that it is almost like following a script. In fact, much of our interaction is scripted (we are able to predict what will happen next with considerable accuracy). We'll have more to say about such scripts later in this chapter. Charles Berger and William Douglas argue that we pay close attention to our own and others' behavior only under rather specific conditions, such as: (1) novel situations where no script exists; (2) when external factors interrupt a scripted interaction; (3) when scripted behavior requires more effort than usual; (4) when the outcome of a situation is not what we expected; and (5) when multiple scripts come into conflict.[2] In most circumstances, we act without being all that aware of what we're doing.

In many cases, such mindless interaction may actually be quite efficient. If we stopped to think about everything we do, our interactions would be filled with more hesitations and awkward pauses than usual. But a steady diet of mindless interaction can take the control of communication right out of our hands. We then run the risk of not learning from successful communication encounters because we can't remember what happened. And of course, bad habits are repeated endlessly when we aren't aware of them.

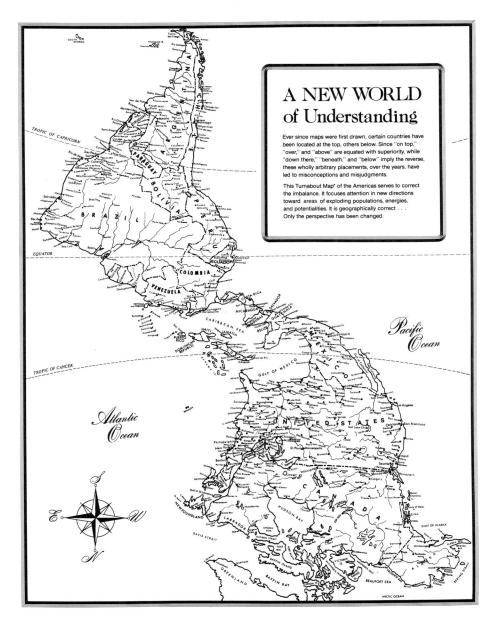

A NEW WORLD of Understanding

Ever since maps were first drawn, certain countries have been located at the top, others below. Since "on top," "over," and "above" are equated with superiority, while "down there," "beneath," and "below" imply the reverse, these wholly arbitrary placements, over the years, have led to misconceptions and misjudgments.

This Turnabout Map® of the Americas serves to correct the imbalance. It focuses attention in new directions toward areas of exploding populations, energies, and potentialities. It is geographically correct . . . Only the perspective has been changed.

Our frame of reference determines much of what we see and hear. In this clever *Turnabout Map of the Americas*, our assumptions are graphically turned "upside down."

Communication Affects Social Cognition

The relationship between social cognition processes and communication is not one-way. Just as the cognitive frame of reference influences how we send and receive messages, the messages we exchange with others can influence and change our own cognitive representations of the social world. As we will see later, one's stereotypes of people who belong to a social group may change as a result of interacting with people who view members of that group differently. We certainly hope that the ideas communicated in this text and in your classroom will affect the way you see your social world, adding some new concepts, rearranging old ones, and eliminating those that hamper your ability to communicate effectively.

As you can see, your cognitive frame of reference does influence the way you communicate. It is not, however, set in stone. There are a number of things you can do to become more mindful of and to alter that frame of reference, so you can get on with the business of communication. The first step is arming yourself with the knowledge of how social cognition processes work. To do that, we begin by looking at the process of perception—how our mind interacts with the physical and social world around us.

THE PERCEPTUAL PROCESS: AN OVERVIEW

There are two ways to think about the relationship between events and our perceptions of them. One view is that physical reality just happens and our senses, as long as they are not impaired, record what is out there in a more or less objective fashion. This suggests that we are *passive* receivers of incoming stimuli—much like the windshield on your car collects insects and dirt particles that happen to come its way. Most theorists, however, believe that perception is an *active* process. Even seeing physical objects as having some existence in reality is the result of a long process of learning to manage our perceptions. For instance, most of us can distinguish our hand from the objects we hold in it. Yet a newborn is unable to make a distinction between her hand and the rattle she is holding. She has to learn to structure her perceptions in a particular way before she draws this conclusion.

Creating Structure, Stability, and Meaning

We construct our own reality by organizing, stabilizing, and relating the stream of stimuli around us in meaningful ways.[3] Normally our culture provides us with a number of ways to structure events. We are not born into a world with no meaning at all. But most of the meaning is social—conventions and agreements created by the members of social groups. For instance, every culture finds its own ways to structure the passing of time. In our culture, a "day" is broken down into smaller units of hours, minutes, and seconds. But we do not perceive every unit of time objectively. On some occasions, such as watching the end of a close basketball game or timing the 100-meter dash, we structure time into seconds and even hundredths of a second. At other times, we structure time so loosely that hours may go by without even registering. We may forget to eat or go to class because we're wrapped up in a good book or involved in a conversation with an old friend we haven't seen in years. We simply don't perceive the passing of time.

During the course of a baseball game, the home plate umpire has to structure and restructure a strike zone for each batter. There is no

BOX 3.1

Perception Goes to the Movies: How Cinematographers Influence What We See

a

Filmmakers are faced with the challenge of communicating their visual message through a limited medium. The "big screen" is only a two-dimensional rectangle, with a dominant horizontal shape. Every scene in a film has to be conveyed within this frame. To create the appearance of depth or extreme heights, a feeling of suspense, or emotional arousal, a director or cinematographer must know quite a lot about the perceptual processes of the audience. They must determine how we are likely to interpret and react to the placement and movement of elements within the frame, the effects of lighting and color, different camera angles, and so on. What do cinematographers know about us that enables them to achieve their intended effects?

Whether their knowledge is implicit or explicit, filmmakers understand a number of perceptual principles that have become the basis for a conventionalized code of filmmaking. For one thing, they know that our attention is most likely to be drawn to the central portion of the screen. We expect elements within the frame to be balanced, with dominant elements near the center, or slightly above center in the case of most medium shots. When a director's purpose is to achieve realism, most shots will be balanced in this way, since that is what he or she knows the audience expects. The result is unobtrusive. But when a sense of drama is needed, the "norm" is usually violated. Dominant figures or elements may be placed near the edge of the screen, perhaps even fading out of the picture.

To create a sense of dominance or power, important elements may be emphasized by placing them in the top third of the screen. Sometimes this is done subtly by focusing the camera clearly on a character in the center third, leaving another character slightly out of focus. The result is a "reminder" of who is really in control (see Photo **a**). Also by using a low camera angle, a figure on the screen may appear more dominant or menacing, as it looks down on us or on other characters or objects.

The opposite effect can be achieved by placing characters in

---

such thing as an objective strike zone. The pitcher, catcher, and batter each see a different strike zone as well. For each of them, the stimulus of a pitched ball and a batter's reaction will be categorized as a ball or strike, a fair or foul ball, and so on. Each is likely to structure the stimulus somewhat differently from the other players or umpires.

People perceive objects as stable and unchanging. The next time you watch television, pay close attention to the size of the images on the screen (and thus on the retina of your eye). When the camera shot is a close-up, a person's face may be as large as the entire screen. As the camera fades away, the head gets smaller. Yet you have no trouble assuming that it's the same

the lower portion of the frame. Characters placed this way look especially vulnerable or helpless, and even more so if the rest of the screen is empty or stark in contrast to the lonely figure at the bottom of the screen. A bird's-eye camera view (directly overhead of the action) is disorienting to the viewer, since we rarely see such a view in ordinary life. Scenes constructed in this fashion are often used to portray a theme of fate or destiny.

In our culture, we also expect forward movement to be conveyed from left to right. By showing movement "against the grain," a filmmaker can create a feeling of tension in the viewer. Downward motion can be used to invoke a sense of danger or vulnerability.

Bright or dark color, as well as special lighting, can dominate a frame. Our attention is drawn to brighter colors and lighted areas of an otherwise dark screen (see Photo **b**). Darkly lit scenes and dark colors may symbolize doom for the characters involved. Color may also be used to balance other compositional

b

features in the frame. A dominant shape on one side of the screen might be compensated for by a bright color on the other side.

These conventions are but a few of the tricks of the trade that cinematographers rely on to communicate through film. Each is based on research in perceptual processes. Can you think of other ways that filmmakers try to manage what you see on the screen?

ADDITIONAL READINGS

Giannetti, Louis D. *Understanding Movies*. Englewood Cliffs, N.J.: Prentice-Hall, 1976.

Nichols, Bill, *Ideology and the Image*. Bloomington: Indiana University Press, 1981.

person with the same size head; you don't think the person's head is constantly expanding and contracting. You are actively processing the stimulus so that it appears stable in size. The point is that the actual image on the retina of the eye is not stable—it keeps changing in size—but we perceive it as stable.

Finally, we relate events or stimuli to each other in ways that have meaning for us. When you develop a headache, you probably try to relate its occurrence to something else in the environment. The jackhammer outside your window, the glare of your computer screen, or the presence of someone you despise at your birthday party may all be leading candidates for the cause of your headache. Actually, none of these may be responsible, but the perception that they are meaningfully related will influence your behavior, as you close the window, turn off the computer, or try to leave the party. Medical researchers engage in the same process of trying to relate environmental stimuli and the body's physiological responses in meaningful ways. They just use more sophisticated theories and statistical models to decide what is "meaningful."

Studies show how ingrained the process is even when no apparent order or meaning exists. In one study, a tape recording of indistinct vowel sounds was presented to people with the following instructions: "This is a recording of a man talking. He is not speaking very plainly, but if you listen carefully you will be able to tell what he is saying. I'll play it over and over again, so you can get it, but be sure to tell me as soon as you have an idea of what he is saying." Surprisingly, people had little trouble identifying intelligible verbal content, unaware that it was entirely their own creation.[4]

It should be clear by now just how much of a role we play in our own perceptions of objects, events, and people. The process can be arbitrarily broken down into a series of steps, even though they may often occur simultaneously. Let's look at how we expose ourselves and selectively attend to some stimuli, add previous knowledge or expectations regarding that stimulus, and integrate what we see, hear, or feel into an organized whole.

Selective Exposure and Attention

There is no shortage of stimuli in everyday life. Regardless of whether the situation is a solitary activity or a communicative event, we are exposed to many more stimuli than our brain can possibly process. Sometimes we go out of our way to expose ourselves to stimuli. **Selective exposure** refers to placing ourselves in or avoiding situations where we will be certain to encounter a specific stimulus. Visiting another country, enrolling in foreign-language or anthropology courses, and listening to international broadcasts on short-wave radio will expose you to stimuli not experienced by many Americans. Turning off the television and avoiding caffeine are also ways of selecting what you are exposed to.

Once in an environment, we will selectively attend to some stimuli and ignore others. **Selective attention** refers to our active participation in determining which of the many stimuli present we will actually perceive. As you read this, stop and try to process as many stimuli as you can. Check all of your senses. What background noises can you bring into focus (for example, the stereo, television, humming of the refrigerator)? What can you feel that you were not aware of moments ago? What can you see in your field of vision if you really concentrate? Now you have some idea just how much there is to be processed at any given moment. Imagine not being able to block out some of these sights and sounds in order to return to the task of reading this chapter.

Fortunately, we can tune in and out the sensory inputs we receive. To a certain extent, this process is outside our awareness. Some environmental features seem to demand our attention. For instance, brightly colored moving objects generally catch our attention more than dull, stationary ones; extremely tall persons stand out in a crowd; speed bumps on highways are hard to ignore because they are such a contrast to the relatively flat road surface. At other times, physiological states may influence what you perceive. People who suffer from allergies such as hay fever notice more pollen in the air, selectively tune in when the pollen count is given on the evening weather report, and rarely pass over a sales ad for allergy medication.

While these examples make it appear that our attention is dictated by external affairs, we

Look at John Haberle's *Grandma's Hearthstone* for a few moments; then look away and try to recall as many objects on the hearthstone as you can. This exercise will give you some idea of just how selective your attention and recall can be.

do exercise a great deal of control over what we perceive. We pay more attention to things that interest us or things that we are mentally prepared to see or hear. The fact that your best friend drives a brown, banged-up Chevy Impala may set you up to notice every brown Chevy Impala that crosses your path.

Past experiences, present motivations, and future goals all play a role in what we choose to attend to out of the myriad of stimuli in the world.

Interpreting and Organizing Stimuli

Once a stimulus has caught our attention, we must classify it in some way and relate it to other known stimulus categories. First, let's look at how we interpret what we perceive.

Interpreting Objects

As an infant, the entire world was new to you. Every object within sight needed to be touched and studied carefully, so you could figure out what to do with it. By now, you've probably seen it all, or most of it, anyway. The difference is that you now perceive many objects as already interpreted. Once you were not so sure. The process of interpreting is done so quickly that we usually don't realize it. When driving to work or school, you immediately interpret a stimulus that is red, octagonal, and attached to a six-foot pole alongside the road. Stop signs are familiar objects to drivers. But what if you suddenly see a small, brownish blur darting in front of your car? Can you categorize it as quickly as you do a stop sign? It may have been a squirrel, a puppy, or a brown paper bag. At times like these you are a little more aware that you are interpreting reality as much as seeing it. If we occasionally have difficulty interpreting concrete objects, imagine the problems we face when interpreting something as abstract as the communication behavior of another person.

Organizing Stimuli

The stimuli we do attend to and interpret do not exist in isolation. As we saw earlier, we connect various stimuli in ways that make them more meaningful. Cognitive psychologists tend to rely on one of two explanations for how the brain integrates all these bits of information. They have also identified several mental models that enable us to organize our perceptions.

Two explanations of organization. Earlier we told you that some theorists believe humans to be passive receivers of stimuli, whereas others grant us a more active role in the perceptual process. The more passive explanations are *theories of association.* Psychologists who hold this view believe that the brain simply records things as they are naturally. Some stimuli occur together more frequently in nature or have similar properties. The brain simply "reads" these co-occurrences or similarities, firing electrical impulses that create stimulus–response patterns of organization.

Other explanations assume a more active role on the part of the perceiver. These approaches, called *theories of construction*, are based on the assumption that the brain creates cognitive models and then imposes them on the stimuli received, rather than vice versa. A simple example will illustrate this. Figure 3.2 is an exaggeration of the kind of "cognitive maps" we impose on our world. No one would argue that this map is "accurate," yet many people deal with the complexities of the modern world by reducing it to much simpler terms.

Think about the path that you take to work or school every day. If you had to draw a map of how to get there, you would not suddenly recall every turn in the road or every signpost along the way. You would forget landmarks and features that do not fit your own mental model of how to get there. It is the cognitive model that you rely on, not the real landscape between home and office.

*Using schema: prototypes, constructs, stereo-
types, and scripts.* Cognitive psychologists use
the term *schema* as a general label for the many
kinds of mental models. A **schema** is a cognitive
structure that helps us process and organize
information.[5] So far, researchers have identified
four basic types of schema that we think are
relevant to interpersonal communication: prototypes, personal constructs, stereotypes, and
scripts.

Prototypes help us to categorize objects,
people, and events. They answer the question
"What is it?" A **prototype** is an organized set
of knowledge that reflects the best example of a
category of persons, objects, or events.[6] Thus
we each have our own prototypical image of a
used-car salesperson, a comfortable chair, and
a good party. No two Doberman pinschers are
identical, yet we have a mental image of what
one looks like. The more any dog looks like the
prototype, the easier it is to classify. In interpersonal communication, prototypes help us
"identify" what kind of person we are dealing
with by matching their appearance, behavior,
and perceived qualities to a known prototype.

A **personal construct**, on the other hand,
allows us to describe things in greater detail
and make judgments about them. Constructs
are mental yardsticks for deciding how two
things are similar, yet different from a third
thing.[7] They answer the questions "What are
its characteristics? What do I think about it?"
For instance, you might judge Dobermans to
be mean and dangerous, while another person
describes them as cute and obedient. The terms
mean, dangerous, cute, and *obedient* are examples
of personal constructs. We will look at other
examples of constructs in perception later in
this chapter.

Stereotypes are closely related to prototypes, but they are not the same thing. A
prototype categorizes people; a stereotype goes
beyond categorizing to the level of prediction.
A stereotype is simply a set of beliefs about the

FIGURE 3.2

**We impose our own cognitive models on the
world we see. Here is what the United States
might look like to a West Coast publisher.**

probable behavior of members of a particular
group.[8] Stereotypes have a certain sense of
"allness" to them, as if every member of a class
always behaves like other members. Thus stereotypes answer the question "What can I
expect it to do?" You might stereotype the
Doberman pinscher as an attack dog, expecting
it to take your leg off if you get too near.
Stereotypes may or may not be accurate. They
may outlive their usefulness and they may be
unfair to individuals, but they do make the
world more organized and predictable.

Prototypes are the "best examples" of a category of people or objects. Robert Bechtle's painting looks like a photograph—but that illusion is just another method the artist uses to comment on the prototypical American family he presents. (*'61 Pontiac*, 1968–69)

Scripts are guides to action. A **script** is defined as a "coherent sequence of events expected by the individual either as a participant or as an observer."[9] Scripts answer the questions "What can we do together? How shall I proceed? What do I do next?" Many scripts such as attending a traditional wedding or going to a Catholic Mass are well defined and make it easy for us to know what to do next. Unscramble the following list of behaviors associated with a "restaurant" script, and place them in the usual sequence:

- waiter takes your order
- pay the bill
- go to the salad bar
- look at the menu
- leave a tip
- host seats you

- waiter brings your meal
- waiter brings water
- ask about the special

Chances are that you know the script pretty well. What other situations do you know that are highly scripted? Can you identify the sequence of events? Which ones are crucial? Which ones could be omitted without ruining the performance of the script?

Prototypes, constructs, stereotypes, and scripts are all extremely useful cognitive schema. Next we will examine how they work in interpersonal situations.

FOUR TASKS IN INTERPERSONAL PERCEPTION

To interact with others successfully requires a wealth of social knowledge. You must be able to perceive enough information in your social environment to know which of the hundreds of schemas in your memory bank are the best ones to pull out of the vault. This is, of course, a very complicated operation. Cognitive psychologists are just beginning to understand how we do it. We have tried to simplify the problem by highlighting what we call the four perceptual tasks that everyone needs to understand: identifying (1) the situation; (2) who the other person is; (3) who you are and what kind of relationship between self and other is implied; and (4) why things unfold the way they do.

Sizing Up Situations

The more we know about the particular situations in which we interact with others, the more likely we are to produce effective messages. We propose three useful ways to manage situations: by identifying episodes, scripts, and potential consequences of following scripts.

Orienting Ourselves: Episode Identification

At one time or another, we have all been in situations where we didn't know what was going on or what to do. Visiting a foreign culture or being initiated into a sorority or fraternity are examples of situations that are not very well defined for us. Knowing the situation can make interactions much easier. In its simplest form, a situation is "a place plus a definition."[10] When we enter a place, our first task is to orient ourselves.

Orientation is a process of establishing a locus in the world, of finding a basis for one's relationship to the world. The clearest example is orientation in space, which means finding a place or set of places in the physical environment from which one's activities can be directed.[11]

Once we have identified the physical setting and our place in it, we must define what we can do socially. Each culture has an array of social episodes or activities for its members to follow. For the individual, **social episodes** are "internal cognitive representations about common, recurring interaction routines within a defined cultural milieu."[12] Some typical social episodes? Having a big family dinner, attending a parent–teacher conference, planning a party, gossiping. To recognize what social episode is appropriate requires that we attend to the "sense of place" (where we are) and the subtle signs that the other person defines the situation similarly. Social interaction is a continuous dance in which participants accept and decline each other's invitations to enact different episodes. For instance, when two old friends have a chance meeting on the street, the question "Can I buy you a drink?" is an invitation to engage in the episode of "talking over old times." Refusing the drink because you are not thirsty would be missing the point—a failure to recognize the other's definition of the situation.

Using Scripts to Guide Interaction: Open, Closed, and Defined Episodes

When people play out an episode, they may also follow a script. As we have seen, a script is a highly predictable sequence of events. Some classroom learning episodes are highly scripted, others are not. For instance, you may be able to predict (from experience) that every Wednesday morning, your history professor will hand out a quiz, call the roll, collect the quizzes, lecture for 20 minutes, and close the class with a humorous anecdote. The more predictable the sequence of events, the more scripted the interaction is.

Scripts and episodes are useful guides to interaction. Knowing the episode narrows the range of possible actions and reactions. Knowing the script makes social life even more predictable. Michael Brenner has proposed that the vast majority of social episodes fall into one of three types: closed, open, and defined episodes.[13]

Closed episodes. This situation is almost completely scripted. Rules for proper behavior are well known in advance and govern the flow of interaction. Rituals such as greetings and religious observances are closed episodes. Many business organizations make interactions within their doors highly scripted by training their personnel to follow carefully devised sets of procedures. If you've ever applied for a loan at a bank, you have probably participated in a closed episode. You have a standard set of questions you want answers to (the loan rate, fixed or variable, length of repayment, and so on) and so does the loan officer (where you work, live, credit references). Other, less formal interactions are also somewhat scripted. The

episode of "small talk" has a limited range of topics, although the sequence in which they are discussed may vary.

Open episodes. When participants enter a situation without any preconceived plan (or with a very general one), they are involved in an open episode. There is greater freedom in such situations to create new forms of interaction and to change episodes in midstream. Some open episodes may actually be frightening, since there is no clear idea of what should be done next. Perhaps you have been in situations where nobody seemed to know what to do. We know of an instructor whose "first day of class" routine was to walk into the class, sit lotus-position on top of his desk, and say nothing for the first half of the class. His point was to show how communication is used to define ambiguous situations. Eventually students would begin talking to one another, trying to figure out what he was doing. From the students' point of view, this was an open episode.

Defined episodes. While closed episodes are known in advance as a result of expectations, many situations are defined "in progress" as participants follow their own personal goals and plans to achieve a working consensus. Even so, the consensus is often temporary. Definitions of the situation may fall apart as quickly as they develop. Brenner argues that ambiguity of meaning and unstructured interactions are common because both partners may be proposing alternative directions for the episode. A not-very-good salesperson might initiate a "sales episode" but eventually succumb to a clever-but-unwilling-to-buy customer's definition of the situation as "shooting the breeze." In close relationships, people may spend a lot of time just deciding what episode to enact next. We know of four friends who, in the course of one evening, proposed over 20

Our individual traits are minimized in many social situations so that our behavior will conform to social expectations. Note how Cezanne emphasizes the card players' concentration on the game—so intent are they that their individual personalities are suppressed. (Paul Cezanne, *The Card Players*)

different activities for that evening. Needless to say, they ended up doing nothing but talking about what they could be doing. No working consensus was ever achieved.

Although we may think that closed episodes are too limiting and value open ones for the freedom they provide, stop and think how chaotic social life would be without any well-defined or scripted episodes. The important thing, of course, is that we recognize the types of episodes others propose so that we can accept the invitation or decline gracefully.

Consequences of Episodes and Scripts

Sometimes it is just as important to perceive the possible outcomes of a situation, like the chess player who sees several moves ahead, as it is to properly label that situation. We can avoid detrimental outcomes if we can see them coming.

BOX 3.2

The Nine Nations of North America: A Matter of Perception

Most of us realize that working in the international business community or taking a vacation to Europe will bring us in contact with members of other cultures. In these instances we prepare ourselves to be more sensitive to differences in verbal and nonverbal codes. We are not so likely to be concerned about a summer visit to the cousins in Oklahoma or a vacation to see the redwood forest. But, according to Joel Garreau, author of *The Nine Nations of North America*, we should be. Our continent is not three nations, but nine. "Each has its capital and its distinctive web of power and influence. A few are allies, but many are adversaries. . . . These nations look different, feel different, and sound different from each other, and few of their boundaries match

the political lines drawn on current maps." The following brief summaries name at least one major feature that characterizes each nation. Imagine how a conversation between members of any two cultures might proceed.

New England. Compared to the members of other nations, there is no doubt that New Englanders see themselves as articulate, traditional, and intellectually superior. But they are also hardy survivors who take an immense pride in their villages and their history. It is perhaps the poorest of the nine nations, but the key to an economic rebound has already begun. This is the first true postindustrial society, and Yankee ingenuity is finding ways to overcome the lack of raw materials and energy.

The Foundry. The key to this nation is the work ethic. These people see themselves as the "real" America. Their habitat is the city. They define themselves by their work. "Ask these people who they are, and before they say man, woman, Methodist, Catholic, American, Canadian, Democrat, Republican, black, white, or brown, they'll say, for example: steelworker."

Dixie. The pace of life and personalized interactions set their culture apart from its Northern neighbors. "If you wish to buy a screwdriver, for example, you first pause, mention the weather, remark on the price of seed, joke with the girl behind the counter, and *then* ask for the tool. Brusquely and impersonally attempting to slap down money and leave with your merchandise marks you as an outsider."

The Islands. Miami is the capital of the Islands and has more in common with Venezuela than it does with the rest of Florida and North America. Drugs, international trade, and tourism are the dominant industries. Spanish is the real language of this culture. Multinational companies are very likely to establish headquarters here. But integration of Anglo and Spanish cultures is far from a reality. Says one Anglo, "'Oh, nobody goes downtown' . . . What they really mean is that nobody who doesn't speak Spanish goes downtown."

Mexamerica. In contrast to the Islands, integration *is* occurring in Mexamerica. Not only are English and Spanish dominant languages, they are blended together frequently. In a depart-

---

Salespeople use the tried-and-true "yes technique" to set up unwitting customers. They ask questions that seem unrelated to selling their product, such as "Are those lovely photographs of *your* children?" "I've had a hard time catching you at home. You must work awfully long hours." The customer's automatic "yes" in response to each question or comment estab-

lishes an habitual pattern that could cost a lot of money at the end of the episode.

Following a script can lead to positive or negative outcomes. Sometimes we know the script so well that we can tell our friends what they are going to say next. If we finish the sentence for them, they may be gratified that we understand them so well or offended that

ment store you are likely to be asked to "presta mi su credit card." The language is "built on Spanish . . . but . . . has a fast-paced, direct, United States style that says what it has to say in a hurry." There are truly three cultures inhabiting this nation: Mexicans, Americans, and Mexican-Americans—and they differ from each other in basic values.

Ecotopia. While most of the Nine Nations espouse the philosophy that "bigger is better," Ecotopians actually believe in people working with nature, not against it. And they vote that way, too. They support environmental policies, holistic medical systems, a ban on nuclear waste and are willing to have a lower standard of living in order to raise their overall quality of life.

The Empty Quarter. This is the nation that still resembles the Old West. It is mineral-rich, but sparsely populated. You can drive for days between cities. The lack of rainfall makes water rights and usage a major political and economic factor. This structures an adversarial relationship with the East Coast decision makers, who largely *(continued)*

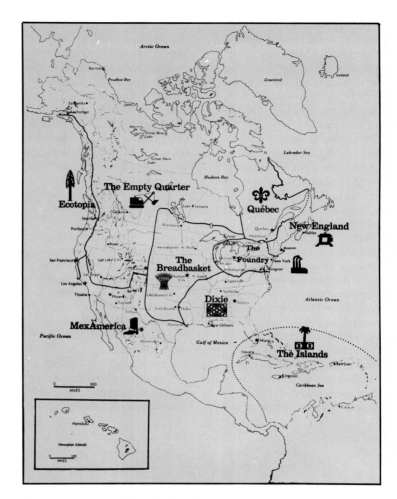

The nine nations of North America

we cut them off. Thus it's important to know something about the other person as well as the situation itself.

Sizing Up People

As we interact, we come to an understanding of what other people are like. Knowing how to size up the individual is another way to reduce our uncertainty about communication. Researchers have studied the process of impression formation, discovering several factors that influence our judgment. We will discuss four of these factors: the use of personal constructs, implicit personality theory, self-fulfilling prophecies, and cognitive complexity.

BOX 3.2, *continued*

ignore these concerns. Citizens of the Empty Quarter are more optimistic about "progress" than their Ecotopia neighbors. The Empty Quarter believes that natural resources can and should be developed.

The Breadbasket. Garreau found the Breadbasket to be the nation most at peace with itself. Eighty percent of the land is devoted to farming, and it produces three-fourths of the continent's wheat and corn. Stability, straightforwardness, and social calm are the primary virtues of its people. These prairie dwellers are somewhat defensive about their lifestyle, especially to Easterners who see the Breadbasket as behind the times and to Eastern politicians who ignore the concerns of farmers. Interaction between plainsfolk and Eastern visitors demonstrates their skeptical relations. Garreau identified

what he calls the "aw shucks" routine. The native, upon learning that the visitor is from the East, begins to put down his own surroundings: "You can't get any good clam chowder" and "There's not much excitement here." But Garreau warns us not to believe a word of it. "He's just trying to find out if the outlander is ignorant enough to bite at the statement."

Quebec. This proud, French-speaking province of Canada is probably the most distinguishable "nation" of the nine, yet it is also the most improbable one. It is distinct because 80 percent of its inhabitants speak French and *think* of their province as a real nation. It is the nation with customs and traditions that are dramatically different from those of its North American neighbors. The improbability of Quebec is that it has survived for more than 400 years surrounded by English-

speaking peoples without losing its own identity. In fact, the English who live in Quebec are often attracted to its uniqueness and want to participate in its language and customs.

According to Garreau, you can forget the map of North America you learned in elementary school. It doesn't really matter anymore. What you can do, as you travel the nine nations, is to look for the differences in talk, values, customs, and politics that characterize each "nation"—as well as the things they have in common—and recognize that intercultural communication does take place right here at home.

Source: *Joel Garreau,* The Nine Nations of North America *(New York: Avon Books, 1981). Copyright © 1981 by Joel Garreau. Reprinted with permission of Houghton Mifflin Company.*

Using Constructs to Judge Others

Earlier in the chapter, we identified personal constructs as mental yardsticks for evaluating objects, events, and people. Here we focus on how we use those constructs to form impressions of those people we communicate with. Since constructs are "personal," no two people will use them in exactly the same way. You and I may both observe Bill eating a sandwich in two bites, ketchup dribbling down his chin. You may think he is "aggressive," while I argue that he is "messy" and "impolite." What we see in others is a combination of their actual

behavior and our personal constructions of their behavior. These constructs say as much about you and me as they do about Bill.

Even though we each use different constructs to judge others, we do use them in similar ways. Steven Duck has noted a typical pattern in the use of four different kinds of constructs.[14] The four types are:

- physical constructs (tall–short; beautiful–ugly)
- role constructs (buyer–seller; teacher–student)

- interaction constructs (friendly–hostile; nice–rude)
- psychological constructs (motivated–lazy; kind–cruel)

Initial impressions are frequently physical. We take stock of the way people are dressed or how attractive they are. These are quickly followed by role constructs as we try to make sense out of each other's position in the social world. As we talk, attention can be focused on interaction constructs, or aspects of the other's style of communication. Finally, we use these observations to infer what makes the other tick—we begin to devise motivations and a personality for the other. When we reach this last stage, we have gone beyond simply interpreting what we see and hear; we've begun to assume that we know things about the person that we can't see.

Organizing Trait Impressions: Implicit Personality Theory

We don't simply form isolated opinions of other people; we organize all of our individual perceptions into a more complete picture by filling in a lot of missing information. One of the ways we do this is referred to as an **implicit personality theory**. This is the belief on our part that certain individual traits are related to other traits. If we observe a trait that we think is part of a cluster, we will assume that the person also has the rest of those traits. Each of us has our own notions of what traits go together. For some, the traits (or constructs) *intelligent, quiet,* and *friendly* may cluster together.[15] If we observe behavior that we interpret as friendly and quiet, we may then attribute intelligence to that person without any first-hand evidence.

Some traits may carry more weight than others in forming impressions and can be described as *central traits*. When present, a central trait changes the way we perceive the whole cluster of traits. In a classic study, social psychologist Harold Kelley presented two groups of students with the following list of adjectives describing a new instructor they were about to meet. One group was told the new instructor was: *warm*, industrious, critical, practical, and determined. The other group heard this description of the instructor: *cold*, industrious, critical, practical, and determined.

Which description do you think led students to form a more favorable impression? If you said the first description, you are in agreement with most of the students in this study. The central trait (warm–cold) changed the way the perceiver judged the other traits, which in turn affected the overall impression.[16]

Another factor that makes some traits stand out is *when* they are first perceived. The tendency for first impressions to be lasting ones is known as the **primacy effect**. When more recent observations change our initial impression, we have the **recency effect**. Which is more likely to happen? Generally, the primacy effect rules. We tend to form impressions quickly and hold on to them. Psychiatrist Leonard Zunin estimates that the first impression is formed solidly within the first four minutes of interaction with a stranger, followed by a decision to continue or terminate the episode.[17]

Prototypes and stereotypes may also affect the emerging impression. Physical traits or key words and phrases used by a person may be so similar to our image of the prototypical "sales manager type" that we have trouble describing him in any other way. Furthermore, if you have an associated stereotype that all salespeople have loose morals and tell insensitive jokes, you can flesh out a complete impression in a matter of a few seconds. Once these cognitive models are engaged, you may selectively attend to behaviors that are consistent with the image

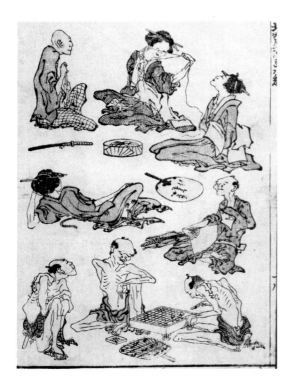 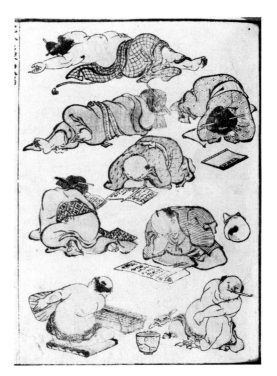

Body type is often taken to be a cue for personality, yet such attributions vary according to culture. Japanese artist Hokusai depicts thin people as energetic and tense; his fat people seem more relaxed and cheerful.

and ignore those that don't fit. Thus we reinforce stereotypes even in the face of contradictory evidence.

Interpersonal Self-Fulfilling Prophecies

Another important perceptual tendency is the self-fulfilling prophecy. Unlike the more passive implicit personality theory (in which traits are associated in the mind), the self-fulfilling prophecy involves both perception *and* behavior. It starts when one person, the observer, believing something to be true about another person, the target, begins acting toward the target as if the belief were fact. This action prompts the target to behave in line with the observer's expectations. If you believe your friend is "touchy," you are likely to avoid sensitive topics and be more hesitant in what you say. The effect of your behavior: Your friend becomes oversensitive because *you* are acting oversolicitous. Unaware that you helped create the touchy atmosphere, you say to yourself, "My God, it's true. You can't say anything to him."

Factors Affecting Impression Formation: Cognitive Complexity

Not everyone forms impressions in the same way. Observers differ in the number and quality of personal constructs they use to evaluate others. A cognitively complex person's system of personal constructs is greater in number *(differentiation)*, includes more abstract psychological categories *(abstraction)*, and has more elaborated ways of connecting various constructs *(integration)*.[18] A cognitively simple person has fewer, less abstract constructs about people and views those constructs as relatively isolated impressions. Let's look at an example comparing the two extremes.

Suppose Pat and Chris observe Marvin on several occasions. They are both present when Marvin (1) cheats on an English test; (2) takes charge and gets everyone out of a burning building; (3) refuses to help with a charity car wash; (4) helps a friend study for a difficult math test; (5) embarrasses another friend by pointing out her faults in front of a large group of people; and (6) always gives blood when there is an opportunity.

If you want to test yourself, you might write down your own impression of Marvin before reading on. Then come back and read the impressions that Chris and Pat have formed.

To Pat, Marvin is "tall and handsome, but extremely selfish, difficult to get along with, and not trustworthy." When reminded of some of the positive things Marvin has done, Pat just shrugs and says, "It's just a front. The real Marvin is a cheat."

To Chris, "Marvin seems selfish when he is unsure of himself, but quite selfless when he knows he can help out. Marvin is also very outspoken and direct—he says what is on his mind. If he believes in a cause, he'll support it. If he doesn't think it's important, he won't give it the time of day." Chris sums up Marvin's behavior as being motivated by his insecurity.

"If he didn't worry so much about being noticed, he wouldn't make himself look so bad. He has real potential."

Why are these two impressions so different? Pat uses fewer, more concrete constructs (for example, tall and handsome) and ignores much of the information that doesn't fit with the emerging impression. If this impression is typical, Pat's construct system is a relatively undeveloped one. Contrast that with Chris, who demonstrates a fairly high level of cognitive complexity. By integrating the apparent contradictions in Marvin's behavior, Chris has arrived at a more subtle understanding of Marvin, recognizing situational constraints as well as psychological motivations.

Research has shown cognitively complex persons to be more accurate in processing information about others, better at placing themselves in the role of the other person, and more patient in weighing most of the evidence before formulating a complete impression.[19] Less complex individuals tend to either stick with their original impression and ignore contradictory information or change the impression to fit the most recent information they have.[20] They lack the ability to integrate the constructs they use into a more complete image of the other.

Considering the differences between more complex and less complex persons, you might get the impression that the more complex the better. Actually, it depends on the situation and the other person. Imagine Pat and Chris trading impressions. They'd probably drive each other crazy. Pat would claim that Chris thinks too much and analyzes everybody. Chris would charge Pat with making snap judgments. It's probably easy to think of situations where the more complex person has an advantage. But can you identify situations where the less complex person would fare better? What about a situation that calls for a quick response?

Children learn who they might (or might not) become by imitating the activities and behavior of their parents.

Sizing Up Relationships

As we read the situation and form impressions of the other, we also face the perceptual task of determining what relevant aspects of *self* fit the situation and how to interpret the emerging *relationship* between self and other.

Self-Monitoring: Deciding Who to Be

Although we will consider the self-concept and communication in much more detail in Chapters 4 and 5, it is important to realize that perceptions of self are frequently connected to our definition of the situation. Just as we form impressions of others, we form and present images of ourselves to others. The awareness of and ability to adapt images of self to the

situation at hand has been referred to as **self-monitoring**.[21] A high self-monitor tends to read the social situation first and then present an appropriate face, as opposed to simply presenting a consistent image of self in every situation.

Mark Snyder characterizes the difference between a high and a low self-monitor in the form of the question each might ask as he defines the situation.

The high self-monitor asks, "Who does this situation want me to be and how can I be that person?" In so doing, the high self-monitoring individual reads the character of the situation to identify the type of person called for by that type of situation, constructs a mental image or representation of a person who best exemplifies that type of person, and uses the prototypic person's self-presentation and expressive behavior as a set of guidelines for monitoring his or her own verbal and nonverbal actions.[22]

The low self-monitor, on the other hand, asks, "Who am I and how can I be me in this situation?" Instead of calling on a prototype to guide his or her actions, the low self-monitor behaves in accordance with an image of her "real" self.

To test yourself, make a list of five or six very different social situations you frequently take part in. Write down how you typically behave in each situation or, better yet, have someone observe you in each of those situations and write down what you do. Then compare your actual behavior to Snyder's self-monitoring questions. Do you normally present a consistent self-image or do you put on a mask for each situation?

Defining Relationships: Self in Relation to Others

When people interact, each presents an image of self to the other. These images are, however, usually quite fluid. We are responsive to the feedback of the other and begin quickly to negotiate a definition of the relationship between self and other. Thus one important perceptual task is the identification of the type of relationship that applies in a given situation. Office workers at a company picnic may perceive that the superior–subordinate relationship with the boss no longer applies during a game of softball. As long as the boss sees things the same way, there's no problem. But what if she assumes she's still in charge and wants to pitch? The difference in perceptions may lead to negative feelings that were never intended.

A wide range of labels for relationships is available to us. We can be casual or longtime acquaintances, friends, close friends, almost friends, just friends, coworkers, neighbors, bowling partners, platonic lovers, husbands and wives, ex-husbands and -wives, blood brothers or sisters, business associates, straightman and funnyman, roommates, counselor and advisee, master and slave, even student and teacher. The list could go on.

Once a relational label is firm in our mind, it tends to limit our perception of what we can do together. Most American couples probably don't even think about drawing up and signing prenuptial agreements about finances or having children. These actions are not perceived as having anything to do with "real" romantic relationships.

Although no empirical studies that we know of have demonstrated the existence of relational prototypes, they probably do exist. In the same way that we have mental images of typical personalities, we may have a cognitive model of the best example of a romantic relationship or a good friendship. No doubt you have heard the phrases "all-American couple" or "Barbie and Ken" to describe prototypical male–female relationships.

Robert Carson has used the term **master contract** to refer to the worked-out definition of a relationship that guides the recurring

interaction of any dyad.[23] This means that as relationships develop, perceptions that were originally guided by a prototype eventually give way to an understanding based on verbalized agreements or silent consent to established patterns of behavior. We will have much more to say about relationships in the remaining chapters of this book. For now, it is important to recognize that identifying what type of relationship you're involved in may be just as crucial as knowing the situation or forming a useful impression of the other.

Explaining Behavior

When all is said and done, we are frequently left with the question "Why did he do that?" Most of the time we're quick to offer some type of explanation. We may feel uneasy when things cannot be accounted for, so we rely on a *causal schema* to explain the behavior we have observed. In this section, we will look at a theory about the types of explanations we provide, and discuss two major perceptual biases that influence our explanations.

Attribution Theory: Accounting for Action

Psychologists who study the process of explaining behavior refer to their research under the rubric of attribution theory. Their concern is not with what actually causes social behavior, but with the process by which we infer particular causes.

Suppose you overheard an argument between two of your friends, Angela and Howie:

ANGELA: Howie! You haven't done the dishes yet? They're left over from last night. Can't you do anything you're asked to do?

HOWIE: It's been a busy morning. I just haven't had time.

ANGELA: No time! You don't have a job. You're not looking for a job. And you can't find 15 minutes to do a dozen dishes?

HOWIE: I've been looking through the classifieds, for your information.

ANGELA: Did you send out any résumés?

HOWIE: No, not really . . .

ANGELA: Here we go again. Do I have to physically *force* you to sit down and write letters of application and send your résumé out?

HOWIE: I'll do it. I'll do it.

ANGELA: You'll do what? The dishes or the résumés? . . .

How do you explain the communication behavior of your two friends? Is Angela the kind of person who constantly nags and belittles others? Or did Howie provoke this tirade? What other explanations could there be?

Attribution research has identified some of the basis types of causes, or attributions, we infer and the conditions under which we infer them.

Four Types of Causal Attributions

Harold Kelley has proposed three classes of explanations and has researched the process underlying each kind of attribution.[24] We have added a fourth category because of our emphasis on relationships. Thus we can account for a person's behavior by attributing it to:

- the actor (the person who performed the behavior)

- the target (the person the behavior is aimed at)

- the situation (circumstances or setting)

- the relationship (the master contract governing actor and target when they interact)

In the example of Angela and Howie, let's focus on Angela's behavior. We'll call her the *actor* in this situation, Howie the *target*. If we believe that there is something about Angela's personality that predisposes her to act this way, we are making an *actor* attribution. If we assume that Howie asked for it, we make a *target* attribution. But what if you knew that Angela had just been told that she was in danger of losing her own job because of budget cuts? You might think that her behavior was more the result of temporary frustration and anxiety, not her personality. In this case, you would be making a *situational* attribution. Finally, you have known both Angela and Howie before they met each other, and you don't think this kind of behavior is really characteristic of either of them. It just seems that when they get together, sparks fly. They're either terribly in love or they're fighting. You might attribute their behavior to the type of *relationship* they have developed.

Can we ever predict which type of attribution will be given? A look at some research on this question may be helpful.

Conditions for attributions: consensus, consistency, and distinctiveness. Kelley's research shows that when we have enough of three types of information about the situation and the parties involved, our explanation will be more predictable. We make causal attributions on the basis of consensus, consistency, and distinctiveness.[25] **Consensus** is judged by asking ourselves if other actors typically behave the same way in similar situations. When episodes are highly scripted and most people follow the script, we are likely to explain their behavior by pointing to the expectations of the situation. If the actor behaves in the same way across a wide range of situations, we have information leading to high **consistency**. If Angela always seems to find a bone to pick, regardless of the situation or the other people involved, her consistency would

When:	We are most likely to attribute responsibility to:
CONSENSUS is low CONSISTENCY is high DISTINCTIVENESS is low	THE ACTOR: The person who performed the behavior
CONSENSUS is high CONSISTENCY is high DISTINCTIVENESS is high	THE TARGET: The person toward whom the behavior is directed
CONSENSUS is high CONSISTENCY is low DISTINCTIVENESS is low	THE SITUATION: The setting or circumstances outside the control of either person
CONSENSUS is low CONSISTENCY is low DISTINCTIVENESS is high	THE RELATIONSHIP: behavior pattern negotiated implicitly or explicitly by both parties

FIGURE 3.3

A model of attribution theory outcomes, based on the work of Harold H. Kelley.

probably lead us to invoke her personality as the prime cause. A judgment of high **distinctiveness** is rendered if we know that no one but the target usually elicits this behavior from the actor. Look at the chart in Figure 3.3 and then think about Angela and Howie again. If we knew that most people don't get upset about dirty dishes or lazy husbands (low consensus), that Angela gets upset frequently and in many different contexts (high consistency), and that

it doesn't usually matter who the target of her anger is (low distinctiveness), then Kelley's theory predicts that you would place the blame (or credit) on Angela herself (the actor).

Attributional Biases

If only life were as simple as consensus, consistency, and distinctiveness. But unfortunately, humans are notoriously irrational at times. There are a number of perceptual biases that affect how we arrive at causal attributions. We rely on some of these biases when we don't have any prior knowledge of the persons being observed, and at other times, the biases just override whatever knowledge we do have.

Personality bias toward others. The most common bias is to explain other people's behavior in terms of their personality dispositions.[26] We are especially prone to this kind of explanation when we observe strangers. We just naturally assume that a stranger who throws a shoe at the television screen lacks self-control or is unstable mentally. The bias is even stronger if the person's behavior is contrary to our expectations.[27] Since we expect people in a restaurant to be eating or drinking, we probably think that only a buffoon would start singing in that setting. Rarely do we look for other explanations—such as the possibility that someone offered him $50 to do it or that the woman he was with accepted his proposal of marriage. Cognitively complex individuals may be less susceptible to this bias, perhaps because of their tendency to engage in role-taking. When we try to see a situation from the other person's point of view, we may see more situational or relational causes.

Situational bias toward self. When we're asked to explain our own behavior, the story is somewhat different. We're more likely to provide a situational explanation. If I throw a shoe at the television, I can explain that it was because of tension built up at the office, a stupid call by the referee, or the loose morals of television producers. One reason may be that I am trying to avoid having others think negatively of me. But another reason is that my vantage point on the action doesn't allow me to see myself doing the action. What I see in my visual field is other people and my external surroundings. It's much more likely that I will

reference the situation as the cause of my behavior.

In addition to these two major biases, we are also likely to be more biased toward personality explanations for members of highly stereotyped out-groups (groups we do not belong to), while giving more situational accounts for members of in-groups such as our own circle of friends.[28]

Relational attributions are far less frequent than the other three types, yet we believe they are equally important. Think about your own behavior with each of three different friends, engaging in the same basic activity (for example, going out for a drink). Chances are that your behavior is different with each friend—and the best explanation is a relational one.

IMPROVING PERCEPTUAL COMPETENCE

One of the themes of this book is improving your competence in communicating with others. But before we can produce messages competently, we must develop **perceptual competence**, or awareness of how we handle the four perceptual tasks outlined in this chapter: defining the situation, constructing a realistic impression of the other, recognizing the type of relationship and self-roles that are appropriate, and assessing what has happened and why.

More specifically, we need to *become aware of our own perceptual blocks.* This may involve overcoming the tendency to rely on simplistic, stereotyped thinking about some situations, some people, and, sometimes, yourself. It may mean that you have to pay more attention to others' nonverbal communication as clues to what they are thinking or feeling. And it means moving away from personality attributions, learning to think more situationally and more relationally. Always check your perceptions by asking, "What did I do that might have contributed to the other's perception and behavior in this situation?"

In addition, *perceptual muscles must be exercised before, during, and after situations*. No doubt this will be difficult at first. You will feel self-conscious and perform awkwardly until the practice becomes second nature to you. But in the long run, you will develop habits that can provide you with greater understanding, prediction, and if you're especially perceptive, greater control of the process.

Finally, *be observant of other people interacting*. Find public places where you can watch people without drawing attention to yourself. Watch films, read novels, and ask questions of others about their interactions. These attempts to become the objective observer can help you cultivate the *distance-from-self* that will enable you to operate on the process level.

Now let's return to the opening scene of this chapter. We asked you to imagine a situation in which you show up at a restaurant for a job interview to be conducted by a friend and one or two other company representatives. Check your impressions of the situation. How did you define the situation and the roles of the three people seated at the table? Were they involved in an episode of "waiting for the interviewee" or an episode of "interviewing a potential job candidate"? That depends on your impressions of each person and their roles. You knew your friend's role, but what about the other male and female? Were they both company representatives or was one of them another job candidate? What nonverbal cues did you pick up on that might help you tell the difference? (Hint: Does one person look more nervous than the others? Is the fact that one person is not having an alcoholic beverage significant?) Was the tone of conversation serious and scripted or light and flexible,

indicating a more open episode? What information is available to help you determine the relationships in this situation? What forms of address were used? How do you interpret your friend's cool and distant greeting? How would you explain her behavior, using attribution theory? Knowing what you know now, how could you best handle this situation?

This chapter has provided you with a lot of information about perceptual processes. We have tried to simplify what you need to know by grouping our knowledge of social cognition processes into four major tasks. We encourage you to become more aware of how you manage these four tasks when you communicate. We also encourage you to continue looking beneath the surface—identifying the perceptual processes that account for what you say and do.

REVIEW TERMS

The following is a list of major concepts introduced in this chapter. The page number where the concept is first mentioned is listed in parentheses.

social cognition (47)
selective exposure (54)
selective attention (54)
schema (57)
prototype (57)
personal construct (57)
stereotype (57)
script (58)
social episode (59)
closed episode (60)
open episode (60)
defined episode (60)
implicit personality theory (65)
primacy effect (65)
recency effect (65)
self-fulfilling prophecy (66)

SUGGESTED READINGS

Gregory, R. L., and E. H. Gombrich. *Illusion in Nature and Art*. New York: Charles Scribner's Sons, 1973. A fascinating look at the nature of illusion and deception as perceptual phenomena. Questions about how we see the world are approached from both scientific and artistic perspectives.

Hall, Edward T. *Beyond Culture*. Garden City, N.Y.: Anchor Books, 1977. An extremely insightful and highly readable book about the role of culture in structuring our perceptions of reality and everyday events.

Hastorf, Albert, David Schneider and Judith Polefka. *Person Perception*. Baltimore: Penguin Books, 1971. A thorough overview of the general principles involved in forming impressions of people. It includes information on ways we structure the world, accuracy in person perception, impression formation, and attribution theory.

Watzlawick, Paul. *How Real Is Real?* New York: Random House, 1976. A wide-ranging look at the ways animals, people, and governments manage reality through ritual, perceptual tendencies, and the use of disinformation. The implications for communication are thoroughly explored.

PROCESS TO PERFORMANCE

TOPICS FOR DISCUSSION

1. Describe conversations you have been involved in where you or the other person selectively attended to some messages and ignored other important ones. If it was the other person who was being so selective, what did you do? Does it ever do any good to point out selective perception to someone? What is the best way to do it?

2. To communicate effectively, we suggested, you have to accurately perceive the situation, yourself, the other, and the relationship between you. In small groups, have each person talk about a recent conversation that left him or her perplexed, without any understanding of what was going on. Then systematically try to determine if the problem was a failure to recognize any of these perceptual problems. Finally, discuss what attributions you made and why.

3. The posters you have seen of the Nerd, the Valley Girl, the Preppy, and the Yuppie are all examples of person prototypes. Identify as many other prototypes of persons as you can. Talk about the characteristics that cluster to form each prototype. Can you do the same thing for situations or relationships?

4. To make sure you understand the difference between a prototype and a stereotype, take some of the prototypes mentioned in question 3 and identify common stereotypes associated with each one. Are all of the stereotypes negative ones? Which stereotypes seem more useful? In what way?

5. Examine your own implicit personality theories. Based on your experience, what traits seem to go together naturally? Why do you think they are associated? What traits are central ones that would drastically change your overall impression of a person?

6. Most of the examples of self-fulfilling prophecy in this chapter show it as a negative perceptual tendency. Does it have to be? Can you think of a time when positive perceptions of others changed their behavior? Discuss what you could do to change a negative self-fulfilling prophecy in midstream.

7. Master contracts are working agreements that govern dyadic relationships. Think of a specific relationship in each of the following categories: (1) student–teacher, (2) parent–child, (3) romantic dyad, (4) best friends, and (5) coworkers. Now try to identify what the master contract of each relationship is. Then identify ways that contract limits your perceptions of things you can do together or limits the range of messages you can use to influence each other.

8. Think about the last major argument you were involved in. Explain why the other person behaved the way she or he did. What type of attributions did you make? Did you use prior information concerning consensus, consistency, or distinctiveness? Now try to generate reasons that you could have made one of the other three types of attributions.

OBSERVATION GUIDES

1. Watch a half-hour episode of a situation comedy or other television program that consists primarily of dialogue. If you can, audio- or videotape the program so you can play it back several times. Choose an interesting segment, such as a misunderstanding, and write down the essence of each message exchanged. Then write down the perceptual factors that best account for why that message was produced or interpreted the way it was.

2. Conduct your own study of attributions. As you observe everyday interactions, make it a point to ask those involved why they acted as they did. Then ask their partner to explain the same behavior. Write down a brief description of the situation, the behavior in question, the actor's account, and the target's explanation. What biases do you find in the results? Are they consistent with those reported in this chapter? If not, can you explain the differences?

CLASSROOM EXERCISES

1. This exercise is designed to measure the way you construct your interpersonal world and form impressions of others. It is based on George Kelly's Role Repertory Construct Test. The end result will be a list of several of your own *personal constructs*. Follow these steps:

a. Look at the list of role titles below and place the name or initial of someone you know personally who fits that category. Place a *different* person in each category. If you can't think of anyone for a particular role, then name some other important person in your life and describe the role he or she plays in relation to you.

Role Category	Name or Initials of Person
1. Mother	_____
2. Father	_____
3. Boyfriend (or girlfriend)	_____
4. Brother (or someone like a brother)	_____
5. Sister (or someone like a sister)	_____
6. Best same-sex friend	_____
7. Best opposite-sex friend	_____
8. A teacher you like	_____
9. A teacher you dislike	_____
10. Most intelligent person you know	_____
11. Someone you pity	_____
12. A boss or superior	_____
13. Someone who threatens you	_____
14. A new acquaintance	_____
15. Yourself	_____

b. Now think about three of the role persons you listed above and compare them (your mother, sister, and someone who threatens you). Try to think of some important ways that two of them are *alike*, but different from the third person. For instance, you might say that two of these people are *friendly* while the other is more *cold-natured*. On a sheet of paper, list as many "constructs" or similarities and differences among these three people as you can. Your list might look like this:

friendly–cold-natured
good-looking–unattractive
talkative–quiet

c. Pick one of the following role sets and repeat step (b) until you have done all of the role sets:

  (1) Father, your boss, a new acquaintance

  (2) Boyfriend, best same-sex friend, best opposite-sex friend

  (3) Liked teacher, disliked teacher, yourself

  (4) Best opposite-sex friend, mother, sister

  (5) Girlfriend, father, mother

d. Your list should be rather long by now. This should give you a pretty good idea of the personal constructs that you typically use to form impressions of others. Compare your constructs with those of your classmates. How similar or different are they? Which constructs that other people use seem unimportant to you? Why do you think people see the world so similarly or differently?

2. Throw an impression-formation party. As a class, design a set of five to ten questions that you can ask strangers in order to get to know them a little better. Then assign several class members to interviewing teams (one interviewer and one camera person). If you can, secure a portable video camera unit and videotape interviews with people of different age, ethnic, or social backgrounds. Make sure you film each person for about 10 to 15 seconds *before* you begin asking the questions (we'll explain why later). If you can't get video equipment, use tape recorders and take several snapshots of each person. Bring the recorders and/or snapshots to class on the designated day. Replay the videos in class, stopping once before any verbal communication takes place and then again at the conclusion of the interview (or look at the snapshots before you listen to the audiotapes). Have each person in the class write down his or her impressions, first on the nonverbal cues alone, then on the total verbal–nonverbal image. Compare your impressions and talk about the perceptual factors that affected those impressions.

CHAPTER FOUR

Masks disguise and create identity. This royal mask, made in the early 16th century at the Court of Benin (Africa), was used to placate spirits. Although some of us may wear actual masks only at Halloween or costume parties, all of us wear social masks most of our lives.

INTERPERSONAL COMMUNICATION AND SOCIAL RULES: ADAPTING TO SOCIAL EXPECTATIONS

A VERY YOUNG CHILD does not know what an "address" is. He knows that he has a home, that he lives there with his sister and his dog, and he may even be able to repeat "47 Pratt Street" when his grandparents ask him where he lives. But he doesn't understand the idea that his home has coordinates and can be located in relation to other people's homes.

Slowly, however, the idea of "address" takes shape. The child learns to differentiate his friends' homes from his own. He knows what it means to go to Grandma's or to visit cousins in New York. Eventually, he will understand much more. He will learn to locate the homes of everyone he knows on a map. Where formerly a letter to a cousin was simply addressed "To Kerry," now the envelope carries quite specific directions: "1200 Elm Street, Newfield, New York, U.S.A., The World, The Solar System, The Universe." The child becomes fascinated with the world and his place in it. As sociologist Peter Berger tells us, "This locating of oneself in configurations conceived by strangers is one of the important aspects of what, perhaps euphemistically, is called 'growing up.'"[1]

Berger points out that as children mature they continue to accumulate addresses—ones locating them on a social rather than a geo-graphical map. "I'm seven years old"; "My dad and mom are divorced"; "I go to second grade, but I'm not very good at spelling"; "My mom is a secretary"; "When I grow up I'm going to learn to fix cars and drive a Trans-Am." As children learn their position on the social map, they also begin to understand just what they can expect out of life and what life expects out of them. They adapt themselves to a larger social system. What this adaptation means for identity and for communication will be the topic of this chapter and the next. In this chapter we will look at some of the ways society shapes and controls us. In the next chapter, we will consider how, despite these social pressures, we manage to create an identity that is uniquely ours.

BEING PART OF THE GROUP: FOLLOWING SOCIAL RULES

One of the fundamental facts about us is that we are social animals. The fantasy of the loner, living a solitary life and answering to no one, may fascinate us; but most of us will spend our lives following rules others have made. To live a "civilized" life means we must be willing to live up to the expectations of others. The competent communicator is one who follows social rules.

Social Control and Conformity Pressures

Why does society place such a high premium on conformity? One reason is that in order to operate effectively, members of social groups must coordinate their activities. Each member must complete assigned tasks and follow rules. Since we belong to many social groups, we are subject to many levels of social control. Berger asks us to think of ourselves at the center of a series of concentric circles, each representing a system of control. These circles represent social coordinates; they stand for the "many forces that constrain and coerce one."[2]

The forces that constrain us are many. Formal economic and legal sanctions control our actions in obvious ways. In addition, more subtle pressures affect us: the desire to uphold the standards and moral customs of our community, our fear of ridicule, our fundamental need for inclusion. Whatever the reason, we are, to a large extent, what our culture wants us to be. Anthropologist Ruth Benedict expresses it this way:

> *The life history of the individual is first and foremost an accommodation to the patterns and standards traditionally handed down in his community. From the moment of birth the customs into which he is born shape his experience and behaviour. By the time he can talk, he is a little creature of his culture, and by the time he is grown and able to take part in its activities, its habits are his habits, its beliefs his beliefs, its impossibilities his impossibilities.*[3]

While we feel that individuals have a bit more room to maneuver than Benedict allows them, we also believe that a large part of who we are and how we communicate is determined for us by social norms. One of the most powerful limits to our freedom comes from social roles. In this section we examine how roles work and how they constrain our communication.

The Nature of Social Roles

Every day we face new situations. If we had to stop and decide how to act in all these cases, we'd have a difficult time of it. Luckily, we act appropriately without very much thought. This is because we know implicitly how someone in our position should behave: We have learned what sociologists call a role, one of the strongest forms of social control.

To understand what a role is, we have to begin by understanding the concept of position. A **position** is a social label that tells people who we are, what our duties and rights are, and where we stand in comparison to others. Some of the positions a society recognizes are occupational (butcher, baker, candlestick maker). Others refer to location in the family (grandparent, parent, son or daughter). Still others indicate age, sex, prestige, or associational groupings.[4] In all cases, positions indicate location on the social map.

Positions are not just empty titles. People are expected to take their positions seriously. Children and adults do not amuse themselves in the same ways. A professional politician and a professional wrestler will address their publics differently. Each position carries with it a set of behavioral guidelines. These guidelines are what we call **roles**: sets of expectations that govern how persons holding a given position should behave. There are several things we should know about roles: (1) they are learned; (2) they are general; (3) they affect our identities; and (4) most of us play multiple roles.

1. *Roles are learned.* We aren't born with a knowledge of roles. We learn to meet social

We learn what to expect out of life very early; our families supply us with information about position and role. (Pablo Picasso, *Family at Supper*, 1903)

expectations in much the same way we learn to ride a bicycle or play the accordion. We learn by observing others, by receiving instruction, by practicing, by experiencing praise or criticism. All of the principles that affect learning in general affect role acquisition. Box 4.1 (pp. 82–83) shows one of the many ways we learn roles: through imitative play.

2. *Roles are generalized guidelines for behavior.* While roles give us a general idea of how to

perform in a given position, they don't spell out every move. We are often left to our own devices when it comes to working out the details of our performances. Most college students, for example, need time to figure out how to be a student. Being a student is more than enrolling for classes; students must act, dress, and even think in particular ways. Freshmen or returning students may have a hard time of it at first, since these issues are rarely addressed in the college catalog. A role is a

BOX 4.1

They Just Like to Be Not the Same As Us: Play Patterns and the Development of Sex Role Identities

In *Boys and Girls: Superheroes in the Doll Corner*, elementary school teacher Vivian Gussin Paley describes how kindergartners' play contributes to sex role development. Paley tells us that by kindergarten age, children have a strong need to define what it means to be boys and girls. Younger children are not concerned with gender. Three-year-olds, for example, fail to distinguish between male and female behaviors. A three-year-old playing the role of a policeman may also cook the food and feed the baby, while one playing a mother may put on a man's vest and hat. Boys may tell you they are fathers and girls that they are mothers most of the time, but occasionally they will say the opposite without feeling uncomfortable.

Around the age of four, children begin to play gender-based roles more frequently. Girls start enacting family dramas, assigning themselves the roles of mother, baby, or sister, and preferring that boys be fathers, plumbers, carpenters, or firemen. Although the girls are sometimes willing to exchange their domestic roles for those of Wonder-woman or Supergirl, it is the boys who specialize in being monsters or superheroes.

By age five or six, gender-based play is firmly established. Not only do the children fantasize sex-based roles, they invent rituals to separate themselves. Although society helps to create the shape of play by providing Barbie dolls and Star Wars action figures, the children themselves often elaborate on gender themes in creative ways. In the group Paley observed, for example, boys hopped to get their milk, while girls skipped to the paper shelf.

What does typical play look like in a kindergarten class? Let's watch the boys play in the doll corner. Jeremy begins. He drags the play oven to the middle of the floor, announcing, "This is the computer terminal." The rest

generalized and idealized model for behavior, not a fully developed script. Competent role performance, therefore, involves experimentation, improvisation, and adjustment.

3. *Roles affect beliefs about self.* It takes time to learn a role, but after a while the strangeness wears off. Eventually people stop noticing their roles. A first-year teacher, for example, may initially feel ambivalent about her authority. But it will probably not be too long before she begins to believe in a teacher's right to instruct and discipline. She may even begin to consider rebellious students as unruly or ungrateful. Similarly, a soldier newly promoted to the rank of officer may be slightly embarrassed by accompanying signs of deference. He will soon become accustomed to being saluted, however, and will begin to resent insubordination.

Enacting a role over a prolonged period may affect one's personality and identity. **Role rigidity** occurs when a role takes over one's identity. Most experts believe it is psychologically necessary to separate self from role. People whose commitment to a single role is too rigid tend to lose perspective. They may find it increasingly hard to relate in any other way. Teachers, for example, may become so used to the role of instructor that friendly conversations turn into lectures. Military officers may treat their children like little "non-coms."

4. *People have multiple roles to play.* People fulfill a number of positions simultaneously.

of the boys quickly begin arranging the rest of the spaceship. Andrew talks into a silver dress-up slipper, "Pilot to crew, pilot to crew, ready for landing. Snow planet down below." Suddenly the boys sight Darth Vader. Andrew takes two sticks, runs over to the paint corner, and asks Mary Ann for red paint to transform them into light sabres.

Then, before rushing into battle, he says gallantly, "Thanks, miss; I won't forget this."

Meanwhile, the girls have decided to build a zoo from blocks. They take four rubber lions and name them Mother, Father, Sister, and Baby and place them in a two-story house. Paley observes, "Girls tame lions by putting them into houses. Boys conquer houses by sending them into space."

Paley notes that the stories boys and girls tell at this age are also very different. Girls tell stories of "good little families" of kings and queens, princes and princesses. Boys prefer tales with bad guys. Paley once asked the girls why boys never told stories about princes. The girls responded that princes are too "fancy" for boys. Boys like characters who are rough. One of

the kindergartners, Charlotte, summed up the discussion: "Here's what I think. They don't want to be fancy because girls do. They just like to be not the same as us."

Source: *Vivian Gussen Paley, Boys and Girls: Superheroes in the Doll Corner (Chicago: University of Chicago Press, 1984).*

ADDITIONAL READINGS

Carmichael, Carrie. *Non-sexist Childraising*. New York: Beacon Press, 1977.

Maccoby, Eleanor Emmon, and Carol Nagy Jacklin. *The Psychology of Sex Differences*. Stanford, Calif.: Stanford University Press, 1974.

Stein, Sarah Bonnett. *Girls and Boys: The Limits of Nonsexist Childrearing*. New York: Charles Scribner's Sons, 1983.

This means they must be nimble in moving between roles. An intern in a hospital, for example, must be a number of different people: At work he or she is a doctor; at home, a husband or wife; at a party, a friend or neighbor; and at town council meetings, a citizen. Our intern must be sensitive enough to recognize the varying demands of each role and flexible enough to adapt to them, for each role calls for a slightly different form of communication. Meeting the communication demands of all of these situations involves a great deal of role versatility. The number of roles an individual can successfully play is called a **role repertoire**. Clearly the larger the role repertoire, the more communicative flexibility one has.

Most of the time people switch roles easily.

Sometimes, however, they experience **role conflict**. This occurs when two or more roles make opposing demands. "Workaholics," for example, often find that professional and personal demands conflict. Attention directed to family concerns is attention taken away from their businesses, and vice versa. Resolving this kind of dilemma is no easy matter; it may ultimately lead to painful choices.

Role conflicts also occur in times of social transition. In the period before an old role has become obsolete and a new role fully accepted, people are often pulled in opposite directions. Our changing understandings of what it means to be male or female and current redefinitions of the shape and purpose of the family are good examples.

CHOOSING OUR ROLES

If it is true that we play multiple roles, how do we decide who to be in a given situation? How, indeed, do we know who we are? George McCall and J. L. Simmons address this question in their role identity model.[5] In order to get through life, they believe, we have to decide which identities to assume. In a sense, we are like circus performers, juggling commitments and role demands, trying not to slip off the tightrope that defines our passage through life.

While we have many role identities, some are more important than others. What determines the salience of a role? McCall and Simmons believe there are three sets of factors: the degree of support we receive for playing a role, the amount of commitment we feel toward it, and the kinds of rewards we receive from it.

Social Support and Role Identity

If those around us support our efforts, we are more likely to embrace a role than if they ridicule us. It is a fact of life that we are constantly being evaluated. Assume, for example, that you dream of becoming a marathon runner. If your family and friends give you support and encouragement, you will go on with your dream. If they laugh at your lack of speed and stamina, you may not believe enough in yourself to keep on.

The Looking-Glass Self

A number of social scientists besides McCall and Simmons have stressed the importance of social support in defining and maintaining a role. Charles Horton Cooley, for example, believes that others act as mirrors, reflecting back to us who we are and how we're doing. Cooley expressed this idea in a two-line poem: "Each to each a looking glass/Reflects the other that doth pass." The **looking-glass self** is the self that comes to us from others.[6] Think about it for a moment. No matter how strong-willed and self-assured you are, if everybody you encounter treats you as incompetent, you will question your abilities. Or even worse, suppose everyone ignored you completely. You'd probably begin to wonder if you were dreaming. It would be like looking into a mirror and failing to see your reflection.

Social Comparison Processes

Social support is essential to most of us. Why? Leon Festinger in his **social comparison theory** gives one reason.[7] He believes that people have a basic need to know how they're doing; they need to know how their opinions and abilities stack up. Since it's hard to find objective scales to measure beliefs and talents, most of us must turn to other people.

We don't turn to just anyone, however. People who are similar to us give us the most useful comparisons. A beginning tennis player would be foolish to compare herself with Martina Navratilova; it would make more sense to look at another beginning player. Similarly, college students gain little information from knowing they're smarter than kindergartners; they need to know how they rate against other students. Most of the time we compare ourselves with those we believe are "in our league" or who are slightly better than we are. Because our need for social comparison is so strong, most of our associations will be with people who are similar.

What Festinger is suggesting is that the need for social comparison leads to conformity pressures. We choose as friends people who are similar enough to reinforce role identities. If unexpected changes in identity are discovered in a relationship, efforts will be made to reestablish similarity. Have you ever been shocked and disappointed when a friend turned out to hold unexpected opinions? If so, you probably exerted subtle pressures to change

Others act as mirrors, allowing us to see ourselves. Their response gives us a sense of who we are. (Pablo Picasso, *Girl Before a Mirror*, 1932)

your friend back into someone you felt more comfortable with. Have you ever been uncomfortable because your abilities were above or below your friends'? Some people will pretend to be better than they are, while others will "play dumb," just to fit in. We try to be what our comparison groups tell us we should be.

Commitment and Role Identity

The amount of material and psychological resources invested in a role also determines how significant it will be. Perhaps you have always admired a runner. Ever since you were a child, you wanted to be like her. Your commit-

The need to maintain face and line is especially strong for members of England's royal family, who fulfill a symbolic function for their nation. A prince must not marry carelessly. Would you be able to cope with the demands of such social roles?

ment will be so great you may persevere even in the face of discouraging feedback. This effect will be doubly strong if you've made a financial investment, say, by buying expensive running shoes and hiring a coach. Commitment and investment are important factors in determining role salience.

Daryl Bem offers a theoretical explanation of why commitment and investment make certain role identities more salient.[8] His **self-perception theory** maintains that one way we learn about who we are is through self-observation. Bem believes that often it is hard for us to tell directly what we are thinking and

feeling. In order to get a clearer idea of our emotions or attitudes, we observe our external behaviors. What we see ourselves doing often helps explain ambiguous emotions or attitudes.

This theory may seem odd to you. Most people think they have direct access to emotions and attitudes. Bem's point, however, is that internal sensations are often hard to identify. Think about it for a moment. How do you feel when you're in love? Does your heart race, do your palms sweat, does your breathing rate increase? Now think about what you experience when you are scared to death. Aren't the sensations pretty similar? One way to tell the difference is to observe external cues. If these sensations occur during the middle of a crucial job interview, it is probably fear you are feeling. On the other hand, if they occur during an intimate candlelight dinner, love is the likely answer.

Bem also believes external cues give us information about our attitudes and values. If we observe ourselves spending a great deal of time and effort doing something, we will probably decide it is important and worthwhile. People often say things like "I must really like the food here; look at how much I ate," or "It must have been a great party; I stayed till dawn," or "I spend all my time training for the marathon; it must be the most important thing in my life right now." The more time, effort, and money we spend on something, the more likely we are to believe we value it.

Rewards and Role Identity

Both intrinsic and extrinsic rewards also determine how important a role becomes to us. It is unlikely that the average person who runs a marathon will be motivated by extrinsic rewards, for runners are not usually highly paid. A runner may receive important intrinsic rewards, however. Amateur runners often feel a sense of pride in accomplishing what few others can do. This feeling of competence goes a long way toward strengthening role allegiance. On the other hand, a runner who fails to complete a race, who experiences painful leg cramps, and who is going broke paying entrance fees may reconsider the importance of running.

McCall and Simmons believe that all of the factors we have discussed interact to determine reactions to roles. Throughout our lives we try on the different roles society presents to us. Those that fit are retained, while those that don't are rejected until we build up a repertoire of roles we're willing to play.

HOW SOCIAL ROLES AFFECT COMMUNICATION

In many ways people are like actors, and everyday interactions are like performances. In the following sections, we'll analyze how people prepare their parts in the social drama of everyday life.

Creating the Ideal Character: The Need for Face-Work

Like stage actors, social actors want to make an impact on an audience. We want to create characters who will be admired and accepted. McCall and Simmons believe "One of man's most distinctive motives is the compelling and perpetual drive to acquire support for his idealized conceptions of himself."[9] Gaining the approval of an appreciative audience is one way to acquire support for the idealized self, and one way of doing this is to create a character who embodies the values of society.

Sociologist Erving Goffman uses the term **face** to describe the part of self presented to others for their approval.[10] As we mentioned in Chapter 1, an individual's face embodies social values; it is an approved identity. **Face-work** is effort spent in presenting face to others. Although the term *face* may seem odd at first, Goffman is actually following common usage. For example, we say that a person who violates social values has "lost face." We describe efforts to avoid embarrassment as "saving face." And some college students refer to time spent impressing others as "face time."

During communication, we present face by taking a **line**. Our lines consist of the verbal and nonverbal behaviors we use during a performance. We must be very careful to take appropriate lines. If we act in ways that aren't "in line" with our position on the social map, others will reject us. The middle-class social climber who tries to pass as a member of the social register or the rich industrialist who tries to relate to his factory workers by acting like "one of the guys" are both out of line. Both will be ridiculed.

During communication we must be careful to preserve our own face and protect that of others. Not only must *we* make a good impression, we must help *others* to make a good impression too. If, for example, we are at a formal dinner party and one of the other guests commits a faux pas, we generally look away, politely pretending not to see that he or she is using the wrong fork. If the social error committed is so obvious that it cannot be ignored, we may try to redefine or diminish it. If our guest unknowingly insults the hostess, we may treat the comment as a joke.

In actively working to maintain our own face, we try to steer clear of situations we feel we can't handle. If someone brings up a topic we're ignorant about, we may change the subject to avoid embarrassment. If we inadvertently offend someone, we can save face by apologizing for our insensitivity or by offering to make amends.

Goffman believes that interpersonal communication is a risky business. We must continually be on our guard for threats to face and line.

> *An unguarded glance, a momentary change in tone of voice, an ecological position taken or not taken, can drench a talk with judgmental significance. . . . There is no occasion of talk so trivial as not to require each participant to show serious concern with the way in which he handles himself and the others present.*[11]

The image presented by Goffman is that of nervous individuals doing their best to avoid disaster. While Goffman may exaggerate the dangers of interpersonal communication, there is certainly some truth to the idea that we are motivated by social approval. Unless you're a completely free spirit, you're probably careful not to do odd or embarrassing things in public. And unless you are completely uncaring and insensitive, you try to keep others from making fools of themselves. Stop and think about it for a minute. You may be surprised to find how much communication centers on protecting face and line.

Getting Ready for the Play: Other Aspects of Self-Presentation

When we go to a play, we expect costumes, lighting, and sets. When we interact in everyday life, we also expect a proper background.

Sets, Costumes, and Props

Goffman divides the arena where our everyday performances take place into two parts.[12] The public part, the stage, he calls the **front**. There are two aspects to front, setting and personal front. **Setting** includes all of the scenery and props that make the performance possible. **Personal front** involves costume, makeup, physical characteristics, gestures, and the like.

When our front is creatively designed, we can give an effective performance. If we don't control a convincing front, however, our performance may crumble. Executives of major corporations know the value of sumptuous surroundings. They spend a great deal of money on impressive office furnishings and artifacts, in the belief that a visitor who spies an original Picasso on the mahogany wall of the reception area is bound to be impressed by their power and wealth. If they're also wearing a $900 suit and are surrounded by a large and respectful entourage, the effect will be increased. Their front acts as a frame for the industrial drama about to unfold.

All of us are viewed against the backdrop of our own front regions. If our personal surroundings are warm and inviting, we're likely to make friends easily. If we have to communicate in a cold and forbidding atmo-

The spaces in which we live help to define the way we communicate.
But think twice before deciding which environment will promote more
rewarding communication.

sphere, we will have to work harder to overcome its effects. The way we set the scene for encounters can affect their outcome. You might find it interesting to analyze what your surroundings say about you and how they affect the ways that you communicate. This is a topic we'll discuss in more detail in Chapter 6. For now, just think about the impressions your environment makes.

Backstage Behavior

If actors had to remain on stage for more than a few hours, they would probably lose touch with reality. Luckily, between acts they can retreat backstage, where they are no longer on call; they can relax and be themselves. The private areas where social actors can escape the critical eye of their audience is called the **back region**. "The faculty lounge, the members-only club, the executive washroom, and the rehearsal studio are examples of back regions."[13] Goffman believes that dedication to role is not always absolute; most of us need a place where we can slip out of our roles and simply be whoever we want to.

The back region answers our need for privacy. By entering it, we escape the rigors of role enactment. But what if we don't have a physical space to flee to? Then we must rely on psychological space. We find a way to let others know the roles we are playing do not completely define us. Goffman calls this **role distance**.[14] Every situation we enter, he says, puts demands on us. Occasionally we resent these demands and try to let others know that there is more to us than meets the eye.

Goffman did much of his research in the medical community, where roles are very well defined. The role of intern is a particularly demanding one. Although interns are expected to be dedicated to their profession, an intern's status in the hospital isn't high. Interns may therefore feel the need to exhibit role distance. There are a number of ways they can do this.

They can use a slightly amused facial expression designed to show the absurdity of their position. They may take longer than necessary to obey a request, forcing others to ask twice. They may flirt or joke, reminding those present of other roles in the outside world. This borderline rebellion allows them to fight back without actually violating role demands. Think back to your school days. How did you and your classmates rebel against your status as schoolchildren? We're willing to bet you used similar tactics.

Ensemble Acting

Most plays are not one-man shows. The success of their performance depends on teamwork. Social actors are in much the same situation. Along with roles come **role sets**, others who help put on a given performance. The role set of a defense attorney includes clients, prosecuting attorneys, judges, law clerks, and office staff. The role set of a rock star may include band members, agents, managers, bodyguards, an astrologer or two, and, perhaps, groupies. These are the people who make performances possible. With them, individuals can become stars; without them they convince no one.

Members of a role set must exercise loyalty, discipline, and circumspection.[15] A politician's family is a good example of a role set. One of their functions is to back up the candidate's performance, presenting an image of wholesomeness and dedication. They must be careful not to give away the act by revealing the candidate's flaws. They must stay in character, never deviating from the party line and never showing anything but delight with their lot in life. And they must never hog the spotlight by seeking personal publicity. According to Goffman, being a particular kind of person is not necessarily a personal matter; it involves a high degree of teamwork.

It is clear that the members of a role set must work together. If members refuse to

An aging gentleman alone with his cat creates quite a different impression from the bouncy, exuberant clown he will become when he steps in front of his expectant audience.

BOX 4.2

A Gathering of Strangers: City Life in the 18th Century

It's important to remember we are products of history, to recall that rules of behavior are only temporary. In *The Fall of Public Man*, Richard Sennett traces the way relationships have changed since the 18th century.

During the 18th century, in the great capitals of Europe, a new class was forming: the mercantile bourgeoisie. When any new social group comes into being, shock waves are felt in all areas of life. New ways of living, dressing, talking, new manners, tastes, and morals manifest the shock of the new.

In the court-dominated society of the 17th century, people's rank and standing were known to everyone. With the rise of a large, mobile middle class in the 18th century, a new set of manners developed. Sennett believes that the 18th-century urban dweller was preoccupied with the need to know who others were without giving away too much about the self. In response to this need, a way of life characterized by great impersonality and artificiality was developed.

If you were to wake up in the Paris or London of the 1750s, you would find the costumes of the crowds puzzling. The upper classes and wealthy bourgeoisie wore enormous wigs, their skin was painted either apoplexy red or dull white, patches of red pigment might be smeared on nose or forehead, and masks were frequently worn. The lower classes wore distinctive costumes with ribbons and buttons identifying rank and occupation. To people of the time, these outlandish costumes were symbols that identified each person's social class. In fact, the law dictated the kind of costume permissible for each person. The body and face were a background on which "ideograms of abstract character and class were mounted." Going out onto the street was like going onto a stage.

Language, too, was theatrical and ornamental. Greetings consisted of stock phrases that could be applied indiscriminately. Mentioning personal details was very bad form. In 1747 Lord Chesterfield wrote to his son: "Of all things, banish the egotism out of your conversation, and never think of entertaining people with your own personal concerns or private affairs; though they are interesting to you, they are tedious and impertinent to everybody else."

The impersonality of the age did not mean that people were isolated. Indeed, it was an intensely sociable era, with public conversation highly regarded. People met in coffeehouses to exchange witticisms about affairs

---

coordinate their acts, chaos is likely. There are several ways to ensure a cohesive performance. One is to choose relational partners who will play their parts reliably. The politician who chooses a spouse merely to further a career uses a method called **altercasting**. While most of us are not that cold-blooded, we often choose friends who will support our definition of self. Morris Rosenberg has said, "Friendship is the purest illustration of picking one's propaganda."[16]

Another technique we can use to ensure smooth performance is that of **mirroring**.[17] Mirroring is the flip side of altercasting. Here we achieve coordination by following the lead of our partner. While both altercasting and mirroring can assure a coordinated performance, they are not very satisfying, since in either case, it is one partner who makes all of the decisions. A more satisfactory technique, from the relational point of view, is **mutual negotiation**. Here both partners work together

of the day. In this atmosphere, one's social class, though clearly visible, was not alluded to, and the only rule was to avoid personal references. Anyone who paid a penny and agreed to abide by house rules was treated with the utmost courtesy. Strangers were welcome partners for conversation both in the coffeehouses and in the streets, where taking a promenade to display oneself and to survey the passing scene was an important social activity.

The values we associate with communication today, the need for individual expression, self-disclosure, and the establishment of similarity rather than difference, were simply unknown. Indeed, to a citizen of the 18th century the idea of interpersonal communication as we know it would be unthinkable. Sennett lets us know that times have changed. Whether for the better it is hard to know.

Source: *Richard Sennett,* The Fall of Public Man *(New York: Random House, 1974).*

ADDITIONAL READINGS

Bellah, Robert N., and others. *Habits of the Heart: Individualism and Commitment in American Life.* Berkeley and Los Angeles: University of California Press, 1985.

Gadlin, Howard. "Private Lives and Public Order: A Critical View of the History of Intimate Relations in the United States." In *Close Relationships: Perspectives on the Meaning of Intimacy,* edited by George Levinger and Harold L. Raush. Amherst: University of Massachusetts Press, 1977.

Lasch, Christopher. *The Culture of Narcissism.* New York: W. W. Norton, 1978.

to construct roles that are mutually satisfactory. To do this successfully we must have the kind of maximal competence we discussed at the end of Chapter 2.

Interpreting Our Scripts: Cultural Elements

Once we have designed the set, made sure all our props and costumes are ready, and assembled a cast of supporting characters, we are ready to speak our lines. Our analysis so far has shown that our choice of lines is not simply a matter of individual style. Our culture is to a large extent our writer and director. While we are not complete automatons, preprogrammed with an entire script, we are also not completely free to speak in any way we wish. In addition to the constraints roles place on us, our culture gives us general attitudes toward speaking. Together these forces are powerful controllers of our actual communicative choices.

A number of scholars have investigated the ways our culture determines the way we actually communicate on a day-to-day basis. As Gerry Philipsen tells us:

Not only do bearers of different cultures speak differently one from another but, more importantly, they hold different assumptions about the value, purposes, and significance of speaking as a mode of human experience. Like religion, politics, and law, so speech, the principle medium of creating meanings in social interaction, itself holds different meanings for the various peoples whose views of the world afford it a place.[18]

Anthropologists tell us different cultures make different assumptions about communication. For example, middle-class Americans are taught that one of the primary functions of speaking in relationships is to share personal experiences. The more important the relationship, the more self-disclosure there should be. One of the purposes of talk is to express one's uniqueness. Speech designed to assert social solidarity is less frequent in this cultural group.

As we shall try to point out throughout this text, other cultures may not share this view. Boxes 7.2 and 13.1 give examples of two very different attitudes toward talk. Our attitudes about how to talk and what to talk about are not only a function of cultural groupings, however; they are also a function of our particular historical period. Box 4.2 shows that over the last 200 years the definition of how to carry on an interpersonal relationship has changed a great deal. Scripts written in the 18th century would give us a different set of lines than scripts written today, and the differences are not simply results of changes in language structures over the years.

COMMUNICATIVE COMPETENCE AND SOCIAL EXPECTATIONS

In our original model of competence, introduced in Chapter 1, we stressed four kinds of competence, one of which involved the ability to adapt to social constraints. This is clearly the kind of competence this chapter has focused on. Our discussion has suggested that we must be aware of the demands placed on us by our social positions. But the social rules we're expected to follow are seldom written down for us. Although etiquette books may codify these rules, we rarely learn them by reading Amy Vanderbilt or Miss Manners. Rather, we learn through trial and error. Part of our competence, then, comes from our sensitivity to unstated social rules.

Another part of role competence comes from creativity in putting on a stylish performance. We don't want to end this chapter with you believing that the competent communicator is a conformist without any imagination. On the contrary, competence involves creativity. If any of you have worked in the theater, you know that putting on a show, even though it is scripted, is an interpretive act involving many design elements. At least as much creativity goes into producing real-life communication performances. Some people have a personal style that makes them stand out from the crowd. Although they follow all the social rules, they do so with originality and verve. Others seem to plod along through life, never establishing command over their role performances. Clearly we differ in our ability to interpret our roles. The individual with maximal communicative competence brings something fresh and exciting to each role.

A final element of competence you might want to consider is the ability to decide when to conform and when not to. There are times when we must deliberately deviate from social norms. We will take up this topic more fully in the next chapter, but it's worth thinking about here. Not all social rules make sense; not all lead to effective communication. When we form relationships, we're in a unique position to make up some of the rules ourselves. This involves transcending simple social instructions. Those of us who don't have the courage to violate social expectations cannot be completely competent.

In this chapter we have focused on the extent to which culture affects us. Our discussion has implied that there is an intimate relationship between who we are and what our culture tells us to be. In the next chapter, we will examine this relationship in more detail.

REVIEW TERMS

The following is a list of major concepts introduced in this chapter. The page where the concept is first mentioned is listed in parentheses.

position (80)
role (80)
role rigidity (82)
role repertoire (83)
role conflict (83)
looking-glass self (84)
social comparison theory (84)
self-perception theory (86)
face (87)
face-work (87)
line (87)
front (88)
setting (88)
personal front (88)

back region (90)
role distance (90)
role set (90)
altercasting (92)
mirroring (92)
mutual negotiation (92)

SUGGESTED READINGS

Benedict, Ruth. *Patterns of Culture*. New York: Penguin Books, 1946. Benedict is one of the most famous of the early cultural anthropologists. In this fascinating book she explores the relationship between culture and personality.

Goffman, Erving. *The Presentation of Self in Everyday Life*. Garden City, N.Y.: Anchor Books, 1959. Goffman is not easy reading, but he is well worth the effort. If you take the time to read him slowly and thoughtfully, you'll find insights on every page. But watch out—Goffman can be addicting. After reading him, you won't view the world the same again.

Hewitt, John P. *Self and Society: A Symbolic Interactionist Social Psychology*. Boston: Allyn & Bacon, 1976. If you want to explore the complex relationship between self, society, and communication, then you need to understand a school of thought known as symbolic interactionism. This is one of the easiest introductions to this important field.

McCall, George J., and J. L. Simmons. *Identities and Interactions*. New York: Free Press, 1966. One of the best treatments of the development of the self-concept around. If you're interested in psychology, this book should tell you everything you wanted to know about role identity and more.

PROCESS TO PERFORMANCE

TOPICS FOR DISCUSSION

1. In *Invitation to Sociology*, Peter Berger tells us: "Where human beings live or work in compact groups, in which they are personally known and to which they are tied by feelings of personal loyalty . . . , very potent and simultaneously very subtle mechanisms of control are constantly brought to bear upon the . . . deviant." Think about some of the ways social groups control their members. How many can you identify? Don't forget mechanisms like ridicule, gossip, ostracism, disapproval. How effective are these mechanisms? Why do you think they work?

2. To what extent are we "creatures of our culture"? Do you agree with Benedict that our possibilities and impossibilities are predetermined by culture? Can you think of examples of why this might or might not be true?

3. What career are you interested in? If you aren't already in that career, what kinds of role changes do you anticipate undergoing when you enter that arena? Can you think of ways this role transition can be made easier?

4. What advice would you give to a high school student who will be entering your school next semester? What do you believe he or she would need to know to be able to "fit in" and assume the student role as defined at your school? What does this tell you about the "ideal" student role identity at your university?

5. Discuss specific social norms designed to help others "save face." Can you describe any situations you've been in where you had to help another save face? What did you do? How did you feel?

6. Although we didn't discuss it explicitly in the text, Goffman says there are times when we engage in aggressive face-work—actions designed to make us look good at the expense of others. Has anyone ever done this to you? How did you handle it? In general, what are some of the ways people engage in aggressive face-work?

7. Discuss some typical "lines" college students use to impress one another. Which are the most successful? Which are the least successful?

8. Box 4.1 discusses male–female sex roles. What is your reaction? If you had children, would you try to prevent or limit the amount of traditional sex role socialization they received or would you encourage it? Does it make a difference what toys and games a child plays when young? Were you raised with traditional or nontraditional sex roles?

9. In *The Fall of Public Man*, Richard Sennett, who wrote the material profiled in Box

4.2, argues that current modes of communication focus too much on establishing instant intimacy. He believes that there is some virtue in maintaining distance and in abiding by norms of politeness and courtesy. What do you think? Do you believe that being polite and showing respect and reserve are good or bad qualities? When should we push for disclosure and when should we remain distant?

OBSERVATION GUIDE

1. How controlled are you by simple social norms? How willing are you to sacrifice face or line? Choose a simple social norm and violate it. Don't do something outrageous that would offend others; simply do something that is slightly odd or atypical. For example, wear an article of clothing that is not quite appropriate. Or sit by yourself instead of joining your friends as you usually do. Carefully note reactions. Be specific. What kinds of pressures were placed on you? Describe your own feelings about doing this. Was it hard to do? Did you feel awkward and uncomfortable? Are you too much or too little affected by social norms? Relate this experience to the social comparison process.

2. Analyze your own style of self-presentation from a dramatic point of view. Think of a particular communication incident where you were trying to make a good impression. What face were you trying to present? What line did you take? How did your setting and personal front either help or hinder you? Describe in detail all relevant props, furnishings, costuming decisions. Was this a solo performance, or did you count on others to help you put on your front? If the interaction was successful, how much was attributable to front? If the interaction didn't quite work out, how would you redirect it if you had the chance?

EXERCISES

1. Working with a partner, list all of the roles you have assumed during the last week. Try to determine the communication expectations for each role. Write out at least three rules of communication behavior for each role you identify.

2. Work with an opposite-sex partner. Plan a skit showing a male–female interaction embodying typical sex roles. Present it to the class, but take the sex role opposite to your own; that is, if you are male, play the female part, and if you are female, play the male part. As a class, discuss the portrayals. What behaviors were used to portray the opposite sex? Were the portrayals accurate? How did you feel while portraying your part, and why? Was this hard or easy, embarrassing or fun?

CHAPTER FIVE

Many artists have an acute sense of their own identity. Vincent van Gogh painted some twenty-four self-portraits during one two-year period in Paris. What do you think are the costs and benefits of so much self-reflection?

INTERPERSONAL COMMUNICATION AND PERSONAL IDENTITY: ESTABLISHING INDIVIDUALITY

W HO ARE YOU?
"I'm Sam I am."
"A butcher, a baker, a candle-stick maker."
"I am a rock. I am an island."
"I've gotta be me."
Who are you, really?

Are you a name? A role? A complex entity molded by needs, desires, and psychological traits into a unique, authentic personality? Or is "the real you" just a concept conveniently used to integrate experiences, physical features, beliefs and attitudes, choices made, ways of talking, walking, and looking at life?

If we had left you at the end of the last chapter, you might think the answer to this important question was determined solely by the society you live in. As we saw, people adapt to the social roles and situations defined by their culture. The starting point for social life is the inheritance of complex signs and symbols from previous generations. The family you were born into had already established roles, rules, and customs long before your arrival, as did the schools, the churches, political parties, and other institutions you may have later joined.

But a funny thing happens when we "join" a family or group and begin to take on a role.

In some subtle and not-so-subtle ways, each of us modifies the social roles we adopt. We only half-learn some rules and break many others to suit our own purposes. As we do this, we begin to forge an "identity" or style that goes beyond the role we play. In some situations, our culture tends to frown upon the intrusion of self-identity in role-structured interaction; in other situations it is encouraged. A cashier is unlikely to show much of his or her self-identity while checking our groceries. On the other hand, the personal life of an actor or actress is expected to be revealed on a talk show. We would probably be disappointed if it weren't.

In this chapter, we want to show how we begin to develop self-concepts out of the roles we assume in everyday interaction. We will define the self-concept and assess its development and change through childhood and into adulthood. We will also examine why our culture, more than many others, encourages us to be "individuals" as much as "conformists." We will see how, once a sense of individuality has been established, the self-concept influences our perceptions and our communication behavior. Finally, we'll talk about what you can do to manage your self-concept and communicate more competently at the same time.

GAINING INDEPENDENCE FROM SOCIAL ROLES AND RULES

As we saw in Chapter 4, a smoothly running society depends on our following socially given roles and rules. We also saw that roles do not totally define us. We exercise some choice in the matter of adopting which of several possible roles to play in any given situation. We play some roles more frequently than others and may become very good at a few of them, internalizing them as part of who we are. But we also "distance" ourselves from some roles and avoid others as much as possible. The *choices* we make concerning the roles we play and how we play them reflect a growing independence from our cultural inheritance. This independence from cultural rules eventually culminates in one or more rather stable self-concepts, which we use to determine when we should conform and when it is in our best interest to resist following social rules. In order to understand how self-concepts emerge and stabilize, we need to first define them.

What Is the Self-Concept?

The **self-concept** is basically each person's own subjective view or image of himself or herself as a person.[1] While it is derived through communication just like any other concept, it remains more subjective than other concepts. Although others are entitled to their own opinions about us and may disagree with one another about what kind of person we really are, our self-concept remains our own private view of ourselves. We actually have several different self-concepts, some of them public, some private.

Public Self-Concepts

How we think of the self when we are in public or "on display" for others to see is the public self-concept. These aspects of self are readily apparent when we play a social role that allows some self-expression. Sports commentators sometimes refer to football teams as reflecting their coach's personality. In such cases, the coach has imbued the role with one of his public self-concepts. It is also possible to derive a public self-concept from one of the social roles that we play frequently and associate closely with our identity. Many people internalize the roles they play at work and see themselves as primarily a police officer, a teacher, a social worker, or a salesperson. A role has been internalized when a person continues to function in that role outside its original or appropriate context. For instance, a father may police his children as if he were still captain of the precinct; a wife may lecture her husband as if he were a student in her class; a social worker may meddle in the affairs of the neighbors as if they were cases in the office.

We all project a certain image of ourselves for others to see (for example, outgoing, reserved, friendly, irritable). Some of these images may be projected on a consistent basis, regardless of the situation. It is more likely, however, that we alter our self-presentation depending on who we're with. If you think about it, you're probably not the same person with every one of your friends. Think about who you are when you're with your family, your friends at home, and two or three circles of friends at school or work. Do you present the same image to all of them? Do you think of yourself in the same way when you're with each group? Chances are that you have at least two or three different public self-concepts.

Private Self-Concepts

Most of us probably think of our private selves as somehow closer to the real thing. These are the aspects of self that aren't so readily apparent to casual passersby or even to relatively close friends. Perceptions of our own psychological traits, personal values, and most frequent emotional states head the list of candidates for how

BOX 5.1

A Minnesota Bird Lost in America: What Is Personal Identity?

The following poem, recited on the radio show "A Prairie Home Companion," offers some insight into the problem of identity and how we maintain it. As you read about the plight of the black-throated gray warbler, think about your own sense of who you are and how much your self-concept depends on your surroundings.

A Book Report on Minnesota Birds
By Garrison Keillor*

We say, "To err is human."
Perhaps to err is also avian.
When a bird is lost, however,
We don't call the National Guard or the Navy in.
We just look up and say,
"Good heavens, what is that black-throated gray warbler
Doing here where all this snow and ice is?"
Maybe the bird looks down and sees it's Minnesota
And has an identity crisis.
He says, "If I'm here in the winter,
Maybe I'm *not* a black-throated gray warbler,"
And broods and broods about it
And feels harbler and harbler,
Until he's too depressed to warble a single note,
For how can he know for sure he's a black-throated warbler,
If he can't see his throat?

*From "A Book Report on Minnesota Birds" © Garrison Keillor, 1980.

---

we describe our private self. One tendency in this regard has been reported by William McGuire and his colleagues as the **distinctiveness postulate**.[2] According to this research, we tend to encode as features of the self-concept those aspects of our own appearance or behavior that are unusual in some way. For instance, one study showed that schoolchildren were more likely to describe themselves in terms of their birthplace, their sex or ethnic background, their hair and eye color, or their height and weight if any of these features were different from the majority of their classmates'.[3] This again shows the important role situation plays in our definition of self-identity. Chances are that as the people around us change, so will

various facets of our self-concept recede into the background (because they are not unusual anymore), only to be replaced by new ways we find ourselves to be distinct from those around us.

Now that we have some idea what the self-concept is and how many versions of it may exist, we want to look at how it develops in individuals from infancy to adulthood.

How Does the Self-Concept Develop and Change?

Although many psychologists and mothers will argue that a newborn shows signs of uniqueness, few will argue that we are born with a

The distinctiveness postulate suggests that we see ourselves in terms of how we are different or unusual from those around us. (*Mr. Patrick O'Brien—The Irish Giant*, 18th-century engraving)

full-fledged sense of personal identity. The self-concept is constructed message by message, act by act, one reaction after another. The social construction of a personal identity takes a good deal of time and is no easy matter. We do know something about the process by which we gain our autonomy from the environment around us, try on various identities, and finally adopt and modify some of them for our very own. Let's begin with this process unfolding in childhood.

Development in Childhood

We enter this world in a relatively undifferentiated state of existence. The psychologist William James described this early existence as "a booming, buzzing confusion." In fact, the newborn infant is incapable of distinguishing parts of his own body from the rest of the environment. The infant has not yet learned from his culture where to draw the boundaries for self and not-self.

One of the pioneers who helped discover how these boundaries are drawn in the Western world was Harry Stack Sullivan. According to Sullivan, the child initially sees himself as simply an extension of the mother (or the person who plays that role), fulfilling the infant's needs for food, warmth and security. When these needs are met, the infant experiences a state of satisfaction that Sullivan described as a "good experience." When a need is aroused and crying fails to bring satisfaction from the other, the infant conceptualizes a "wrong experience." The need is not met and tension is not reduced. On occasion, the mothering that's done (say, breastfeeding or holding the infant) may satisfy the biological need but may at the same time communicate a feeling of nervousness. Sullivan called this circumstance a "bad experience," believing that repeated experiences of this type might lay the groundwork for anxiety about one's personal identity.[4]

Relying on the work of Sullivan and several other researchers, Dennis Smith and Keith Williamson have proposed a four-stage process for the development of personal identity in childhood:[5] (1) personification, (2) imitation, (3) role-playing, and (4) symbolic role-taking.

Personification   As the infant gradually realizes where her own body begins and ends, she transfers the previous states of global experience to the mother figure: "good mother," "wrong mother," or "bad mother." Eventually, the child can also transfer responsibility to a "good me," "wrong me," or "bad me." This sense of self is initially just the realization of a separate body and different states of satisfaction, but in time, and especially with the acquisition of language, the child can begin to use the linguistic label "me" to refer to her own momentary desires and later to refer to herself as the source or agent performing some set of behaviors. Sullivan refers to the ability to recognize a single self or a single other performing multiple roles as **personification**. The possibility of being a separate person is crucial to future development of a self-identity.

Imitation   Once the child is capable of personifying, she begins to imitate the behavior of significant others. **Imitation** is the simple repetition of behavior observed without any understanding of what is being done. For example, a two-year-old observes her pregnant mother holding her stomach and sighing heavily every time she sits down or stands up. The child imitates the behavior but has no idea that she is behaving like a "mother with child."

Role Playing   Gradually, the child may come to differentiate the things that her mother does when she is pregnant from those she does when she is not pregnant. Then the child will be able to engage in **role playing**, or imitation accompanied by some degree of understanding. She can stuff a pillow under a shirt, wear mother's high heels, sigh wearily, and *know* who she is supposed to be. At this stage, the child has the ability to try on many different roles and can practice being many different kinds of people.

Symbolic Role Taking   While communication plays an indisputable role in the earlier stages of development, it becomes even more crucial during the **symbolic role taking** phase. This stage involves learning to take a role mentally without having to do so physically. At this point, a wide world of selves is opened up to the young child, limited only by the power of her imagination. Communication with others is also enhanced as the child can now begin to see what the world might look like to other people.

As the child tries on various roles, the significant others in her world are constantly reacting to her performances. Some role presentations meet with overwhelming approval, others with a reprimand, and still others get mixed reviews or some other ambiguous response. In effect, these interactions take the form of the parent telling the child, "That's you!" or "That's *not* you!" And since the parents are seen as godlike authorities by the young child, she seldom doubts that the parents' feedback is not true. Repeated acts of role-play followed by parental (and later peer) confirmation or disconfirmation certainly have a great deal of influence on the self-concepts we develop.

Development in Adulthood

By now it should be clear that our self-concepts develop slowly over many interaction episodes with both significant others and relative strangers. As we move through adolescence and into adulthood, our self-concepts seem to stabilize. As a result of repeated interactions and consistent feedback, we begin to think of our identity in more and more limited terms. Yet it would be a mistake to think that we enter adulthood as a finished product. In some very subtle ways we continue to change and yet remain much the same person in our own minds. Subtle changes can occur as a result of what we call the residual self, self-perception, and self-talk.

Changes in the Residual Self   If our identities are constantly open to change, how is it that we seem to maintain stability in our sense of who we are? William Wilmot explains how we stabilize our identity by referring to the **residual self**.[6] As Wilmot sees it, we enter every social transaction with some kind of self-concept, derived from our past experiences in similar situations, present expectations, and any further consequences we foresee. Thus there is always a "residue" of our past identities in every encounter. If we project essentially the same residual identity in a new situation, and others offer their approval of that identity, then little or no change takes place in the self-concept. Horace thinks of himself as a "nice, friendly guy" when it comes to meeting new people. He makes new friends easily and his old friends tell him he's too nice for his own good. He attends a social gathering where he engages in a half-dozen pleasant conversations with strangers, all of whom seem genuinely pleased-to-have-made-your-acquaintance. His self-concept can remain intact.

At other times, however, the self we project may not be reinforced. We may sense that others see us quite differently than we see ourselves. When this happens, we are likely to find some way to incorporate both views, and we leave the situation with a slightly "new" residual self. Suppose Horace, the socialite, attends another gala event and acts the way he always does when meeting strangers. This time people don't warm to his friendly conversations. He overhears one person call him "Mr. I-Am-Friendly," while another labels him "a fraud." Horace leaves this encounter with a slightly altered self-concept. He still thinks of himself as friendly, but now maybe a little too sugar-coated.

Some writers refer to this event-by-event building of the residual self as a "biographical" or "historical" self. In other words, even though we may present a different self in each of several interactions, the one fact that ties all the selves together is that they emanate from the same physical self. Thus no matter which self we present—as long as it seems appropriate, is approved by others, and does not consciously conflict with another important aspect of our self-concept—our sense of who we are will probably remain stable. In fact, Anthony Greenwald has identified three cognitive biases that help to preserve the sense of a stable identity: egocentricity, beneffectance, and cognitive conservatism.[7]

The first bias, **egocentricity**, refers to the fact that we have a better memory for information that is highly relevant to our conception of self. If you see yourself as a genius, you're more likely to remember SAT scores and comments about how good your ideas are, or how well you play Trivial Pursuit. You may forget comments about such mundane matters as burning the brownies or not picking your clothes up off the floor.

A second bias, **beneffectance**, enables us to perceive ourselves as more responsible for positive outcomes and less responsible for negative ones. Thus our friend Horace could reconcile the reactions to his friendly self-concept by taking credit when being friendly pays off, and invoking the maxim "You can't please everyone" when it does not.

Finally, as we look back on our lives, we tend to apply the principle of **cognitive conservatism**, seeking out information that confirms our own self-concept and revising our own biographical memory so that it fits better with our present self-concept. You can test this principle yourself by writing a brief autobiography sometime when you are down on your luck and then writing another one when you are feeling on top of the world. Then compare the two when your self-concept is on a more even keel. This principle suggests that you would interpret the same events quite differently depending on how you saw your self at the time you wrote about them.

Changes through Self-Perception Cognitive biases, such as those just discussed, help reinforce our self-concepts. But on occasion, simple observation of our own behavior leads to the development of new self-concepts. As you may recall from Chapter 4, Daryl Bem proposed his **self-perception theory** to explain how many of our self-definitions come about and are changed. Bem suggests that we come to know who we are by observing our own behavior "after the fact" and then inferring what kind of person we must be.[8]

Suppose you're cleaning your apartment and notice that your garbage can is full of paper and aluminum cans. On a whim, you decide to take them to a recycling center. Later that day as the temperature drops below zero, you think about turning the heat up but decide against it. Finally, you catch yourself just as you are about to toss a gum wrapper out of your car window. You put it in the ashtray instead. As you take stock of your behavior, you may be led to the

Our fascination with the question of who we are is an endless source of amusement, at least in our culture. (Albrecht Dürer, *Self-Portrait at Age Twenty-two*, 1493)

conclusion that you are fast becoming a "conservationist." This may also happen when friends point out aspects of your behavior that you have overlooked. In effect, you may say to yourself: "I did give money to the college fund. I do stop to help people who have flat tires. I must be a charitable person."

Changes through Self-Talk Sometimes we talk ourselves into altering our self-concepts.

Some people spend considerable time in self-reflection, prayer, or just talking to themselves. These internal dialogues can be persuasive and are often directed at self-improvement. Through symbolic role taking, we can imagine ourselves as another person or having a totally opposite personality. We can produce one or more "ideal" self-concepts and convince ourselves to try them out.

As we have seen, the development of a self-concept is a process of learning social roles and identifying closely with some of them. At the same time, we try to distance ourselves from social roles so that we are not totally defined by them. As we grow up, our parents and peers encourage us to play some roles more than others and to spice them up by adding in elements of our own personality. The process continues into adulthood, although there are a number of ways we convince ourselves that we have a consistent or stable self-concept. The end result is that we think of ourselves as "unique individuals," unlike anyone else. Why do we place so much emphasis on individuality? We address that issue next.

STANDING OUT IN THE CROWD: BREAKING SOCIAL RULES

In many non-Western cultures, the freedom to deviate from socially prescribed roles is severely restricted. The notion of a "self" apart from the social roles one has learned is foreign to many cultures. In cultures that have operated on the basis of long-established traditions, one plays a role as it was meant to be played and does not improvise. It is the character of our own culture, however, to allow and even encourage creativity in role enactment. This opens the door for people to leave a personal mark on the roles they play. As a result, we tend to devote as much time and attention to caring for our identities as we do feeding and clothing ourselves.

Although there are probably many reasons that our culture emphasizes individuality and self-identity, we want to focus on two of them. One reason has to do with the complexity of our culture, the fact that there are so many diverse groups that vie for our attention and allegiance. The second reason is perhaps even more fundamental. Our culture values the individual as the basic unit of society. Let's look more closely at these two reasons that being unique—and breaking the rules—is so attractive to most of us.

Influence of Multiple Systems

As a society becomes larger and the number of subcultures and groups within it increases, the individual in that culture is inevitably faced with more choices for his communication behavior. The person who is a member of both a bowling league and a chapter of Alcoholics Anonymous may have to choose between following the bowling group's implicit rule that "we always go out for a few beers after we bowl" and the other group's rule that doesn't allow for social drinking. The decision to follow one set of rules often means breaking another set. This would rarely happen if all the rules were negotiated by and applied to all members of the society at large. But a large society, especially in the absence of old traditions, will inevitably become a loosely structured conglomerate of many smaller institutions. Each individual will likely belong to a number of different groups and no one group will have his or her undivided loyalty. This fact alone makes the individual, rather than the group, the focal point of decision making.

Individual decision making stands in stark contrast to primitive and traditional cultures where the group reigns supreme. Perhaps you recall the discussion in Chapter 1 of the !Kung and their ritual of insulting the meat (see Box 1.2). In small social groupings such as this, there is an ever present danger that an emphasis on any one individual will destroy the social bond of the group. In larger societies, this risk is minimized. It is ironic that in modern culture we are freer to flex our personalities precisely because we are ultimately replaceable—we don't threaten the survival of the group.

Influence of Western Cultural Values

It is obvious to even the most casual observer that Eastern and Western cultures operate under very different systems of thinking. A number of scholars have noted that the principal difference is in the way each views the *relationship* of humans to the rest of the natural order. According to Eastern philosophy, humans are viewed as intricately woven into the fabric of nature, neither above nor below other forms of life. In the West, the tendency is to view ourselves as *separate* from nature and from each other. Not until we go out of our way to "develop a relationship" with another person do we generally see connections among ourselves. This Western notion of compartmentalizing nature leads us to make finer and finer distinctions, and ultimately, to end up with the individual as the basic social unit, the building block of society. As Edward Hall in *Beyond Culture* puts it:

Culture has always dictated where to draw the line separating one thing from another. . . . We in the West take the many entities that are enclosed in a single skin and supported by a single system of bones and muscles and say that this is one thing—a person. . . . None of this can be applied to the Pueblo Indian, for something akin to lineages in the Pueblo are the viable unit. No human being outside of these groups has significance independent and distinct from the group.[9]

Our personal identity is actually a collection of selves that we monitor and use in different situations. (Pablo Picasso, *The Red Armchair*, 1931)

Thus our own cultural blinders direct us to see the individual and to place a priority on his or her continued existence. Cultural messages encourage us to "stand out in a crowd," "rise head and shoulders above everyone else," and above all, the old paradoxical injunction, "be unique."

Thus far we have followed the development of the self-concept from its rudimentary beginnings in childhood role playing to its status as a flexible, yet apparently stable, representation of our personal identity. We have also seen why the self-concept is so important to those of us in Western societies, especially in American culture. Next we hope to gain a better understanding of how self-concept affects our own behavior and our communication with other selves.

HOW SELF-CONCEPTS AFFECT COMMUNICATION

What good is a self-concept? What does it do for us? One major function of the self-concept is that it acts as a guide, channeling what we perceive, how we should act, and what we remember. In addition, the self-concepts we adopt contribute to the style of communication we employ in each social encounter. Let's look first at how a self-concept affects our perceptions.

Self-Concepts Shape Perception and Judgment

Although cognitive psychologists have only recently shown renewed interest in studying the concept of self, their efforts have shed some new light on how the various self-concepts are related to each other and to other concepts. In this section, we will look at the influence of four aspects of self-concepts: (1) self-schemata, (2) life scripts, (3) self-esteem, and (4) self-handicapping strategies.

Self-Schemata

It must be obvious by now that each of us has not one but several self-concepts. You probably think about your self in somewhat different ways when you are at work, with your parents, alone, or with an intimate friend. Even though they are different, these various self-concepts are related. Cognitive psychologists have been investigating the ways people organize their self-concepts. They refer to **self-schemata** as

cognitive structures that organize and guide the processing of self-related information.[10]

People use different organizing principles for making sense of their collection of self-concepts. Hazel Markus has identified several of them. For some people, independence or dependence is the central principle in their self-schema. For others, masculinity or femininity may be dominant.[11] Whatever the organizing principle, it affects how we perceive ourselves and our social world. For instance, someone whose self-schema is based on the organizing principle of "being competitive" is likely to remember more incidents in which she was competitive and fewer in which cooperation occurred. There is also evidence that such a person is likely to hold the view that "everyone is competitive" as a way of justifying her own competitiveness.

Life Scripts

Sometimes an organizing principle becomes elaborated into a **life script**, a relatively fixed way of thinking about the self and relating to others. Eric Berne originated the concept and defined four very general life scripts: "I'm OK, you're OK," "I'm OK, you're not OK," "I'm not OK, you're OK," and "I'm not OK, you're not OK."[12] Each of these scripts represents a basic view of self and others and influences how we perceive social situations. Barnett Pearce and Vernon Cronen offer an extended definition of a life script as "that repertoire of episodes that a person perceives as identified with him/herself."[13] The life script of a "practical joker," for example, would entail a number of episodes such as "hiding things from people," "placing a thumbtack or whoopee cushion on another's chair," and other similar escapades.

Self-Handicapping Strategies

While most people no doubt adopt life scripts that they believe will result in positive public images, on some occasions a life script can be used as an excuse for a potentially negative self-presentation. A person who fears that he won't be capable of performing a new dance step may decline an invitation to dance by invoking his life script of "A real man doesn't. . . ." He may thus be using his life script as a self-handicapping strategy. In their research on this subject, Steven Berglas and Edward Jones defined a **self-handicapping strategy** as a technique for manufacturing protective excuses ahead of time to prevent possible failure in the future.[14] The research has shown that some people will talk or act in ways that protect them from bearing the brunt of future failures. They'll make excuses in the event that they fail an exam, make a mistake in a financial report, or miss a crucial free throw. Supposedly, the excuse planted ahead of time (had to work, company came over, the old wrist is acting up again) takes the heat off the individual and places the blame on the circumstance.

Self-Esteem

Finally, it is not only the particular self-concept, life script, or handicapping strategy that guides our actions, but also our general level of **self-esteem**: how worthwhile we feel in regard to our goals and achievements. Obviously, being successful at the things that are important to us raises our self-esteem and failure lowers that esteem. Repeated episodes of failure may be serious enough to warrant a temporary lowering of our goals, at least until we hit a better streak of luck. Repeated success, on the other hand, gives us additional confidence to attempt new goals or perhaps even try on new identities.

Self-Concepts and Relational Styles

Besides the self-concept's impact on our perceptions of social interaction, the self-concept can also affect the way we communicate verbally and nonverbally. In fact, the relationship between our identity and our communication behavior is a reflexive one. That is, the residual self that we enter a situation with shapes the way we communicate, and in turn, the way we communicate can influence and revise what we think about ourselves.

For example: A young woman enters her boss's office during her first week on the job, to talk about how to approach her first "real" client. She has had considerable sales experience in a previous position with another company. She sees herself as an "aggressive and competent salesperson." This identity shapes the way she communicates with her boss. She walks into the office with confidence, engages in a little small talk, and then proceeds to lay out her plan for snaring the client. Along the way, however, she uncharacteristically stumbles over her words, forgets a major step in her proposal, and almost knocks the boss's coffee cup off the desk. While these behaviors do not completely shatter her competent-salesperson image, they do dent it a bit around the edges. The feedback she receives from observing her own behavior plus the boss's reaction modifies her self-identity; she won't see herself in quite the same way the next time she enters the boss's office.

This reflexive relationship between self-identity and communication should make us realize that our self-concept is always under construction, and therefore open to change. Remember, one of the most troublesome of human traits is that we create or reify social realities (like the self, the government, and so on), and then forget that we created them in the first place. We aren't stuck with our personalities—we just tend to rebuild the same ones time after time. We can, in cooperation with those around us, alter who we are. This is by no means an easy task. It involves a great deal of communicative skill on our part. We must be able to manage *communicator styles*, develop a *rhetorically sensitive* self-schema, and, for some of us, learn to deal with high levels of *communication apprehension*. The inability to master these aspects of style will severely limit our potential. Let's look briefly at each of these three factors.

Communicator Style

The concept of communicator style has been defined by Robert Norton as "the way one verbally, nonverbally, and paraverbally interacts to signal how literal meaning should be taken, interpreted, filtered, or understood."[15] Norton identifies nine prominent communication styles that not only color the meaning of messages, but establish personal identities as well. One's style may be dominant, dramatic, contentious, animated, impression-leaving, relaxed, attentive, open, or friendly (see Table 5.1 for definitions and examples of each style).

A style is usually established by the simple repetition of behaviors associated with that particular style. Others soon begin to expect the person to act that way on a regular basis. A person who repeatedly turns a clever phrase or states her observations in offbeat ways may be regarded as having an impression-leaving style. The more she uses that style, the more likely it is that others will associate it with her personality. She doesn't always have to be clever or offbeat to maintain the style. Once established, it is likely to affect the expectations of those who know her. You may hang around just in case she says something striking.

According to Norton, people don't usually rely on a single communicator style, but instead develop what might be called a "style profile"— a combination of style variables. One person may tend to communicate by blending a dominant style with a friendly and attentive style. Another may be equally effective using a combination of dominance with some aspects of the impression-leaving and contentious

styles. You might want to inspect Table 5.1 and see if you can discover your own style profiles. Which one style or combination of styles do you use most frequently with your best friend? When interacting with your instructors or an employer? Can you identify situations in which the style you use may not be the most effective one? Think of a particular situation, such as telling a friend about one of your recent accomplishments. To what extent does your self-concept affect your communicator style in that situation? Which styles does your self-concept encourage? Which ones does it prohibit or discourage? A useful exercise is to practice using different communicator styles until you can turn them on and off easily. Then you can manage your style rather than having it manage you.

Rhetorical Sensitivity

Another way to think about the self-concept and communication is in terms of rhetorical sensitivity. In the view of Donald Darnell and Wayne Brockriede, there are three basic types of communicators: Noble Selves, Rhetorical Reflectors, and Rhetorical Sensitives.[16]

The Noble Self   This kind of person has a self-schema that emphasizes consistency above all else. Darnell and Brockriede defined these people as ones who "see any variation from their personal norms as hypocritical, as a denial of integrity, as a cardinal sin." A Noble Self who has an organizing principle of honesty may struggle frequently with issues such as how to respond to a friend who asks, "Do you think I'll get the job?" or "How do I look?" The Noble Self will feel a strong obligation to say exactly what he thinks, no matter how it affects the other person.

The Rhetorical Reflector   At the other extreme are those who "have no Self to call their own. For each person and each situation they present

TABLE 5.1

Communicator styles and their manifestations

Communicator style	Verbal and nonverbal manifestations
Dominant	Tendency to come on strong, take charge of social situations, speak frequently, and otherwise control conversations.
Dramatic	Likes to act out the point physically and vocally. Tells jokes, stories, and often exaggerates to make the point. Speech tends to be picturesque.
Contentious	Loves to argue, quick to challenge others, precise about defining things, and often insists that others show proof to back up their arguments. Once wound up, hard to stop.
Animated	Very expressive nonverbally: constantly gesturing, using a wide variety of facial expressions; face and eyes usually reveal emotions and feelings.
Impression-Leaving	What this person says, and the way he or she says it, is almost always memorable. People usually don't forget such a person easily.
Relaxed	Comes across as calm and collected during interaction, especially under pressure. The rhythm and flow of speech is rarely affected by feelings of nervousness.
Attentive	Listens to others very carefully and lets them know it by giving nonverbal feedback such as eye contact and nodding. Shows empathy and can usually repeat back exactly what the other said.
Open	Readily reveals personal information. Openly expresses emotions.
Friendly	Gives positive feedback to recognize, encourage, and reinforce other people.

Derived from Robert Norton, *Communicator Style: Theory, Application, and Measures* (Beverly Hills, Calif.: Sage Publications, 1983), pp. 64–72.

a new self."[17] This kind of person is most concerned about being "appropriate." She will follow the social rules of the situation or will try to be the kind of person the other wants her to be. In response to the friend's "How do I look?" question, the Rhetorical Reflector will say what she thinks you want to hear.

The Rhetorical Sensitive. In contrast to these two extremes, the Rhetorical Sensitive has a much more complex self-schema. Roderick Hart and Don Burks characterize this kind of person as an "undulating, fluctuating entity, always unsure, always guessing, continually weighing . . . the values, attitudes and philosophical predispositions of others."[18] Once he understands the complexity of the situation, the other, and the self, he "swims in a sea of probabilities" before actually communicating. Such a person:

1. realizes there is no Single Self; therefore any situation will require one of several selves.

2. avoids communicative rigidity; doesn't try to be overly consistent or arbitrarily follow social conventions.

3. avoids making messages without regard for the other, yet doesn't simply try to placate others.

4. realizes that there are times when an idea should *not* be communicated.

5. seeks a variety of ways to communicate ideas and feelings.[19]

Being rhetorically sensitive requires that we think about the way we communicate before, during, and after we interact with others.

It should be clear from this discussion that a rhetorically sensitive communicator is one who can monitor situations, determine which self would be most appropriate, enact an effective communicator style, and make any necessary adjustments. No doubt we would judge such a person as highly competent. And of course, now that we know what to do, we can work at becoming rhetorically sensitive ourselves. All we need to do is practice. There may, however, be one major obstacle in our path that practice alone will not overcome: a debilitating anxiety known as communication apprehension.

Communication Apprehension

Communication apprehension refers to "an individual's level of fear or anxiety associated with either real or anticipated communication with another person or persons."[20] According to the research of James McCroskey, as much as 20 percent of the U.S. population can be categorized as highly apprehensive.[21] Most of us are anxious about communicating in one situation or another: public presentations, job interviews, first dates. Being apprehensive in these situations is fairly normal. Those people who are highly apprehensive tend to feel anxious in a wide variety of communication situations, including talking to people they already know.

When communication apprehension strikes, the results are very predictable. All our knowledge about communicating effectively goes out the window. For instance, even though we know that a more dramatic communicator style would grab an audience's attention and give us a better chance of being heard, the feeling of fear strangles our expressiveness. Fortunately, researchers have discovered several facts about this anxiety that make it much more manageable.

Communication apprehension is not an innate disability but a learned reaction to physiological arousal. When we're called upon to perform an important task, the body begins pumping more adrenaline into the blood to provide energy. Physically we feel an increase in arousal; cognitively we label that arousal as fear.[22]

The fear of communicating can be overcome, first by labeling the arousal as energy rather than fear, and then by focusing on the potentially positive rather than negative outcomes of any communication transaction. Although you shouldn't expect an overnight transformation, you can begin to approach communication situations with a different perspective, one that puts you (and those you interact with) in mutual control of social forces, rather than letting the forces control you. One way to do this is to increase our awareness of our own self-presentations.

IDENTITY: AWARENESS AND PRACTICE

It should be clear by now that how we think about our self can either limit or expand our ability to communicate. We cannot overemphasize the need to give ourselves options for communicating in a world where the only question about change is how fast it will occur, not if or when. To manage our communication in such a world requires that we (1) increase our awareness of the self we present to others; (2) avoid the tantalizing but unfruitful search for our "real self"; and (3) discover ways to balance the tensions between conformity and individuality.

Self-Monitoring

Throughout this chapter we have discussed several features of our self-concepts and how they develop. One of the first steps in managing our communication is to become more aware of those aspects of self that influence communication. We can begin by learning to monitor our behavior for evidence of how our self-concept influences it.

In Chapter 3 the concept of self-monitoring was discussed as a perceptual tendency, the degree of awareness one has of the situation at hand and of the kind of self-presentation appropriate to that situation. Here we wish to expand the concept to include not only awareness but the ability to exercise control over self-presentations. If you recall, the person defined as a high self-monitor shows a much greater awareness of and ability to tailor identity to the changing conditions of the situation. The low self-monitor, on the other hand, pays less attention to situational cues and relies to a much greater extent on inner feelings, attitudes, and a more predetermined image of self. The low self-monitor shows more consistency in self-identity across situations (like the Noble Self), but is unable to adapt easily when the preferred self obviously doesn't fit the situation. The result is that low self-monitors often appear to observers to be less friendly, outgoing, and extroverted and more worried, anxious, and nervous than high self-monitors.[23] Mark Snyder explains this finding by drawing a distinc-

tion between "background" and "foreground" self-presentations. He argues that high self-monitors display a consistent background image of being friendly and at ease, while constantly adapting their foreground image (for example, being dramatic or serious or contentious) to the interaction at hand.[24]

This research suggests that one of the keys to communication effectiveness is the ability to be aware of and manage the foreground persona that we present to others in changing social episodes. One way to increase your awareness is to monitor for one or two days how many different situations you faced and which self you projected in each one. Determine whether any other self would have been more appropriate. Imagine yourself in that situation, trying on the new identity. Role-play the situation with a classmate. Before long you will go beyond awareness to regulating and controlling those impressions.

Aspects of Self to Monitor

Let's assume you have already begun to develop a habit of monitoring your own behavior and identifying which self-concept you project in various situations or relationships. Now you can begin to reflect on these situations and ask yourself additional questions raised in this chapter. You could begin by considering what your overall self-schema is like—what organizing principles tie these various self-concepts together? Are you more concerned about the consistency of your self-image (Noble Self) or simply adjusting who you are to the demands of the situation (Rhetorical Reflector)? Or do you show signs of Rhetorical Sensitivity across these situations? (Look again at the five attitudes of rhetorical sensitivity on page 112.) Which of the four basic life scripts best characterizes you? What episodes are important in maintaining your life script? How frequently are you guilty of relying on self-handicapping strategies to ease the pain of possible failure? Is it possible that these strategies actually bring about failure? Remember the "self-fulfilling prophecy" discussed in Chapter 3? How do you feel about yourself in these situations? Which situations affect your self-esteem the most?

You can also become more aware of how the self-concept influences your communication behavior. The next time you have an argument or misunderstanding with a friend, stop and think about what you actually said and the communicator style aspects of your behavior. If your style is to be dramatic and your friend is asking you to "tell the honest truth," it might be a good time to alter your style and stick to the facts.

Avoiding the Extremes

It is possible to become overly concerned with your identity. Some people concentrate so much of their energy on trying to find out who they are that they lose sight of other important aspects of effective interpersonal communication. There are two extremes to be avoided: the narcissistic search for "the real self" and the path of the Rhetorical Reflector, the person who always lets others define the situation and then tries to fit in.

The Narcissistic Self

One reason so many people are unable to manage situationally relevant self-images is that they believe in the idea of one authentic and "real" self. Our culture has in fact perpetuated this belief, leading some social critics to describe the 1970s as "the me decade" and the pursuit of self-knowledge as an empty exercise, unable to fulfill its promise. Social critic Richard Sennett has even argued that an entire culture of people focusing their energies on the "search for self" risks losing the ability to communicate in public.[25] While conceiving of one authentic self is not necessarily bad, it can lead to problems if it becomes a rigid standard

In Greek mythology, the young Narcissus fell in love with his own reflection and pined away until he was turned into the flower that bears his name.

for every situation. In the extreme form of clinical narcissism, a person suffers from pervasive feelings of inner emptiness, depression, and intense feelings of rage combined with a belief in his own right to seek gratification.[26] The result is an endless cycle of searching for a self that cannot be found.

Think about it for a moment. How much value do you place on talking to total strangers just for the sake of conversation, to exchange thoughts about current political or social events? Sennett argues that too many of us devalue the art of public communication because it cannot help us determine "who we really are." The only interpersonal relationships we do value are intimate ones, because we can "find ourselves" only when others help us discover ourselves through intimate self-disclosures. As a result of focusing on their "real" selves, people spend less time engaged in community action and doing something about world issues. Whether Sennett's thesis is true or not, it is an intriguing one. And it suggests a number of possible dangers in the search for the one true self. Rather than worrying about "the real me," we might better spend that time honing the various selves we need to use in the variety of situations we face daily.

The Rhetorical Reflector

The other extreme has already been discussed in this chapter, but bears repeating here. The Rhetorical Reflector self-image can be carried to excess. A person who is overly concerned about being appropriate or making others happy can lose any sense of uniqueness. In some cultures this may not be detrimental. We remind you again of the !Kung and their ritual of insulting the meat to ensure that individuality doesn't interfere with the community's survival. Likewise, some Eastern philosophies, such as Zen Buddhism, encourage their followers to purge the concept of self from their minds (see Box 5.2, pp. 116–17). When an entire culture or group follows such a practice, the results may be quite beneficial to all concerned. In mainstream American culture, the Rhetorical Reflector doesn't usually fare so well. While he may be seen as a saint by some, most will view such a person as a doormat or a burden. The classic example is the martyr who always gives up his own self-interests, allowing (or in effect, forcing) others to make all the decisions.

Relating Self-Concept and Social Knowledge

In Chapter 1 we presented a model of communicative competence that suggested four processes that must be mastered to attain interpersonal competence: (1) interpreting perceptual cues; (2) planning personal goals; (3)

adapting to role requirements; and (4) encoding and decoding messages. You must synchronize all four processes; especially important is the balance that must be struck between maintaining the self-concept (personal goals) and maintaining the social system (adapting to role requirements). How this tension is balanced may determine your overall level of communication competence. As we saw in Chapter 2, three levels of communication competence are possible: minimal, satisfactory, and optimal.[27] Let's look at each of these levels of competence again, this time focusing on how they relate to achieving personal goals.

Minimal Competence

Sometimes you know just enough about the situation to get by. Your perceptual competence lets you figure out the basic role requirements and what messages to use, but that's about it. When you don't understand all or most of the role requirements and/or the messages that satisfy those requirements, but know enough to initiate and conclude a social episode, you are minimally competent. Many people are only minimally competent at the art of conversation. They can get one started, but they may have a lot of trouble keeping it flowing smoothly from topic to topic or knowing what's appropriate or inappropriate to talk about in a given instance. Awkward silences or poor conversational regulators may dominate the talk. Achieving personal goals is rather difficult because they don't know quite how to manipulate the roles and rules.

Satisfactory Competence

When you learn to master most of the nuances of a given situation, you may be considered satisfactorily competent in that situation. When you know all the social system or culture can tell you about an episode, you can usually achieve a wide range of personal goals while at the same time meeting most of the role

BOX 5.2

Zen and the Art of Selflessness: "What Is Your Original Face Before Your Mother and Father Were Born?"

Our culture values people as isolated, separate individuals. We spend a great deal of our time reflecting on who we are. But not every culture attaches so much importance to the individual and ego involvement in social life. In fact, in Japanese Zen Buddhism, practitioners strive to eliminate self-identity altogether, to achieve a sense of *mu*, or nothingness. They reject the idea that a person's essence or being can be an object of thought.

The ideal of personal activity in Zen is "nondoing," or what some call a "state of no-mind." According to T. P. Kasulis, the author of *Zen Action, Zen Person*, it is the ability to be "unselfconsciously responsive," or in harmony with the surrounding social context and interpersonal relations. Lao-tzu, the founder of Taoism, once suggested that the ideal person was like water—responsive and yielding, but not fatalistic. By yielding (or being in harmony with the situation), water follows its path and eventually wears away the rock obstructing it (thus it is not fatalistic).

Of course, this philosophy is quite complementary with much of Japanese culture. Social situations are highly defined in Japan, so that knowing one's role and being in harmony with the situation is much easier than it is in our own culture. The self is defined to a much greater extent by social relationships with parents, children, husbands and wives, and in-laws.

All these important relations or "betweennesses" are stripped away when a person enters a Zen monastery. The result, if Zen training is successful, is a person whose self-definition has been essentially erased, since there is little sense of a private self to begin with. Rinzai, a well-known Zen master, refers to this achievement as becoming "a true person of no status."

According to Zen philosophy, the self is a social fiction that gets in the way of truly experiencing life. Kasulis describes the process of writing at his desk, including the pen, paper, and other paraphernalia around him: "These are not merely things in my experience; they *are* my experience. My self does not relate to these things, my self *is* these things." Contrary to our Western view of a person apart from, yet moving through, one context after another, the Zen view is that an individual is a person only insofar as he or she is *in* one of these contexts. Private feelings may exist, but the individual's

requirements and personal goals of the other person as well. Satisfactory competence, then, is knowing how to manage a given episode, achieving as many personal goals for self and other as possible within the conventional system of roles and rules established by the culture. Most of us strive for this level of competence by learning all the rules, watching how competent communicators manipulate those rules, and then following suit. If you've ever worked for a large organization, or observed closely how your college bureaucracy works, you have probably known people who knew the system so well that they could accomplish all sorts of personal goals by bending, but not breaking, those rules.

Optimal Competence

A person's ability to creatively break out of the normal role and rule requirements in order to achieve personal goals is termed optimal competence. At this level of competence, you know

For the Japanese, the emphasis would be not on the individual who is responsible, but on the relationship, or the "betweenness" of the two:

A: The indebtedness *does not end.*
B: Oh no, the indebtedness goes this way.

There is little doubt that the self is one of our many socially constructed realities. But for us, it is one that seems so natural we can hardly imagine living without it. For a Zen person, the self is *the problem* that distorts perception of events and relationships. The Zen master poses the problem in one of the most popular koans in Zen training: If identity is so fundamental, "What is your original face before your mother and father were born?"

Source: *T. P. Kasulis,* Zen Action, Zen Person *(Honolulu: University Press of Hawaii, 1981).*

meaning as a person is predominantly public—and observable in relationship to others. Like a chess piece without a chessboard or a rulebook to play by, the solitary person has no meaning. Kasulis contrasts the two views in the following example of two people exchanging apologies: For Westerners, the discourse would go something like this:

A: Oh, excuse me.
B: Oh no, excuse me.

what is expected of you but choose to "step outside the system" or "follow the beat of a different drummer." Artists, historians, poets, and others who have exposed themselves to different cultures and ideas often have the capability to pick and choose when they wish to follow their native culture's ways. According to Linda Harris, a person may be optimally competent in one of two ways: by becoming alienated from the social system or by transcending it.

The person who is *alienated* is one who steps outside the system and then finds it difficult to participate again and gain any sense of satisfaction. Someone who outgrows particular religious practices or realizes that there are other equally valid ways to be religious may become alienated and unable to enjoy what was once a vital form of interaction.

Those who *transcend* the social system realize that every such system is a product of communication and they more or less revel in that discovery. They experience a great deal of satisfaction from participating in many different kinds of social systems but feel bound by no particular system. They frequently step outside the system to gain a better perspective on it and then look for possible ways to improve it. Social activitists are good examples of this level of competence. Mahatma Gandhi's ability to creatively break the rules of the British government and eventually free India from British rule illustrates how one can transcend a particular social system to achieve goals in a highly competent manner.

Try thinking about your own level of communication competence in any given social situation. Determine what you need to know about the situation, how to adapt to its role requirements, what your own and others' personal goals are, and what kind of message exchange will result in the level of competence you want to achieve.

IDENTITY AND COMMUNICATIVE COMPETENCE

As we indicated earlier, our identities are constructed in the process of communicating with others. This means that to be ourselves we must manage others' impressions of us through the messages we exchange with them. One of the best ways to do this is by increasing our repertoire of message options: verbal and nonverbal strategies, a working vocabulary, the range of communicator styles we can use comfortably, and so on. In the following chapters we'll encounter a number of communication tactics that will serve us in this regard. The important thing for you to do at this point is to make a commitment to yourself to develop *your* ability to use a wide range of communica-

tion strategies. You might begin now by making a list of some specific communication behaviors or skills that you don't perform as well as you'd like. Seek out opportunities to work on these skills so that you can add them to your repertoire and call on them when you need them. By doing so, you'll be building the kind of identity that is adaptable enough to enjoy the best of times and survive the worst of them.

REVIEW TERMS

The following is a list of major concepts introduced in this chapter. The page where the concept is first mentioned is listed in parentheses.

self-concept (100)
distinctiveness postulate (101)
personification (103)
imitation (103)
role playing (103)
symbolic role taking (103)
residual self (104)
egocentricity (104)
beneffectance (104)
cognitive conservatism (105)
self-perception theory (105)
self-schemata (108)
life script (108)
self-handicapping strategies (109)
self-esteem (109)
communicator style (110)
rhetorical sensitivity (110)
the noble self (110)
rhetorical reflector (110)
rhetorical sensitive (111)
communication apprehension (112)

SUGGESTED READINGS

Berne, Eric. *Games People Play*. New York: Grove Press, 1964. A highly readable book about the influence of life scripts and game playing on interpersonal relationships. By identifying these games in your own relationships, you can determine whether the self-concepts these games reinforce are really worthwhile.

Cushman, Donald, and Dudley Cahn, Jr. *Communication in Interpersonal Relationships*. Albany: State University of New York Press, 1985. This book focuses on interpersonal communication as the major force in developing, presenting, and validating individuals' self-concepts. No other book we've seen emphasizes the role of self-concept as much as this one.

Rubin, Theodore, M.D. *One to One: Understanding Personal Relationships*. New York: Viking Press, 1983. This popular-press book also emphasizes the role of three basic "character types" (people who move toward, against, or away from other people) in relationships. All possible combinations of personality types are explored in terms of the relationships we are likely to develop with others.

PROCESS TO PERFORMANCE

TOPICS FOR DISCUSSION

1. Think of five or six interpersonal situations in which there are clear role requirements: teacher–student, doctor–patient, and so on. Now think of several real people you know who play those roles. Draw distinctions between those communication behaviors, rules, and obligations that are role-related and those that emanate from the self-concepts of the individuals involved. What potential advantages and disadvantages arise when people add self-expression to their social roles?

2. Discuss the distinctiveness postulate (page 101) in terms of what makes you different from your various groups of friends, family, and other acquaintances. Compare the ways that you differ from one social circle to the next. To what extent are you really a different person to each group? How does the distinctiveness postulate help account for this? Are some distinctions more important than others (for example, sex, age, height, weight, attitudes, personality)?

3. Self-perception theory (page 105) suggests that we often behave first and then decide what kind of person we must be based on observations of our behavior. Can you think of examples of this happening to you? Have you ever pointed out behaviors to a friend that led him or her to revise a self-concept? In what ways do we block out perceptions of our own behavior in order to protect a self-concept?

4. Do you agree or disagree with the statement that we do not have one "real" self, but many selves? What do you think are the strongest arguments for your point of view?

How would you convince someone who held the opposite point of view?

5. Talk about the advantages and disadvantages of each of the three types of communicators: Noble Self, Rhetorical Reflector, and Rhetorical Sensitive. Are people really distinct types or are there some aspects of self that we try to maintain consistently (Noble Self)? When would the Rhetorical Reflector be a positive and healthy self-concept?

OBSERVATION GUIDES

1. For this Twenty Questions Statement Test, you will rely on the observations of at least two close friends. The objective is to discover aspects of your self-concept that are consistent or at least apparent to both yourself and several of your friends. You should write down 20 two- or three-word statements *about yourself* by completing the following phrases:

a. "I am . . ."
b. "I like . . ."
c. "I have done . . ."

Ask your friends to do the same thing, except they will complete the statements about *you*, not about themselves. Now compare lists, identifying those self-concept statements that appear on all or most of the lists. What similarities or discrepancies surprise you the most? Are most of the statements self-identity ("I am . . ."), evaluative ("I like . . ."), or behavioral ("I have done . . .") statements? What does this tell you about your self-concept(s)? Conclude your observations by writing a brief analysis of your self-concept in each of the relationships involved. Why do you think you appear the way you do to each person?

2. Visit a day-care center or early childhood learning center. Ask permission to observe and possibly talk to some of the children during their playtime. Look for examples of self-concepts in development. Record examples of verbal or nonverbal communication that reflect the stages discussed in the chapter: personification, imitation, role playing, and symbolic role taking. Ask questions such as "Who's your favorite hero?" or "Who do you like to be when you play?" What do their answers tell you about their developing self-concepts? What behaviors or roles are reinforced by playmates or attending adults? Ask your instructor whether you can present some of your findings to the class.

CLASSROOM EXERCISES

1. This exercise should be conducted in groups of four. Initially, two people will role-play a conversation while the other two will act as observers. Later you will reverse roles. The objective is to improve your ability to enact a wider range of *communicator styles*. You should follow the steps below. Step (a) may be done prior to class to save time.

a. Individually, write down your own *ideal* communicator style profile for meeting new people. Write down how would you like to come across in terms of the styles described in Table 5.1. Also write down a style you feel is very difficult for you to enact and a situation in which you would like to be able to use this style.

b. Decide who will role-play and who will observe first. One observer should record the behavior of Role Player #1, the other should observe Role Player #2. Observers should make a list of the nine communicator styles and write down examples of each style they witness during the role-play. Plan to provide feedback at the conclusion of the role-play.

c. The first role-play is a conversation between two strangers. After exchanging greetings, you will hold a two-minute conversation about your choice of topics: sports, movies, careers, campus or world events, for example. Throughout the conversation, role players want to enact their ideal communicator style profile. Don't tell the observers what that style is, just try to come across in the preferred manner. Begin the conversation.

d. After a couple of minutes, cut the conversation off and let the observers provide feedback to each role player. Compare style observations with what the role player was trying to do. Suggest ways to improve the enactment of each aspect of the style profile.

e. Switch roles and repeat steps b, c, and d.

f. If you have time, continue the exercise by working on the *difficult* situation and style profile that each person has written down. Conclude the exercise by talking about how you can improve your range of styles in actual situations.

2. Bring to class examples of media messages that encourage or reinforce the narcissistic self and the search for "the real you." Discuss these examples and talk about how they influence interpersonal relationships. Do these messages really encourage us to place less value on conversations and relationships that do not involve talking about ourselves?

3. As a class, make a list of five important social episodes that most people need to participate in regularly to be accepted on campus, at work, or in the community. Divide the class into five groups. Assign an episode to each group. Each group should discuss, prepare, and present a series of very short skits to demonstrate how one could be incompetent or minimally, satisfactorily, or optimally competent (reread pages 115–118). Focus on the communication behaviors, rules, and roles that are appropriate or inappropriate as well as the possible *personal goals* one might want to achieve. Enact each skit in front of the class, concluding with a brief explanation of what makes the person minimally or optimally competent in that situation.

CHAPTER SIX

Dance, which involves a complex synchronizing of body movements, is a form of both art and communication. (Pieter Brueghel the elder, *The Wedding Dance*, c. 1566)

CODING INTERPERSONAL MESSAGES: NONVERBAL COMMUNICATION

I F YOU'VE EVER taken care of a small child, you're probably familiar with the following scene. While engrossed in a book or television program, you notice little Johnny slink into the room, hugging the wall, hands behind his back. He looks full-face in your direction, but only occasionally lifts his lowered eyelids. At the moment you give him your full attention, he blurts out, lower lip not quite quivering, "I didn't do anything!"

There is, of course, little doubt in your mind that something quite wrong has been done and that someone feels very guilty about it. The verbal denial only underscores your belief in the contradicting nonverbal messages being sent.

As we saw in the model presented in Chapter 1, accurate perceptions and knowledge of the self and social system are not enough for effective communication to take place. We must be able to integrate perceptions and knowledge into appropriate verbal and nonverbal codes. In Chapter 7 we will look at the way we code messages verbally. This chapter will discuss the variety of nonverbal channels through which coded messages can be sent and received.

Nonverbal messages are powerful, especially when they contradict verbal ones. But we often overlook the importance of more subtle nonverbal messages. Studies of small-group communication demonstrate that those who talk more often become leaders while those who actively listen and provide nonverbal feedback seldom get any credit for their contribution. Our inattention to nonverbals may have prompted British novelist John Fowles to remark, "The British mean far more than they say; Americans say far more than they mean."[1] We do, however, give some credit to those who work well in the nonverbal mode. People especially competent at reading others' nonverbal messages are labeled "intuitive," while those who send more nonverbals are called "expressive."

To make it in our culture, a person must first be articulate, then add in elements of intuition and expressiveness. (Clint Eastwood may be the exception here. He usually doesn't have to *say* anything to be effective.) We hope that by focusing on nonverbal codes first, you will become more aware of their function in everyday communication. You already know a lot about diagramming sentences and increasing your vocabulary, but how many classes have you had on nonverbal communication?

We want to discuss nonverbal communication first for two other reasons. One has a simple historical basis: Nonverbal communication is an *older* form of communication. Animals share, and we share with them, a number of nonverbal signals that communicate within and across species. The marking of territories, threat displays when territorial bounds are violated, and relaxed, open-mouth expressions that signal approachability are examples of widely shared gestures rooted in a common biology, modified only by environment and culture. These rudimentary forms of communication preceded the evolution of the human brain's neocortex, which made language possible. The tendency to believe nonverbal messages when they contradict verbal ones (as in the opening example) may well be traced to the fact that nonverbal communication has a much longer evolutionary history. Language is, in the scheme of things, the new kid on the block. Nonverbal communication, having been around, is like an old trusted friend.

Second, we rely on nonverbal communication before initiating most verbal interactions. Breaking into a conversation often involves a complex dance of eye contact, head movement, preliminary gesturing, and vocalized throat-clearing if we do not want to be seen as rude. Greeting friends while walking across campus is preceded by a set of acknowledged approachability cues: eye contact, a flash of the eyebrows, perhaps even an abbreviated waving gesture. These nonverbal cues are not accidental; they are crucial regulators of conversation.

For these reasons, we think a good starting point for improving our ability to encode and decode messages is to attend to our own and others' nonverbal behaviors. They provide us with a context for interpreting many of the positive and negative connotations of messages. To begin, we will define nonverbal communication, describe what makes the nonverbal such a powerful message system, examine in detail each of the nonverbal codes and how they function in interpersonal situations, and then summarize how we balance these cues to establish and maintain interpersonal relationships. We will end the chapter with some suggestions for improved use of nonverbal codes.

WHAT IS NONVERBAL COMMUNICATION?

Suppose that as you are taking an exam, you notice that the person across the aisle from you keeps twitching his head and shoulder, then glances quickly in your direction. Your eyes don't meet and nothing is said, but the other person has a very puzzled look on his face. Would you say that nonverbal communication has taken place?

Many scholars would say yes, others would say no. For the first group of scholars, all behavior has communicative potential and therefore should count as an instance of communication. In the example above, nonverbal behavior has occurred and has been noticed by another person, so some information has been exchanged. Other scholars argue that we have to place some limits on what we call communication. If we don't establish limits, the term *communication* becomes too vague and loses its meaning. To counter this tendency, two conditions are attached to nonverbal behaviors before they are considered acts of communication: There must be some degree of intentionality and some level of consciousness on the part of *either* the sender or the receiver.[2]

One way to narrow the definition would be to stipulate that nonverbal behavior must be (a) perceived consciously by either the sender or the receiver; (b) intended as a message by the speaker; or (c) interpreted by the receiver as intended. Thus if the twitching behavior of the exam taker was an attempt to signal you for help, we might call it a poor attempt at communication, but an act of communication nonetheless. How would you *know* it was

Children have a more difficult time disguising their feelings than adults do. This young boy's posture and facial expression suggest that he is guilty as accused.

intentional? You might not know for sure, in which case you'd have to interpret it as an intentional attempt to get your attention and induce a state of guilt, so that you'll help him cheat. If the behavior was simply a sign of nervousness and didn't lead you to attribute it as having any message value, there is no reason to count it as an act of communication.

In a similar vein, we can limit the realm of nonverbal communication to those behaviors that are consciously attended to by sender, receiver, or some third party. Frequently, we may not be aware of the nonverbal messages we send to others. As long as no one else is aware of such messages, there is no point considering them as communication. For instance, most people are not very aware of how their voice sounds to others. A person whose

voice has a nasal quality may sound to some people like he or she is whining, while others don't consciously perceive the nasality at all. Those who notice the nasal quality may infer some attitude or personality trait. In this case, a message has been received, or "leaked," even though it was not intended or interpreted as intentional.

The Power of Nonverbal Codes

Once we have identified a nonverbal message, our next concern might be deciding how much credence to give that message. In some situations, nonverbal messages speak more powerfully than verbal ones. The opposite is true in dozens of other cases. It is really a matter of matching the capacity of a verbal or nonverbal code to the social situation. Below we list five aspects of nonverbal communication that make it so powerful.

1. *Nonverbal codes are older, more trusted forms of communication.* As we have noted, nonverbal codes have been in use longer than verbal ones. And since we live the first 12 to 18 months of life relying totally on nonverbal communication, it is little wonder that when in doubt, we tend to give credence to the nonverbal message. Of course, this trust can backfire. Suppose you want to buy an insurance policy. The salesman's nonverbal communication may seem to indicate a genuine concern for your welfare, and he may discourage you from reading the fine print of the policy because it's all "mumbo-jumbo." If you relied on the salesman's nonverbal expression of concern, you might well be relying on the wrong code.

2. *Nonverbal codes are more emotionally powerful.* Nonverbal behaviors tell people about our emotional state. It takes a good deal of practice to hide our true feelings from others—and even then, close friends will often see through our attempts. When we want to convey how we feel about someone, language often fails us. Desmond Morris refers to the myriad gestures that express emotional bonding (interlocked arms, shoulder embraces, holding hands) as "tie signs" that physically connect people in ways words cannot.[3]

3. *Nonverbal codes express more universal meaning.* Members of different linguistic groups must spend a lot of time and effort to learn each other's verbal codes, but they can communicate instantly by smiling or wrinkling their faces in disgust. The work of Paul Ekman and Wallace Friesen has shown a number of emotions to be expressed in the same way by members of different cultural groups.[4] Happiness, anger, disgust, fear, surprise, and sadness are all conveyed by using the same facial muscles in much the same way. There are differences, but primarily in the rules that govern *when* it is appropriate to show the emotion in public or *how much* emotion should be displayed. Facial expressions are probably the most universal of the codes because of their prominence in face-to-face interaction. Other body movements and gestures have multiple and sometimes contradictory meanings within and across cultures, as we shall see later in this chapter.

4. *Nonverbal codes are continuous and natural.* Because gestures and body movements flow into one another without obvious beginnings and endings, they seem to be a more natural part of our existence than words. Words are also strung together, but unless you have a bad case of mumbling, your words don't slur into one another as nonverbals often do. Nonverbals are immediate—that is, they are physical extensions of our bodies, and their form resembles their message more than words' do. A gesture signaling someone to "come here" imitates the movement of a body from a far place to a closer proximity. Words, perhaps because they can be written and stored away from the body, often seem more distant and more unnatural.

5. *Nonverbal codes occur in clusters.* Verbal communication is limited to a single channel at a time, but nonverbal communication operates in much the same way as recording studios use multitrack taping systems. Several channels are operating simultaneously and usually in concert. When different nonverbal codes send the same message, the impact is intensified. While you can repeat or rephrase verbal messages to achieve redundancy, it will take more time and still not mirror the intensity of the combined forces of touch and tone, facial expressions, body positioning and movement, and so on.

Given the unique capacity and power of nonverbal codes, we will now examine what they accomplish in everyday interactions.

THE FUNCTIONS OF NONVERBAL CODES: THREE WAYS TO USE THEM

We use nonverbal codes to achieve some very specific purposes. While researchers have proposed several ways to classify these functions, we have grouped them into three general types. Nonverbal codes may be used to express meaning in and of themselves, they may modify verbal messages, and they are used to regulate the flow of interaction.

Expressing Meaning

Nonverbal messages are often used to convey how we feel about other people and how we see our relationship to them. Albert Mehrabian suggests that there are three fundamental dimensions of feeling expressed through nonverbal communication: liking, status, and responsiveness.[5] It is easy to recognize that nonverbals express **liking** or disliking, as when people smile or turn up their noses at one another. **Status** is conveyed by nonverbal cues indicating how important or influential we think we are in relation to others. Staring at a subordinate may communicate snobbishness or dominance. **Responsiveness** indicates how aware we are of the other person and the level of involvement we feel with him or her. Bursting into tears or laughing heartily would indicate high responsiveness; a blank stare or an ever-so-slight chuckle would be low. In Chapter 8 we'll elaborate on the ways we send each other these relational messages.

Modifying Verbal Messages

While some nonverbal messages stand on their own, others work in conjunction with verbal messages. Nonverbals can complement, accent, repeat, substitute for, or contradict verbal

In ancient Egypt, statues such as this were commissioned for placement in the tombs of prominent officeholders. This statue is unique because of the way the woman embraces her husband, suggesting that she was the legitimate owner of the tomb. (*Memy-Sabu and his wife*, Gizeh, c. 2420 B.C.)

BOX 6.1

Drawing on the Right Side of the Brain: Processing Nonverbal Communication

Improving your ability to process nonverbal cues may have a curious relationship to the uncultivated habit of doodling. According to some experts, the ability to draw depends on a particular pattern of brain activity. It is this same pattern that may also influence how we detect nonverbal cues.

Most of us have the sense that we are one body, one person. But there is increasing evidence that suggests there are at least two of us, in a sense. The human brain is divided into two hemispheres, and each half seems to experience a reality of its own. The left hemisphere specializes in the processing of language. It operates in a logical and rational manner, breaking information into discrete units and reassembling them sequentially, much like a computer does. The right half processes information in a more rapid, holistic, and intuitive fashion. It specializes in processing visual, auditory, and spatial forms and patterns; in short, the many modes of nonverbal communication.

Thus in any given situation, the two halves of the brain are perceiving different aspects of the world. For normal human beings, the two hemispheres communicate via the corpus callosum, a major network of nerve fibers that connects the two brains. In spite of this ability to integrate information from both hemispheres, there are times when one side is dominant. The other half takes a back seat and is more or less turned off. Research indicates that for most of us, most of the time, the left, or more verbal, hemisphere is the dominant one. At other times, the two halves are in conflict, each interfering with the other's ability to process what it does best.

Peter Andersen and his colleagues define nonverbal communication as a process of sending and receiving messages that are governed primarily by the right side of the brain. If this is true, our ability to perceive nonverbal messages would be vastly improved if we could find some way to engage the right brain more frequently. Help in this regard comes from a rather fascinating source.

In her book *Drawing on the Right Side of the Brain*, Betty Edwards argues that we have been taught to use the left brain to a much greater extent than the right brain. In the process, we lose the natural ability to paint, sketch, or draw because we have lost touch with the way the right

---

messages. **Complementing** is the nonverbal elaboration of the verbal message. When friends say they are sick, their flushed faces, unsteady gait, and pained looks help us determine the extent of their illness. **Accenting** refers to nonverbals that underline or focus attention on a specific word or phrase. Pounding the table with your fist at the same time you say "I've had it!" makes that particular phrase stand out. Sometimes we give a verbal message and then try **repeating** it nonverbally to help the receiver process the total message. For instance, when someone asks a favor, we may say "Yes" and then nod our head to make sure the person knows our response was genuine. At other times, we avoid the verbal response altogether, and the nonverbal serves a **substituting** function. A cold stare may say "No!" better than any verbalized refusal could. Some situations require substitution. Deep-sea divers

brain "sees" things. The left brain interferes too much, trying to get us to "name" what we're drawing rather than attending to simple lines and shapes. For instance, when most people draw a face, they verbalize the parts as they draw them: nose, eyes, lips, hair. Edwards has taught would-be artists to improve their drawing skills by first becoming ab-sorbed in a "right-brain mode of experiencing." One of the exercises she suggests involves drawing a sketch by looking at a copy of it turned upside down (see illustration). Drawing this way forces you to focus on patterns of lines and shapes, keeping the left brain at bay and putting the right brain in control. If you try this, you will find that you soon become so absorbed in drawing that you forget the passage of time. In this relaxed but alert state of mind, you'll be more in tune with the nonverbal mode.

While there is as yet no hard scientific evidence that exercises such as this will improve your ability to decode nonverbal cues, the prospect is an interesting one. Now is a good time to consider developing the right hemisphere and some of the skills we rarely use.

ADDITIONAL READINGS

Andersen, Peter, John Garrison, and Janis Andersen. "Implications of a Neuro-physiological Approach for the Study of Nonverbal Communication." *Human Communication Research* 6 (1979): 74–89.

Edwards, Betty. *Drawing on the Right Side of the Brain.* Los Angeles: J. P. Tarcher, 1979.

cannot speak verbally, so they rely on hand gestures and other body movements to indicate what they want one another to do.

You may frequently find nonverbal messages **contradicting** verbal ones. When they do, you have a choice to make. One of your professors may say she has plenty of time to go over a quiz with you, but if she remains standing, doesn't offer you a seat, and keeps fidgeting with her watch, you may question the sincerity of the verbal remark. As noted before, we generally believe the nonverbal message when a contradiction occurs. However, this is not always the case. Young children, perhaps because of their fascination with newly acquired language skills, often believe verbal statements, especially in cases of sarcasm.[6]

Other studies demonstrate that some people consistently rely on the verbal channel, others on the nonverbal channel when presented with contradictory cues.[7] One explanation for these channel preferences is that they are learned habits, another that they are related to left–right brain dominance (see Box 6.1).

Regulating the Flow of Interaction

Finally, nonverbal codes function to regulate the flow of talk. When two people converse, nonverbals are primarily responsible for the smoothness of taking turns, avoiding long pauses, changing topics, even signaling when it is appropriate to end the conversation. In many professional contexts, the function of nonverbal communication is simply the administration of a *service* or *task*.[8] Thus, the nonverbal act of holding a patient's arm while the doctor administers an injection functions to make the task easier. A similar behavior in some other setting may function quite differently.

So far we have talked about nonverbal communication in general. We have defined nonverbal communication, seen what makes it such a powerful system, and we have identified three ways we use nonverbal cues. Now we turn our attention to each separate channel of nonverbal communication. We call each of these channels a nonverbal "code."

THE STRUCTURE OF NONVERBAL CODES: SEVEN CHANNELS FOR MESSAGE MAKING

Nonverbal codes are structured in many ways. While a single message is almost always transmitted via more than one channel, we will discuss each code as if it stood alone. Seven codes will be analyzed: proxemics, physical appearance, gaze, facial expression, kinesics, vocalics, and tactile communication. Some scholars also include chronemics and olfaction as codes. *Chronemics* refers to the study of and interpretation of time as message. Time is related to status in our culture. A doctor's time is considered more valuable than the patient's time, for instance. Rather than discuss chronemics as a separate code, we have chosen to emphasize the importance of timing as it relates to the other codes discussed. *Olfaction* has to do with the messages we attach to smells emitted by the body. Since humans rely on this code much less than other animals, and since there is very little research on how humans do communicate in this mode, we won't include it as a major nonverbal code.

As you read about each of the codes, keep in mind the functions that have been mentioned. Ask yourself how you could use each code to express a particular meaning, to modify a verbal message, or to regulate a conversation. The first code we will examine has to do with the way people use space.

Proxemics

Approaching other people is a more delicate proposition than most of us realize. Take the mundane matter of walking across campus or strolling through a busy shopping mall. As soon as visual contact is made or we sense that another body is nearby, we begin manipulating our own body movements and anticipating the movements of the other in order to avoid getting too close or bumping into one another. Ashley Montagu and Floyd Matson have pointed out that "there are virtually as many rules, customs, and conventions governing the conduct of 'sidewalkers' as there are for car drivers, the difference being that the sidewalk rules are unwritten and tacit and . . . completely unnoticed."[9] The next time you stop to talk to someone, notice how each of you shifts your body back and forth to establish a comfortable speaking distance. Watch when two people move from an open lobby area to a cramped, crowded enclosure such as a hallway, elevator,

Proxemics
Environmental preference
Territoriality
Personal space

Touch
Types of touch
Contexts

Eye Gaze
Eye contact
Expressiveness
Regulation
Looking
Seeing

**Facial
Expression**
Universal expressions
Facial blends
Cultural display rules
Leakage cues

Vocalics
Vocal qualities
Vocal characterizers
Vocal segregates

Kinesics
Emblems
Illustrators
Affect displays
Regulators
Adaptors

**Physical
Appearance**
Body types
Clothing
Artifacts

FIGURE 6.1
Seven nonverbal codes.

or cafeteria line. What actions result from this change in distance? People may actually stop talking or change to a more impersonal topic of conversation. Each of these situations is an example of how people use or adjust to changes in the spatial environment. Investigators call

the study of messages sent in this mode **proxemics**.

How many ways do we use space to communicate? Architects design interior and exterior spaces to make personal, philosophical, or cultural statements. People grow hedges around the edges of their property to discourage trespassers. And perhaps the most powerful proxemic statements are made during conversation itself, by the simple measurement of how much distance we keep between ourselves and those we talk to.

Environmental Preferences

While each of us reacts to the environment in some unique ways, we are also programmed genetically and culturally to react in more similar ways. When we feel comfortable in a physical setting, we are more likely to communicate effectively. Or perhaps we should say, when we feel uncomfortable we communicate less effectively and may even attribute these negative feelings to the people in that environment. In a classic study, Abraham Maslow and N. L. Mintz asked people in three different environments to rate a series of photographs of faces (actually negative prints). One room was set up to be "beautiful," another "average" and the third "ugly." People consistently rated the photographs higher in energy and well-being in the beautiful room and lower in the ugly room.[10] This study supports the notion that the environment has a spillover effect on social interaction.

Other factors that fill up environmental spaces can have a dramatic effect on our social behavior. Physical features of an environment (such as lighting, color, noise, and extremes in temperature) affect our preference for that environment.[11] In addition, more subjective perceptions (such as familiarity, novelty, and mystery) have been shown to affect whether we will approach or avoid the environment.[12]

According to Albert Mehrabian and James Russell, the combination of these environmental factors and our own predisposed mental sets produce emotional reactions along three dimensions: arousal–nonarousal, dominance–submissiveness, and pleasure–displeasure.[13]

For instance, a visit to the Grand Canyon would probably give most people a moderate level of arousal, a submissive feeling, and a strong sense of pleasure, which combine to produce a sense of awe. For some people, social conversation is very difficult in a bar or nightclub because they are unable to screen out all the background noise and flashing strobe lights. The level of arousal is so high for them that concentrating on talk is too difficult. Most of us feel more dominant in those settings that are very familiar to us. We are more likely to tell someone what to do when they are on our turf, or territory, than when we are on theirs.

Territoriality

The concept of territoriality refers to the legal or assumed ownership of space. Lawrence Rosenfeld and Jean Civikly define territoriality as "the assumption of proprietary rights toward some geographical area, with the realization, at least for humans, that there is no basis for those rights."[14] Animals mark their territory by building nests, leaving excrement, and fending off intruders. Humans use a great variety of territorial markers, ranging from where they stop mowing the grass to the placement of personal photographs on otherwise institutional-looking desks.

Stanford Lyman and Marvin Scott have distinguished four types of territoriality in human interaction.[15] *Public territory* is owned by no one, accessible to anyone. City streets, park benches, and plazas exemplify this kind of territory. Each of these may, from time to time, become *interactional territories*, as when a softball team takes over a park to use as a practice field. Other spaces are designed for interaction. These include courtrooms and tennis courts. *Home territories* allow for an even greater degree of privacy. Strangers will rarely intrude on a space they consider to be someone else's home. This includes more than physical violations. A neighbor who constantly peers through your windows is considered rude and will usually not persist if you stare back. *Body territory*, the final classification used by Lyman and Scott, is more frequently referred to as personal space by other researchers.

Personal Space

This term has been used to describe an imaginary bubble extending out from our bodies, an area considered to be almost as private as the body itself. Movement into personal space is reacted to strongly—only small children and intimate family and friends are allowed to enter this space without apology. Anthropologist Edward T. Hall has done the most to draw our attention to personal space and other forms of conversational distance.[16] In observations of middle-class Americans, Hall has distinguished four interaction zones:

1. *Intimate distance* (0–18 inches). Reserved for lovemaking and very private conversations.

2. *Personal distance* (18 inches–4 feet). The range at which one is comfortable with friends and acquaintances.

3. *Social distance* (4–12 feet). Used for business transactions and role relations.

4. *Public distance* (12–25 feet). Appropriate for public ceremonies, speechmaking, classroom lectures, and so on.

The actual distance at which you are comfortable talking to others may vary according to your personality and age, sex, status, or cultural differences in relation to those you interact with. For example, Edward Hall describes an experience with an artist in northern Germany. Talking to a young woman on the porch of her apartment house, Hall could see an artist in conversation with someone inside his first floor studio. Assuming that they had nothing to do with one another, Hall ignored what was going on inside. A few minutes later the artist came outside and began yelling at Hall for intruding without even a sign of greeting.[17] The difference was simply a matter of interpreting space. For Americans, there was enough space between the groupings to allow them their separate activities. For the German, his space had already been invaded.

Some people simply need more space than others. Unless you are aware of this, you may find yourself trying to move closer to others (to make yourself more comfortable) while they compensate by moving away (to reestablish their comfort zone). Hall points out one problem that may arise: "Since none of us is taught to look at space as isolated from other associations, feelings cued by the handling of space are often attributed to something else."[18] The most likely result is that you will form negative impressions of these people.

Research also demonstrates that those similar in age stand closer to one another than age-discrepant pairs, and that male pairs space themselves farther apart than opposite-sex pairs, who usually stand farther away than female pairs.[19] Occasionally, the norms for personal space are violated without incident because one of the parties is viewed as a nonperson, as a mere object—for example, waiters, servants, and people in crowded elevators or stadiums.

Stop and think about the communicative functions that proxemics serve. We may use spatial distance or closeness to communicate feelings of liking, or to achieve some sense of privacy, or even to threaten or remind the other person of our status. Can you identify ways we use proxemics to regulate conversation or to modify the nature of our verbal statements? For instance, we may stand closer to someone we find physically attractive. Physical appearance is another code that often operates in conjunction with proxemics.

Physical Appearance

Appearance alone can be a powerful message. Each culture defines its own prototypes of physical beauty as well as stereotypes about what physically beautiful or unattractive people are like. We will look first at the message potential of the human body itself, then at the artifacts we adorn our bodies with.

Characteristics of the Body

Facial features and beauty, color, length, and style of hair, skin color, the general shape of the body, and posture are among the physical features that people pay close attention to when they first make visual contact. The role of these features in communication depends on our awareness of them and the belief that the sender intended some message by his or her appearance. When a husband puts on a little weight, and others notice this fact, communication may or may not be occurring. If you are his wife and you believe that body weight can be controlled, you may interpret his appearance as saying, "I don't care what I look like to you anymore. It's more important that I enjoy myself than look good for you."

The communication value of most natural body features is limited. Stereotypes aside, there is no message value in the natural color of one's hair or skin. Thus we should pay attention to what people do to enhance, display, alter, or conceal their bodies. These are the real messages directed at us, because there is some element of control on the sender's part.

Even so, we rely on these constant features a great deal in deciding whom to communicate with. Research demonstrates that most cultures have strong prototypes about physical beauty.[20] Many people believe that our own culture's

prototypes are magnified by the media, influencing the evaluation of and desire to be with other people. One study, conducted by Ellen Berscheid and Elaine Walster, involved college freshmen who signed up for a computer date to a dance. Pairs were actually matched at random rather than by interest or compatibility. When asked to indicate satisfaction with their date and desire to date again, physical attractiveness was the only predictor of either one.[21] Another study showed how physical attraction serves as a central trait in many of our implicit personality theories. A physically attractive person was consistently rated as more sociable, outgoing, poised, interesting, and sexually warm and responsive than an unattractive one.[22]

We tend to believe that physical beauty is intrinsic and interpreted the same way the world over, but Desmond Morris reminds us how temporary our prototypes are in his comparison of vital statistics in today's beauty contests with carved figurines of past epochs:

If we consider [the Venus of Willendorf] as Miss Old Stone Age of 20,000 B.C., then, had she lived, her vital statistics would have been 96-89-96. Moving forward to 2000 B.C., Miss Indus Valley would have measured 45-34-63, and in the late Bronze Age, Miss Cyprus of 1500 B.C. would have registered 43-42-44. Later still, Miss Amlash of 1000 B.C. would have offered the startling proportions of 38-44-78, but Miss Syria of 1000 B.C., only a short distance away, would have measured an almost modern 31-26-36.[23]

While prototypes also exist for the ideal male physique, our point is simply to remind you of how temporary any ideal image is, and to realize that physical beauty standards vary across time and across cultures. Not only do people's evaluations of physical characteristics vary, but their assessments of material adornments do too.

Clothing and Personal Artifacts

People go to great lengths to adorn their bodies with a variety of objects. Fashionable clothing and accessories, tight or loose-fitting garments, changing the color of hair, attaching earrings, and wearing your shoelaces untied are all forms of adornment.

Clothing has been recognized for a long time as a way to communicate social status, group identification, and personality.[24] The popularity of books and magazine articles about what clothing to wear to job interviews and business meetings indicates our concern with the status implications of clothing. In one study, various styles of men's clothing were ranked for social status and then placed on models who had been independently ranked for status according to facial and head features alone. Invariably, higher-ranked clothing increased, and lower-ranked clothing decreased, the perceived status of the models.[25] In many large companies, status distinctions are maintained by subtle factors such as suits made of more expensive fabric, while group membership is maintained by similarity in the basic type of apparel (professionals wear dark suits, staff wear simple dresses or shirtsleeves and slacks, maintenance personnel wear uniforms). People often identify with one another by wearing the same or similar clothes. The next time you visit an amusement park, watch groups of people and look for ways they identify with each other through clothing. The most obvious examples will be families where Mom, Dad, and all the kids are wearing T-shirts with the family's last name printed across the back. In what other subtle and not so subtle ways do people say they are together?

Finally, dress may convey messages about the self, whether intentional or not. A friend reported turning down a good job offer because she didn't think the people she would have to work with were very stimulating. Her first impression was that "there was beige every-where. Most of them wore two or three shades of beige, and their faces had a beige cast to them, and I would have to say their personalities were equally as beige." At other times, physical appearance may be so eye-catching that the person becomes the focus of our visual field.

Gaze

Our eyes aren't just instruments for receiving stimuli, they are themselves messengers. Even the simple act of appreciating physical beauty requires that we proceed with caution. Erving Goffman has recommended that we "discipline our eyes" until we have mastered the skill of knowing how to look without appearing to be looking.

One of the first contributors to the literature on visual communication was Adam Kendon, who proposed that gaze served three primary functions in communication: an expressive, a regulative, and a monitoring function.[26]

The Expressive Function of Gaze

Gaze plays an important role in the communication of emotions. Although identification of most emotions requires the decoding of complete facial cues, the eyes are especially expressive in conveying fear and surprise.[27] Likewise, gaze broadcasts interest in and liking of the other person, and researchers have found that people gaze more when they receive or want to receive approval, especially from someone who is higher in status.[28]

In addition, gazing can frequently create arousal in those being stared at. Imagine eating your lunch alone, enjoying your private thoughts, when you suddenly become aware that someone is watching you. You glance in the person's direction, expecting him to look away, but he does not. How do you react? According to P. C. Ellsworth and Miles Patterson, that depends on the attributions you make.

If you sense that the other person's motives are harmless, or you find him interesting in some way, you will probably reciprocate by smiling and looking in that direction again later. If you attributed the other person's behavior negatively, you are more likely to compensate by turning away, giving a nasty look, or leaving the other's presence.[29] We will have more to say about Patterson's work at the end of this chapter because it applies to how we react to a wide range of nonverbal cues.

Using Gaze to Regulate and Monitor Interaction

Gaze, along with other nonverbals, serves to regulate and monitor the other's reactions during conversation. Gaze first signals that we're available for communication. Averting our eyes says just the opposite. When you're in a hurry and can't stop to talk, you may pretend not to see the other. Or you may simply opt for the "eyebrow flash"—a common sign of recognition that involves a look, a smile, a raising of the eyebrows, and a nod.[30] It may be used to acknowledge the other without committing yourself to converse.

Once conversation has begun, eye behavior helps keep turns and transitions flowing smoothly. The general pattern for Americans is to look more when they listen than when they speak, and to very rarely look at each other for more than a split second. Why do we follow this pattern? When we listen, gaze shows interest in what the other is saying and allows us to receive complementary or contradictory nonverbal cues. When we begin a speaking turn, we are busy concentrating on what we want to say, and thus do not look at the other as frequently or as long.

Women, it seems, gaze more than men and are more uncomfortable when visual contact is cut off.[31] Some speculate that this is a function of traditional socialization, which teaches women to be more concerned with social affiliation. A greater difference has been noted in the gazing patterns of blacks and whites. Clara Mayo and Marianne LaFrance have shown that whites gaze too much for blacks and that blacks look more when talking and less when listening, just the opposite of whites.

The White may feel he is not being listened to while the Black may feel he is being unduly scrutinized. Further, exchanges of the listener–speaker roles become disjunctive, leading to generalized discomfort in the encounter.[32]

Blacks use more "backchanneling" gestures; that is, they give more verbal and nonverbal feedback to a speaker while he or she is still talking. Because of this, it makes sense that a black speaker would look more while talking: he or she is simply trying to monitor the feedback others are giving. The fact that we use our eyes to monitor feedback has raised the question of where our vision is usually focused during interaction.

Looking versus Seeing

What do you focus your vision on when you talk to other people? Do you look into their eyes, in the direction of their eyes, or at the whole upper body? D. R. Rutter, in a comprehensive review of visual communication, makes a distinction between looking and seeing.[33] **Looking** refers to gazing in the direction of the other's eyes, whereas **seeing** is defined as visual contact with the whole person. Rutter argues that seeing is more important than looking when regulating and monitoring feedback. It was once thought that people used gaze to signal turn taking. Now it appears that seeing the whole person is necessary for picking up *other* turn-taking cues such as nods and gestures. This relegates gaze to a lesser role in regulating interaction. Eye contact (mutual looking) plays even less of a role. Some research shows that eye contact occurs no more frequently than chance in most encounters.[34] We

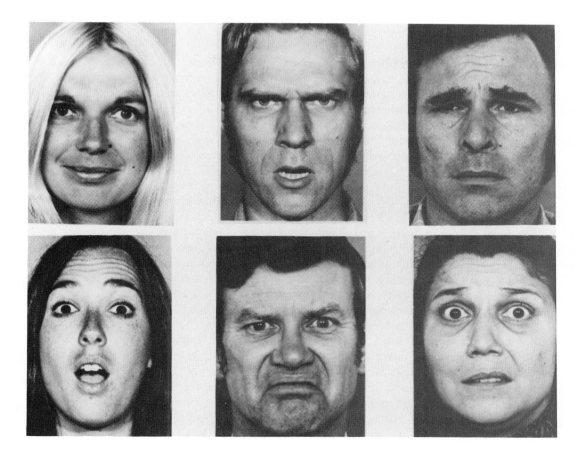

FIGURE 6.2

The six universal facial expressions. Can you identify what emotion is being expressed in each of the photographs above? Researchers Paul Ekman and Wallace Friesen have studied facial expressions across cultures and have found these six (surprise, anger, happiness, fear, disgust, and sadness) to be universal. Paul Ekman and Wallace F. Friesen, *Pictures of Facial Affect* (Palo Alto, Calif.: Consulting Psychologists Press, 1976).

encourage you to test these findings yourself. Keep in mind the distinctions between eye contact (mutual looking), gaze (looking), and seeing (gazing at the whole person). Which occur more often in your own conversations and what functions do they appear to serve?

Facial Expression

One reason for getting a full view of the other person rather than gazing in the direction of the eyes is to pick up entire facial expressions, which may well be the single most important channel of nonverbal communication. People read a lot in our facial expressions. They infer some personality traits and attitudes, judge reactions to their own messages, regard facial expressions as verbal replacements, and, primarily, use them to determine our emotional state. Since most of the research has focused on emotions, so will our discussion. We will examine how six universal expressions are created and controlled, and why we sometimes misread facial expressions.

Universal Expressions

The study of facial expression owes a great deal to two researchers, Paul Ekman and Wallace Friesen. The comprehensiveness and quality of their work gives us confidence in their findings. They have demonstrated the universality of expression in conveying six basic human emotions.[35] Regardless of culture, the emotional states of happiness, sadness, surprise, fear, anger, and disgust are communicated with remarkable similarity (see Figure 6.2).

Ekman and Friesen discovered three separate sets of facial muscles that are manipulated to form these expressions: (1) the brow and forehead, (2) the eyes, eyelids, and root of the nose, and (3) the cheeks, mouth, most of the nose, and the chin. All of these facial regions are combined in a particular way to produce a representation of a pure emotional state. For instance, surprise is announced by (1) raised eyebrows, (2) eyes wide open, and (3) the dropping of the jaw and parting of the lips. Look at the other five emotions in Figure 6.2 and identify how they are expressed in each of the three facial regions. You may wish to consult Ekman and Friesen's book *Unmasking the Face* for further practice photos.

A key factor is that facial expressions are often short-lived. We rarely hold a look of surprise for long. If you can't believe the astronomical amount of your phone bill, surprise may quickly give way to disgust or anger.

The person with you may see traces of both emotions on your face. The result is called a **facial blend**. Since social interaction usually consists of rapid-fire exchanges, we are constantly changing expressions. What others see are usually blended expressions rather than pure emotional states.

But, you may be saying to yourself, people's facial expressions aren't always genuine. It is true that although emotional expressions are universal, *when* they are displayed is not. **Cultural display rules** often control this. We know that it is quite improper to laugh at someone who falls down, no matter how funny it strikes us. We are supposed to act surprised when an unannounced party is given in our honor, even though someone spilled the beans earlier. Business practice requires that salespeople show enthusiasm for vacuum cleaners, vegetable dicers, and other products that do not intrinsically excite them. Most people have personal display rules, ingrained early in life, such as "never show your anger in public."

Women, at least in American culture, are generally more nonverbally expressive than men. This is also true with respect to facial expression. Most of the studies to date show adult women to have significantly more facial reactions and general facial activity than men.[36] Many people, regardless of sex, display a characteristic style of facial expression (see Figure 6.3). Withholders, for instance, may inhibit facial muscle so much that others marvel at how they can talk without moving their mouths.

But controlling the face is not quite so easy as we might think. Professional actors might be regarded as specialists in controlling their faces, but the rest of us don't fare so well. We give ourselves away to the perceptive observer by producing momentary **leakage cues**, unintended signs of our real feelings, which are largely but not completely masked in normal facial management. When trying to maintain

Withholder

This person's facial expression doesn't show how he feels. He isn't trying to deliberately deceive; he just shows very little expressiveness.

Revealer

Revealers tell all with their faces. They are very expressive and often say that they just can't help showing how they feel. You always know when a Revealer does or doesn't like the birthday present you gave her.

Unwitting Expressor

This person shows emotion without realizing it. He says things like, "How did you know I was angry?"

Blanked Expressor

Blanked expressors think they are showing an emotion when in fact they show little if any expression at all. They just have a kind of neutral look on their face at all times. They differ from a Withholder in that the Withholder usually knows that she is not expressive.

Frozen-affect Expressor

The frozen-affect person constantly shows one emotion (such as happiness) when she is not experiencing that emotion at all.

Substitute Expressor

These people feel one emotion and think they are expressing it, but most onlookers would say some other emotion is being expressed. The person who feels angry but looks sad would be an example.

Ever-ready Expressor

This person almost instinctively shows the same emotion as his first response to any new event. Such a person may express surprise to good news, bad news, or the announcement that he has just been fired.

Flooded-affect Expressor

This person frequently displays more than one emotion. One of the emotions is characteristic of the person, similar to the Frozen-Affect Expressor. When another emotion is felt, it is mixed with the old characteristic expression. A person may look fearful, for instance, and thus show both fear and anger when he is angry.

FIGURE 6.3

Do you have a characteristic style of facial expression? Paul Ekman and Wallace Friesen have identified eight different styles of facial expression in their research. Which one best fits you? Adapted from Ekman and Friesen, *Unmasking the Face* (Englewood Cliffs, N.J.: Prentice-Hall, 1975), pp. 155–57. Illustration from *Men* (Dover Books), p. 3

our composure in the face of the announcement that a coveted award went to another contestant, we let disappointment leak out when we momentarily turn down the corners of the lips, quickly replacing it with "a stiff upper lip." Box 6.2 (pp. 142–43) describes some of the latest research on detecting leakage cues related to deception or lying.

Misreading Facial Expressions

Even when people spontaneously express an emotional state, we may not perceive it. Norms regarding eye behavior are partly responsible. We look at the other person's face only about 50 percent of the time during conversation. Ekman and Friesen point out that this is due to more than just being polite and not staring at the other. Often we don't want to be burdened with the knowledge of how the other feels. This may reach comic proportions, as when a parent exasperated with a pouting child says, "I'm *not* looking at you!"

Other reasons for misreading the face include attending to competing verbal and nonverbal channels, not paying close attention to the context of interaction, and not knowing the target person's usual repertoire of facial expressions. When we are concentrating on what the person is saying or distracted by nervous gestures, we are likely to miss the momentary expressions that might reveal how the person really feels. Likewise, failure to perceive the context accurately may cause problems. When a friend or acquaintance is also your interviewer for a job, she may try to neutralize her expressions as much as possible so as not to show favoritism. If you think of her as a friend rather than an interviewer, you may read the expressionless face as genuine and think she doesn't want you to get the job. Finally, Ekman and Friesen suggest that you can improve the accuracy of your judgments by learning the idiosyncratic ways the other person uses facial expressions. This means making a concerted effort to record what the person does with his face in various situations, when you know for a fact that his reaction is or is not genuine. Facial expressions are, however, only one way we manipulate our bodies. We also communicate by managing other body movements known as kinesics.

Kinesics

The study of body movements such as gestures, posture, head, trunk, and limb movements is known as kinesics. Facial expressions are also considered kinesics, but we have discussed them separately because of their overwhelming contribution in face-to-face interaction. At any rate, these kinesic behaviors help us determine when people consider themselves to be of equal or different status, when they are nervous, want to emphasize a point, and so on. Ekman and Friesen have proposed five categories of kinesic behavior: emblems, illustrators, affect displays, regulators, and adaptors.[37] We will look at each of these categories in turn.

Emblems

These are gestures that can easily be translated into verbal statements; there is widely shared agreement as to what they mean. When you doubt someone's sanity, you can indicate so by raising your hand to your temple and moving the forefinger in a circle. Almost every culture has developed different nonverbal symbols for saying yes and no. The way someone sticks out his tongue may indicate that he dislikes you (Rude Tongue), that he wants to be left alone (Concentration Tongue), or that he is flirting with you (Sexy Tongue).[38] In each case, the placement or movement of the tongue is the crucial factor.

Illustrators

Nonverbal behaviors that accompany speech, often emphasizing particular words or painting

Sculptors are often intrigued by the significance of kinesic and tactile communication. (Gustav Vigeland, *Father, Mother, and Child*)

a picture of what is being said, are called illustrators. Hand batons are common examples. When people talk, they may raise a forefinger, or wag it at the other person; hold their palms up, down, in front of them, or sideways; they may slam their fist through the air or clasp their hands together. None of these gestures has a meaning in and of itself, as an emblem would. Illustrators depend on, but also add an emphasis to, verbal messages.

Affect Displays

While emotions are communicated primarily via the face, some postural and gestural cues also work to convey how we feel. A child throws her entire body to the ground and kicks arms and legs wildly in reaction to parental refusal. Such a tantrum is usually intentional and has a twofold purpose: It expresses the emotion felt—rage—and is also an attempt to annoy or embarrass parents until they give in.

People may also synchronize their actions, consciously or not, to physically demonstrate an affective, or emotional, relationship among themselves. Children imitate the posture and gestures of their parents or heroes; people simultaneously lean forward to hear some choice gossip; and a group of "cool" teenagers mirror each other by leaning casually on one leg and resting their thumbs in their belt loops.

BOX 6.2

The Big Lie: Can You See It Coming?

An important and potentially damaging piece of information about your past has suddenly become a hot item on the gossip circuit. There are only two people, both close friends (or so you thought), to whom you had revealed this information. You question them and they both deny having broken your trust. One of them is definitely lying to you, but you don't know which one. You ask yourself: Are there any communication behaviors that reveal the truth about lies?

There is no *easy* answer to your question. But thanks to the careful research of Paul Ekman and his associates, as well as other social scientists, a more sophisticated picture of lying and lie detection is emerging. Ekman has pieced together a fascinating look at the issues, the research studies, and the ways to identify deception in his book *Telling Lies*.

So what cues should we attend to? How can we increase the likelihood of detecting a lie? Ekman is adamant that there is no one single sign of deceit itself, but he does believe that we should look for two things in a suspected liar's behavior: (1) problems with the *content* of the lie, and (2) clusters of "reliable" nonverbal expressions of *emotion* during the telling of a lie.

In terms of content, a person may lie to us by either not telling the truth (concealment) or by fabricating an untruth (falsifying). Concealment is obviously an easier way to lie—you don't have to make anything up. There is no content to be checked out. If you know that a friend's spouse is having an affair, it's much easier to remain silent than to deny knowledge of the affair or to offer plausible cover stories for the spouse's whereabouts. But fabricating a story can create problems for all but the most exceptional liars. First of all, the liar may not anticipate when it will be necessary to lie. Having to fabricate on the spot may result in pauses that are too frequent, too long, or too short; speech errors such as nonwords like "ah" and "uh-uh-uh," or an inadequate story line that doesn't hold up under further questioning. In addition, the liar must remember the false content if you question him at some other time.

Expressions of emotion play a vital role in lie detection as well. A lie is harder to pull off if it involves emotions that are felt at the moment. Anger, for instance, is difficult to conceal and even harder to fabricate. Researchers describe two kinds of nonverbal clues to look for: leakage and deception clues. *Leakage clues* occur when a liar accidentally reveals her true feelings while trying to conceal them. Typical leakage clues are "micro expressions" and "squelched expressions," which are flashed momentarily and then are concealed. A complete look of disgust may register for only a microsecond before giving way to a smile, or only part of an expression is revealed before it is squelched. *Deception clues*, on the other hand, don't tell you what the liar is actually feeling; they only suggest that the feeling being expressed is a false one.

In both cases, most people ignore the important clues because they focus on the nonverbals that are easiest to control. Liars can and do manipulate their words and many of their facial features. Amazingly, those are the behavioral aspects that most people attend to. The research suggests that body movements (posture, arm, leg, and feet movements) leak emotions, but are rarely controlled by liars because most people don't bother watching them. According to Ekman, the face is a good source of leakage and deception clues also, but you have to know what to look for and what to ignore. The "reli-

Communication can be used to deceive, as we see in this painting of a young man being told his fortune as an accomplice of the charlatan lifts the man's pocket purse. (Georges de La Tour, *The Fortune Teller*)

forehead is normally a highly reliable expression that is absent in false expressions.

Ekman is hopeful that further research will uncover more precise expressions for different emotional blends: enjoyable anger, self-righteous anger, and so on. Such research may further enhance our ability to distinguish false from felt emotional expressions. He is also quite sure that the research will make little difference unless people are willing to learn the subtle complexities involved in detecting deception.

ADDITIONAL READINGS

Ekman, Paul. *Telling Lies.* New York: W. W. Norton, 1985.

Knapp, Mark L., and Mark E. Comadena. "Telling It Like It Isn't: A Review of Theory and Research on Deceptive Communications." *Human Communication Research* 5 (1979): 270–85.

Morris, Desmond. "Nonverbal Leakage: How You Can Tell If Someone's Lying," *New York*, Oct. 17, 1977, 43–46.

able" facial muscles—those that are hardest for most people to control—are one of the keys to uncovering lies.

A couple of examples should illustrate some typical deception clues. When the emotion of happiness is truly felt, a number of facial muscles react involuntarily. Ekman has identified as many as 18 different smiles that people produce. The most reliable sign of a *felt* smile is the use of the zygomatic muscle, which produces raised cheeks, bagged skin below the eye, and crow's-feet wrinkles at the corners of the eye. A *false* smile does not usually involve the muscles around the eye. It almost always is limited to action in the lower part of the face. In addition, the timing of a smile is important. People tend to let a false smile disappear too quickly from their face. For fear or sadness, the muscle in the

Regulators

These are nonverbals that help control interaction flow. When you want to break into conversation, you may use preliminary gestures such as leaning forward or tilting your head forward while raising your hand to a position where it may be used as an illustrator. What kinesic cues would you use to tell the other person that it is his turn to talk, or to hurry up, or to indicate that even though you have to pause to catch your breath, you have one more point to make before yielding the floor?

Adaptors

This final category includes any body movement designed to manage anxious, emotionally charged, or novel situations. **Self-adaptors** are manipulations of your own body: pressing a hand against your mouth, chewing your nails, crossing your arms, or brushing your hand through your hair. Since touch is often reassuring, we may touch ourselves to calm down or just to feel better. Self-touch may also indicate a desire to withdraw from interaction, to be left alone.

Object-adaptors are material objects used in the tension-management process. Smoking cigarettes, tapping a pencil on your desk, caressing a stuffed animal, or chewing on a straw are examples. Their only communicative value seems to be that they tell onlookers we're nervous or uncomfortable.

In summary, many kinesic movements (with the exception of emblems) may operate as unconscious messages on the sender's part. Habitual illustrators, regulators, and adaptors may either help or hinder our communication efforts. Since receivers are usually more aware of these gestures, we may be sending messages we don't want to send. But most people resist seeing themselves on videotape—perhaps we really don't want to know about our unconscious messages. Communication is hard

enough without adding new pieces to the puzzle.

The nonverbal codes considered so far have been visual in nature. We now turn our attention to a code that is entirely auditory.

Vocalics

Words are spoken through the medium of the voice, which has characteristics of its own, apart from the content of what is said. These characteristics are called vocalics, or paralanguage. *What* is said is frequently less important than *how* it is said. What we convey in our voices can accent, alter, or flatly contradict verbal meaning. Sarcasm is often a product of vocal inflection. Our investigation of the vocal channel will begin by looking at the qualities of the human voice that have message potential, followed by an examination of the role these characteristics play in impression formation and emotional expression.

Vocal Characteristics

While researchers have classified vocalic cues in several ways, we simply want you to be aware of the many components that make up the vocal system.[39] **Vocal qualities** include such things as loudness, pitch, inflection, tempo, rhythm, intensity, articulation, and resonance. **Vocal characterizers** are more specific sounds that we may occasionally recognize as speech acts themselves. Laughing, crying, moaning, yelling, and whining are examples. **Vocal segregates** are sounds that get in the way of fluent speech, including "uhs" and "ums," stuttering, and uncomfortable silences. The combinations of these cues produce the unique voice patterns of each person. You probably know someone whose voice is especially high-pitched or raspy or nasal or monotone. How do these qualities affect your impressions of such people? People from different cultures or regions within the same culture usually differ from each other in characteristic ways called *dialects*. How do you react to those whose dialect differs from yours?

Messages in the Voice

The voice is often used to infer personality traits. When you talk to a stranger on the telephone, what image of the person do you form as you listen? David Addington's research on voice types and perceptions shows some of the more common attributions people make about the personality that goes with the voice. An example should suffice. A "breathy" male voice led listeners to infer that the speaker was younger and more artistic. The same characteristic in a female voice led to the stereotype of a more feminine, prettier, more petite, effervescent, yet shallow individual.[40] The accuracy of such impressions has never been proved. It's more likely that vocal cues are just one more aspect of our implicit personality theories. We factor in the vocal cues alongside others that then trigger a more complete prototypic impression.

We also use vocal cues to infer emotional states, especially when facial cues are unavailable or suspect. One review of the research on vocalics and emotion concluded that two emotions were most likely to be interpreted accurately: joy and hate. The hardest to communicate were love and shame.[41] The ability to judge emotions in the voice does vary, however. Some people are remarkably good at it while others cannot make the auditory distinctions or don't listen carefully. At certain times, the context makes vocal cues more salient. In one study, alcoholic patients were more likely to seek additional treatment when a doctor made the referral in an "anxious" voice.[42]

From the auditory mode, which is one of the "distant" senses, we move to a consideration of the tactile mode, probably the most "immediate" sense.

Tactile Communication

From the time we are born, the nonverbal code of touch is extremely important. Studies with infants have shown how tactile stimulation triggers social, emotional, and even intellectual growth.[43] Advocates of the human-potential movement have stressed the need for adults to touch and be touched. In spite of this, we know very little about the role of touch as a message system. According to one reviewer, the research that has been conducted tends to emphasize only the positive role of touch.[44] Few investigators have studied how touch is used to dominate or threaten others. Yet we know from everyday experience that touching conveys a wide range of emotions and meanings.

Types of Touch

Touching may be the most ambiguous of the nonverbal codes because its meaning depends so much on the nature of the relationship, the age and sex of the other, the situation, where we are touched, how much pressure was applied, whether we think the touch was intentional or accidental, and how long the touch lasted. In addition, touch may be applied by brushing, patting, squeezing, stroking, embracing, slapping, kicking, and even tickling. The texture of touch may even be meaningful. Shaking hands with someone whose palm is sweaty is not very pleasant and may be interpreted as a sign of nervousness. The manner in which you place your hand on someone's arm may be the difference between reassuring or patronizing that person. The warmth or coldness of other cues, such as the tone of voice, may add meaning to being touched.

The Contexts and Functions of Touch

Touching may be used to signal aggression, status, friendliness, sexual interest, or simply to regulate interaction. But these meanings are

No one knew the value of tactile communication better than Helen Keller, who could neither see nor hear. Here she returns the well-known grin of President Dwight Eisenhower.

mediated by context. Richard Heslin has classified the meanings of touch according to the relational context in which they occur.[45] The *professional/functional* context legitimates any kind of touch necessary to accomplish impersonal ends or services. Doctors and hair stylists are allowed to touch us in ways that other people cannot. *Social/polite* relationships allow for a minimum of touching during greetings, goodbyes, and conversations. A handshake is acceptable, as is a brush on the arm to get another's attention. The meaning of other forms of touch in this setting is more difficult to determine. Brenda Major believes that touch may simultaneously communicate warmth and

dominance, but that men and women pay attention to different messages. When an equal-status stranger initiates touch, men more often see it as an act of dominance; women see it as a friendly gesture.[46] Higher-status individuals seem to have more rights regarding touch. They can initiate touch more frequently, and it is rare when a lower-status person feels comfortable enough to reciprocate that touch.[47]

Friendship encourages a number of touching behaviors associated with liking. A shoulder embrace, a greater frequency of brushing the hand or arm, a slight squeeze are examples of appropriate actions. In *love/intimate* relations, we find more hand-in-hand, arm-in-arm, bodies leaning against one another, and more touching in general. Finally, *sexual* relationships forbid very few forms of touch. But even in sexual relationships, the meaning of touch may vary.

Heslin has proposed a curvilinear relationship between forms of touch and liking. In the initial stages of acquaintance, intimate touch is taboo and should lead to strong dislike. As a relationship becomes defined as loving or sexual, intimate touch becomes pleasurable. There is a danger, however, that the quantity of touching may lead to the view of the other person as a "sex object," reducing, sometimes drastically, the pleasure of touch. Although Heslin didn't include it in his scheme, we would add an *adversarial* relationship context. This could encompass professional wrestlers, brothers and sisters, and normal folks during the course of an argument. You may grab someone by the shirt collar in an attempt to threaten her, or if things deteriorate, you may push or shove her.

Touching is only one of many nonverbal codes. And, as we have reminded you all along, none of the codes stands alone. They operate as a complex, mixed-message system every time we interact with one another. How we can make sense out of and react to the total nonverbal package is the subject of the next section.

BALANCING NONVERBAL CODES: COMPENSATING AND RECIPROCATING

Most people on a crowded bus avoid looking at each other or limit their visual behavior to random glances. But what would you think if a stranger kept looking in your direction, and as seating opened up, moved closer to where you were sitting, and then offered someone else his seat and stood even closer to you, occasionally brushing his arm against yours? How would you react?

One way to look at this stranger's behavior is to define his advances as increasing the physical and psychological immediacy or closeness between you. Our guess is that unless you were extremely attracted to this stranger, you would probably *compensate* for his behavior by distancing yourself in one or more ways. You might get up and change your seat, turn and look out the window, or bury your head in your newspaper.

We don't always avoid increases in nonverbal immediacy. Sometimes we *reciprocate* another's invitations. Is there any way to predict when we will compensate or reciprocate? Let's look at one theory that tries to account for these differences.

Equilibrium Theory

Equilibrium theory is one explanation of how the various nonverbal codes interact. It is the work of Miles Patterson and a number of earlier contributors whose theories Patterson has modified.[48] The first theory Patterson drew from was Michael Argyle and Janet Dean's equilibrium model. This suggested that in any situation, people establish a comfortable level of nonverbal intimacy by balancing various nonverbal cues. They maintain the normal level of involvement by **compensating** when something happens that increases the level of intimacy between them. During the course of developing a more personal relationship, they may escalate the level of involvement by **reciprocating** when the other initiates an increase in nonverbal intimacy. The proper balance of cues may be defined by cultural norms or a negotiated preference of the two individuals.

The next time you shop at the mall, observe the seating patterns of strangers in the food court. Most strangers will not share a table, except under the most crowded circumstances.

Note how they compensate to maintain equilibrium if forced to share. They'll sit on opposite sides and ends of the table. They may avoid interaction altogether, staring off in opposite directions. If they do talk, they are likely to have very limited and brief eye contact. If either engages in any intimacy behaviors—excessive staring, prolonged smiling, or intimate statements—the other will probably compensate. Equilibrium theory predicts that if one of these strangers increases the level of involvement beyond what was normal or comfortable, the other will *compensate* by reducing involvement in one or more codes (for example, if one moved closer, the other would avoid any eye contact). No doubt you've been in situations where something like this has happened.

But on other occasions, you may have noted that increases in nonverbal involvement are matched by the other person. When someone cries and repeatedly looks up at you between sobs (in effect increasing the level of involvement), you may move closer to him, put your arm around his shoulder, and ask if you can help. In other words, you *reciprocate* by a further increase in intimacy. Equilibrium theory did not account for such reciprocity. To explain these two different reactions to the increase in nonverbal involvement, Patterson proposed that *changes in arousal* and *cognitive labeling* of that arousal change are important.

Many factors can cause a change in arousal, either by increasing or decreasing it. Being stared at or enclosed in an elevator with others may increase what was once low arousal, whereas being comforted and touched may decrease a high arousal state. In addition, arousal may increase when the other person violates our expectations, causing us to become uncertain about what is going on. Once a change in arousal does occur, we go through a cognitive labeling process to determine if the emotion being felt is positive or negative. If we make a negative attribution (for example, fear or anger), compensation is the most likely response. If we label the arousal positively (excitement or love), then the model predicts that reciprocity will occur. For example, suppose your very good friend sneaks up behind you and tries to surprise you. She sticks her forefinger in your back and says, "Stick 'em up!" This behavior may startle or frighten you (a negative attribution), in which case you'll probably jump away and put your arm in front of you for defense as you turn around. You would be compensating for the increased level of nonverbal involvement. The opposite reaction might occur if you recognized your friend's voice or expected some routine like this from her (a positive attribution). You might then reciprocate by turning around and embracing your friend.

Compensating and Reciprocating in Everyday Life

How well does equilibrium theory explain everyday interactions? We think you'll find that it can help you understand the give-and-take of nonverbal communication. One of the principal themes of this text is the way communication is used to regulate the tension between feeling independent and feeling like a part of the social systems around us. When we feel closed in by a relationship, we may compensate by reducing the level of nonverbal involvement. You can probably remember your early teenage years when you desperately needed to present yourself as an adult, not a child. At this point in life, too much nonverbal involvement with parents, such as holding their hands or staying close to them while shopping, suggests that you are still a child. Compensation becomes a tool for establishing your own identity and your status as an adult.

Understanding the various nonverbal codes we have described is an important part of interpersonal communication. Even more important is understanding how they work in conjunction with one another and with verbal messages. Recognizing how people compensate and reciprocate for increases in nonverbal intimacy can help you manage your nonverbal communication more effectively.

IMPROVING NONVERBAL COMPETENCE

This chapter has emphasized the structure and function of nonverbal codes. Nonverbal communication is structured such that messages may be coded in at least seven or eight different channels. We have also mentioned some major functions that these codes serve: modifying the content of a message, structuring relationships, and managing the flow of conversation.

Simply knowing that these different channels and functions exist should make you more aware of and better able to read nonverbal cues. Reading additional research on each code and how they function together can give you more insight into appropriate ways of communicating. But the best thing you can do is continue to be observant of the ways people use nonverbal codes and how they place an emphasis on one code in order to get their meaning across. But be careful not to read too much into any one nonverbal code—avoid the simplistic how-to-read-a-person-like-a-book approaches that suggest a different meaning for each nonverbal gesture. They simply don't work that way. Remember, the power of nonverbal codes rests in their clustering to produce the same message in several different ways.

Although our culture stipulates the parameters of nonverbal use and meaning, individuals do produce their own unique nonverbal styles. This makes it important to be aware of the normal nonverbal repertoire of those close to you or with whom you frequently interact. By knowing another's nonverbal habits, you will be in a better position to recognize subtle contradictions or modifications that might signal a problem in your relationship or in the other's self-confidence or demeanor.

Finally, work on your own nonverbal communication. Ask yourself if your vocal tone is as reassuring or as forceful as you want it to be, or if you might not crowd others too much during conversation. Make an inventory of your own use of each nonverbal code, separately and in combination with other codes. Observe the reactions of others when you try to alter your normal pattern of interaction, noting positive, negative, or ambivalent responses. Do this for several weeks until awareness of nonverbal communication becomes second nature to you. You will become a more competent communicator.

REVIEW TERMS

The following is a list of major concepts introduced in this chapter. The page where the concept is first mentioned is listed in parentheses.

liking (127)
status (127)
responsiveness (127)
complementing (128)
accenting (128)
repeating (128)
substituting (128)
contradicting (129)
regulating (130)
proxemics (130)
territoriality (132)
personal space (133)
physical appearance (134)
gaze (135)
looking (136)
seeing (136)
facial blend (138)

SUGGESTED READINGS

Ekman, Paul, and Wallace Friesen. *Unmasking the Face*. Englewood Cliffs, N.J.: Prentice-Hall, 1975. A classic guide to understanding emotions from observations of facial expressions. Chapters on why we make mistakes in reading faces, how to recognize facial deceit, and how to check your own facial expressions are very interesting. In the process, you will learn a great deal about nonverbal research methods.

Mehrabian, Albert. *Public Places and Private Spaces*. New York: Basic Books, 1976. A close look at nonverbal behavior in residential, work, therapeutic, play, and communal environments. Suggestions for making environments more conducive to interaction are especially useful. This book is recommended precisely because it blends a theoretical perspective with practical ways to manage the environment's influence on us.

Montagu, Ashley, and Floyd Matson. *The Human Connection*. New York: McGraw-Hill, 1979. A very readable exploration into the nonverbal codes involved in approaching, meeting, signaling, and communicating with others.

Morris, Desmond. *Manwatching: A Field Guide to Human Behavior*. New York: Harry N. Abrams, 1977. From the postural echo to hybrid gestures to the "twenty basic ways of moving from place to place," this practical handbook will enable you to identify and label a wide range of nonverbal behaviors. It is worth glancing through for the pictures alone; worth reading for the insights into the historical origins and cultural variations of many gestures.

PROCESS TO PERFORMANCE

TOPICS FOR DISCUSSION

1. In small groups, discuss the advantages and disadvantages of the "limited" definition of nonverbal communication presented in the text (pp. 124–25). Decide for yourselves if we should include *all* nonverbal behavior as communication or whether some limits are necessary. Then try your hand at defining nonverbal communication.

2. The research in this chapter identifies facial expressions as the most universal of nonverbal gestures. Are there any other codes that you think might approach universal meaning (that is, people from different cultures would interpret the gesture the same way)? Can you arrange the codes in order from most universal to least universal? What implications does this have for interpreting and sending nonverbal messages in everyday interactions?

3. What are your own preferences in terms of personal space or conversational distance? How close do you like to stand when talking with friends, acquaintances, or strangers? Can you recall an episode in which conversational distance had a dramatic impact? What happened? How did you (or the other) respond to the violation of expectations? What was the outcome of the conversation?

4. Identify as many nonperson roles as you can (see p. 133). What do people say and do in the presence of these role persons that they would avoid if they met the same person in another setting?

5. Discuss the role of *norms* in nonverbal communication. Consider norms for two or three different codes. What are the advantages and disadvantages of following these norms? Can a person be too normal? How far can someone go in violating the norm before most people label them as abnormal? What positive outcomes can be achieved when norms are violated? When do norms become too limiting?

6. One study mentioned in the text pointed out differences in gaze between black and white Americans. Identify other ethnic, regional, or cultural groups you have interacted with and discuss the differences in nonverbal norms that you noticed. Can you think of appropriate ways to improve communication when such differences are apparent?

OBSERVATION GUIDES

1. Make your next trip to the zoo an investigation into nonverbal communication. Visit a large metropolitan zoo where you can observe primates and other species close to humans on the evolutionary scale. What similarities and differences do you see or hear? Organize your observations according to the various codes discussed in the text (facial, gaze, kinesics, and so on). What gestures seem to be used primarily for communication? What functions do they serve? Identify any gestures humans use that might have originated with earlier species. How has the meaning of such gestures changed?

2. Specify a particular block of time and try using nonverbal codes as a substitute for verbal ones. When people ask you questions, do not verbalize beyond unintelligible vocalizations such as grunts or groans. Vary the types of responses you make (vocalized only, facial only, combined responses, and so on). Keep track for a couple of days and try to formulate some general principles about when substituting works best.

3. Observe people in naturally occurring conversations, recording the specific nonverbal codes used to regulate the flow of interaction. Which cues are more characteristic of smooth turn-taking? Which cues seem to cause awkward transitions or silences? Compare your observations with those of published research (your instructor can recommend journal articles or textbooks that summarize these behaviors).

4. It is a rare semester when students are not involved in at least one group project.

Take advantage of these opportunities to observe nonverbal interaction more closely. Take a few minutes during each meeting to observe how different group members communicate nonverbally. As unobtrusively as you can, record facial expressions, body posture and movement, gaze, gestures, and vocal characteristics. Also note the situation at hand so you won't interpret nonverbals out of context. What do these observations tell you about the interest level, status relations, and interpersonal competence of group members? What gestures are shared or imitated by other group members? What does this suggest about the bonding of group members together?

CLASSROOM EXERCISES

1. Identify people you think are especially accurate at reading others' nonverbal cues or are very good at getting their message across nonverbally. These should be people who aren't members of your class. Formulate (in class) a set of interview questions to ask these people. You might want to ask what behaviors they attend to most often when they want to know what the other thinks or feels, and how they know when someone is deceiving them. For message sending, ask people how aware they are of their own nonverbals, which codes they use intentionally, and which they think are most important. Would they rather use verbal or nonverbal messages to give instructions, or convey emotions? You should think of other types of messages to ask them about. Interview a dozen people outside of class and compare the answers you get. Prepare a short presentation to the rest of the class, focusing on what you have learned about nonverbal communication competence.

2. Assemble groups of four or five. Have each person remove any cash, valuables, and "really embarrassing" items from their wallets. Place the wallets in a basket and give them to your instructor, who will redistribute the wallets to another group. Each group should analyze the contents of each wallet, writing down a brief profile of its owner. The profile should be based *only* on inferences made from the artifacts found in the wallet. It can include the person's sex, age, personality, nature of appearance, interests. Once the profile of each wallet is written, enclose it in the wallet and return them to your instructor, who will return them to the original owners. Group members may then read the profiles written about them to each other or introduce one another to the class by reading the profiles aloud. Conclude the exercise by discussing the accuracy of the profiles and what particular artifacts were most influential in communicating those impressions.

3. Divide the class into six groups. Each group is assigned one of the following communicative functions: (a) exercising social control, (b) regulating interaction, (c) expressing intimacy, (d) expressing emotion, (e) facilitating service or task goals, and (f) modifying the content of verbal messages. Each group should then compile a list of the ways each nonverbal code helps to accomplish that function. During the week, group members should bring to class audiovisual examples of how this is done (family photos, magazine photos, film clips, audiotapes, and so on). Try to find both stereotypical and unusual examples to illustrate these functions. Groups could be given the last five to ten minutes of two or three class sessions to discuss what they have found and prepare a 10- to 15-minute presentation to the class. Presentations could be conducted the following week.

CHAPTER SEVEN

The desire to bind time by recording spoken communication is universal.
The message in these hieroglyphs, written over 3,000 years ago, is accessible
today to those who know how to break the verbal code. (*King's Scribe
Amenhotep and His Wife Renut*, c. 1275 B.C.)

CODING INTERPERSONAL MESSAGES: VERBAL COMMUNICATION

O N JUNE 27, 1880, a remarkable woman was born. Although she graduated cum laude from Radcliffe College at the age of 24 and later became a famous author and lecturer, Helen Keller had to battle almost insurmountable odds. Many of you know her story. When she was a child she was struck with an illness that left her both blind and deaf for life. It was impossible for anyone to penetrate her dark and silent world. She developed a crude sign language, but she was constantly frustrated by her inability to communicate, often screaming and crying until she was exhausted.

All of this changed when Anne Sullivan became her teacher. Perhaps you recall the scene from *The Miracle Worker* in which the seven-year-old Helen first learns the meaning of language. She and Sullivan were in the wellhouse of the Keller home. Sullivan placed Helen's hands beneath the pump and spelled the word "w-a-t-e-r" into them. As she felt the cool liquid spill over her hands, Helen realized for the first time what words were. As she wrote later:

That living word awakened my soul, gave it light, hope, joy, set it free! . . . I left the well-house eager to learn. Everything had a name, every

object which I touched seemed to quiver with life. That was because I saw everything with the strange, new sight that had come to me.[1]

There are two ways to respond to this story. We can dwell on what Helen lacked and the obstacles she overcame. Or we can concentrate on what she gained that day at the wellhouse. What she gained was language and with it history, literature, and culture. When she acquired language, she acquired access to the same symbolic world the rest of us inhabit. From that moment on, she didn't have to see or hear the world directly. She could share others' experiences.

This chapter is about what happened to Helen and what happens to each of us simply because we use language. It's about what language is, how it is put together, and how it affects us. We'll begin by defining language, paying particular attention to the ways the verbal code differs from the nonverbal. Next we look at language structure, examining semantic, syntactic, and pragmatic levels. We will then consider how language affects our thoughts and behaviors. Finally we'll look at ways of overcoming language confusions in order to increase message competence.

WHAT IS LANGUAGE?

In this section we will compare verbal and nonverbal codes and describe some of the power that comes to us through language.

Differences between the Verbal and Nonverbal Codes

One of the major differences is that language is a digital code, while nonverbal is classed as analogic. Before we explain the differences between these codes, see if you can discover them for yourself by considering the examples shown in Figures 7.1 and 7.2. In the first, you see a drawing accompanied by a verbal description. Both the words and drawing describe the same subject, using different codes. The way the drawing conveys information is analogic; the way the written description conveys it is digital.

Now look at the second example. Figure 7.2 shows a braille translation of Helen's description of her experience at the well-house. This is in a digital code. Next to it is a still from *The Miracle Worker* in which actors convey Helen's experience analogically. As a third example, think for a minute about the difference between a sundial and a digital clock. A sundial shows time by reflecting the actual movement of the sun across the sky, while a digital clock displays separate numbers that change at fixed intervals.[2]

Try listing adjectives that describe the analogic examples. What do the movement of the shadow on the sundial, the gestures of the actors, and the lines of the drawing have in common? Next, try to describe the digital examples. What similarities are there between the digital readout, the braille letters, and the written words? If, for the first set, you came up with words like *natural, continuous, immediate, similar,* or *relational,* you have grasped the nature of analogic codes. If, for the second set,

TOADS are found in almost every part of the world. Members of the family Bufonidae, they are squat and fat, have short legs and a warty skin. They secrete a poisonous substance from the parotoid glands behind the eye. They feed on the larvae of harmful insects.

FIGURE 7.1

you chose words like *artificial, abstract, arbitrary, separate,* or *logical,* then you've discovered the essence of digital codes.

Analogic codes indicate meaning by being similar to what they convey. The actors' movements are like those of real people experiencing real emotions. The lines in the drawing trace the natural shape and form of the object they represent. The movement of the shadow on the face of the sundial mirrors the passage of time. In analogic codes, an expression and what it indicates are naturally connected. Many of the nonverbal behaviors we studied in Chapter 6 convey meaning analogically.

FIGURE 7.2

Analogic and digital representations of Helen's experience at the well-house

In **digital codes**, meaning is conveyed symbolically. **Symbols** are units of meaning that are arbitrary and conventional. They're arbitrary because the relationship they have to the things they represent is artificial rather than natural. Consider the word *joy*, for example. The fact that that particular combination of sounds and letters was chosen to represent the emotion is an arbitrary one. There is nothing particularly joyful in the word j-o-y. The word stands for the emotion because people agreed that it should. Symbols are conventional, based on social agreement. We could easily change the meaning attached to the words in our language—if everyone within our language community agreed. Maybe the reason people react so emotionally to language changes is that such changes violate basic social contracts. At any rate, without knowing the conventions used to assign meaning to symbols, digital codes are impossible to understand.

We have seen that the way meanings are expressed differs in the two codes. The kinds of meanings they can express also differ. Analogic codes (especially those consisting of expressive behavior) seem to be best at conveying relationships and immediate emotional states. Digital codes are useful for more abstract, logical meanings. Assume that you don't know the story of Helen Keller. How much of it could you gather by looking at the picture from *The Miracle Worker*? You could easily recognize that it involves two characters experiencing intense emotion. You might also understand what they're doing and what they feel for one another. What you could not understand is the history of their relationship or their interpretations of it. For this, you would have to turn to digital reports.

The Power of the Verbal Code

In Chapter 6 we listed some of the reasons nonverbal codes are so powerful. Language has a different kind of power. Four characteristics of the digital code make it uniquely different from the analogic code and allow us to act in otherwise impossible ways:[3]

1. *Verbal codes consist of discrete, separable units.* The structure of language is unique. It consists of units of sound and meaning that are discrete and separate. This fact gives language immense flexibility, for the units that make it up can be processed and manipulated more readily than those of the nonverbal codes. Words and sounds can be modified, combined in unique ways, and transmitted singly or in combination across time and space. They can be easily saved, stored, and retrieved. This is impossible in analogic codes. Although there have been attempts to break analogic displays into units and to write grammars describing their combinations, most have failed.[4]

2. *Language encourages us to create new realities.* One of the unique things about language is that it allows us to talk about absent or nonexistent things. Words don't need to have actual referents in the physical world. Of course, this is a mixed blessing. Language allows creativity, but it also allows us to deceive one another. In fact, Umberto Eco has defined language as "everything which can be used in order to lie."[5]

3. *Language gives us the ability to think in new and more complex ways.* Abstract nouns, logical words such as *and, or, all,* and *none* and grammatical markers can't be expressed analogically. Such words allow the development of complex philosophical and mathematical systems. Language enhances our ability to think rationally and logically, although this doesn't mean we always do so.

4. *Verbal codes are self-reflexive.* Language can comment on itself; it allows us to talk about the way we talk. This quality is known as self-reflexiveness. It's what allows us to think about language and modify it when it doesn't work. Without this aspect of language, studying and improving communication would be impossible, for we would have no way to talk about it.

THE FUNCTIONS OF LANGUAGE

Stop for a minute and think of all the things you normally do with language. Think of as many examples as you can, like commenting on the weather, reminiscing with old friends, describing last night's NFL telecast, memorizing facts, cursing, telling jokes, talking to yourself, writing poetry, telling white lies, cheering a team to victory. It's pretty clear that language isn't just a vehicle for exchanging facts and seeking information. In this section, we'll list some of the functions of language.[6]

1. *We often use language to conquer the silent and the unknown.* We all have a need to escape from silence. When alone in a dark or quiet place, we often talk simply to make sound. Somehow, unbroken silence can be oppressive and frightening. By talking, we defend ourselves against the unknown. We also conquer the unknown by labeling it. Things without names are threatening and mysterious. We can reduce them to more human and manageable proportions by naming them; perhaps we believe something that is named can be controlled. If so, we are not far from a belief in the magical qualities of language.

2. *Language allows us to express and control emotion.* Some talk may simply be an attempt to reduce inner tension. Many psychologists believe that we have a biologically based need to vent emotions. Shouting in joy or cursing in anger are examples of this function. Of course, language can also be used to inhibit emotion. For example, we can talk ourselves into calming down. In a classic episode of "The Honey-

mooners," the Jackie Gleason character repeats "Pins and needles, needles and pins, the happy man is the man who grins," and then counts to ten, hoping by the time he's finished he'll have forgotten what he was angry about.

3. *Language can reveal or camouflage our thoughts and motives.* What goes on within us remains hidden unless we choose to show it to others. We can discuss inner feelings directly or reveal them more subtly. Freud was one of the first to turn our attention to the meanings of linguistic errors or slips of the tongue. He called these errors *parapraxes* and believed they were caused by inner conflicts.[7] If, for example, a speaker were to say quite sweetly, "We'll do whatever I—I mean you—want," the substitution might indicate a hidden need for control. Although to the trained ear parapraxes reveal inner feelings, they are attempts to hide true desires and designs from both self and other. Of course, we can use language as camouflage more directly; we can hide behind overt lies, evasions, and half-truths.

4. *We employ language to make and avoid contact.* Language connects us to others. The telephone company slogan "Reach out and touch someone" reflects this basic function. Telling someone "I just called to hear your voice" is using language to bridge distance. Of course, we can also talk to keep others away. A compulsive talker can avoid contact. Language can be a wall as well as a bridge.

5. *Language enables us to assert individual and social identity.* Each of us has a unique style; talk enables us to present it and thus an image of how we want to be perceived. At the same time, it also allows us to submerge ourselves in a group. Slang, jargon, and shared language games can signal social solidarity and belonging.

6. *Language may be used to give or seek information.* It almost goes without saying that language is an important medium for information exchange. It allows us to categorize and interpret the environment. Through language we can state, assert, describe, explain, and demonstrate the order we see around us. We also use language to gather information from others. Even seemingly trivial small talk, or phatic communication, can serve as social reconnaissance. Because survival is based on accurate predictions about the world, linguistic means of reducing uncertainty are essential.[8]

7. *Language allows us to control and be controlled by the world.* Language is power. It can be used to influence, regulate, persuade, or dominate. From making a good impression to brainwashing, we use language to control our worlds. Of course, language also controls us by affecting the way we perceive and think about the world. In many ways, we are prisoners of language.

8. *Language can be used to monitor the process of communication.* As we noted earlier, language is self-reflexive; it allows us to metacommunicate, to communicate about the communication process. When two people discuss a topic of interest such as politics or religion, they are communicating. When they discuss their discussion, they are metacommunicating. Metacommunication occurs when we use language to check communication channels ("Did you understand what I said?"), regulate the flow of talk ("Wait a minute. Let me finish making this point."), or comment on language patterns ("I know I change the subject whenever you make a good point. It's just that I can't stand to be on the losing end of an argument.")[9]

THE STRUCTURE OF LANGUAGE: THREE LEVELS OF MEANING

Now that we know some of the functions of language, let's look briefly at how language is

structured. Language can be analyzed on a number of levels.[10] The three we believe most important to the study of interpersonal communication are the word, the sentence, and the speech act. To understand and use language, we have to understand all these levels of meaning.

Semantic Meaning: Language at the Level of the Word

Actually, to be technically correct, we should use the term *morpheme* rather than *word*. A morpheme is a linguistic unit of meaning. Although in most cases morphemes are equivalent to words, some word fragments also carry meaning. For example, the *s* that tells us a word is plural has meaning in its own right. Therefore a word like *dogs* is actually made up of two morphemes; the word *dog* and the plural morpheme *s*.

The study of meaning at this level is called **semantics**. While a full discussion of semantic meaning is beyond the scope of this book, we can at least begin by considering two kinds of word meanings: denotative and connotative.

Denotative and Connotative Meanings

Denotative meaning is public, conventional meaning. It is, in a sense, the meaning that was agreed upon when the language code was constructed. This kind of meaning belongs not to the individual but to the language system itself. To find out the denotative meaning of an unfamiliar word, we simply turn to an authoritative source such as the dictionary. That is why denotative meaning is often referred to as "dictionary meaning." **Connotative meaning** is private, often emotionally charged, meaning. It becomes attached to words through experiences and associations. Here, individuals rather than the language system are the final authority.

Consider the term *baseball*. Our dictionary tells us that its denotative meaning is:

a game played with a ball, bat and gloves between two teams of nine players each on a large field centering on four bases that form the corners of a square 90 feet on each side, each team having a turn at bat and in the field during each of the nine innings that constitute a normal game, the winner being the team that scores the most runs.[11]

While this definition expresses (albeit awkwardly) at least part of the meaning of baseball, it seems curiously flat. There is more to meaning than what is in the dictionary. Part of what is missing is connotative meaning.

We chose this example because we, your authors, have very different attitudes toward baseball. For one of us, baseball is a neutral concept. That author can recall attending only one major league game (when a team called the Senators played in Washington, D.C.). If asked to identify famous baseball players, she could probably list only those whose names are associated with candy bars. For the other, baseball has much stronger and more positive meanings. As a child, he played baseball every day of the summer, using flour from the kitchen to mark out a diamond on a homemade playing field. He memorized batting averages and followed every aspect of fellow Oklahoman Mickey Mantle's career. Even today he shows up at the office at the beginning of spring training wearing a Yankees baseball cap. For the two of us the term *baseball* has different connotations, as it does for each of you. There are as many connotations for a word as there are unique experiences with it.

The Importance of Semantic Competence

Mastering the semantics of one's language is important, for no one can communicate competently without an appropriate vocabulary. People who use words incorrectly may talk on for hours without realizing they are conveying messages they never meant.

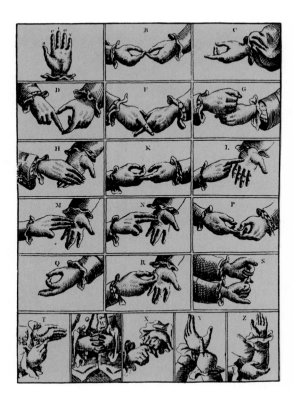

This 18th-century flysheet shows a finger spelling system used to communicate with the deaf. Although gestural, this code is actually digital. Can you think of other verbal codes that are not spoken?

Lack of semantic competence can also lead to feelings of isolation and rejection. Group membership is often associated with access to special words. If you have ever heard others talk in unintelligible technical terms, you know how incompetent and left out you felt. It's impossible to fit into a professional or social group without mastering the jargon that group favors.

Sensitivity to connotations is also an important part of semantic competence. Many arguments start because one party inadvertently uses a word that has negative connotations for the other. Calling a woman you do not know well "honey" or referring to her as a "girl" are good examples. While some women may not mind, others find this usage belittling. Words like *love* and *commitment* and *responsibility* also carry strong emotional charges. They can cause relational problems if individuals attach different meanings to them. To be fully competent, it is necessary to realize that words call up different reactions in each of us.

Syntactic Meaning: Language at the Level of the Utterance

Of course, words are rarely used in isolation; they usually occur in phrases or sentences. The study of the process by which words are combined and ordered into grammatical sequences is called **syntactics**.

Order As Meaning

It's important to be able to order words appropriately. Had the previous sentence been written, "Important it's words appropriately order to be to able," you would have been confused at the very least. Probably you would have decided that your authors were suffering from some kind of mental disorder. Part of a word's meaning is its relationship to the words that precede and follow it.

Although in English a single word may mean several things, context usually makes its meaning clear. *Port*, for example, means something different in the context of "No, not starboard, you fool! Port!" than it does in the context of "Please don't drop that bottle of priceless vintage port."

Consider the difference between the sentences "The ship sails" and "Ship the sails."[12] The words are the same, but their order differs. Meaning based on word order is called **syntactic meaning**. For a more interpersonal example, consider the two sentences "Sam wants to

marry Claudine" and "Claudine wants to marry Sam." Although the words are the same, the meanings are not. And it could make a real difference to both Sam and Claudine whether one or both meanings are intended.

The Importance of Syntactic Competence

Strict rules govern sentence form. If we fail to abide by these rules, most people will react negatively. Syntax is thought to be a mark of social and economic status (which it often is) and also an indication of intellectual ability and moral rectitude (which it definitely is not.) We often believe people who use "incorrect grammar" (grammar that violates *our* set of rules) are too "dumb" or "lazy" to use language "the right way," and we let this perception shape our impressions.

Pragmatic Meaning: Language at the Level of the Speech Act

In order to understand communication, it is necessary to go beyond the semantic and syntactic levels. Having a good vocabulary and knowing the rules of sentence construction will not guarantee adequate communication. We have to know how to use sentences in actual conversation. **Pragmatics** investigates language as it is used in actual interaction.

Language in Use

People don't generally talk just for the fun of it. When we use language, we use it to do things. The things we intend language to do for us are called **speech acts**.[13] Examples of speech acts are promising, questioning, threatening, praising, declaring, warning, requesting, and so on.

We said earlier that sentences can help us figure out the meanings of words. Speech acts can do the same for sentences. Knowing a sentence's meaning involves knowing its intended speech act. Let's say that you've just written a poem. You're not sure how good it is, so you show it to a friend. Your friend reads it, thinks for a moment, and says, "I've never seen anything like it. It's unique." But what does this mean? Puzzling over the syntax and semantics of the sentence won't help you. In order to understand the message, you have to know what your friend was trying to do: compliment you, engage in literary criticism, or try to weasel out of saying anything at all. To be able to communicate, we must be able to assess the speech acts of others and formulate our own.

CMM: Interpreting and Producing Speech Acts

How do we know what speech acts mean? And how do we know when and how to use them? A theory called the coordinated management of meaning (CMM for short) helps answer these questions.[14] According to CMM, we know how to use language because we follow rules that tell us how to understand and produce speech acts. There are two kinds of rules in CMM theory: **constitutive rules**, which tell us how to recognize speech acts, and **regulative rules**, which identify, in a given context, the speech acts that are appropriate and inappropriate. Before looking at examples of these rules, let's consider how context affects communication behavior.

CMM theory tells us we have different rules for different contexts. What is appropriate in a heart-to-heart conversation is not appropriate at a formal dinner party. What is effective in showing a boss how responsible you are will not be effective in impressing a date. What works at home may not work at school. To communicate effectively, people must take into account the situation, their relationship, their self-images, and relevant cultural rules. Figure 7.3 (p. 164) shows the contexts that CMM identifies as important.

The top portion of 7.3 shows the CMM contexts. As you can see, contexts are nested within one another, with higher levels including lower ones. Let's start near the bottom with the speech act. Speech acts make sense only when we understand the episode in which they occur. An **episode** is made up of a set of speech acts that fit together naturally. If you were to ask communicators "What are you doing?" their answer would name the episode they're involved in. "Going for pizza," "shooting pool," "buying groceries," "having a barroom brawl," "closing a big deal" are examples of episodes. Clearly we expect different speech acts in different episodes. What is appropriate for the barroom may not be for the boardroom. If we know the episode in which an utterance occurs, we can fix its speech act more easily than if we hear it out of context. We'll also know which additional speech acts are appropriate and which would be out of place.

Another important context is the **relationship** between communicators. If you were to ask communicators "Who are you to one another?" their answer would identify their relationship. Examples are student–teacher, husband–wife, boss–worker. Relationships determine episodes. Episodes such as "discussing one's fears and hopes," "showing affection," and "borrowing money and clothes" are usually appropriate for the relationship we call best friends. But they are not particularly likely if the relationship is professor–student. If we know a speaker's relationship to us, we are likely to understand his meanings. We will also be in a better position to do or say the correct thing.

The next context is **life script**. Your life script is your sense of self. It answers the question "Who am I or who do I wish to be?" For example, a "person at peace with nature and the universe" enters into relationships, episodes, and speech acts different from those of "an executive determined to make it to the top at all costs." The ways these two individuals interpret the world and the acts they consider

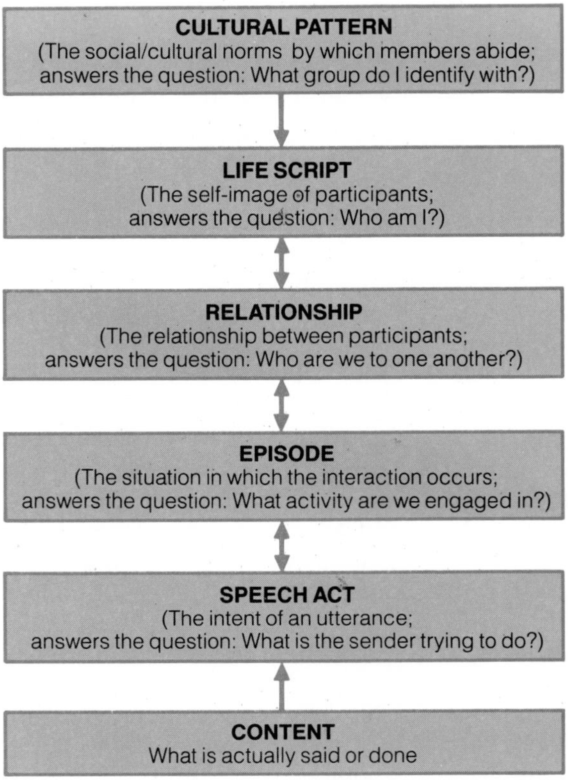

FIGURE 7.3
Levels of hierarchical meaning in CMM theory

CULTURAL PATTERN
(The social/cultural norms by which members abide; answers the question: What group do I identify with?)

↓

LIFE SCRIPT
(The self-image of participants; answers the question: Who am I?)

↕

RELATIONSHIP
(The relationship between participants; answers the question: Who are we to one another?)

↕

EPISODE
(The situation in which the interaction occurs; answers the question: What activity are we engaged in?)

↕

SPEECH ACT
(The intent of an utterance; answers the question: What is the sender trying to do?)

↑

CONTENT
What is actually said or done

	(Situation 1)	(Situation 2)	(Situation 3)
Cultural Pattern:	Middle-Class American	Middle-Class American	Middle-Class American
Life Script:	Educated Professional	Wild & Crazy Guy	Cold-blooded Egoist
Relationship:	Doctor/ Patient	Pals	Rivals
Episode:	Medical Exam	Kidding Around	Business Meeting
Speech Act:	Diagnosis	Joke	Put-down
Content:	**"You look terrible today"**		

Each level adds meaning to levels above and below. Communication makes sense only in reference to the context in which it occurs.

legitimate are likely to be diametrically opposed. If we know who someone is, we're in a better position to understand his meanings and respond effectively to him. Finally, **cultural patterns** affect all other levels, since the groups we belong to determine the nature and function of talk.

Using Pragmatic Rules in Interaction

How does all of this work in practice? Assume you hear the words "You look terrible today" and you want to know what the speaker meant. To interpret the speaker's intended speech act, you must consult your set of constitutive rules. To pick the right rule, you must use contextual cues; words have different meanings in different contexts.

If the statement is uttered by a physician in the episode of "physical examination," you will probably decide to count the words as a medical diagnosis. If it is uttered by a friend in an episode of "joking around," you will interpret it as the first move in a game of joking insults. Finally, if it is uttered in public by a subordinate who dislikes you, it may be seen as a "challenge to authority." Over the course of our lives, we build up a repertoire of interpretive rules that help us understand communication in a variety of contexts.

To respond to any comment, it is necessary to consult a regulative rule. Regulative rules tell you what speech acts are appropriate given your goals and your understanding of the context. In the case of the physical examination described above, your goal is probably to get information about your health. Your regulative rule set will tell you that insulting the doctor ("You think *I* look bad? Have *you* looked in a mirror lately, doc?") or asserting your authority ("That's quite enough. I'll see you in my office in half an hour.") are not appropriate. Of course, these speech acts might be exactly the right thing to do if you are just joking around or if your authority is questioned. Your rule for

the medical episode may read, "Given this context and my desire to get advice from my doctor, the proper speech act for me to perform is a polite request for further information." You then translate this speech act into something like, "What treatment do you suggest?"

The Importance of Pragmatic Competence

Communicating appropriately isn't easy. Embarrassment results when contexts are misinterpreted or rule sets are inadequate. If you have ever burst into a conversation with some trivial remark, only to realize that you interrupted a serious discussion, you know how important it is to label episodes correctly. If you have ever come on too strong too soon with someone, you know how tricky reading relationships can be. If you have ever interpreted an innocent remark as a threat to self, you have seen the way life scripts affect perception. Part of mastering pragmatic competence is being able to identify contextual levels accurately.

Communication is a complex, rule-bound process. If we learn to do it well, our relationships will be easy and rewarding. If we have trouble with pragmatic rules, the world can be a hostile place. In fact, it's been argued that many interpersonal problems result from differences in pragmatics. Box 7.1 (pp. 166–67) discusses another aspect of pragmatics, conversational style, and how it affects interpersonal relationships.

LANGUAGE, THOUGHT, AND BEHAVIOR

While language is a powerful way to control the world, many people feel that if we aren't careful, language can control us. In this section we'll look at theories that suggest that language, thought, and action are associated. We'll start with the controversial Sapir-Whorf hypothesis. Then we'll look at some of the research on the

BOX 7.1

Please Pass the Conversation: Conversational Styles and Relational Definitions

Unless you're a hermit, you talk with many people during a typical day: bus drivers, clerks, cashiers, waiters, secretaries, professors, friends. When these conversations go well, you feel satisfied with your world, for, in the words of linguist Deborah Tannen, "a perfectly tuned conversation is a vision of sanity—a ratification of one's way of being human and one's place in the world." Of course, when conversations go awry, the world can seem a very hostile place. There is something deeply disturbing about conversations that don't mesh.

All conversations are governed by implicit pragmatic rules. When people share these rules, conversations go smoothly. When their rules differ, however, misunderstandings and misattributions can easily occur. Well-meaning people, sincerely trying to get along, can experience conflicts simply because their conversational styles differ.

Tannen has written a number of books and articles explaining how the way we talk (our conversational style) can affect how we get along. In one she presents a detailed analysis of a Thanksgiving dinner. Three of the guests, including Tannen, were from New York, two from California, and one from Canada. Tannen taped the dinner conversation and then analyzed it carefully. What she found was that the three New Yorkers differed considerably from the others in the way they talked. They were louder and quicker, frequently interrupting one another. They showed their interest in a topic by bombarding their conversational partner with rapid-fire, personal questions. When they wanted to speak, they persisted until the others gave way, rarely stopping to invite the others to talk. Their style was direct, friendly, informal, energetic— and somewhat overwhelming.

The non-New Yorkers were a lot quieter. They had a hard time getting the floor, and when they did, they talked for shorter periods of time in a more formal and "polite" style. They showed less involvement but more consideration. Overcome by the New Yorkers' steady stream of talk, they found it difficult to

relationship of social class and gender to language behavior. Finally, we'll discuss some of the pitfalls inherent in English.

Linguistic Determinism: The Sapir-Whorf Hypothesis

The influence of language on thought has been strongly articulated by two linguists, Edward Sapir and Benjamin Lee Whorf.[15] Their analysis of the effects of language on cognition, the Sapir-Whorf hypothesis, has two important parts. The first, **linguistic determinism**, says that language determines the way we interpret the world. In the words of Sapir, "We see and hear and otherwise experience very largely as we do because the language habits of our community predispose certain choices of interpretation."[16] The second part of their hypothesis, **linguistic relativity**, follows from the first. If language determines thought, then speakers of different languages will experience the world differently. Thought is relative to language.

Let's look at some evidence for this hypothesis. If you have studied a foreign language, you know that other languages often make

keep up. In fact, the harder the New Yorkers tried to establish rapport, the more inhibited the others felt. Thus the dinner guests were working at cross-purposes.

How can we explain what happened? Tannen finds the answer in conversational style. She believes that conversants simultaneously want to (1) signal friendship and closeness; (2) avoid imposing their will on others; and (3) show their independence and distance from one another. Different speakers attach different degrees of importance to these conflicting goals. Some, like the New Yorkers above, will use a high-involvement style, refusing to stand on ceremony. In doing so, however, they run the danger of appearing rude. Others will use a high-considerateness style, following more formal rules. Of course, their politeness may be seen as coldness and lack of interest. When two people with different styles and expectations talk, they're likely to run into difficulties.

By analyzing conversation for details like pacing and pausing, loudness, pitch and intonation, expressive reactions, degree of persistence, tolerance for noise or silence, and use of involvement devices, conversational styles can be uncovered. They can then be compared and discussed to see whether they are likely to lead to harmony or discord.

Source: *Deborah Tannen,* Conversational Style: Analyzing Talk Among Friends *(Norwood, N.J.: Ablex, 1984).*

ADDITIONAL READINGS

Gumperz, John J. *Discourse Strategies.* London: Cambridge University Press, 1982.

Lakoff, Robin. *Language and Woman's Place.* New York: Harper & Row, 1975.

Tannen, Deborah. *That's Not What I Meant!* New York: William Morrow, 1986.

distinctions we don't. In English, for example, we simply say *you* when we want to talk to someone directly. In Spanish there are two forms of *you*, a polite form *(usted)* to be used with older persons, strangers, or those of high status, and a familiar form *(tú)*. In Spanish it is grammatically necessary to mark that point in a relationship when participants change from being mere acquaintances to close friends.

Not only do different languages tell us how to talk to one another, they also specify what to talk about. Different languages recognize different categories of experience. The words for colors are a classic example. In English there are seven basic colors in the spectrum (purple, indigo, blue, green, yellow, orange, and red.) In Bassa, a Liberian language, there are only two *hui* (which includes our purple, indigo, blue, and green) and *ziza* (which covers yellow, orange, and red.)[17]

Another frequently cited example is the fact that Eskimos have many more words for snow than we do. These words enable them to talk about distinctions most non-Eskimos could not perceive. This doesn't mean that Liberians couldn't learn to make fine color distinctions or that Southerners could not learn to see different kinds of snow. It only means that it will be harder to do these things. Without a name for something, it takes longer to distinguish that thing from other things, and the distinctions are less stable.[18]

Both the color and snow examples illustrate how our language separates things that are continuous in nature. The color spectrum is just that, a spectrum, not a collection of separate things. As Whorf tells us:

English terms, like "sky, hill, swamp," persuade us to regard some elusive aspect of nature's endless variety as a distinct THING, almost like a table or chair. Thus English and similar tongues lead us to think of the universe as a collection of rather distinct objects and events corresponding to words. Indeed, this is the implicit picture of classical physics and astronomy—that the universe is essentially a collection of detached objects of different sizes.[19]

Some American Indian languages preserve the unity of nature more fully than English. Sentences in these languages don't consist of nouns and verbs. If, for example, an English speaker were to see a light flash in the summer sky, he or she would say, "The light flashed." The action that took place would be indicated by a verb, while that which caused the action would be indicated by a separate noun and article. The Hopi speaker, however, would not divide what was seen into two parts. To the Hopi, the flashing and the light are one and indicated by one simple "verb," *rehpi*.[20]

The Sapir-Whorf hypothesis tells us that English speakers don't normally see the world the same way Hopi speakers see it. While we may not be complete prisoners of our language, we are deeply affected by its structure. Every language encourages and aids its speakers in some endeavors, while making other kinds of thoughts and actions more difficult.

The Effects of Group Membership on Language Use

The groups we belong to often use language differently. According to the Sapir-Whorf hypothesis, this means they will encourage us to think and act in special ways. Two groups often used as examples are social class and gender. Box 7.2 (pp. 170–71) gives an example of how both these factors affect language use.

Language and Social Class: Elaborated and Restricted Codes

The British sociologist Basil Bernstein studied the way class membership is related to language usage.[21] He found that working-class language employs shorter, simpler, and more conventionalized grammatical forms, while middle-class syntax exhibits more variety and complexity. Middle-class speakers make more complex grammatical decisions; Bernstein refers to their code as **elaborated**. Working-class speakers tend to use grammar in more rigidly determined ways, employing commonly shared forms; for this reason he calls their language code **restricted**.

More interesting are pragmatic differences. Bernstein believes that the primary purpose of elaborated codes is to convey information. Elaborated-code speakers try to use language precisely, being careful to fill in all of the details a listener might need. Restricted-code users, on the other hand, emphasize the social aspects of language, using it as a tool for building social identity and binding the individual to the group. They assume listeners don't need to have background information spelled out. The following dialogue is a good example of a restricted code.[22] Gary and George are friends who are discussing their plans for the evening.

GARY: How's about Trucker's tonight?

GEORGE: A little stick, eh?

GARY: Why not?

GEORGE: Okay, mine or yours?

GARY: Oh no! Every man for himself . . . wife, you know.

GEORGE: (to new neighbor) Why don't you come along too?

NEIGHBOR: (with no idea of what he is getting himself into) Sounds great!

Although our original source didn't give a direct translation into elaborated code, we can imagine that it would go something like this:

GARY: How would you like to go to our favorite country-western bar tonight, the one called Trucker's?

GEORGE: Do you mean to play pool?

GARY: Yes, why not?

GEORGE: OK, let's go together. Should we take your car or mine?

GARY: Oh no, we'd better go separately. My wife wants me to come home early tonight.

GEORGE: (to neighbor) Why don't you come along too?

NEIGHBOR: (understanding completely) Sounds great!

As you can see, restricted codes are not well designed for use with outsiders. They rely heavily on shared assumptions and expectations, and they encourage social solidarity. They're often found in groups who are, or want to be, set apart from society at large. Prison inmates and adolescents are examples cited by Bernstein. The "dorm talk" college students use with roommates and friends may be another.

Elaborated codes, on the other hand, do little to emphasize group identity. They encourage a more distant approach to communication. While there is a correlation between code and class, code switching can and does occur. Bernstein's point is that the economic and social conditions associated with class make it likely that the classes will use language differently much of the time.

Because of these differences, members of different classes may devalue each other's speech. To restricted-code users, those with elaborated codes may seem cold and stilted. To the elaborated-code user, restricted-code speakers may seem illogical and overly emotional; their slang may not be perceived as a bond but as a lack of precision. These differences can cause problems in cross-class communication. Think, for example, of how code differences might affect the relationship between a working-class child and a middle-class teacher.

Language and Gender: Instrumental and Expressive Talk

Gender may also play a part in language use. There have been many studies of male and female language patterns.[23] Men and women seem to have different vocabularies, in part because social rules focus their attention on different parts of the world. Women, for example, are reported to make finer color distinctions than men, while men have greater mechanical–technical vocabularies. It has also been suggested that women are more likely to use words such as *lovely, adorable, precious,* and *cute,* adjectives that some feel are trivial. Finally, women have been shown to use less intense words to express themselves. While men are often permitted to curse a blue streak, women have less freedom to do so.[24]

There also appear to be syntactic differences. Women tend to use more tag endings (fragments such as "right?" or "OK?" tacked on the end of sentences), qualifiers (words like *maybe* and *perhaps*) and disclaimers (sentences that ward off criticisms like "Well, I may be wrong, but . . .") While the use of these forms makes women seem more polite, it also makes them seem unsure of themselves.

BOX 7.2

Talking Tough in Teamsterville: Male Role Enactment in an Urban Community

Talk is not valued the same in every community. Some cultures encourage talk, while others inhibit it. But all develop strict rules about how to talk. In Teamsterville (the label for a blue-collar neighborhood in Chicago) talk is carefully regulated. The men in Teamsterville grow up with circumscribed ideas about the value of talk. Let's look at these ideas.

Teamsterville men know that talking in certain situations will cast doubt on their manliness. For example, self-disclosure or serious talk with women or children is not considered manly. Responding to an insult or to insubordination by talking it out is definitely bad form. The Teamsterville man demeans himself if he responds to a challenge verbally rather than physically. Teamsterville men also avoid talking to status superiors. Talk with authority figures or strangers is mediated through professional speakers like local precinct captains, Catholic parish priests, or union stewards.

When does the Teamsterville man feel free to converse? When he is with his male friends. The place most appropriate for speaking is the street, sidewalk, and to a lesser extent, the porch.

Teamsterville men devalue talk in cases where other men would value it. Compare Teamsterville rules with those followed by white-collar suburbanites or black Americans in urban ghettos. In both of

---

Finally, there are pragmatic differences. Talk concerned with getting things done, usually through an exchange of factual information, is **instrumental talk**. If a student needed to be directed to the registrar's office, it would be instrumental to say, "It's on the second floor of Job Hall. Make a left as you leave the office and follow the corridor through the next three buildings. Then take the stairs next to the reception area." Talk concerned with feelings is **expressive talk**. If you were to say to the same student, "You look like you're having a terrible day!" or "Cheer up; I'm sure everything will be fine," you would be using expressive talk. In general, women's speech uses more person-oriented expressive talk, while men's speech is more fact-oriented and instrumental.

Of course, not everyone fits the stereotype. Traditionally, however, women have been taught to be more polite and indirect than men, while men's speech has been "more literal, direct, and to the point. It employs stronger statements and forms that tend to press compliance, agreement, or belief on the listener."[25]

The point is not that one kind of speech is better than the other. Social and economic factors put varying pressures on us to use language to adapt to our assigned roles. As Barbara and Gene Eakins point out, "The damage comes when women and men cannot readily switch from one style to the other to meet the demands of the situation."[26] What seems to be called for today is more flexibility in language functions.

Language Confusions: A General Semantics Approach

The Sapir-Whorf hypothesis gives no specific analysis of English. For this, we must turn to an area known as **general semantics**, which

these cultures, being verbal is considered an advantage. The ghetto dweller takes pride in his ability to play word games like the dozens (see Box 13.1). The white suburbanite believes that talking things out is appropriate way of building relationships.

And the places for talk also differ by culture. Talk in an upper-middle-class suburb takes place in private, sheltered areas, in living rooms or backyards. Visitors are usually from outside a ten-block radius. Adults don't socialize on front porches or in front yards.

It might be tempting for some of us to consider Teamsterville men as linguistically deprived. That conclusion, however, misses the point. All of us are constrained by cultural norms for using language. All of us feel comfortable speaking in some situations and with some people, and uncomfortable elsewhere. The meaning and value of communication is set down for us by our culture.

Source: *Gerry Philipsen, "Speaking 'Like a Man' in Teamsterville: Cultural Patterns of Role Enactment in an Urban Neighborhood,"* Quarterly Journal of Speech *61 (1975): 13–22.*

ADDITIONAL READINGS

Hymes, Dell. "Models of the Interaction of Language and Social Life." In *Directions in Sociolinguistics: The Ethnography of Communication*. Edited by John J. Gumperz and Dell Hymes (New York: Holt, Rinehart and Winston, 1972).

Philipsen, Gerry. "Places for Speaking in Teamsterville." *Quarterly Journal of Speech* 62 (1976): 16–25.

describes some of the confusions in our language.[27]

One of the problems with English is that single words can have multiple meanings. Thus two people may believe they agree when in fact they are bypassing one another. Assume I say, "I want that report in the morning," and you say "Fine, it'll be on your desk." If what I mean by "morning" is 7 A.M. and what you mean is any time before noon, it is easy to see why I might label you as irresponsible and you might think of me as unreasonable.

One word that's used in multiple ways is the word *is*. Consider the following sentences: "It is raining outside"; "Green is the color of grass"; and "Joanna is immoral." These three sentences use the verb *to be* differently. In the first, *is* is a report of a fact about the world. In the second, *is* is a statement that's true by definition. In the third, *is* indicates a subjective opinion. Confusing them can mean trouble. If,

for example, we fail to understand how *is* is used in the third statement, we can confuse opinions with reality. Unfortunately, when we describe someone as being immoral, we may think we are stating a fact about their nature. But a person is not immoral in the same way that grass is green or rain is falling. When we say that Joanna is immoral, we really mean "Joanna has acted in a way that I find unacceptable given my value system at this time." We often confuse opinions with statements of fact.

Our language also encourages us to make static evaluations, to overlook the fact that people change and grow. Names often tend to make people appear more unchanging than they are. Sue at 12 and Sue at 19 are in many ways very different people. In some societies, when people reach crossroads in their lives, they are actually given new names. Our society generally does not mark change in this way, although if Sue should marry, she may take on

Through symbols we can refer to the fantastic and mythical as well as the mundane. (Detail of an imperial court robe, Chinese, T'ung Chih period, 1862–74)

you have ever been the victim of prejudices, you know the problems connected with false generalizations.

Finally, our language encourages polarized thinking, seeing things in either–or terms. In English most words have an easily identifiable opposite. We know, for example, that the opposite of *good* is *bad* and the opposite of *hot* is *cold*. While it is easy to identify these extremes, it is rather difficult to talk about anything in between. This characteristic of language is easy to demonstrate. Below are a series of continua. We have filled in one end; we ask you to fill in the other by writing in its opposite.

good _____ _____

hot _____ _____

virtue _____ _____

happy _____ _____

old _____ _____

male _____ _____

Now try to label the midpoints. (No fair using words like *sort of* or *semi* to modify the original words.) We're willing to bet it will be hard to do. Now try dividing the continua in half again. This should illustrate that our language encourages dichotomies and discourages graded thinking.

The general semanticists are fond of saying, "The map is not the territory." They mean by this that there are things about the world our language overlooks or discourages us from seeing. After all, a map is only a rough guide to the territory it covers. If we think that everything we talk about (everything on the map) exists in the way we talk about it, we are apt to be in error. Considering the differences between words and things may help us find ways of speaking more effectively.

General semanticists offer some guidelines for using language effectively. They tell us that

a new last name to mark her new status. Her husband, however, will retain his name as though nothing particularly different had happened to him.

Other words encourage us to make false generalizations. The word *all* is one. Our language makes it as easy to talk about "all the people who grew up on Long Island" as it is to talk about "all the books on Tom's top shelf." The difference, of course, is that I can verify statements about Tom's books by walking down the hall and looking. What I "know" about all the people born on Long Island is at best an inference and at worst a stereotype. If

if we mentally index and date words, we may remember to use them more accurately. By *indexing* they mean being aware, for example, that love$_1$ (my use of the word) may not be the same as love$_2$ (your use). *Dating* reminds us that things change over time, so morality$_{1958}$ is not confused with morality$_{1988}$. They also suggest that we put mental quotation marks around abstract words to remind us that they are symbolic constructs. "Reality" is a good example. Finally, they urge us to hyphenate words referring to objects that occur together in reality but are separated by language, such as *space–time*. Although actually using these devices would be awkward, thinking about them may alert us to potential problems.

IMPROVING MESSAGE COMPETENCE

To communicate effectively entails mastering all three parts of language: semantics, syntactics, and pragmatics. While all are important, pragmatics probably has the closest relationship to communication effectiveness.

Competent communicators are sensitive to pragmatic nuance, skilled at uncovering the meanings in others' messages, and flexible and creative in expressing their own. It is a fact of language that people usually say less than they mean and understand more than what is actually said. This means that as receivers, we must become adept at reading between the lines. We must be able to identify others' intentions correctly. This skill is partially a result of experience and partially a result of perceptual sensitivity, both of which can be increased and improved through practice.

As both senders and receivers, we must be sensitive to context. We cannot talk the same way in every situation; we cannot treat everyone identically. To do so is to ignore personal and social differences. The competent communicator is rhetorically sensitive, knowing how to phrase a message in different ways, depending on context.

The competent communicator is also cooperative. The general semanticists tell us that meanings are not in words but in people. We can modify that further by saying that meanings are not only in people, but in relationships. When we form relationships, we must coordinate our meanings with others', creating new ways of thinking and acting. If we are insensitive or inflexible, we will find ourselves at cross-purposes with one another. If we really communicate, we act as a unit, developing a shared speaking style that allows us to express mutual meanings.

REVIEW TERMS

The following is a list of major concepts introduced in this chapter. The page where the concept is first mentioned is listed in parentheses.

analogic code (156)
digital code (158)
symbol (158)
semantics (160)
denotative meaning (160)
connotative meaning (160)
syntactics (162)
syntactic meaning (162)
pragmatics (162)
speech act (162)
constitutive rule (163)
regulative rule (163)
episode (163)
relationship (163)
cultural pattern (165)
Sapir-Whorf hypothesis (166)
linguistic determinism (166)

SUGGESTED READINGS

Gleeson, Patrick, and Nancy Wakefield, eds. *Language and Culture*. Columbus, Ohio: Charles E. Merrill, 1968. An anthology containing important excerpts and short essays from writers like Sapir, Jespersen, Whorf, and Langer. Full of stimulating ideas and excellent examples of the relationship between language and culture.

Hayakawa, S. I. *Language in Thought and Action*, 4th ed. New York: Harcourt Brace Jovanovich, 1978. A representative and entertaining introduction to general semantics. The illustrations, exercises, and applications are still among the best in this area.

Keller, Helen. *The Story of My Life*. New York: Doubleday, 1905. If you haven't read this since you were in grade school, it bears a second look. If you've never read the book, then you should certainly do so. Mark Twain said that the two most interesting figures of the 19th century were Napoleon and Helen Keller.

Pearson, Judy Cornelia. *Gender and Communication*. Dubuque, Iowa: William C. Brown, 1985. There's a lot to be said about the relationship between language and gender. Pearson offers an up-to-date discussion of male–female differences in communication, including a discussion of how language produces images of men and women.

Slobin, Dan I. *Psycholinguistics*. Glenview, Ill.: Scott, Foresman, 1971. An intelligent and articulate discussion of such topics as language development, the nature of meaning, and the connection between language and cognition, as well as an excellent and easy-to-follow introduction to syntactics.

PROCESS TO PERFORMANCE

TOPICS FOR DISCUSSION

1. It has been said that we live in a symbolic universe made up not of physical things, but of things that can be talked about. Discuss this statement. Think of things important to you that do not have physical existence.

2. In what kinds of communication situations is it most appropriate to use analogic messages? In what situations are digital codes a better choice? Try to think of instances in which using the wrong code could lead to interpersonal problems.

3. During spoken communication, the verbal code is always accompanied to some extent by the analogic. Think of situations where the two codes could contradict or compete with one another. How could .this be avoided or solved?

4. Have you ever been involved in a conflict that arose because of a disagreement in connotative meaning? What happened and how did you resolve it?

5. Proper names often have strong connotations. We associate them with certain physical and mental characteristics. Do the following names have associations for you? If so, describe your idea of a(n): Leland,

MaryEllen, Justin, Bambi, Tad, Kristine, Jane, Billy Joe. Do you like your own name? If you could change it, what would you change it to and why? If you marry, will you be willing to change your last name to that of your spouse? (Men, answer this one too.)

6. Discuss ways that your life script limits your communication. What kinds of talk would you avoid because such talk would say something negative about you?

7. Think of several different groups of people. If you wanted to impress members of these groups, how would your language change? Are there episodes you would either avoid or try to enact for each of these groups? Are there certain speech acts that would be off limits for one of these groups but not for the others?

8. What strategies do you use when you find yourself in a social situation with no rule to tell you how to act? How would you suggest a person go about developing rule sets?

9. How can language be used to increase social solidarity and group cohesion? Give some examples. What is your reaction to this kind of language use?

10. General semanticists argue that our language's lack of precision is a severe drawback to rational thinking. Can you think of any value in imprecise or unoriginal remarks such as ambiguous statements or clichés?

OBSERVATION GUIDE

1. Keep a diary of interactions for half a day. Begin by making brief notes every time you speak to someone, indicating what it was you spoke about. Later, go back and indicate the function each fulfilled. Analyze how you typically use language. How much of your communication is spent in gaining or acquiring information? How much is spent in controlling or persuading others? Is your speech primarily expressive or instrumental?

2. Observe people talking in public places. Compare the topics discussed by all-male, all-female, and mixed couples. Compare the ways language is being used. Did you find any gender-related differences? If so, why do you think these differences exist, and how do you think they affect you?

3. Choose a recent conversation in which the outcome surprised you in some important way (examples: things turned out really bad; you didn't achieve the goals you wanted; things went far better than you had anticipated; and so on). Write a brief description of the situation and your relationship to the other person. Then write the conversation in **dialogue form** as accurately as you can. Place descriptions of gestures, tone of voice, and so on in parentheses.

Next apply the Coordinated Management of Meaning (CMM) model discussed in this chapter. Identify how *you* interpreted the various message exchanges in terms of:
a. the "speech act" as *intended* by the sender and/or *interpreted* by the receiver (the constitutive rule)
b. the antecedents and consequents influencing the production of each speech act (the regulative rule)
c. your definition of the "episode" and how that influenced message choices or interpretations

d. how you saw the "relationship" in this situation and how that influenced message choices or interpretations

e. how your own "life script" may have influenced message choices or interpretations

Follow this up by "taking the role of the other person" and trying to determine how he or she saw the same five elements (a–e above). Discuss how this analysis could help you handle similar situations more successfully in the future.

EXERCISES

1. According to Hayakawa (in Chapter 3 of *Language in Thought and Action*), there are differences between facts, inferences, and judgments. To Hayakawa, a fact can be directly verified; it is a report of something we have seen, heard, or felt. An inference is a statement about the unknown made on the basis of the known, and a judgment indicates an expression of approval or disapproval. Discuss the extent to which the following statements involve facts, inferences, and/or judgments. (See pp. 44–45 of Hayakawa's book for additional examples.)

a. She swore, threw the book across the room, and started to scream.

b. She was angry.

c. She is high-strung and bad-tempered.

d. Overweight people should not wear stripes, plaids, or excessively bright colors.

e. The grade-point averages of student athletes and student nonathletes are not significantly different.

f. Athletes are just as smart as nonathletes.

g. Poor people generally have lower morals than middle-class people.

h. And Adam lived an hundred and thirty years and begat a son in his likeness, after his image; and called his name Seth. (Genesis 5:3)

i. My lover is faithful to me.

j. X is the best-looking guy in my class.

k. The standard of living in the U.S.A. is one of the highest in the world.

2. Take a play, situation comedy, or soap opera script. For each line of dialogue, identify the speech act being performed. Indicate when a character switches from one speech act to another and when characters enter new episodes. Analyze how you would portray the character. What relationships does your character have with the others? How would you describe each character's life script? How would you say each line to make clear the meaning of the dialogue? How could nonverbal codes help to increase the effectiveness of your portrayal?

3. Below you will find a scale used to measure connotative meanings. According to Charles Osgood, its originator, whenever we come in contact with an object, we (1) evaluate its goodness; (2) judge its potency; and (3) decide how active it is. The first two items below are evaluative; the next three measure potency; and the final three measure activity. By asking people to fill out this scale for any given concept, you can get a sense of what the concept means to them.

Semantic Differential Scale

Concept: _____

For each set of adjectives below, circle the number which best indicates where you would locate the meaning of the concept listed above.

good 1	2	3	4	5	6	7	bad
valuable 1	2	3	4	5	6	7	worthless
large 1	2	3	4	5	6	7	small
strong 1	2	3	4	5	6	7	weak
heavy 1	2	3	4	5	6	7	light
active 1	2	3	4	5	6	7	passive
fast 1	2	3	4	5	6	7	slow
hot 1	2	3	4	5	6	7	cold

a. Choose a partner. Think of a number of common activities and objects; for example: playing tennis, mountains, snakes, church, demolition derby, marriage. Individually, fill out semantic differentials for each concept. Compare your semantic profiles. Discuss how you came to have these associations. How might your meanings affect your interpersonal relationships?

b. Take the name of any product, say "oatmeal" or "potting soil." Ask at least 20 people to fill out a semantic differential scale on the product. Compile the average scores for the evaluation, activity, and potency dimensions. Now plan an advertising campaign for the product. You want to increase those dimensions of meaning on which your product is low. Come up with a plan to give the product more favorable connotations. How could music, color, camera movement, narration, and so on make your product appear better, more potent, and more active?

CHAPTER EIGHT

Degas, who knew the Bellelli family, captured their dynamics in this
portrait. Posture, costume, touch, facial expressions—all reveal alienation
between husband and wife, as one of the daughters attempts to bridge the
gap. Try analyzing snapshots of your own family. Do they reveal
relationships? (Edgar Degas, *La Famille Bellelli*)

AFFECTING OTHERS: SENDING RELATIONAL MESSAGES

T HE FOLLOWING TAKES place at a company picnic. The hero is Johnson, who has been with the firm for only a few months. Not knowing anyone, he gravitates toward his immediate supervisor. While they are chatting, the vice-president for planning, Mr. Bigelow, comes up.

BIGELOW: *(ignoring Johnson and speaking directly to the supervisor)* Hope you didn't have any money on last night's game. Did I call it, or did I call it?

(Our hero stands forgotten as his two superiors discuss the game. When a lull occurs, the supervisor remembers to introduce him.)

BIGELOW: *(with obvious lack of interest)* Nice to meet you, Jackson.

JOHNSON: *(wondering if it is appropriate to correct a vice-president)* Very glad to meet you sir. Actually, my name is . . .

BIGELOW: *(cutting in)* I've heard good things about you. Keep up the good work. I'm always on the lookout for enterprising young men with fresh ideas. You'll find my door is always open.

JOHNSON: *(seizing his opportunity to offer a fresh idea)* You know, sir, one idea I've been considering . . .

BIGELOW: Right, fine. *(Turning to the supervisor)* What we need is a drink. So how about those Mets! Think they have a chance?

(Deep in conversation, the supervisor and vice-president move off toward the refreshments, leaving our employee feeling distinctly foolish. Just then, Johnson is hailed by a vaguely familiar figure whom he finally places as a fellow worker, Frazier.)

FRAZIER: Hey Johnson, how ya doing? See you got to meet Mr. Big. Did he by any chance tell you *(imitating Bigelow)* "I'm always on the lookout for enterprising men with fresh ideas?"

(Both men laugh.)

FRAZIER: Glad to see you. I read your report and, while I think you're dead wrong, I found it interesting. Let me buy you a beer while I give you the benefit of my experience. Your first mistake . . .

JOHNSON: *(surprisingly, beginning to warm up*

to Frazier) Wait just a minute. What mistake? My plan is excellent. You're going to have to do some hard talking to convince me I'm off base.

The two men spend the next hour arguing, and Johnson leaves feeling he is finally being accepted in the organization.

How did it happen that Johnson felt better about himself when he was challenged than when he was complimented? Why was the cordial conversation with the vice-president less pleasant than the argument with the brash young coworker? In this chapter, we'll try to answer these questions. We'll look at the kinds of relational messages we send and the way these messages affect us. We'll also examine the way relational patterns define and constrain interactions.

WHAT ARE RELATIONAL MESSAGES?

In the situation above, two kinds of messages were being sent simultaneously: content and relational messages. **Content messages** consist of what is actually said about a topic. They are what we would transcribe if we were precisely recording an interaction. In the situation with Mr. Bigelow, the content consisted of a compliment. In the conversation with Frazier, it was a criticism. In our scenario, however, something else was happening that was more important to Johnson than content. Relational messages were being sent.

The Nature of Relational Messages

Relational messages are cues that tell us what sort of a message a content message is to be taken as.[1] They let us know whether a statement is a put-down, a sincere overture of friendship, a sarcasm, or a joke. They indicate the speech acts behind the content. By telling us how to interpret a speaker's comments, they let us know what a speaker thinks of us. As Paul Watzlawick, Janet Bavelas, and Don Jackson point out, every message "not only conveys information but . . . at the same time it imposes behavior."[2] To understand how relational messages impose behavior, let's turn to another example.

You're at your high school reunion. An old rival sees you. She stares at you for a minute, looks at your brand-new outfit with thinly veiled amusement, and adjusts her impeccably tailored jacket. She glances briefly at her date, shrugs her shoulders almost imperceptibly, and drawls, "Great to see you. Care to join us?" Without saying anything directly, she has indicated her high opinion of herself and her low opinion of you. She has also indicated what she hopes you will do. The unspoken message is clear: "I'm inviting you to join us only because my manners are as well tailored as my suit. I hope, however, you will have the good grace to refuse."

Now let's rewrite the scene, this time supplying you with an old friend. She sees you, her eyes light up, and a big smile crosses her face. She gives you a hug, stands back and looks you up and down. Keeping her arm around your shoulder, she guides you toward her date. "Great to see you. Care to join us?" This time you know you're sincerely wanted, and you accept with pleasure. Although the content message was the same, there was a world of difference on the relational level.

Sending Relational Messages

Relational messages are often conveyed indirectly and may therefore escape our attention. They are easiest to read when signaling a change in mood. For example, when a parent,

Relational messages are often subtle and complex, not readily deciphered by outsiders. The meanings in the scene are highly charged yet enigmatic. What do you think the relationship is between these three figures? (Piazetta, *Il fiorellin d'amore*)

exasperated by his child's behavior, finally loses patience, the child usually responds to the relational shift. He can tell that this time, when Father says "Go to bed," there is an additional relational message that says "And I mean it!"

In most cases, relational messages recede into the background. If a couple is getting along, their relational messages may acknowledge that fact, saying, in effect, "Our relationship is going fine. Let's keep it as it is." In fact, in most healthy relationships, attention is directed to content, and relational meanings are scarcely noticed. Troubled relationships, however, "are characterized by a constant struggle about the nature of the relationship, with the content aspect of communication becoming less and less important."[3]

Relational messages are often sent unconsciously, through nonverbal channels. In their classic work on the subject, Watzlawick and his colleagues equate content messages with verbal statements, and relational messages with nonverbal behaviors. While people generally convey relational matters through unspoken dialogue, direct relational talk is possible.[4] When we tell someone how much we care, or when we give them direct orders, the relational message is stated directly.

BOX 8.1

The Children of Bulldogs Banks: A Study of the Development of Group Culture

In 1945, six German-Jewish orphans arrived in England and took up residence in a country house named Bulldogs Banks. Their parents had been killed by the Nazis when the six were infants; they had subsequently been passed from refugee to refugee until becoming inmates of the Ward for Motherless Children in the Tereszin concentration camp. They lived there for about two and a half years, until the camp was liberated by the Russians. At the time of their entry into England, they ranged in age from three to nearly four years. None had ever known any life but a group setting; they had never experienced anything remotely resembling a normal family. Nevertheless, they forged strong bonds, creating their own relational culture.

The one thing that was clearest when they arrived at Bulldogs Banks is that they "cared greatly for one another and not at all for anybody or anything else." Adults were virtually nonexistent, except as the source of basic necessities. They lived entirely for one another and could not bear to be separated for more than a few minutes. While it is normal for children of this age to show jealousy, rivalry, and competition, the children of Bulldogs Banks were remarkably altruistic. If one child was given a treat, he couldn't be happy until all of the others were also given treats. For example, when Paul was offered a pony ride, a treat he had looked forward to, he cried because the others couldn't go. Since Ruth didn't like to go for walks, the others would often give up this privilege (one they all enjoyed) to stay with her.

They were extremely solicitous of each other. All would spontaneously share food, willingly giving away the largest and choicest portions. When one child was unhappy or afraid, the others would try to comfort him. One day, for example, John refused to get up, crying uncontrollably. All of the children were concerned, refusing to leave him. Ruth brought his clothes, urging him "Why don't you put them on?" while Miriam gave him her favorite doll and smiled sweetly until he calmed down. Their degree of identification with one another was intense. Leah came to Bulldogs Banks six months later than the others. When she arrived, the others reverted to earlier behaviors (speaking only German, acting wild and uncontrolled) for about a week, giving

Relational Messages and Relational Definitions

When relational messages accumulate, they lead to **relational definitions**; that is, they give us an overall sense of who we are to one another. Relational definitions are mental models that label and classify relationships and specify how members should treat one another. As we get to know other people, we let them know what we think about them. We indicate the degree of affection we feel, the amount of attention we expect, and the kind of commitment we're willing to make. These messages define who we are as a unit and guide our behaviors.

For example, two individuals may arrive at the following relational understanding: "We are close but not intimate. We feel affection and trust but are not romantically involved. We are friends." Once they define themselves in this way, they will be bound by the norms and obligations of friendship and will try to act as friends should. Their relational definition will direct future behaviors.

The interpersonal literature describes relational definitions in a number of ways. Two of

of the fears a normal three-year-old shows. Since adults were unimportant, they couldn't catch their fears from adults; they also had the group as protection. Children who grow up with parents often compete for parental attention. Without any idea of what a mother or father was, they turned their love toward each other and created their own patterns of interaction.

Source: *Anna Freud and Sophie Dann, "An Experiment in Group Upbringing,"* The Psychoanalytic Study of the Child, *vol. 6 (New York: International Universities Press, 1951), pp. 167–97.*

ADDITIONAL READINGS

Burlingham, Dorothy T. *Twins.* London: Imago, 1951.

Freud, Anna, and Dorothy Burlingham. *Infants without Families.* New York: International Universities Press, 1944.

her a chance to adapt to her new surroundings.

There was no identifiable dominance hierarchy. Rather, the children formed an intensely cohesive group with shifting leadership patterns. Although they had their personal favorites (Paul and Miriam were especially close, and Leah was least liked), they all stuck up for one another. There was almost no physical aggression, and verbal arguments generally trailed off or were redirected toward a nearby adult. The only child who showed any "normal" signs of sibling rivalry was Ruth, who was also the only child who had formed any mother attachments during her days in the camp.

The group was remarkably free of anxieties. Although intensely afraid of dogs and vans (fears from the concentration camp experience), they had few

---

the most important equate relational definitions with cultures and with contracts.

Relationship As Culture

Culture, in its most general sense, is an acquired set of beliefs, attitudes, and values that people use to interpret their world and guide their actions. As we have seen in other chapters, cultural understandings are necessary for social harmony. While it isn't hard to grasp what culture is, it *is* hard to decide on the boundaries between cultures. Sometimes we use the term to refer to very large groupings (for example, Western versus Asian culture); other times we use it to refer to smaller groups (for instance, punk rockers or IBM employees). Julia Wood has suggested that if two people develop common orientations and behaviors, they can form their own **relational culture**.[5]

Like larger cultures, relational cultures guide members' perceptions of the world. Members of relational cultures create shared constructs, schemata, and scripts. They develop common language habits and codes of conduct. All the mechanisms that allow larger cultural units to develop work in miniature within relationships. Understanding a relationship, therefore, involves uncovering and analyzing these mechanisms.

Sometimes relational cultures mirror larger cultural patterns; sometimes, when individuals are cut off from "normal" society, they manufacture their own unique patterns. Box 8.1 describes how six children, separated from their families in infancy, created a culture that helped them survive the ravages of war.

Relationships As Contracts

The cultural metaphor is not the only way to think of relational definitions. A number of theorists have used a contract-negotiation metaphor to explain relationships. Robert Carson sees relationships this way.[6] When people negotiate a legal contract, they state what they expect to receive from one another, indicate mutual obligations, and outline any exceptions or contingency clauses. Carson tells us that the same thing happens implicitly during the negotiation of a **relational contract**. "The members of the dyad never quite state the 'rules' under which they are operating, but the rules are there nevertheless, and they are often followed in an utterly reliable fashion by both parties."[7]

A couple, Amy and Mark, might develop their contract in the following way. Amy tries out a behavior, perhaps by disclosing details of her past and expecting Mark do the same. He, however, may nonverbally back off, change the subject, or refuse to respond. He wants a clause added to the contract: "There should be boundaries placed on what we discuss. Our pasts should be off limits." Amy may be willing to abide by this rule in most instances but may wish to add the condition "when a self-disclosure can help us understand or solve a problem, then we should talk about the past." If Mark agrees, the amended version becomes part of their unstated contract.

When this rule is coupled with other rules concerning privacy and involvement, a general definition of the depth–superficiality dimension of their relationship is arrived at. Although Mark and Amy may not realize they have negotiated a contract and may not be able to list its rules, they can usually sum up their general understanding. For example, they may agree that "We respect each other's privacy." In Carson's terms they have negotiated part of an overall "master contract" that defines their relational identity. In Wood's terms, one part of the relational culture has been specified. Whatever metaphor we use—culture or contract—the fact remains that couples build up all kinds of unstated rules, normative standards, role definitions, and relational labels.

Our definitions are often strongly influenced by outside sources. For example, we may try to follow religious or community-based images of "good" relationships. And whether we rebel against them or try to follow them, family models are also important to intimate bonds. Regardless of where our original definitions come from, when we enter relationships, we present them to our partners, and they are accepted, rejected, or modified.

THE CONTENT OF RELATIONAL MESSAGES

While only a few years ago it was assumed that the range of relational topics was quite narrow, current research shows that they are much more varied and complex than we first thought.[8] For example, Judee Burgoon and Jerold Hale have identified seven major and five minor **relational themes**. Their research indicates that we communicate about the following issues: dominance–submission, emotional arousal,

TABLE 8.1

Types of relational messages

1. **Dominance–Submission**
   "In this relationship I want to take control."
   "In this relationship I want to relinquish control."
2. **Emotional Arousal**
   "I am actively involved in and excited about what is happening."
   "I feel passive and unresponsive."
3. **Composure**
   "With you I am relaxed and in control of myself."
   "With you I am tense and out of control."
4. **Similarity**
   "We are like one another; we have something in common."
   "We are different; we have nothing in common."
5. **Formality**
   "Our relationship is guided by formal, cultural-level rules."
   "Our relationship is guided by informal, individual rules."
6. **Task–Social Orientation**
   "Our primary focus should be on the task at hand."
   "Our primary focus should be on each other and our relationship."
7. **Intimacy**
   "We are closely bound by ties of attachment and involvement."
   "We have little attachment; we are not close."
   a. **Affection–Hostility**
      "I feel positive emotions toward you."
      "I feel negative emotions toward you."
   b. **Trust**
      "I know that you won't hurt me."
      "I fear that you will harm me."
   c. **Depth–Superficiality**
      "I wish you to know personal things about me."
      "I wish to keep myself hidden from you."
   d. **Inclusion–Exclusion**
      "I wish to be with you."
      "I wish to be distant from you."
   e. **Intensity of Involvement**
      "You are a central focus of my thoughts and feelings."
      "You are of no interest to me."

Adapted from Judee K. Burgoon and Jerold L. Hale, "The Fundamental Topoi of Relational Communication," *Communication Monographs* 51 (1984): 193–214.

Status and dominance are relational messages conveyed in many ways. Posture, facial expression, costume, and position all indicate clearly which of these three figures has the highest status.

composure, similarity, formality, task–social orientation, and intimacy.[9] Table 8.1 gives examples of these relational topics. We'll examine each in more detail.

Sending Dominance Messages

Of all the relational messages identified, messages concerned with dominance have received the most attention. These messages focus on control, telling us "who has the right to direct, delimit, and define" the actions of a dyad.[10] They tell us who is in charge.

It is common to talk about three types of dominance messages. Those that indicate a desire to take control or limit the action of others are called **one-up messages**. During conversations, they often take the form of denials, disagreements, interruptions, topic changes, and the like. Messages that indicate a desire to give in or relinquish one's freedom are called **one-down messages**. Agreeing, acquiescing, giving up the floor, or allowing the other to direct the conversation are examples. Finally, statements indicating equivalence or not implying control are **one-across messages**.

Communication researchers often find it useful to code conversations in order to examine dominance patterns. Commonly, they indicate one-up messages with a ↑ , one-down messages with a ↓ , and one-across messages with a →.[11] Coding dominance isn't difficult. To see for yourself, code the following dialogue. Be sure to consider how what is said relates to the rest of the conversation. To code the interaction, place the appropriate arrow next to each statement.

(   ) ALLAN: Well, I'd say that you make most of the decisions about household matters.

(   ) LOU: Yes, I guess I do.

(   ) ALLAN: Sure you do. You have complete freedom because I trust your judgment.

(   ) LOU: Yes, I . . .

(   ) ALLAN: (interrupting) For example, when you decided to paint the den green, did I say anything?

(   ) LOU: No. Sorry about that.

We've made your task easy. The control pattern here is not subtle. Allan's comments are all one-ups. Even though he says that Lou has control, his style belies his words. He takes control of the conversation, interrupts Lou, and finishes Lou's sentences. Allan is clearly

These women don't have to say a word to indicate their smug narrow-minded approach to life. Their relational messages clearly convey their attitudes. (Grant Wood, *Daughters of Revolution*, 1932)

saying, "I'm the one in charge." Lou is clearly in the one-down position and appears to be saying, "Go ahead. I'll follow your lead."

Talk, of course, isn't the only way to indicate dominance. Many behaviors demonstrate control. The executive who picks up the chalk at a meeting and stands in front of the blackboard signals her desire to direct the group. Conversely, the person who takes an inconspicuous seat in the back of the room may be trying to avoid taking control.

Indicating Emotional Tone

In the Burgoon and Hale system, two themes indicate emotion: emotional arousal and composure. Emotional arousal refers to how responsive we are to others; it lets others know whether we are excited or bored. People generally find it easy to read arousal cues. And often arousal is contagious. Talking to someone who is excited can increase our excitement level, while trying to tell a joke to an apathetic listener can dampen our enthusiasm. As Burgoon and Hale point out, arousal messages can "run the gamut from highly manic activities to complete passivity (as when sleeping)."[12]

Composure, the other common emotional theme, indicates self-control. It shows we're capable of calmness and detachment, that we won't give way or fall apart. Sometimes such an attitude can seem cold, for it says, in effect, "I can control my emotions and act with poise. Nothing you do will cause me to react emotionally." In most cases, however, we value those with composure and draw on their strength. Although composure and emotional arousal may seem to be simple opposites, Burgoon and

Hale believe they are separate relational dimensions, for "it is possible for someone to be both highly aroused and highly controlled (as when expressing contempt) or nonaroused and uncomposed (as when showing restless boredom)."[13]

Showing Similarity

Similarity, another important relational cue, has powerful effects on attraction and credibility.[14] Although we often hear that opposites attract, research shows that it is more often the case that birds of a feather flock together. People generally seek out others who are similar in appearance and actions to themselves. If you doubt this, ask yourself how willing you are to communicate with someone whose behavior is totally different from yours or what your first reaction is to people who look strange. Most people find it difficult to deal with the odd or unusual.

Defining Episodes

Because we need to know what kinds of rules to follow, we usually scan episodes for formality cues. In formal episodes, we stick to general, cultural-level rules of conduct, while in informal episodes we can deviate from these rules and act more naturally.

In shared work situations, we must also decide on the level of task–social orientation we wish to maintain. We need to let our partners know whether we intend to stick to business or have fun. For example, assume you have been assigned a very attractive lab partner in a tough science course. You must decide whether to concentrate on work or whether to spend time getting to know your partner. This involves some fairly tricky relational negotiations, for if you set the wrong tone, both task and social outcomes can be adversely affected.

Indicating Intimacy

The relational message with the greatest potential to define a relationship is probably that of intimacy. Intimacy messages are central to the growth and development of interpersonal trajectories. Whether our goal is to create a private relationship or to maintain distance, we must control intimacy cues. Perhaps because they're so important, intimacy cues are often hard to express directly. We sometimes become awkward and tongue-tied when we try to convey closeness and concern.

Intimacy messages are complex. Burgoon and Hale have wisely broken intimacy down into subcategories, each describing a different dimension of attachment and involvement. Some of the most vital intimacy messages are those that signal affection–hostility. Very early in our lives we learn how to identify anger and love. Children become adept at knowing how far their parents can be pushed before affection turns to annoyance. Messages along the affection–hostility dimension are easy to decode, perhaps because they are usually conveyed by a number of channels working in concert.

Another key intimacy dimension is trust. People who are trusting are open to risk; they let others know how vulnerable they are, willingly placing themselves in positions where they may be hurt. People who are trustworthy won't exploit others' vulnerabilities. We know that relationships don't progress very far toward intimacy unless those involved are both trustworthy and trusting.

Depth–superficiality is another intimacy dimension. It indicates the extent to which partners are willing to give each other access to personal information. In intimate relationships, participants engage in self-disclosure. Those who refuse to open themselves to others indicate that they prefer to keep the relationship at a nonintimate public level.

Closely related to depth–superficiality is the inclusion–exclusion dimension of intimacy. Messages that fall along this continuum indicate a willingness to associate with others. People generally described as "warm" or "welcoming" are indicating inclusion. Those described as "cold" may be giving off exclusion messages.

Finally, intimacy is signaled by intensity of involvement. If you are intensely involved with someone, he or she is central to you, the focus of all your attention. If you are uninterested, unwilling to listen, or inattentive, involvement is minimal.

Intimacy, then, is a complex blend of many factors that can combine in different ways. When people are in love, for example, all of the positive aspects of intimacy work together. Lovers convey affection, trust, openness, closeness, and intensity of involvement. This, however, is only one form of intimacy. Many other combinations are possible. For example, people are sometimes bound together by mutual hostility. Intimacy is not an all-or-nothing affair. To indicate the kind and degree of our intimacy, we send many relational messages.

In your own way, you are always sending relational messages. The way you stand and move, your facial expressions and gestures, let others know what you think of and want from them. Check out the messages you send. Ask a friend to describe your relational style. You may be sending messages you don't mean to.

HOW RELATIONAL MESSAGES AFFECT US

One of the most important aspects of relational messages is that they affect receivers' self-concepts. When we tell others how we feel about them, we can either enhance or diminish their feelings of self-worth. Let's look at some of the ways relational messages affect identity.

Confirming and Disconfirming Messages

One of the best discussions of the relationship between interpersonal communication and self-concept is given by Evelyn Sieburg. She argues that whenever we communicate with people, we present them with a version of ourselves.[15] Their response invariably tells us something about the success of this self-presentation. Responses that make us value ourselves more are known as **confirming messages**. Those that make us devalue ourselves are known as **disconfirming messages**. Although each dyad is unique, Sieburg felt it was possible to identify responses that confirm and disconfirm most people. Table 8.2 (p. 190) defines and gives examples of these responses.

To understand these responses better, let's look again at the scenario that opened this chapter. Johnson, the new employee, was anxious to make a good impression on his boss by presenting the best self possible. Bigelow's responses served to disconfirm him in several ways. By failing to acknowledge Johnson's presence, Bigelow was being impervious. He told him, in effect, "You are not worth noticing." By failing to match his tone of voice to his cordial words, he confused Johnson. Bigelow's words and actions were incongruous.

Bigelow also interrupted Johnson, cutting him off in mid-sentence. Furthermore, he changed the subject when Johnson began to talk. Because Bigelow minimally acknowledged Johnson's contribution before he took the conversation in another direction, his response was tangential rather than totally irrelevant. Bigelow's tendency to hide behind impersonal clichés was also disconfirming because it kept Johnson at a distance. About the only thing

TABLE 8.2

A taxonomy of confirming and disconfirming messages

Disconfirming responses	Definition	Example
Impervious	When B fails to acknowledge, even minimally, A's message	A: Hi! B: (continues working, ignoring A)
Interrupting	When B cuts A's message short	A: So then I . . . B: Nice chatting with you. Bye!
Irrelevant	When B's response is unrelated to what A has been saying	A: So then he left me. B: I'm thinking of going to Bermuda on break.
Tangential	When B acknowledges A's message but immediately takes the talk in another direction	A: I just don't know what to do. B: Gee, too bad. Have you seen my new car?
Impersonal	When B conducts a monologue or uses nonimmediate, cliché-ridden, overintellectual language	A: How can I improve my grade, professor? B: Adequate classroom performance is a function of cognitive and affective integration.
Incoherent	When B's response is rambling and difficult to follow	A: Tell me what's wrong. B: Well, uh, see, it's a . . . gosh, hard to say.
Incongruous	When B's nonverbal and verbal messages are contradictory	A: Are you angry with me? B: No. Of course not. Why should I be? (said sarcastically)

Confirming responses	Definition	Example
Direct acknowledgment	When B reacts directly to A's message	A: Can we talk? B: Of course. Come over.
Agreement about content	B reinforces opinions offered by A	A: I've definitely noticed a change in Joe lately. B: Yes. I have too.
Supportive	B expresses understanding and reassurance to A	A: I feel just awful. B: I understand. I think you did the right thing.
Clarifying	B tries to clarify A's message	A: I'm not sure what to do about it. B: So you're confused and upset, is that it?
Expression of positive feeling	B expresses positive feelings about A's message	A: No, I think we should tell him about it. B: Now I know what you mean. Good idea!

Adapted from Frank E. X. Dance and Carl E. Larson, *Speech Communication, Concepts and Behavior* (New York: Holt, Rinehart and Winston, 1972), pp. 141–43.

Bigelow did not do was become tongue-tied and flustered, a response that would have signaled incoherence. No wonder Johnson felt unhappy about the meeting. He felt he was being told, "You are unimportant and unworthy."

One of the reasons Johnson liked Frazier was that Frazier used no disconfirmations. Although he disagreed with Johnson, he did so in a way that said, "You are a worthy opponent. I may not agree with you completely, but I respect you." As you can see in Table 8.2, there are a number of responses that lead people to value themselves more. These confirming responses include direct acknowledgment, agreement about content, showing support, clarifying responses, and expression of positive feeling. All of these are ways to improve another's self-concept.

Paradoxes and Double Binds

Contradictory messages are called paradoxes, and repeated exposure to them can cause us to doubt the validity of our own perceptions. There are two kinds of paradoxes that can damage the self-image: paradoxical definitions and paradoxical injunctions.[16]

In **paradoxical definitions**, speakers present themselves in contradictory ways. A classic example is the statement "I am a liar." If the speaker is really a liar, then the statement must be true. But a speaker who describes himself truthfully cannot be a liar. If this is confusing, you have the idea. Paradoxical messages always confuse us; they challenge our belief in rationality and consistency. And what is oddest about them is that although it is the speaker who is being illogical, it is the receiver who feels confused and disconfirmed. Any time a message is delivered that defines a relationship in contradictory ways ("I am your friend but I don't want to be around you," "I respect your

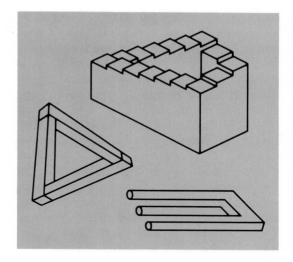

For most people inconsistencies and paradoxes are vaguely unsettling. Although the impossible figures drawn here fascinate us, they also confuse and disconcert our sense of reality.

ideas but I can't support them"), it can be considered to be a paradoxical definition.

Another kind of paradox, a **paradoxical injunction**, gives us an impossible order, one that must be disobeyed in order to be obeyed. "Stop giving in to me" is a good example. If you obey the command, you are giving in. If you refuse to give in, you are giving in because you are obeying the injunction. Other examples are "Dominate me!"; "Be spontaneous"; "Disagree with everything I say"; and "Love me for myself, not because I ask you to." While paradoxes may be fun to think about if you like brain teasers, during interaction they are much less benign. They undermine our belief in logic and put us in a situation where we're "damned if we do and damned if we don't."

Imagine that you are a child whose mother says to you, "I want you to be more affectionate." But when you show affection by trying to touch her, she stiffens and backs off. Or you are a young adult whose father tells you, "I want you to be independent and have a life of your own." But when you do strike out on your own, he develops severe chest pains. Such a situation, where there is no "correct" response, is called a **double bind**.[17] In a true double bind: (1) the relationship between the two people involved must be an intense and important one; (2) the "victim" must be presented with a contradictory injunction; and (3) he or she must have no way of escaping, either by recognizing the paradoxical nature of the message or by withdrawing from the interaction. The victim must react, although reacting "correctly" is impossible.

Imagine being the victim of a habitual double bind, with no way of returning to a more logical world. After a while, this kind of treatment could make you question your own sanity. You might begin to act in ways normal people would consider "crazy." Even mild cases of contradictory behavior can be upsetting. Some people habitually use sarcasms and jokes so that we're never really sure what they think of us. For most of us, this is disquieting, for we can't be sure whether we are being accepted or not. These kinds of messages are also double binding.[18]

PRAGMATIC PATTERNS AND RELATIONAL SEQUENCES

While we react strongly to others' relational messages, our own are often invisible. How then can we diagnose communication problems? The only real way is to pay more attention to our own actions. By uncovering repetitive sequences of behavior, we can often discover why our relationships are going the way they are.

Looking for Meaning in Patterns

Before we begin discussing pragmatic patterns, there are three points to consider. All three have been implicit in our previous discussions.

1. *Relational definitions are created not by a single individual, but by both members of a relationship working together.* The fact that one person has a domineering personality does not necessarily mean that she will be a dominant member in all her relationships. Her partner has a great deal to do with how dominance–submission patterns get worked out.

2. *To understand relational definitions, we need to become aware of patterns of behavior.* In relationships certain sequences of acts become favored and repeated over time. To diagnose a relationship, we need to uncover these patterns of repeated acts.

3. Participants often blame the patterns they do recognize on their partners. *It is generally unproductive to blame individuals for the way a relationship progresses;* it is more productive to place any blame on co-created patterns.

These points are part of a perspective developed by researchers known as the Palo Alto group.[19] These researchers, primarily psychotherapists, wanted to learn why some relationships were so destructive. They felt the answer could be found in communication patterns. While our interest is with a more normal range of behaviors than those investigated by the Palo Alto group, the insights they provide can quite easily be applied to everyday interaction.

Patterns versus People: The Locus of Dyadic Communication

The Palo Alto group argues that when people enter a relationship, it is the relationship itself that most affects them, not their individual personalities. With some people we are relaxed and happy; with others we are at our absolute worst. Does this mean our personalities change when we are with different people? The Palo Alto group says no. What changes is our communication system. To understand relationships, we must understand the behaviors that make up the dyadic system.

But how do we go about looking at behaviors that are usually invisible? What should we look for? First, we should look at sequences rather than individual acts. Unless we know how an individual act is connected to other behaviors, we cannot understand its relational meaning. Let's take an example. Suppose you hear a laugh. Can you assume that it means someone is happy? Of course not. It all depends on what happened before. The laugh may have been an appreciative response to a good joke. Or it may have been a scornful response to a desperate request. The smallest unit to carry relational meaning is not a single act, but at least two acts in sequence, or what is called an **interact**.[20]

To understand a relationship fully, we must often look at a number of interacts. Let's assume that the laugh we heard followed an apology. To understand this interact's relational meaning, we must connect it to other interacts. Perhaps the following scenario applies. Lee habitually gets mad and insults Adam. When this happens, Adam usually responds by threatening to leave Lee, who, terrified that Adam will make good on the threat, begs for forgiveness. At that point, Adam scornfully laughs at Lee, which causes the whole process to start over. The laugh takes on a sinister aspect in this scenario, for it is clear that the sequence is a disturbed one.

Of course, this unpleasant pattern is not the only explanation for the apology–laugh. Perhaps when tired, Lee acts irritably but usually realizes and apologizes immediately. Adam, understanding this, laughs good-naturedly to let Lee know everything is OK. A very different meaning can now be assigned to the laugh. The point here is that we can understand and control relationships best by looking for patterns. If necessary, we can then intervene to break the pattern.

The Problem of Punctuation

Even among people who can identify patterns, there is often a stumbling block to solving them: the tendency to **punctuate** sequences inappropriately. In grammar, punctuation marks are ways of dividing words into units that belong together. In punctuating a sentence, we use a capital letter to show where it begins. When we punctuate a relational sequence, we do essentially the same thing. We decide where it begins.

Let's consider an example that occurs often in real life, although the position of husband and wife may be reversed. A couple is locked in a pattern in which the wife, feeling ignored, nags at her husband. The husband responds to this attack by withdrawing. The more he withdraws, the more she nags, and the more she nags, the more he withdraws. They are enmeshed in a self-perpetuating pattern.[21]

Even if they recognize what's going on, they may spend all their energy arguing over who started it. The wife punctuates the sequence by saying it was the husband's fault. The husband punctuates it by saying he withdrew only because she began it all by nagging. Of course, none of this does any good; the conflict only worsens.

Types of Patterns

Although each dyad works out its own relational patterns, some occur with enough frequency that they can be labeled and described. In this section we will review several common relational patterns.

Complementarity and Symmetry

One of the easiest ways to classify patterns of interacts is to consider whether they are similar or different in relational meaning. When the acts in a sequence are relationally opposite, we have what is called a **complementary pattern**. A sequence characterized by a repeated pattern of one-ups followed by one-downs would be so labeled. A pattern consisting of acts that are similar is called a **symmetrical pattern**. If such a pattern consists entirely of one-ups, it is considered to be an example of **competitive symmetry**. If it includes only one-downs, it is **submissive symmetry**. Look at the following conversations and see if you can tell which is complementary, which is competitively symmetrical, and which is submissively symmetrical.

Conversation 1

JOAN: Let's begin by defining the problem.

JANE: OK, that's fine.

JOAN: We'll make a chart showing all the negative forces.

JANE: Sounds good. Should I . . .

JOAN: No, I'll do it. Hand me that paper.

JANE: OK.

Conversation 2

JOAN: Let's begin by defining the problem.

JANE: We did that last time; we don't have time now.

JOAN: We need to review it. I'll make a chart . . .

JANE: You can do that later. Anyone have any solutions?

JOAN: Wait a minute! Who made you the expert?

JANE: Don't be a jerk!

Conversation 3

JOAN: How would you like to begin?

JANE: Whatever you suggest is just fine.

JOAN: I'll agree with whatever you say.

JANE: No, really, you decide.

JOAN: I'd be happy to go along with what you think.

JANE: I really have no preference.

It's not very difficult to label these conversations. The first is complementary. Joan takes control and Jane acquiesces. Their control behaviors are opposite and therefore complement one another. Conversation 2 is characterized by competitive symmetry. Here both Joan and Jane want to direct the activity. Such a conversation may signal a fight for leadership. The final conversation illustrates submissive symmetry. Although the two seem agreeable, they are actually in a contest to see who can force the other to take control.

Is one sequence better than the others? Not really. Although the complementary relationship shows the least amount of disagreement, it's not necessarily the best. Habitual complementarity can trap participants in rigid roles. When we are young, it is natural for our relationship with our parents to be complementary. But how natural would it be if we still let Mom and Dad make all the decisions when we were 30?

While on the face of it symmetrical patterns seem to be negative, since they are characterized by struggle, there are times when they can be positive. The clash involved in competitive symmetry can sometimes motivate partners to be more creative. And sometimes the willingness to give in characterized by submissive symmetry can signal care and concern. What is unhealthy is any pattern so rigid it cannot change. If, for example, a dominant member in a complementary relationship becomes ill and can no longer make decisions, it may be necessary for the submissive member to take over. If the members cannot make the switch, severe problems of adaptation are possible.

Evolving Patterns: The Problem of Spirals

Over time, relational roles may become more and more extreme. When the actions of each party intensify the actions of the other, we have a **spiral**.[22] Spirals often arise where there is competitive symmetry. Assume you and a friend are in competition for a prize. The harder you work and the better you do, the harder she works and the better she does. As you near your goal, you redouble your efforts, and she does the same when it looks like you are about to win. While healthy competition may lead you to reach your potential, unchecked competition may become an obsession and spiral out of control.

There are times when intensifying a relationship makes it better. If by showing affection you increase a friend's confidence so that he acts more lovable, you will probably feel even more affection. The relationship can develop in a positive direction. This is a progressive spiral. Unfortunately, the opposite can occur. If, for example, you lose trust in a friend, that friend may decide that it is useless to act in a trustworthy manner. He may therefore violate your trust, and the relationship will degenerate. This is a regressive spiral.

William Wilmot believes that most relationships are characterized by alternating spirals that fluctuate between being progressive and regressive. He argues that most couples place limits on how high or low a spiral can go. When a spiral reaches one of these limits, it must change directions or the relationship will dissolve. Our nagging wife and withdrawing husband cannot keep up their regressive spiral for long. It will have to reverse if they are to stay together.[23] Box 8.2 (pp. 196–97) further discusses how spirals define roles and looks at some of the social mechanisms for restraining runaway escalation.

Unwanted Patterns: Controlling URPs

If relational patterns are negotiated, you would think that people would steer clear of destructive sequences. Unfortunately, many patterns are undesired and undesirable. In **unwanted repetitive patterns (URPs)**, participants feel out of control. Have you ever known someone who just rubbed you the wrong way? Every time you got together, a fight would inevitably ensue. If so, you have experienced an URP. In most URPs the following conditions will occur: (1) There will be a clear sequence of alternating messages so that each participant will know exactly what comes next; (2) the URP will be recurrent; (3) it will occur regardless of topic or situation; (4) the sequence will be unwanted; and (5) the participants will both share the perception that it could not be avoided. They will feel a compulsion to see it through to its conclusion.[24]

It is not completely clear why URPs occur. They appear to be an immediate reaction to "triggering" messages. Participants respond automatically, without considering the consequences. They touch off simplistic, almost childish, responses in one another. Perhaps these responses are somehow connected to core beliefs about the self.

What can be done about URPs? The first step is to recognize them for what they are and to try to overcome the tendency to punctuate them inappropriately. The next step is somehow to break the sequence. Wilmot offers five suggestions for stopping spirals that seem applicable to all kinds of URPs.[25]

1. *Change your behavior.* For example, if a partner is afraid of commitment and your insistence is only making her more afraid, perhaps you should stop asking for commit-

Schismogenesis: Patterns of Role Differentiation in a New Guinea Village

In the 1930s, anthropologist Gregory Bateson first described the complementary and symmetrical interaction patterns we have discussed. At the time, he was working among the Iatmul of New Guinea, one of whose characteristics was extravagant competitive exhibitionism by the men, accompanied by the women's passive admiration. Bateson was interested in under-standing this extreme behavior, which clearly placed a strain on its practitioners.

To explain the progressive differentiation in roles he observed, he coined the word *schismogenesis*, meaning an escalation in the intensity of a behavior caused by one's partner's reactions. He noted that schismogenesis could be complementary (as when exhibitionism was increased by admiration and admiration by exhibitionism) or symmetrical (as when rival moieties competed in bullying novices during initiations).

Bateson felt that schismogenesis, unless restrained, could destroy relationships. He also felt that it could develop in all long-term interactions between intimates. He noted that the result of uncontrolled schismogenesis was hostility, inability to empathize, and mutual jealousy. After long-term complementary schismogenesis, partners feel disgust for one another's behavior.

One of the most interesting parts of Bateson's discussion centers on cultural mechanisms for restraining schismogenesis. Bateson suggests a number of them:

1. It is possible that adding a small amount of complementary behavior to a symmetrical relationship may stabilize role differentiation. For example, if management plays basketball once a year with labor, this small dose of symmetry may ease feelings of difference.

2. A couple experiencing complementary schismogenesis may try to change its topic by focusing on different behaviors. A couple acting out a dominance—

ment and instead treat the relationship more casually. Wilmot suggests that if doing more of the same doesn't work, doing less of the same might.

2. *Use third parties* such as friends, counselors, or relatives to provide new perspectives and break problem patterns.

3. *Reaffirm your relational goals.* If your partner is very important to you, try to recall how the relationship developed and what your original goals and commitments were. If it is with a casual acquaintance, think about why it is necessary for you to work together. Discuss this with your partner.

4. *Try to spend either more or less time with the person.* You may succeed in breaking the pattern either by sharing more of yourself or by taking time out to be alone.

5. *Try changing an external situation.* Maybe a change of location, even a vacation together, may succeed in upsetting relational habits and providing new patterns of behavior.

IMPROVING RELATIONAL COMPETENCE

There seem to be two keys to controlling relationships: an awareness of patterns and sequences and a willingness to change.

The first thing to consider is that you always send relational messages. You may be too preoccupied to notice them, but that

submission pattern may convert that pattern to nurturing—weakness, a more acceptable kind of role differentiation.

3. Refocusing symmetrical rivalry may also be effective. For example, true hostility may be shifted to mock aggression. Box 13.1 gives a good example of this process.

4. The groups or individuals experiencing schismogenesis may be united in opposition to a common enemy. We know, for example, that during war, nationalist sentiment overcomes internal political rivalries.

5. Hierarchical organization may ease the strain of complementary relationships by allowing an individual to dominate the group below while being submissive to the group above. For example, the husband who is powerless at work can dominate his children.

6. Inverse schismogenetic patterns may restrain one another. For example, love, a positive escalation of emotion, may counteract rivalry, a more negative emotion.

Source: *Gregory Bateson,* Naven, *2nd ed. (Stanford, Calif.: Stanford University Press, 1958).*

ADDITIONAL READINGS

Bateson, Gregory. *Steps to an Ecology of Mind.* New York: Ballantine, 1972.

Watzlawick, Paul, Janet Beavin Bavelas, and Don D. Jackson, *The Pragmatics of Human Communication*. New York: W. W. Norton, 1967.

doesn't mean your relational partner won't. For example, you may let the fact that you are tired or worried slip into your voice without realizing it. Although the furthest thing from your mind may be sending a negative relational message, a friend or coworker may easily read your tone as a criticism. Whether you intend to or not, relationally you cannot *not* communicate. Becoming aware of what it is you are communicating is one way to increase competence.

The opposite side of the coin is to learn not to be overly sensitive. It's easy to read all kinds of relational meanings into a message. If in doubt, check your perceptions. Ask yourself if you are projecting your own insecurities onto your partner. If you aren't sure, then talk about your feelings.

Of course, one person cannot change a relationship alone. Sit down with your partner and try to diagnose the kinds of messages characteristic of your relationship. Ask yourself whether your dyad specializes in disconfirming messages. Also check to see whether there are any positive relational messages you'd like to be able to send but find difficult. If you both agree you'd like to be warmer or more confirming, practice until you feel comfortable.

Try to identify patterns of interacts and sequences that habitually lead to conflict. Check your tendency to punctuate the sequence unfairly. Try to observe as objectively as possible the kinds of behaviors causing URPs and spirals.

Finally, don't be afraid to metacommunicate. Talking about what is going on in a supportive and confirming way is the best method of solving interpersonal problems. By becoming more aware of relational messages and by being willing to try new patterns, you can gain control over this crucial aspect of interpersonal communication.

REVIEW TERMS

The following is a list of major concepts introduced in this chapter. The page where the concept is first mentioned is listed in parentheses.

content messages (180)
relational messages (180)
relational definitions (182)
relational culture (183)
relational contract (184)
relational themes (184)
one-up message (186)
one-down message (186)
one-across message (186)
confirming message (189)
disconfirming message (189)
paradoxical definition (191)
paradoxical injunction (191)
double bind (192)
interact (193)
punctuation (193)
complementary pattern (194)
symmetrical pattern (194)
competitive symmetry (194)
submissive symmetry (194)
spiral (195)
URP (195)

SUGGESTED READINGS

Bateson, Gregory. *Steps to an Ecology of Mind.* New York: Ballantine, 1972. Bateson is one of our most original thinkers. This is a collection of his ideas about communication and interaction. It's impossible to read Bateson without gaining insights.

Laing, R. D. *Knots.* New York: Vintage Books, 1970. A fascinating look at some of the "psycho-logics" that lead us into relational binds and paradoxes.

Watzlawick, Paul, and John H. Weakland, eds. *The Interactional View.* New York: W. W. Norton, 1977. A collection of essays by members of the Palo Alto group.

Wilmot, William W. *Dyadic Communication*, 2nd ed. Reading, Mass.: Addison-Wesley, 1979. An excellent introductory text. Wilmot's discussion of relational intricacies is particularly relevant.

PROCESS TO PERFORMANCE

TOPICS FOR DISCUSSION

1. Why do you think people prefer to use nonverbal codes rather than verbal codes to express relational messages, especially since nonverbal codes are often less explicit and hard to decode accurately? Could there be some advantage to ambiguous coding?

2. Most of the time relational codes go unnoticed. When and under what conditions do people pay attention to relational codes? See if you can construct a theory of some of the factors affecting this process.

3. Review the relational themes in Table 8.1. Discuss how each of the nonverbal codes discussed in Chapter 6 can be used to convey each theme.

4. Analyze the way the relational themes are conveyed by students and teachers in classroom contexts. Be specific.

5. Imagine you are on a job interview. What kinds of impressions would you like to convey? What relational messages would it be most appropriate to send? How could you convey these messages most effectively in an office setting during a 20-minute screening interview?

6. It has been argued that many traditional patterns of male–female interaction (men holding the door for women and paying for dates) are relational messages indicating dominance. What is your opinion?

7. Research has shown that women are often more sensitive to subtle relational cues than men are. Why do you suppose women have traditionally been more subtle and men more blunt in their relational messages? What implications does this have for cross-sex interactions?

8. Evaluate the metaphors of culture and contract as descriptions of the way people define relationships. Are these useful ways to think of relational development? In what ways do they break down?

9. Build a model describing how couples reach consensus on relational definitions. What factors are involved? What steps take place?

10. Try to come up with a list of suggestions to stop URPs.

OBSERVATION GUIDE

1. Think of a situation in which you were disconfirmed by someone. Describe the disconfirmation. How did you feel about it? How was the situation resolved? Now think of a situation in which you felt confirmed. What was done or said to give you that feeling?

2. Have you ever been in an URP? If so, describe the pattern in detail. What was the sequence, how did you feel, what did you do about it? If the URP was resolved, how was this accomplished? If it was not resolved, what do you think might have worked? If you have never been in an URP, you have probably observed them. Answer the questions above about an observed URP.

3. Think of a current relationship. What is your relational definition? How did you arrive at it? What kinds of agreements and norms characterize the relationship? Think of a rule that took some negotiation and describe this process. If the negotiation process was easy, what made it so? If difficult, why? What could have been done to ease the situation?

EXERCISES

1. Take a play, a recording of a favorite TV show, or a tape of a real-life conversation. Working with a partner, choose a segment and code it, using the following system (from B. Aubrey Fisher, *Small Group Decision Mak-ing*, 2nd ed. New York: McGraw-Hill, 1980, pp. 327–29).

Dominance (↑ +) : An attempt to severely restrict the freedom of the other.

Structuring (↑) : An attempt to control the other while leaving him or her some options.

Equivalence (→) : An attempt at mutual identification or equality.

Deference (↓) : A willingness to follow while retaining some freedom.

Submission (↓ +) : An extreme willingness to be led by the other.

Discuss the coding until you agree. If possible, record your discussion using a portable tape recorder. What kind of pattern do you see? Is it complementary or symmetrical or mixed? How would you sum up their relationship? (To make this even more interesting, go back and listen to the tape of your own interaction. Together analyze the control dimension that occurred between you during this exercise.)

2. This exercise is designed to give you practice in sending and receiving relational messages. Begin by forming groups of four or six. Turn to the 12 relational themes identified by Burgoon and Hale. Take a pack of 3×5 cards and print the names of each relational theme on a separate card, making cards for both positive and negative expressions of a theme (that is, make one card for dominance, and another for submission; one for affection and one for hostility).

Now shuffle the cards and deal an equal number to each member. The person who begins chooses a card from his hand and acts out the relational message. The only words that can be used are the letters of the alphabet recited in order. As a player acts out the message, each member of the group should write on a scrap of paper the message being conveyed. After all members have made their guesses, they should compare answers. Award five points to the player if he manages to match at least one group member; award five points to all who guessed correctly. Once the points have been awarded, the current player discards the card that was played, and the next person acts out one of her cards. Continue until all the cards have been played. In case of a tie, have the players involved play a runoff round.

Discuss how difficult it was to convey the messages. Are you an emotionally expressive person? Why or why not? Are you sensitive to others' messages? Why or why not?

CHAPTER NINE

Interpersonal influence is as old as the human race. For good or bad we are often persuaded by those closest to us. (Albrecht Altdorfer, *The Fall of Man*, c. 1535)

AFFECTING OTHERS: INTERPERSONAL INFLUENCE

EVERYONE THOUGHT PAUL was headed straight for success. At college he had been an above-average student, motivated and bright. He had a small but close circle of friends and a good relationship with his family. In fact, his parents were so proud of him, they gave him a trip across the country as a graduation present. Because they knew their son made friends easily, they weren't surprised when he called them from San Francisco to tell them he was going to explore the coast with some kids he'd met. Before hanging up, Paul told them he loved them and promised to call in a week. That phone call was the last any of Paul's friends or relatives heard from him until, six months later, a private detective found him wearing saffron robes and selling flowers on a street corner in Seattle. Like thousands of other young Americans, Paul had joined a cult.

Paul's family and friends were stunned and confused. What had happened to cause such a radical change in Paul's behavior? What techniques of mind control could so rapidly turn a normal boy into a true believer? Had Paul been, in fact, as normal as he seemed, or did he have some fundamental psychological flaw that everyone had overlooked? Who was responsible for what happened?

When a boy like Paul makes such a radical departure, it's natural to look for explanations.[1] Most people place the blame either on the personality of the "victim" or on the extraordinary methods of mind control used by cult members. But people who have studied cults professionally have made some surprising findings. In most cases, they tell us, cult recruits are ordinary people, reasonably well balanced, well educated, and well brought up. And the techniques used, far from being mysterious forms of "brainwashing," are actually ordinary modes of interpersonal influence, similar to the methods you and I might use to make new friends, convince a candidate to accept a job with our firm, or persuade a member to abide by club bylaws.[2]

In this chapter we introduce you to a number of theories that explain processes of persuasion and attitude change. As you read, try to apply these theories to Paul's situation. By the end of this chapter, you should have a clearer understanding of why Paul made the choices he did. To start you off, Box 9.1 describes techniques used to recruit cult members.

Moon for the Misbegotten: Methods of Cult Conversion

Enough first-person accounts of conversion experiences now exist to allow us to piece together the techniques cults use to recruit new members. You may be surprised to discover how simple and yet how effective these methods are. What is clear is that they depend very heavily on the creation of interpersonal bonds. The account given here is based on experiences of former members of Rev. Sun Myung Moon's Unification Church, but similar methods are used by many cults.

The first step in recruitment is for a cult member to approach a target of about the same age and background. The recruiter, usually attractive and friendly, strikes up a conversation, inviting the target to a picnic or similar social event. There an attempt is made to determine whether the target's beliefs and values make him eligible for further influence. No direct identification of the cult or overt proselytizing takes place at this time.

If the target seems suitable, he is invited to a retreat, usually in a beautiful, secluded area outside the city where contact was first made. No pressure is exerted. It is important that the target's decision to accept be voluntary. Once at the retreat, the target is cut off from all the hassles of the outside world; there are no TVs, radios, or telephones, no difficult decisions of any kind. He is surrounded by attractive role models who seem sincerely happy, vital, energetic, and unconditionally accepting both of one another and of the target. The atmosphere and activities are reminiscent of a summer camp. Simple games (dodge ball, tug-of-war, red rover) immerse the target in competitive group play. Traditional songs and rhythmic chants and cheers evoke an elementary school atmosphere where simple obedience, pleasure, and belonging are key.

Group beliefs are expressed in simple language incorporating popularly accepted values such as

EXPLAINING SOCIAL INFLUENCE: TARGET NEEDS

People who are good at persuading others—politicians, evangelists, con artists and the like—usually have a good understanding of human needs and goals. They realize that influence is not a one-way street; it is a communication transaction. Targets are not passive receivers of information; they actively involve themselves in the persuasion process, changing only if a persuasive appeal touches them in some way. Change agents must therefore know what people need and want. In this section, we examine three human needs: the need to achieve rewards and avoid punishments, the need for stability and consistency, and the need for a positive self-image.

The Need for Rewards

Why do people engage in some behaviors while avoiding others? For some the answer is simple: People act so as to maximize rewards and minimize punishments. Actions associated with positive stimuli will be repeated, while actions associated with negative stimuli will be

unity, peace, and love. Teachings take the form of truisms, tautologies, and comforting but difficult-to-pin-down slogans. ("When you possess the egoless ambition which is not centered on the self, you have many shields around you; you will be safe no matter what you do"; "Love is everywhere and has every motivation.") If the target tries to question these beliefs, members show concern and deep disappointment, urging the recruit to suspend judgment and wait for enlightenment. Afraid of offending his "hosts" and of being excluded from the love of the group, the target seeks meaning and understanding. This effort at self-persuasion is met by return of group acceptance and affection.

The need to belong is a key to understanding the recruitment process. Cult members create a perfect interpersonal relationship in which everything is shared: food, clothes, love, faith. For the period of commitment, the target becomes part of that relationship, experiencing the innocence and security of early childhood.

What happens to cult members? It has been estimated that 90 percent decide to leave after about two years. Many see the experience as beneficial. Although they abandon the cult, few of those who leave of their own volition have bad feelings about their stay. Instead, they take with them lasting values, which they integrate into their new lives.

Source: *Philip G. Zimbardo, Ebbe B. Ebbesen, and Christina Maslach,* Influencing Attitudes and Changing Behavior *(Reading, Mass.: Addison-Wesley, 1977),* and Saul V. Levine, "Radical Departures," Psychology Today *18, no. 8 (August 1984): 20–27.*

ADDITIONAL READINGS

Lofland, John. *Doomsday Cult: A Study of Conversion, Proselytization, and Maintenance of Faith.* Englewood Cliffs, N.J.: Prentice-Hall, 1966.

Stark, Rodney, and William Sims Bainbridge. *The Future of Religion: Secularization, Revival and Cult Formation.* Berkeley and Los Angeles: University of California Press, 1985.

---

avoided. People who hold this view of motivation are called learning theorists.

To understand their position, let's begin with the concepts of stimulus and response. A **stimulus** is any unit of sensory input; a **response** is any unit of behavior. When a doctor tests a patient's reflexes, the blow of the hammer is the stimulus; the knee jerk that follows is a response. Learning theorists believe that all behavior consists of stimulus–response chains following one another in a never-ending series.

Let's look at an example. It's time to take Rover for a walk. Rover's owner, Mrs. Walker, removes his leash from the closet. Rover hears the clank of the chain and rushes toward the door, knocking over the water dish in his excitement. Mrs. Walker cries, "Rover, just look what you've done! No walk for you, you bad dog," as she hauls out the mop. Rover slinks off with a hangdog expression. "Never mind. It's not your fault. Let's go out," Mrs. Walker sighs, and she retrieves the chain. Rover barks, runs around in circles, and wags his tail so hard he scatters trash all over the kitchen.

Let's look at all this from Mrs. Walker's standpoint. Going to the closet for the leash is a behavior, and therefore a response (R). It is followed by Rover's accident with the water dish, which serves as a stimulus (S) for her actions of scolding and mopping (R's). Rover's guilty reaction (S) prompts Mrs. Walker to reassure her pet (R). From Rover's viewpoint, everything is reversed. The rattling of the leash is a stimulus (S) that causes Rover to run into the water dish (R). The spilling water and the owner's scolding (S's) let him know he is in trouble and had better show contrition (R). And so it goes. Each action and reaction continues the chain of stimulus and response.

A reasonably intelligent person (or dog) soon realizes that the consequences of behavior can be either pleasant or painful. Learning occurs when an organism actively discriminates between positive and negative stimuli, seeking out those that are rewarding and avoiding those that are punishing. It follows that people are influenced by the rewards and punishments associated with their behavior.

There are several models of learning: classical conditioning, operant conditioning, and social learning are three of the most important. The classical conditioning model focuses on what happens before a response (the S-to-R relationship), while the operant conditioning model focuses on what happens after a response (the R-to-S link.) Social learning modifies both by taking into account the nature of the human being involved in the S-R chain.[3] Let's look briefly at each model.

Classical Conditioning and Learning

Certain stimuli naturally result in certain responses. For example, most people wince when they get an injection. There is nothing very surprising about this. What is more surprising is that the response to one stimulus can be transferred to another. Just reading about getting a shot or just passing a doctor's office may be enough to make some people cringe. When two stimuli are paired so that the response to one (the natural or unconditioned stimulus) becomes attached to another (the conditioned stimulus), **classical conditioning** has taken place.

Many of you are familiar with I. P. Pavlov's experiments in classical conditioning.[4] Pavlov knew that without any conditioning, laboratory dogs salivate when given meat powder. The unconditioned stimulus of meat powder is naturally followed by the unconditioned response of salivation. His experiments demonstrated the effects of associating a new stimulus, a ringing bell, with the meat powder. After a number of trials the bell alone (the conditioned stimulus) began to cause the dog to salivate. The dog learned to respond in a new way. Figure 9.1 gives a further example of classical learning.

Classical, or associational, learning plays a large part in interpersonal situations. Many responses to others are based on associations. It's not unusual to feel instant dislike for a stranger simply because he or she reminds you of someone from your past. It's also not uncommon to let responses to context color your impressions. You may dislike people you meet under trying or uncomfortable conditions, while you may be overly impressed with those you meet in luxurious surroundings. The ugly room–beautiful room study we discussed in Chapter 6 is a good example of how associations determine perception.

People respond positively to stimuli associated with rewards. That's why advertisers pair their products with attractive stimuli. And it's why movie stars like to display themselves in glamorous surroundings. Think back to Paul and the cult members. His initial experience was very pleasant. Members were friendly and fun-loving and wholesome. In many ways, being with them must have been like being a carefree child again; living at their farm must have been like being back at summer camp.

Classical Conditioning
situation: As a child, every time Tim made funny faces, his friends and relatives laughed and he felt good. Clowning was associated with praise and laughter.

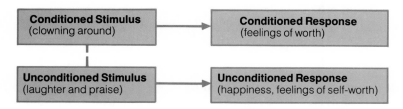

Operant Conditioning
situation: In high school, Tim enters the talent show; audience response determines his future responses.

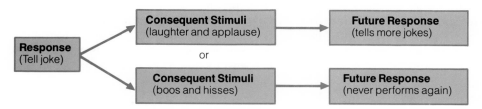

Social Learning
situation: Tim observes the success of a famous comedian; he imagines himself becoming famous, too. He imitates his hero.

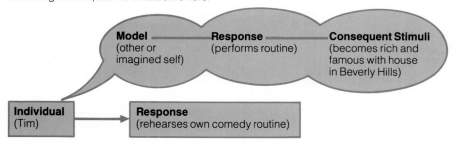

FIGURE 9.1

A comparison of three learning theories

Operant Conditioning and Learning

Associational learning is not the only way rewards and punishments affect people. Actions are also controlled by their consequences. According to **operant conditioning**, if a response's consequences are rewarding, the response will be repeated; if punishing, it will cease.[5] Controlling the consequences of an action is called **reinforcement**. Parents reinforce their children by making sure that treats follow good behavior and punishments follow bad. If you were ever "grounded," you were the target of operant conditioning. Figure 9.1 compares operant and classical learning.

Behaviors occur because of the reinforcements that follow them. But what kinds of stimuli provide the best reinforcement? The answer isn't easy. While money and power are effective reinforcers in our culture, even they don't work with everyone. The only way to know whether a reinforcer will be successful is to try it. If it increases or decreases a target behavior, it is a reinforcer. If it has no effect, then it's not.

For most schoolchildren, a teacher's scoldings are negative reinforcers, while a teacher's praise is positive. But not always. The class clown is a good example of someone who may be encouraged by disapproval. The more the teacher shouts and scolds, the more likely it is the clown will continue. Because people find different stimuli appealing, the first step in operant conditioning is to find what stimuli will be effective reinforcers.

Acts of interpersonal approval or disapproval, called **social reinforcers**, are usually potent forms of influence. Social reinforcement plays a large part in the cult conversion experience, as it does in everyday life. Cult members dispense smiles and praise freely whenever a visitor agrees with them, but when he shows doubt, these reinforcers are withdrawn. In order to keep receiving positive reinforcement, a prospect may censor his uncertainty. This reaction is not so unusual. Think for a minute about what happens when people you value criticize or tease you. You probably change your behavior. It takes a very unusual person to keep on doing things that others obviously dislike.

Social Learning

So far we have looked at learning that results from active exposure to positive and negative stimuli. **Social learning theory** emphasizes indirect learning, learning that involves anticipation and imagination.[6] According to social learning theory, one of the most important ways we learn is by observing others being rewarded or punished. This kind of learning is called **modeling** or **vicarious learning**. What happens to someone else shows what may happen to us. If a schoolchild sees a classmate punished for acting out in class, she learns that such behavior leads to trouble. If she sees her friend gain popularity as a result, however, she may decide to follow suit.

Media presentations are important sources of vicarious learning. Not only do ads show models being rewarded for using a sponsor's products, but sitcoms and movies also provide images for imitation and identification.

Not all models are equally influential. We are most influenced by models similar in attitude, gender, or age. In addition, models who are reliable and competent, who are of high status, or who are attractive will have greater impact. Finally, the more people we see being rewarded for a given behavior, the more we are likely to try that behavior.[7] These principles help to explain why cult recruiters are so successful, for they are usually young and attractive.

Another way people learn is by rewarding themselves when goals are met. This is called self-reinforcement. A person who tells himself

"As soon as all my work is done, I'm going to treat myself to dinner in a good restaurant" or "I'm going to keep rehearsing until I can play this piece perfectly, no matter how long it takes" is using principles of social learning to control his own behavior. Punishments and pleasures may be actively self-imposed.

A final way we learn is as a result of symbolic representations of consequences. Social learning theory is based on the belief that humans are thinking beings. Through our ability to reason, we can imagine an action's consequences. We can also respond to others' persuasive arguments. Rewards and punishments mediated through thought and talk are a powerful mode of control.

Learning and Interpersonal Exchange Processes

Learning theories have been used to explain a number of interpersonal processes, among them the reasons relationships form and dissolve. **Social exchange theory** is a learning model that states that if given a choice between two relationships, we will choose the more rewarding one.[8] Most people give up on relationships when the punishments begin to outweigh the pleasures. In general, people avoid costly relationships, although they may endure a short string of losses if they believe they'll get a return on their investment in the long run. According to social exchange theory, while every successful exchange may not involve a large profit, it should at least allow us to break even.

In the last chapter we discussed the fact that every interaction involves relational messages. In exchange theory, objects or actions that carry relational meaning are called **relational currencies**.[9] Gifts, favors, time, access rights, and so on are all examples. Even food can carry relational meaning. When you visit home after you have been away, a special meal may be prepared. What is significant is not the food itself, but the affection it stands for.

Exchange can be very complicated. Like economic currency, relational currency can become devalued or inflated over time, partners can fail to agree on appropriate exchange rates, and relationships can even go bankrupt if the exchange is mismanaged. If, for example, one of the parties feels she is doing all of the giving and receiving nothing in return, trouble can result. If Melanie was brought up in a family that expresses love through expensive gifts and Carlos wasn't taught to value material goods, there may be conflict. She will think he doesn't respect or care for her, while he may think her shallow and grasping. Neither will get adequate rewards, and the relationship may fail. When we think of the effects of rewards and punishments on behavior, we must remember to include relational currencies.

The Need for Stability and Consistency

Is all behavior a result of learning? Some say no, believing that our primary motivation is not for rewards but for cognitive consistency. These people believe that internal contradictions are deeply troubling. When confusions and inconsistencies occur, people do their best to return to a state of consistency. Theories based on this supposition are called consistency theories.[10]

Maintaining Relational Balance

According to **balance theory**, we feel comfortable, or balanced, when valued others agree with us on important issues.[11] When people we like oppose us or when people we dislike take our side, we are confused and uncomfortable. This state of discomfort is called imbalance. The typical situation described by balance theory involves a person (P), another person (O) who is related to P, and a stimulus (X) about which both P and O have opinions. If P's relationship to O and X is out of balance, P will try to change it. Figure 9.2 describes ways a P-O-X relationship can be either balanced or imbalanced.

Let's consider the relationship between Peggy (P), Oscar (O), and the stimulus, heavy metal rock music (X). If Peggy and Oscar are friends, and if both like this kind of music, then their relationship is balanced. There is a positive relationship between all three elements of the triad. This state of affairs is illustrated in the first of the balanced states diagrammed in Figure 9.2. Under these conditions, Peggy will be happy with her relationship to both O and X.

Unfortunately, not all relationships are balanced. If Peggy detests rock music on aesthetic or moral grounds, knowing that her friend Oscar likes what she hates will cause discomfort. Her relationship with O and X will be out of balance. She can correct this in three ways: by changing her attitude to Oscar, by changing her taste in music, or by trying to convert Oscar. While pressures toward balance may be very mild if one's relationship to O or X is trivial or inconsequential, they can be quite powerful if the relationship is important. For example, when we discover a close friend acting dishonorably, the strain may be severe. Something has to be done to get things back in balance.

Balance theory explains why we are attracted to similar others and accounts for some conformity pressures. Consider Julie's statements in the following dialogue.

JULIE: That was a pretty good movie, wasn't it?

JEFF: Well, I don't know, I thought it was kind of slow.

JULIE: Oh, well, yes, it was slow. But the acting . . . ?

JEFF: A bit stilted.

JULIE: Oh. Yeah. I guess it could have been a lot better.

Julie wants Jeff to like her, so when they disagree, she amends her statements. Her desire for balance makes her easily influenced. While her attraction to Jeff remains high, she will make every effort to agree with him.

In general, balance theory tells us that people who are liked and admired have a great deal of influence over the attitudes of others. Advertisers, of course, have always known this; celebrities are paid huge sums of money for endorsing products. But the effect is not limited to the world of advertising. The principles of balance theory are very relevant to interpersonal situations. Have you ever agreed with others just to get them to like you? Have you ever threatened to leave someone unless he or she changed?

Congruity Principles

According to balance theory, there are only three ways to reduce inconsistency: We change our attitude to X *or* we change our attitude to O *or* we try to change O's attitude to X. But are those really all the possibilities? Think about it. If a friend says something you don't particularly like, isn't it possible that you might change toward *both* your friend and his idea? You might like him a bit less because his views aren't what they should be, but you might also like the idea a bit more because he thought of it. And wouldn't your response depend on how good a friend he was and on the issue of disagreement? If your best friend likes lime sherbet instead of orange, it is unlikely you will resolve the imbalance by dropping him. Balance theory doesn't take these factors into account. **Congruity theory**, however, does.[12]

Every day speakers make statements about objects. Sports figures endorse products, judges

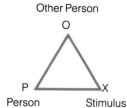

Other Person

O

P   X

Person   Stimulus

situation: A person (P) holds either a positive or negative attitude toward another person (O) and toward a stimulus (X). O also holds an attitude toward X, and P is aware of O's attitude.

Balanced States   The P-O-X relationship is stable; P need take no action.

Unbalanced States   The P-O-X relationship is unstable; P must restore balance.

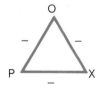 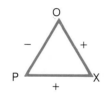 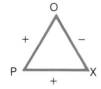

To restore balance P can:
1. change own attitude toward O
2. change own attitude toward X
3. try to change O's attitude toward X

FIGURE 9.2

Balance theory

rule for or against defendants, politicians take stands. Congruity theory allows us to predict the effects of these statements; it lets us know whether these statements will damage or increase the source's credibility.

Let's say that an average citizen reads in the morning paper that a presidential adviser has been indicted for fraud. Since the citizen already has a mild aversion to the adviser, this news doesn't bother her. She gets upset, however, when she reads that the president, whom she admires and respects, has decided to stand behind the adviser. According to congruity theory, when a well-liked source says something positive about a disliked object, a state of cognitive discomfort called incongruity occurs.

To reduce incongruity, *both* the attitude toward the president and the attitude toward the adviser will have to change. The amount of change will not be equal in both cases, however. The most strongly held attitude will change less, while the weaker attitude will change more. Since our newspaper reader reveres the president and only mildly dislikes the adviser, her attitude toward the adviser will change more. This case is illustrated in Figure 9.3.

Congruity theory allows us to compute the actual amount of attitude change that will occur. Congruity theory calculations always use a scale ranging from -3 (indicating a strong negative attitude) to $+3$ (indicating a strong positive attitude.) Let's assume that the original rating of the president is $+3$ and that of the adviser is -1. As you can see in Figure 9.3, there are four scale units between the two attitudes. Change will be inversely proportional to the original positions, so the president's rating will go *down* one unit and the adviser's will go *up* three units. Our citizen now rates both the president and the adviser at $+2$. The adviser has gained credibility, while the president has lost. For those of you who are mathematically minded, Figure 9.3 gives a formula that can be used to compute congruity in this and other situations.

The ability to make predictions based on scale ratings is a valuable one for professional pollsters, political consultants, and marketing executives. In the average interpersonal situation, however, attitude scales aren't often used. What is important in interpersonal interactions is knowing that in cases of incongruity, attitudes toward both source and object are likely to change. Every time you advocate something that displeases your friends, their attitude toward you decreases a bit; every time you associate yourself with things they approve of, your attraction increases. It is useful to remember that your attraction is always fluctuating as a result of the attitudes you reveal. Only if you are very well liked can you get away with advocating unpopular views. People who stand by their views in the face of disapproval often pay a high price in terms of popularity.

Congruity theory also explains changes in attitudes as a result of group conformity pressures. If one close friend advocates a position you dislike, you will increase your liking for that position only a small amount. If another friend also favors the position, however, it increases a bit more in attraction. If all your friends agree, you may finally reach the point of approving wholeheartedly of the idea.

Reducing Internal Dissonance

Our final consistency model is **cognitive dissonance theory.**[13] The most general of all the consistency models, it maintains that whenever a person becomes aware of holding a cognition inconsistent with other cognitions, there will be pressure to reduce the inconsistency. This pressure is called *dissonance*. Dissonance always occurs as a result of a decision between alternatives.

Let's say that upon graduation you have a choice between two jobs. One is in Albuquerque, New Mexico, a city that intrigues you. The other is in a suburb of Buffalo, New York. You decide on the latter. How you feel about this decision will depend on all of the cognitions you hold about the two jobs and the two cities. Some cognitions will be consonant, or consistent, with your choice of the Buffalo job; for example, believing that the Buffalo job provides opportunity for advancement. Some beliefs may be dissonant, or inconsistent, with your decision; for example, hating cold weather. Still other beliefs will be irrelevant; liking Woody Allen movies or believing yourself to be an honest person have little if anything to do with the decision.

situation: An observer holds an attitude toward a source and toward an object. The observer hears the source making an assertion favoring the object. If the observer's initial ratings of source and object are identical, congruity exists. If the observer's initial ratings are unequal, incongruity exists, and attitude change will be necessary.

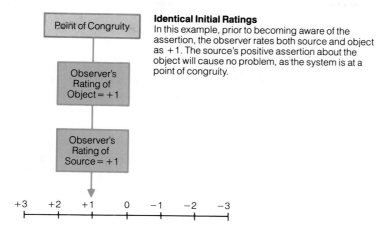

Identical Initial Ratings
In this example, prior to becoming aware of the assertion, the observer rates both source and object as +1. The source's positive assertion about the object will cause no problem, as the system is at a point of congruity.

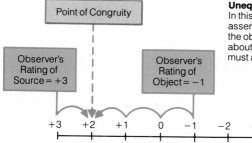

Unequal Initial Ratings
In this example, prior to becoming aware of the assertion, the observer rates the source as +3 and the object as −1. The source's positive assertion about the object will cause incongruity. The observer must adjust attitudes to point of congruity, +2.

To restore congruity the observer must decrease liking for source and increase liking for stimulus. Amount of change will be inversely proportional to initial rankings. Congruity point may also be computed by using the following formula:

$$R_o = \frac{|A_o|}{|A_o| + |A_s|} A_o + (d) \frac{|A_s|}{|A_o| + |A_s|} A_s$$

Where R_o = congruity point for object, A_o = initial attitude to object, A_s = initial attitude to source, d = direction of assertion, +1 if positive, −1 if negative. A bracket around a symbol indicates absolute value (value without + or − sign). Note: Example is for case where assertion is positive; with negative assertions, congruity occurs when ratings are mirror images (for example, +2, −2 indicate congruity when source speaks against object).

FIGURE 9.3
Congruity theory

According to dissonance theory, the dissonance you feel after any decision is a function of the number and importance of the perceptions you hold about that decision. This relationship is illustrated in the following formula:

Amount of dissonance after decision =

$$\frac{\text{\# of dissonant cognitions} \times \text{their importance}}{\text{\# of consonant cognitions} \times \text{their importance}}$$

If there are a number of career advantages to moving to Buffalo, if the only dissonant element is a dislike of cold weather, and if climate is not very important, then dissonance will be low. If, however, you have a lot of objections to the Buffalo move and each is very important, then dissonance will be high, and you will have to do something to reduce it.

There are several ways to reduce dissonance. The most obvious is to turn down the Buffalo job and move to the Southwest. If that is impossible, you can manufacture cognitions consonant with your decision. You can convince yourself that housing costs in Buffalo are very low; that it has a good orchestra and exciting professional sports teams; that its location on the Canadian border will give you easy access to international travel. At the same time, you can reduce dissonance even further by thinking unpleasant thoughts about Albuquerque. You can act as your own change agent by providing yourself with positive information about your decision and negative information about alternatives.

How does this apply to influence? Let's look at an example. Perhaps you want to persuade a friend to stop smoking. If you point out that it makes no sense for someone who values his health and dislikes wasting money to smoke, perhaps your friend will reduce the ensuing dissonance by giving up cigarettes.

There is another way dissonance can lead to interpersonal influence. Most people don't like their actions to violate their beliefs. If they act in ways contrary to their attitudes, they may

reduce dissonance by changing their beliefs. This influence strategy is known as **counterattitudinal advocacy**. For example, one way to encourage kids to take more pride in their country might be to involve them in an essay contest. While at first they may think of patriotism as "corny," by the time they finish researching the subject, writing their composition, and delivering it with enthusiasm, their private beliefs may change to match their public actions.

The effects of counterattitudinal advocacy will be stronger if it is voluntary, if a lot of effort is involved, if the sponsor is not particularly attractive, and if the reward for participation is not great. In all these cases, there are no external justifications to explain away compliance. As a result, the only way to reduce dissonance is through attitude change. If we do an unpleasant task for a large reward, we can always rationalize our behavior by saying, "I hated it, but I needed the money." If, however, we work long and hard for free, the only way to make sense of our actions is to say, "Actually, I liked doing it." This principle explains why we value things we have to work hard for. The fraternity or sorority that is the hardest to get into and has the most difficult initiation ceremonies is often the most popular. The commitment we make voluntarily will be more lasting than one made under duress. This is why cult members try to convince recruits that their decision to join is voluntary. The stronger the dissonance created by an action, the more likely it will be that it will lead to internal attitude change.

Uncertainty Reduction

According to some theorists in our field, the need for consistency explains a lot about how and why we communicate.[14] They believe people have a basic drive to reduce uncertainty. The more uncertainty we experience, the less we can predict events. In a situation of total uncertainty or randomness, purposeful action would be impossible. Communication provides a means of reducing uncertainty. Through communication we gather information about the world. The need to live in a predictable and consistent universe is one of the chief reasons we communicate.

The Need for Self-Respect

We have nearly finished our discussion of the forces that motivate action. There is one more we should look at briefly, however, one already discussed at some length in Chapter 4: the need to present a proper face to the world. A number of theorists hold that people need to respect themselves and be respected by others.

In his **value theory**, Milton Rokeach tells us the self-concept is a powerful guide to behavior.[15] Each of us has an identity we try to live up to. For Rokeach, the clearest reflection of people's identities is their values. A value is simply a belief that some goals and paths to goal achievement are better than others. Some people, for example, believe that altruism is more worthwhile than self-interest; they therefore act with kindness and charity. Others believe it is important to achieve personal success. They may value ambition and material security above everything else. Table 9.1 lists some of the values Rokeach believed are basic to all people. If you were asked to rank these, which would you consider the most important?

Rokeach believes people can be influenced by appeals to their value systems. If, for example, bravery is high in your hierarchy of values, you may undertake very foolhardy actions in order to avoid being labeled a coward. You may be highly influenced by challenges or dares. If you believe that stealing is wrong, anticipated guilt may stop you from shoplifting. Values are key parts of our life scripts. One of our strongest motivations is to remain true to what we believe is right.

Characteristics attributed to sources can enhance or inhibit their ability to persuade. When source and message "match," influence will be high.

Not only do we need to be true to private images of self, most of us also need to present favorable public images. Young children may begin smoking in order to appear older and more sophisticated to their peers. They may even get together and practice until they can smoke without feeling sick or looking foolish.

TABLE 9.1

Terminal and instrumental values

Terminal values—preferable end states of existence

A comfortable life (a prosperous life)
An exciting life (a stimulating, active life)
A sense of accomplishment (lasting contribution)
A world at peace (free of war and conflict)
A world of beauty (beauty of nature and the arts)
Equality (brotherhood, equal opportunity for all)
Family security (taking care of loved ones)
Freedom (independence, free choice)
Happiness (contentedness)
Inner harmony (freedom from inner conflict)
Mature love (sexual and spiritual intimacy)
National security (protection from attack)
Pleasure (an enjoyable, leisurely life)
Salvation (saved, eternal life)
Self-respect (self-esteem)
Social recognition (respect, admiration)
True friendship (close companionship)
Wisdom (a mature understanding of life)

Instrumental values—preferable modes of conduct

Ambitious (hardworking, aspiring)
Broad-minded (open-minded)
Capable (competent, effective)
Cheerful (lighthearted, joyful)
Clean (neat, tidy)
Courageous (standing up for your beliefs)
Forgiving (willing to pardon others)
Helpful (working for the welfare of others)
Honest (sincere, truthful)
Imaginative (daring, creative)
Independent (self-reliant, self-sufficient)
Intellectual (intelligent, reflective)
Logical (consistent, rational)
Loving (affectionate, tender)
Obedient (dutiful, respectful)
Polite (courteous, well-mannered)
Responsible (dependable, reliable)
Self-controlled (restrained, self-disciplined)
Terminal values are associated with life goals; instrumental values define appropriate means for achieving these goals. Both guide action.

Reprinted with permission from Milton Rokeach, *Beliefs, Attitudes, and Values* (San Francisco: Jossey-Bass, 1968). Copyright 1968 by Jossey-Bass.

For them, smoking is a form of self-presentation. What kind of interpersonal appeal will discourage them? Probably not rational arguments about health hazards. A better approach might be to convince them that smoking is unattractive and unsophisticated: that it makes them look silly and juvenile.

Value theorists believe that people often engage in unrewarding and inconsistent behaviors simply to act out a valued life script. The "macho" man, for example, may have to do a lot of unpleasant things to prove himself. Think about it. Have you ever sacrificed rewards because getting them would involve violating a value? Have you ever done things that were irrational and inconsistent in order to act out a social role? If so, you may agree with value theory.

Summary: Choice and Motivation

As we have seen, learning theories hold that people are motivated by the rewards and punishments accompanying their behaviors, consistency theories state that people need to make their belief systems stable and consistent, and value theories tell us that people act so as to create favorable images. But which theory is right? It's possible that they all are. At various times we may try to fulfill all of these needs. Daniel Katz, for example, believes that people form and maintain attitudes for several different reasons.[16] He identifies four functions of attitudes: adjustment, knowledge, value expression, and ego defense. The first three correspond pretty closely to learning, consistency, and self-validation theories. The last is based on the individual's need to defend the ego from psychological threat and is based on psychoanalytic theory.

Katz makes two important points about motivation. The first is that people are motivated at various times by various forces. Although Katz doesn't explain why our motivations shift, it's possible that people have different motivational schemata that guide actions. When the reward–punishment schema is uppermost, we tend to judge an action in terms of gains and losses. When a value schema is in place, we will take a more noble stance. And when the consistency schema is being used, we try to act rationally. If this is true, then part of being a successful change agent involves calling up the correct schema in our audience. There are probably things a persuader can do to switch a target from concern with reward attainment to concern with value exemplification. Think about it. What would you do to change the focus of a target's attention from self-interest to self-sacrifice?

Katz makes a second point worth considering. Different methods must be used to change different kinds of attitudes. If a behavior is driven by a need for adjustment, then it can be changed by promises or threats. If it helps the individual maintain a stable world view, then rational arguments should be used. Katz tells us that interpersonal influence must be flexible and varied.

EXPLAINING SOCIAL INFLUENCE: SOURCE CHARACTERISTICS

While an understanding of target needs plays a big part in interpersonal influence, it's not the whole story. Source characteristics are also important. Communication scholars have known for a long time that not all speakers are equally persuasive. While Aristotle was the first to recognize that a speaker's character, knowledge, and good will are an important part of persuasion, others since him have acknowledged the significance of the attributions receivers make about sources.[17] Think of all the ways we have of describing persuasive speakers. We refer to their credibility, expertise, dynamism, charisma, and the like. It is clear that the characteristics a source manages to convey to an audience provide him or her with a great deal of power.

Power and Interpersonal Influence

Power and influence go hand in hand. A powerful person is one who can control a situation, and this control can come in many ways. John R. French and Bertram Raven believe there are five kinds of power: reward, coercive, expert, legitimate, and referent.[18]

A source perceived as controlling rewards has **reward power**. The employer determining who gets a raise, the political boss deciding on the next candidate for governor, the guy in the bar standing drinks for his buddies, or the teenager lending out the latest albums are all wielding reward power. When people own things we want or need, they become important to us, and their importance is in direct proportion to our need. Control of physical or emotional resources is a prominent aspect of power.

Of course, the ability to dispense rewards is not the only base of power. The person who can inspire fear has **coercive power**. Most people comply with the requests of an armed criminal or a burly bully. On an interpersonal level, fear of being excluded or unmasked can lead to psychological coercion. People often rule with threats as well as promises.

Sometimes a source is influential because he or she has special knowledge or skill. This influence base is called **expert power**. In an age in which it is impossible to know everything, people must rely on specialists. We seldom question the recommendations of physicians or engineers or scientists.

While intelligence and training are significant sources of power, sheer attractiveness can also lead to influence. The people we admire have **referent power**. Rock stars have their groupies, gang leaders their faithful lieutenants, and teenagers their adoring kid brothers and sisters. In each case, these figures embody some moral or physical attribute others admire. Imitation is not only the sincerest form of flattery, it is an indication of interpersonal influence.

Of course, sometimes the actual characteristics of a source are not as important as his symbolic characteristics. When people become representatives of social institutions, they take on **legitimate power**. Most law-abiding citizens obey a police officer without question. Compliance has almost nothing to do with the officer's personality or ability; he represents the power of the state and therefore has the "right" to control actions. While you may question the fairness of a particular assignment your professors may make, you seldom question their right to make assignments. The academic setting legitimizes teachers' requests.

Self-Presentation Strategies

Having a power base is all very well, but it counts for nothing unless others know about it. Power is largely a matter of attribution. How, then, do you make sure others know you're powerful? One way is by employing self-presentation strategies to translate power bases into observable behaviors. Edward Jones and Thane Pittman have described five methods of strategic self-presentation used in interpersonal influence situations: ingratiation, intimidation, self-promotion, exemplification, and supplication.[19]

According to norms of reciprocity, we generally like those who like us. It is hard to mistreat people who appreciate us; indeed, we often feel we owe them something in return. This suggests that we can influence others by appearing to like them and by being pleasant

Teachers influence and control in many ways. All of the power bases discussed by French and Raven may be used at some time or other. How do teachers show legitimate, reward, coercive, referent, and expert power? (Winslow Homer, *The Country School*, 1871)

and friendly. This strategy is called **ingratiation**. The ingratiator uses charm, helpfulness, and flattery to control others.

While many people are sincerely nice, the ingratiator is strategically nice. In practice this is somewhat tricky. If the ingratiator is too nice, the target will be suspicious, and the strategy will backfire. The classic case of the ingratiator is the "yes man" who tells others whatever they want to hear in order to curry favor. While this is an extreme behavior, most of us have been taught that we should be pleasant if we want to influence others. As the saying goes, you can catch more flies with honey than with vinegar.

People who use **intimidation** aren't at all concerned with being nice. Instead, they want to appear dangerous. We generally give in to people who get ungovernably angry or violent. Young children often throw tantrums to get their way, while older people bully and threaten. Sometimes the destruction the intimidator threatens is self-destruction. Having an asthma attack or a dizzy spell whenever we are crossed is one way of controlling those around us.

Self-promotion is another strategy. Self-promoters want to be perceived as competent. They emphasize expert power. Others are so impressed with their training and experience that they have little choice but to agree. The dilemma facing the self-promoter is how to present an impressive list of credentials without seeming to brag. One way is to ensure the aid of a friend who can enthusiastically describe the promoter's accomplishments, allowing the promoter to look modest and slightly embarrassed. While self-promotion can be carried to extremes, most people try to appear as competent as possible. We all like to look as though we know what we're doing, especially in public situations. Every time we attempt to build credibility, we are engaging in mild forms of self-promotion.

Another way to influence is through **exemplification**. Exemplifiers control others by personifying the values they admire. They project so much integrity that others feel either admiration or guilt. Think of the influence wielded by religious prophets or saints; they are extreme examples of exemplifiers, people whose goodness is power.

Most of us don't go that far, although we do use exemplification in many influence situations. The child who acts like "a little angel" to impress his folks, the student who asks the teacher for extra reading assignments, and the employee who is always willing to work late if the boss needs her are all using this presentational strategy. Of course, exemplification doesn't always lead to popularity. Students have highly uncomplimentary labels for other students who try to impress teachers; exemplifiers make everyone else look bad in comparison.

The final strategy outlined by Jones and Pittman is called **supplication**. Here the presentation is that of helplessness. The supplicator appears so weak and defenseless that others feel a duty to act as protector. Not so long ago, women were taught that men resented strong women. Advice columns urged women to play dumb if they wanted to get a man. Women had to pretend to be bewildered by machines, too weak to carry anything heavier than a handbag, and too scatterbrained to balance a checkbook. A competent man would then step in and solve all of the problems. Through helplessness, women achieved a certain kind of influence. Most of that has changed now, and most people feel the change is healthy, for the supplicator often pays the price of diminished self-worth. People who play helpless for too long, whether male or female, may come to think of themselves as helpless, and that is not a particularly good feeling. "Learned helplessness" is the label given to people who have actually lost particular abilities or skills because of fear or practicing long-term supplication.

While all of these strategies can be unhealthy if carried to an extreme, we probably all use modified forms of them. Think about it for a minute. When you want something from someone, do you ever use these techniques? Probably. They are common ways of influencing others. You might find it interesting to see if you know people who are ingratiators, intimidators, self-promoters, exemplifiers, or supplicators. Most of our students have no difficulty thinking of examples from among their friends or acquaintances.

Influence As Self-Persuasion

We hope that we haven't given you the impression that influence is something a source does to a target. We don't want you to think that clever sources have complete control over their targets. Keep in mind that sources can set up conditions that will enhance influence, but it is receivers who ultimately convince themselves. Box 9.2 gives a good example of how receivers participate in their own persuasion.

Cognitive response theory stresses the large part played by the receiver during the influence process. It states that during persua-

American artist George Bellows was fascinated by evangelist Billy Sunday, whose charismatic style caused havoc in his audience. Sunday embodied the influence strategy of exemplification. (George Bellows, *The Sawdust Trail*, 1916)

Caveat Emptor: Techniques of Confidence Tricksters

P rofessional confidence tricksters rarely use a "hard sell" when setting up their marks. In fact, it is often the mark who begs to be let in on the deal, believing he's putting something over on the con artist. Con artists know that getting their targets to persuade themselves is their most effective technique. Two things are essential in a well-run con game: The mark must believe it's possible to get something for nothing, and the con must seem absolutely trustworthy. How do con artists

manage to make their marks believe their unbelievable tales? By knowing the mark's weaknesses and by putting on a credible front.

One of the most imaginative and stylish of all confidence tricksters was "Count" Victor Lustig. Early in his career he managed to sell the Eiffel Tower, not once, but twice! Throughout his life he assumed many identities and created many unusual "business opportunities" for gullible investors.

A classic example was the "money machine" he sold to a hardheaded businessman for $25,000. In the winter of 1925–26, Lustig turned up in Palm Beach hoping to find the perfect mark, someone whose greed was equaled by his need for status. Lustig's first step was to acquire an appropriate front. Hiring a chauffeur-driven Rolls-Royce, he checked into an expensive suite

at one of the finest hotels and waited. Before long, opportunity presented itself in the person of Herman Loller, a self-made millionaire frustrated by his lack of

---

sion, receivers generate cognitions about the messages they hear. Receivers search their cognitive files for preexisting attitudes, knowledge, and feelings and try to make sense of a source's message in light of what they already know. Messages supported by prior beliefs will probably be accepted; unsupported messages may have a negative or boomerang effect. Influence targets are active generators of information rather than passive receivers. In a real sense, we cannot influence others; we can only hope they will influence themselves in ways we want them to. Like all communication, influence is an active transaction between source and receiver.

PLANNING PERSUASIVE MESSAGES: COMPLIANCE-GAINING STRATEGIES

In the previous pages we looked at general explanations of social influence. But how is all of this translated into communication? When faced with actual influence situations, what does the competent communicator do? If you were in situations like the following, what influence strategies would you use?

Your aunt who lives nearby and with whom you are close has a large basement with a finished

social importance. To someone like Loller, knowing a cultured European aristocrat was extremely flattering. As they became friends, Loller confided some business setbacks. Lustig reluctantly revealed that he, too, had had money problems but that they had been solved by his "money-making machine," a box that would duplicate any paper currency so accurately that no bank could tell the difference. To "romance" the story, Lustig revealed that the machine had originally been developed by the Germans to undermine Allied currencies during World War I. It had fallen by chance into the hands of a Rumanian friend. It was, of course, the only one of its kind in the world.

Loller begged for a demonstration. Lustig showed him a beautiful mahogany box into which he placed a $100 bill. Six hours later, he removed two damp bills, identical to the last detail. They looked perfect, as they should have, since both were completely genuine. Lustig had merely altered the threes and eights of the serial numbers on one bill to make it identical to the other. He calmly suggested that Loller take each bill to a bank to make sure it was genuine.

Loller was hooked. He begged for a copy of the box. Lustig demurred. When Loller offered $25,000, he reluctantly gave in. Loller was so taken by Lustig's story that when the box failed to work, he convinced himself that he was operating it incorrectly. It was almost a year before he began to suspect and went to the police.

If you feel that Loller must have been particularly gullible, consider the fact that Lustig pulled off the same scheme again, selling his machine to a sheriff for $10,000 and the chance to escape from jail. It appears that people will believe just about anything if they really want to.

Source: *Colin Rose, ed.,* The World's Greatest Rip-Offs *(New York: Sterling, 1978).*

ADDITIONAL READINGS

Mackay, Charles. *Extraordinary Popular Delusions and the Madness of Crowds*. New York: Farrar, Straus & Giroux, 1932.

Wade, Carlson. *Great Hoaxes and Famous Imposters*. Middle Village, N.Y.: Jonathan David, 1976.

recreation room. You have a very tiny apartment and would like to have a big party in your aunt's basement. However, she can be finicky about cleaning and sometimes minds noise.

You are going away for a weekend and need someone to take care of your cat. You have spoken to your neighbor, Marty, once or twice in the past year. He seems to be home most weekends. You want him to feed the cat while you are gone.

Your car has stalled out and the battery is dead. You need to call the service station to get your car jumped but do not want to leave the car. A teenager approaches. You want her to call the service station and report where you are.[20]

These situations represent just some of the cases studied by researchers interested in an area of interpersonal influence known as **compliance gain**. These researchers have spent a great deal of time trying to understand the conditions in which communicators will use different kinds of message strategies.[21]

Kinds of Message Strategies

A number of social scientists have developed lists of compliance-gaining strategies. One of the earliest, and perhaps the best known, was developed by Gerald Marwell and David Schmitt. They believed that there were at least

16 ways a communicator could get someone to respond to a request.[22] Table 9.2 describes these strategies. Others have described similar but slightly different sets of strategies.[23] While no one completely satisfactory list has been developed, it is certainly clear that there are many ways to communicate to influence to others.

The success of these strategies seems to depend on the situation. Research is currently being conducted to find out what situational factors people take into account when they choose a strategy. Initial indications seem to suggest that intimacy (how close source and target are to one another), dominance (their relative feelings of power), resistance (whether the target will comply easily or resist the request), rights (how justified the request is), personal benefits (whether the request is selfish or altruistic), and consequences (the long-term effects of the request) will affect choice of a strategy.[24] Certainly this makes sense. We don't ask a friend for a relatively inconsequential favor the same way we ask a stranger to do something that will involve a great deal of effort. You might find it useful to look at Table 9.2 and ask yourself if you have ever used any of the strategies. Try to figure out when and with what kind of people you use a particular technique. Which have been the most successful for you and why?

The Structure of Requests

Recent studies have examined the kinds of strategies most often chosen. Although evidence is sketchy, it appears that people avoid the more complex strategies and favor direct, positive requests. One study found that appeals to altruism (do it for me) and promises (I'll do you a favor one day) were the most frequently used strategies and that subjects don't generally choose negative sanctions.[25]

The same study also looked at the ways people structure their requests. It concluded that most messages making a request consist of two basic parts. The speaker begins by establishing a reason for making the request. He then politely asks whether the target is willing to comply. Both of these techniques help to define the request as reasonable rather than as an arbitrary order. How would you respond if someone said to you, "Go get me a glass of water"? In most situations, this would be rude. You probably will respond more positively to a message that establishes need ("Gosh, I'm thirsty") and asks rather than orders ("Would you mind getting me some water?"). It is important to include components that define the nature of the communicative speech act.

A competent communicator must also be aware of the face needs of the target. Messages vary in the extent to which the sender takes account of the positive and negative face of the receiver.[26] "Positive face" attempts acknowledge the need of the target to be liked and appreciated and are indicated by the presence or absence of greetings, gossip, and reference to the relationship. Compare "Hi, how are you doing? Remember Tim? Well, he sends his regards. You know, I would really appreciate it if you could do me a favor" with "Hello. Would you do me a favor?"

"Negative face" techniques acknowledge the target's desire to feel autonomous and uncoerced. The competent communicator softens a request by indicating uncertainty as to the outcome and a reluctance to impose. Compare "Would you mind?" or "Please let me know if it's an imposition" with "Do it!"

Messages may also vary in the extent to which the source tries to enhance her own face. A source who needs to borrow money may make some attempt to show she isn't a deadbeat. The person who says "I need to borrow 50 bucks" may leave us in doubt as to our

TABLE 9.2

Sixteen methods of gaining compliance

1. Promise
(If you comply, I will reward you)
You offer to increase Dick's allowance if he increases his studying.

2. Threat
(If you do not comply, I will punish you)
You threaten to forbid Dick the use of the car if he does not increase his studying.

3. Expertise (Positive)
(If you comply, you will be rewarded because of "the nature of things")
You point out to Dick that if he gets good grades he'll be able to get into a good college and get a good job.

4. Expertise (Negative)
(If you do not comply, you will be punished because of the "nature of things")
You point out to Dick that if he doesn't get good grades he won't be able to get into a good college or get a good job.

5. Liking
(Actor is friendly and helpful to get target in "good frame of mind" so that he will comply)
You try to be as friendly and pleasant as possible to get Dick in the "right frame of mind" before asking him to study.

6. Pre-Giving
(Actor rewards target before requesting compliance)
You raise Dick's allowance and tell him you now expect him to study.

7. Aversive Stimulation
(Actor continuously punishes target, making cessation contingent on compliance)
You forbid Dick the use of the car and tell him he will not be allowed to drive until he studies more.

8. Debt
(You owe me compliance because of past favors)
You point out that you have sacrificed and saved to pay for Dick's education and that he owes it to you to get good enough grades to get into a good college.

9. Moral appeal
(You are immoral if you do not comply)
You tell Dick that it is morally wrong for anyone not to get as good grades as he can and that he should study more.

10. Self-feeling (Positive)
(You will feel better about yourself if you comply)
You tell Dick he will feel proud if he gets himself to study more.

11. Self-feeling (Negative)
(You will feel worse about yourself if you do not comply)
You tell Dick he will feel ashamed of himself if he gets bad grades.

12. Altercasting (Postive)
(A person with "good" qualities would comply)
You tell Dick that since he is a mature and intelligent boy, he naturally will want to study more and get good grades.

13. Altercasting (Negative)
(Only a person with "bad" qualities would not comply)
You tell Dick that only someone very childish does not study as he should.

14. Altruism
(I need your compliance very badly, so do it for me)
You tell Dick that you really want very badly for him to get into a good college and that you wish he would study more as a personal favor to you.

15. Esteem (Positive)
(People you value will think better of you if you comply)
You tell Dick that the whole family will be very proud of him if he gets good grades.

16. Esteem (Negative)
(People you value will think worse of you if you do not comply)
You tell Dick that the whole family will be disappointed (in him) if he gets poor grades.

Reprinted with permission from Gerald Marwell and David R. Schmitt, "Dimensions of Compliance-Gaining Strategies: An Empirical Analysis," *Sociometry* 30 (1967): 357–58.

chances of being repaid. The person who lets us know "I have some money saved, but I need another 50 bucks for the down payment. I get paid at the end of next week. I wonder if I could borrow . . ." is more likely to be successful. In influence situations, as in all others, concern with face is an essential aspect of communicative competence.

Compliance-gain research is a fairly new area of investigation. So far it has raised more questions than it has answered. But the questions are interesting ones. We do know, from current research, that it is important to gear requests to situational and social demands.

INTERPERSONAL INFLUENCE AND COMPETENCE

Interpersonal influence is a complex process that takes a great deal of sensitivity and awareness. In order to persuade others, the competent communicator must understand the theoretical principles underlying social influence processes. These principles are not hard to apply. There are certain basic ways to enhance influence that cut across all theories. First of all, communicators should be aware of their own bases of power. Others respond to us according to the attributions they make about us; we want those attributions to be favorable. The persuasive speaker should build credibility; the interpersonal communicator should present himself as attractively as possible.

Second, it is important to frame appeals that take into account the needs and desires of others. If we know people are motivated by rewards, we can convince them by offering rewards. If we know they are troubled by inconsistency, we can show that our proposals will lead to stability. If we understand their values, we can appeal to them. The competent

change agent matches technique to receiver needs.

Third, we should realize that if we can get receivers to influence themselves, our work will be done for us. Encouraging a target to behave in ways related to our proposals is a cardinal influence principle. If we can get someone to try our product, to act on our ideas, to testify to our beliefs, we have gone a long way toward persuading her. Only the incompetent communicator sees persuasion as a one-way process.

In summary, competent communicators must be sensitive to the context, to their own self-presentations, and to the target's needs and vulnerabilities. They must then be able to translate this into rhetorically acceptable message forms. While we cannot give you all of the ways to do this, we can urge you to observe what works and what doesn't and to form your own theories of interpersonal influence.

REVIEW TERMS

The following is a list of the major concepts introduced in this chapter. The page number where the concept is first mentioned is listed in parentheses.

stimulus (205)
response (205)
classical conditioning (206)
operant conditioning (208)
reinforcement (208)
social reinforcer (208)
social learning theory (208)
modeling/vicarious learning (208)
social exchange theory (209)
relational currencies (209)
balance theory (209)
congruity theory (210)
cognitive dissonance theory (212)
counterattitudinal advocacy (214)

SUGGESTED READINGS

Bettinghaus, Edwin P. *Persuasive Communication*. 3rd ed. New York: Holt, Rinehart and Winston, 1980. A basic text on persuasion practice and theory. Easier to handle than Zimbardo, with more emphasis on communication.

Lofland, John. *Doomsday Cult: A Study of Conversion, Proselytization, and Maintenance of Faith*. Englewood Cliffs, N.J.: Prentice-Hall, 1966. A participant observer's firsthand account of the beginning of the Moon cult.

Mackay, Charles. *Extraordinary Popular Delusions and the Madness of Crowds*. New York: Farrar, Straus & Giroux, 1932. People will believe anything, and in this fascinating book, Mackay traces the history of some of the world's most bizarre beliefs.

Zimbardo, Philip G., Ebbe B. Ebbesen, and Christina Maslach. *Influencing Attitudes and Changing Behavior*. Reading, Mass.: Addison-Wesley, 1977. This book introduces major theories of persuasion in social psychology. For the beginning student, its interest will probably lie with the case studies, including Zimbardo's analysis of the 1974 Patty Hearst kidnapping case. (He was an expert witness at the trial.)

PROCESS TO PERFORMANCE

TOPICS FOR DISCUSSION

1. Think about the ways household products are named (Tide, Mr. Clean, Fab, Biz, Lestoil, and so on). Analyze the kinds of associations the manufacturers hope you will make. Think also about packaging and presentation. Discuss the effectiveness of this influence ploy.

2. If you are a parent, what kinds of reinforcers work with your children? If you are not, think back to the ways your parents used reinforcement principles to control you. What techniques were used, and how effective were they?

3. You may have gone to a school that used a token economy as an incentive to learning. If so, share your experiences. If you did not, do you think it is a good way of influencing children? (In a token economy, kids are paid in tokens for good behavior; these tokens can be redeemed for treats or privileges.)

4. What do you think of the economic model used in social exchange theory? Do

you think it's a good way to describe relationships? If not, why not? If so, can you extend the metaphor?

5. Modeling says we pick things up by watching others. Have you been influenced by models since you came to college? If so, who were your models, what did you learn from them, and why were they successful?

6. When you were very young, what media figures (TV or radio or books) served as models for you? What effect did they have on you?

7. Have you ever experienced the kind of pressures described by balance theory—for example, finding yourself disliking a friend because of his or her beliefs? How did you resolve your imbalance? Does balance or congruity theory come closer to describing the way you resolved the situation?

8. Think about the last fairly important decision you made. Did you do anything to avoid dissonance, such as rationalizing your decision or exposing yourself only to information that told you you were right? Describe what you did to protect yourself from dissonance.

9. Think of the person you most trust. What personal characteristics give that person credibility? What suggestions would you give the average person who wanted to increase his or her credibility?

10. Refer to the situations that open the section on compliance gaining (page 223). What techniques would you use in each situation to get the person to comply? Describe specifically what you would say or do.

OBSERVATION GUIDE

1. Schools are in the business of influencing people. What are some of the ways the institution you attend now tries to influence you? How did they get you to come? How do they control you once you're here? How will they affect you once you are an alumnus? Don't forget things like architecture and interior design of dorms and classrooms, layout of campus, college handbooks and advertising materials, peer influences, course selection, and so on. How successful is this influence?

2. Analyze your own power. When you want others to do things, how do you go about it? What bases do you use? How could you improve and increase your power bases? Outline a plan to become more powerful.

3. Observe people you know who are ingratiators, intimidators, self-promoters, exemplifiers, and/or supplicators. Describe in detail how they go about achieving power. Describe your feelings about them. Do you find yourself using any of these techniques? What is the outcome?

EXERCISES

1. Bring a number of popular magazines, ones with advertisements, to class. Form small groups and look through the magazines to find examples of each theory of influence. Keep looking until you have uncovered uses of all three learning theories, of each of the consistency theories, and of value theory. A single ad or article may use several at the same time. Once you have found examples, report to the class. Which of all the examples was the most effective in your mind? Why?

2. Form groups of four or five. You have just been hired to mount a campaign to improve the image of the city of Mudville. Think of the worst city you can imagine; Mudville is at least that bad. Its civic leaders have decided to try to improve the morale of its citizens and the image it projects to the rest of the world. Your group is to come up with a public relations campaign. Report your plan to the rest of the class, explaining the theories behind each technique. (Make up any information about Mudville itself that you feel you need.)

3. Choose a partner. Individually rank the terminal and instrumental values given in Table 9.1. Give a rank of 1 to the value most important to you personally; give a rank of 2 to the second most important value, and so on. Once you have finished, think about what these rankings say about you. Are you altruistic or egoistic? Are you a realist or an idealist? Discuss with your partner. Explain why you feel the way you do. (This is also a good exercise to do with people who are close to you. It will allow you to examine one another's value structures.)

PART III

RELATIONAL CONTEXTS

CHAPTER TEN

Look closely at this family portrait. What can you decipher about the relationships from this painting? (John Singleton Copley, *The Copley Family*, 1776–1777)

FAMILY INTERACTION PATTERNS

We are a family that has always been very close in spirit. Our father was drowned in a sailing accident when we were young, and our mother has always stressed the fact that our familial relationships have a kind of permanence that we will never meet with again. I don't think about the family much, but when I remember its members and the coast where they lived and the sea salt that I think is in our blood, I am happy to recall that I am a Pommeroy—that I have the nose, the coloring, and the promise of longevity— and that while we are not a distinguished family, we enjoy the illusion, when we are together, that the Pommeroys are unique. I don't say any of this because I'm interested in family history or because this sense of uniqueness is deep or important to me but in order to advance the point that we are loyal to one another in spite of our differences, and that any rupture in this loyalty is a source of confusion and pain.[1]

So begins John Cheever's short story "Goodbye, My Brother." This description of the fictional Pommeroy family is striking in its portrayal of the mixed emotions of family life. Here is a man who views his family as close, permanently bonded, and loyal. At the same time he admits it is undistinguished, built on illusion, and not a frequent subject of his thoughts.

Families are indeed a varied lot. They can be as quiet and inconspicuous as the Pommeroys or as public and powerful as the Kennedys. Even people who have no shared bloodlines often consider themselves family. Organizations as varied as churches, clubs, even businesses describe themselves as "one big happy family."

From the perspective of this book, the family is a social construction, another context in which communication takes place. In fact, it is one of the richest sources of communication patterns that we have. In order to better understand the impact the family has on our communication, this chapter examines the family as a system, and the communication patterns found within that system.

MAINTAINING FAMILY TIES

As you read this chapter, you may find yourself looking for some magic formula, some specific set of communication patterns or skills that will enable you and your family to reach the zenith of family life. You should know by now that you won't encounter any such formula in this book. The interpersonal communication patterns that lead to success or failure are many, and their creation and variety should be a source of celebration as much as sorrow. In fact, many family therapists and researchers agree that the myth of the "ideal family" is a problem in itself.[2]

What is the myth? You probably know it well. The ideal family inhabits a home where stress rarely occurs. Members of the family can and do talk to one another about almost anything, regardless of differences in age, sex, or viewpoint. They smile comfortably with one another even when they disagree. They don't yell or scream. They hug a lot. They listen to one another with ears pricked for maximum reception—something an expert might call "total listening." They frequently sit and look at each other for long periods of time—just thrilled to be a family unit. They play, pray, stay, say "hey," and are A-OK together. They indulge in practical jokes and other forms of good, clean fun.

So maybe we exaggerate a little. But the fact is that "normal" families don't always get along. They have built-in differences in perspective and conflicts of interest. There are typical stages in family life that produce "crisis points." Outside interests of family members and social–economic changes require adaptation and change by the family as a unit. Yet for all the difficulties any family must face, it is perhaps the best-equipped social unit in society.

Families are conservative by nature, providing a buffer between a rapidly changing society and the individual's need to maintain a stable identity. The family, even a troubled one, provides the sense of permanence in an otherwise changing world. The family is our first "social reality" and the source of many of the communication patterns and types of relationships we will repeat later in life. Virginia Satir has characterized the family as a "factory" where different kinds of people are made.[3] It is the family as a factory that we wish to investigate here.

As a producer of persons, communication patterns, relationships, and other social realities, any family can be judged as doing its job very well or quite poorly. In some cases the results may appear to speak for themselves, as when one family turns out several productive citizens while another family consistently produces social deviants. In most cases, the results are mixed, and many other social–environmental factors have to be considered. Rather than identifying any one "ideal" family type, this chapter will describe the family as a *system* of elements that operate together, producing communication patterns that enable its members to either adapt to or resist outside influences and typical crises within the family system. Once you understand the *processes* underlying family interaction, you should be a better judge of your family of origin (the family that produced you) as well as any family you help produce in the future. In fact, once you understand the patterns of interaction that were forged in the family you grew up with, you may be surprised to find yourself repeating many of those same patterns in your current intimate relationships (see Chapter 11). Let's begin by looking at the system of relationships we call a "family."

THE FAMILY AS A SYSTEM: STRUCTURE AND FUNCTION

To describe the family as a "system" may sound like we have given in to the technology of our times, making something full of life seem dull and mechanical. This is, of course, not our goal at all. On the contrary, we have found that thinking about the family as a system brings it to life, provides new insights, and gives us a vocabulary for talking about family communication (metacommunication). In Chapter 2 we introduced the basic concepts of systems theory: open and closed systems, wholeness, interdependence, nonsummativity, and equifinality. You may wish to review that discussion before you read on.

Scholars differ on the precise definition of what a family is. Some prefer to emphasize the traditional values of our culture and define the family in terms of marriage and biological kinship. We prefer to use a somewhat broader definition that includes groups of people who think of themselves as "family" even though they may not be related by blood or marriage. Kathleen Galvin and Bernard Brommel define the **family** as "a network of people who live together over long periods of time bound by ties of marriage, blood, or commitment, legal or otherwise."[4]

Family rules and interactions may be observed at the level of the whole unit ("As a family, we always had a big Sunday dinner at Grandma's—she was the only one with a place-setting for 24.") or at the level of one of its many subsystems ("Annie and Chris always fought over whose turn it was to do the dishes."). **Subsystems** may vary from the husband–wife, parent–child, or brother–sister dyad to temporary coalitions formed by one group of family members against another.

Something to remember about a family as a system is that each family member is one of its parts. And even though each part is a unique individual, he or she is also a working component of the whole system. Like any mechanical system, there must be some working order among the individual parts. (In a human system, we would call the working order between any two parts their "relationship." The various working orders developed by the entire family could be called the **family structure**. The structure of the family keeps it working smoothly, coordinating the efforts of its various subsystems. The family system can also be analyzed in terms of its **functions**, that is, the services it provides for its members and the

Individuals and subsystems within the family system. (Marisol, *The Family*, 1962)

society at large. The most obvious functions of a family are to provide socialization, food and shelter, and emotional support for its members. For society, the family serves as a major means of passing on cultural beliefs to succeeding generations.

Finally, every human system goes through a process of **evolution**. No family system remains static. The evolution of the system refers to how the family adapts to the developmental changes and personal needs of its members as well as to the changing social and economic needs of the culture. We will look at each of these aspects of the family system in turn.

Family Structures

A family may have as many different structures as it has events or issues to deal with. There may be a power–authority structure for dealing with family discipline problems, a decision-making structure for determining how the family will manage impending changes or make use of its free time, and perhaps an interaction network that indicates which family members are more likely to talk to one another about problems, share secrets, or form coalitions in order to increase their influence. Each of these structures consists of family members playing different roles and relating to other family members in unique ways. These roles and relationships are built up as members repeat patterned episodes of communication.

Power–Authority Structure

Each of us learns a great deal about how to handle and express authority by observing how it worked in our own family. Ronald Cromwell and David Olson define **power** in the family as the "ability (potential or actual) to change the behavior of other family members."[5] In most families, power is legitimately held by one or both parents. Parents are allowed to discipline their children, but not vice versa. However, as most parents know, children quickly develop their own power bases. Little Johnny knows that putting on his "cute face" will usually make his father laugh rather than punish him, and he also knows that crying will wear his mother down until she allows him to have some ice cream.

Some families establish very clear lines of authority, others allow individual members to determine how much influence they want to exert. Basil Bernstein refers to the first type of family as having a **positional structure**; the second type he calls a **person-oriented structure**.[6] In a positional family, lines of authority are hierarchically arranged. In a traditional family, power may ultimately rest with the father. In his absence, the mother takes charge, and in her absence, temporary power is passed on to the oldest child, and so on. Some research indicates that positional families make greater use of restricted language codes (see Chapter 7). In other words, there are limited opportunities for children to verbalize their own opinions, since they don't have much influence. Person-oriented families, on the other hand, rely to a much greater extent on communication as a means of influence. All members of the family are usually allowed to state their opinions and to defend or explain their actions prior to any discipline. As a result, these families teach their children to use elaborated language codes, a skill that enables them to adapt to a wider variety of social circles. Not every family can be labeled as positional or person-oriented. Bernstein describes the two types as opposite ends of the spectrum. Your family probably falls somewhere in between.

Decision-Making Structure

In some families, the power and decision-making structures may be almost identical. This may be the case if the parents make all of the family decisions, set the rules, and are the only ones who enforce them. But this is not true of every family. In some families, many decisions are made as a group, but the enforcing of decisions is left up to the parents. Even when decisions are made on the basis of group discussion, there are a variety of ways those decisions can be made. And the roles that family members play in the process may vary.

Roles In any decision-making group, people play various roles in the process. Family life is no different. See if you can identify who plays the following roles in your own family. Someone must play the role of the **task leader**—bringing up topics for the family to discuss, guiding that discussion, seeking (or preventing) input from other family members, suggesting the *means* for decision making, and in general taking charge of the situation.

Another family member may play the role of **social leader**. This is the person whose main concern is that everyone gets along, that no damage is done to family relationships while decision making takes place. Although parents take on the leadership roles most of the time, it is not uncommon for even a small child to play the social leader. While planning a weekend outing, the entire Smith family erupts into an argument about what sporting equipment to bring in their already crowded station wagon. Six-year-old Jennifer screams, "Stop fighting! I want us to have fun."

Every family needs to acquire up-to-date information in order to make the best decisions. As a result, some members specialize as **information providers**. The information provider knows—or can find out—where the neighbors went for the weekend, the best places to eat out, and the latest cultural trends.

Anyone who repeatedly points out the negative consequences of a decision or argues the opposite point of view is called the **devil's advocate**. Most experts suggest that this role be passed around, since the person who plays it too much can become an object of group outrage. However, the family that doesn't have a devil's advocate may find itself making decisions that are poorly conceived. If you've ever gone on a long trip only to later discover that there was a much shorter route, you know what we mean.

There are a variety of other roles family members may play. A **tension releaser** interjects a little humor to break up uncomfortable situations, a **silent observer** usually just listens and comments only when he thinks the process is getting out of hand, someone is being unfair, or the group needs a summary of what it has done. When a member's input reflects only her own interests and not the whole family's, that

person is labeled a **self-centered follower**. The family member who always agrees with everyone else plays the role of **conformist**. Think about your own family for a moment. Try to identify which roles each person plays most often, which ones are shared by several members, and which ones are missing. Try to imagine what it would be like if different family members switched roles.

Decision-Making Styles   How does your family make decisions? Before you read on, think about some recent family decisions. What types of problems or decisions are brought to the entire family's attention? Who decides if a problem should be discussed? How much discussion occurs prior to such decisions? Are all decisions made in the same manner or does the family handle "important" decisions differently than "mundane" ones? Who exerts the most influence in discussion? Who has the final say, if anyone? The answers to these questions will tell you a lot about your family's decision-making style.

Ralph Turner has identified three common family decision-making styles: consensus, accommodation, and de facto.[7] Perhaps one of them fits your family. The least common, but most admirable, style of decision-making is called **consensus**. A family reaches consensus when its members try to make a unanimous decision, seeking input from all members, negotiating differences of opinion or values, and trying to reach a solution that everyone feels is satisfactory. This method requires a great deal more talk than the other two styles. In many cases, true agreement among family members is an almost impossible task. It may well be that the process of *trying* to reach consensus is more important than the actual outcome.

A more frequent style of making decisions is **accommodation**, a process in which less articulate or less dominating members of the family give in to those who hold the power or are more persistent. Decision by vote is a form of accommodation. Turner suggests that members usually accommodate because they don't see the value of further discussion. They see the handwriting on the wall and figure it isn't worth their time to argue when others indicate no room for negotiation. In the long run, this style may have a negative impact on family life, especially if the same few are allowed to dominate decision making and "discussion" becomes a meaningless term. There is also a tendency to avoid conflict with this style, which means that problems may not be aired and tensions may resurface more often. However, this need not always be the case. An accommodating style can be managed successfully if everyone gives in on occasion, so that each family member has a sense of being able to influence the rest of the family when an issue is important to him or her.

When neither of the first two methods works, many families resort to de facto decision making. A **de facto decision** is one in which a single member of the family acts alone or the matter is decided "by events," usually after a period of unproductive discussion. A typical example of this style occurs on family trips. A 20-minute discussion about where to stop for lunch seems to be going nowhere. After passing a dozen fast-food restaurants, the driver of the car finally pulls over in exasperation: "We're eating here!" Or a sign along the interstate warning "Last services for 50 miles" makes the decision for them.

No doubt one of these styles characterizes the way most families make decisions, yet you may find that your family has one or more unique patterns of communication when making decisions. If you can describe that pattern and its outcomes (who it favors, how satisfactory it is to most family members, and most important, what quality of decisions it pro-

duces), you will be in a better position to understand and change the process when necessary.

Interaction Structure

Another way to look at the structure of the family is to describe the communication channels that are most frequently used within it. Some family members may spend more time with one another; some may talk to each other more than they do to other family members. The typical patterns of interaction within a family (who talks to whom most frequently) are its **communication network**. The structure of family networks may vary a great deal. A family with a *centralized* network has a single member who interacts a great deal with all the members and may or may not pass information along to the rest of the family. This central member acts as a go-between, keeping family members in touch, even though they may not physically speak to one another very often. In an extended family, a parent or grandparent may play this role. Sons and daughters living away from home may phone their parents rather than each other, since they know they'll find out what's happening that way.

Families that are highly cohesive tend to reflect a *decentralized* network, one in which frequent interaction is likely to occur among all or most family members. Extended families of this type may have large phone bills, since everyone wants to hear the news from the source. When something exciting happens to one member, she shares it with everybody, not just the central figure.

Look at the diagrams of different communication networks in Figure 10.1 and see which one best represents your own family network. In fact, your family may have more than one network. Many families alter their communication patterns in order to deal with different situations or events. Since individuals have

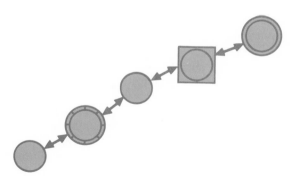

THE CHAIN NETWORK. Family members relay messages to one another via a series of other family members. It is typically used when members see each other occasionally but are rarely all together at once. Messages are, however, prone to distortion as they are passed along.

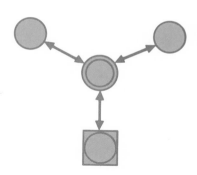

THE "Y" NETWORK. A centralized network where one member serves as a "gatekeeper," allowing some but not all messages to be exchanged among members. One parent may monitor the children's requests of the other parent, or an older child may summarize her siblings' desires to the parents.

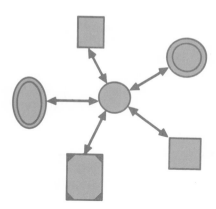

THE WHEEL NETWORK. A highly centralized network found in families that communicate through one key figure. Most members do not talk directly to one another. They find out about each other from the central figure.

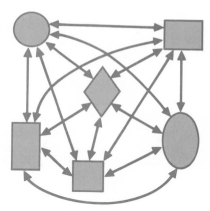

THE ALL-CHANNEL NETWORK. The most decentralized network of all. It is characteristic of families that spend a lot of time together as a unit and in separate dyads. All or most of the communication channels are open and utilized.

FIGURE 10.1

Four family communication networks

different likes and dislikes, one or more members may be automatically left out of the network when certain types of information are being exchanged. The prudish sister who thinks gossip is a form of evil is more likely to be the subject of the family rumor mill and less likely to hear about it. The brother who eschews sports is not included in the summer-long discussions of the pennant race, even though he may often be within earshot of those discussions. Younger children, especially, are often told to go outside and play when a family problem has to be dealt with. They are not yet a part of the problem-solving network.

Let's take a look at some of the structures we've been talking about in a hypothetical family, the Clicks. At the simplest level, the family role structure consists of a father (Bic, age 38), a mother (Barbara, age 36), an elder daughter (Brenda, age 15), a middle son (Buck, age 12), and the baby (Binky, age 6). The power structure in this family is a positional one, with the father and mother having the most influence, followed by Brenda, with less influence exerted by Buck and Binky. Although no one has ever stated the power structure, the children "know" that Mother is more likely to enforce rules regarding table manners and foul language, whereas Father makes sure everyone does assigned chores. In the parents' absence, Brenda is allowed to enforce rules, but she cannot actually punish her brothers.

The decision-making structure is a little different. When important decisions are made, such as where to go on vacation, everyone gets to make a pitch for where he or she would like to go. Buck has developed the habit of researching his places of interest (this year he wants to visit several outdoor historical museums and see a Red Sox game), so he is often more persuasive than his brother and sister. Although the parents tend to rule out some places because of expense or distance, a family decision is usually reached by majority vote. Most family decisions are made this way. (This decision style reflects a mix of consensus and accommodation.)

Finally, the interaction structure in the Click family is an interesting one. Brenda is very close to her father, primarily because she's interested in his work as a race car mechanic. She's always asking him questions about how things work. Oh, yes, she's also very protective of Binky and hates Buck's guts. Buck is the isolate in the family. He reads a lot about history and loves baseball. He talks a lot about his interests, but not to anyone in particular. If pressed, he would say he gets along with Binky better than anyone else in the family. Binky is his mother's favorite. They frequently form a coalition in the family decision-making process. The three Click family structures are visualized in Figure 10.2.

The structured relations of the Click family are not necessarily typical of most families. Every family establishes its own patterns and means for handling recurring situations. You may want to analyze some of your own family's structure and how they have changed since you were younger.

Characteristics of Family Structures

Family structures evolve over time as family members establish and repeat patterns of interaction. These structures have a number of characteristics in common, including the differentiation of members into roles, the creation and maintenance of boundaries, and the coordination of subsystems.

Role Differentiation In a given family structure, members perform different tasks in relation to one another. In an efficient family structure, these roles are complementary. When a parent disciplines, a child is supposed to obey. This ideal isn't always achieved, of course, but the system won't function very well if it is rarely achieved. Tension often arises in families when two members compete for the same roles, as when one parent intentionally counteracts the authority of the other: "I don't care what your mother said, you can't go!" The point here is that there must be enough complementarity of roles for the system to function, yet not so much specialization of roles that the family cannot adapt to the absence of the member who usually plays a particular role.

Boundaries According to Salvador Minuchin, a noted family therapist, it is essential that a family establish and maintain clear boundaries among its members and between itself and the outside world. The **boundaries** of a subsystem consist of "rules defining who participates and how."[8] Inside the family, there are often physical boundaries such as separate bedrooms, toys, or clothing, and corresponding rules for who is allowed to enter, play with, or wear such belongings. Parents may even impose boundaries on themselves to give their children room to breathe or grow, or simply to avoid being overwhelmed by demands. Not interfering as two younger children settle their own dispute or telling them "I can't help you out—you'll have to solve this problem yourselves" is an example of setting boundaries. It says in essence, "No adults allowed."

Likewise, families may regulate the extent to which the outside world is allowed to penetrate the family's day-to-day world. David Kantor and William Lehr identified three basic types of families that differed largely in how they deal with the society at large.[9] An **open family** is one that encourages its members to experience a wide variety of social life and then share those experiences with the rest of the family, providing a constant source of new ideas. This kind of family adapts to changes in the culture and is typified by the prototypical parent/chauffeur rushing children off to dance class, piano lessons, baseball practice, and the movies before taking in an adult education

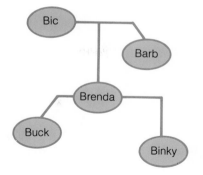

a. Power–Authority Structure
A Modified Chain Network

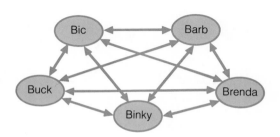

b. Decision–making Structure
All-Channel Network

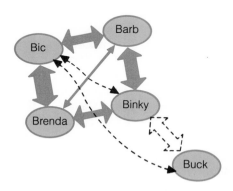

c. Interaction Structure

FIGURE 10.2
Three family structures—the Click family

Family members often specialize in their roles. Cultural stereotypes may influence the way these roles develop.

course at the local community college. The boundaries between family life and the rest of life are quite flexible, each influencing the other.

A **closed family** reacts to the larger society with a little more suspicion or indifference. "The family that plays together stays together" is a maxim that represents the values of the closed family. Many outside activities are restricted or participation is monitored very closely by the authority figures in the family. At any rate, family always comes first in relation to outside activities. Boundaries are often reflected in different sets of rules—one for appropriate behavior with family members, another for how to behave in the presence of strangers.

In contrast to the close-knit relations and high degree of sharing in both open and closed families, the third type of family is much more independent and unpredictable. This type may go months without much interaction among family members and then suddenly spend the next three weeks in constant companionship. Plans for a family get-together may be made and then changed several times because of the fluctuating interests of family members. Because life is so unpredictable in such a family, Kantor and Lehr called it a **random family**. The boundaries in random families are not very clearly drawn and may be a frequent source of misunderstanding and dispute.

Minuchin describes the boundaries of a family system along a continuum that ranges from "enmeshed" at one end to "disengaged" at the other extreme.[10] An **enmeshed system** is one that sacrifices the autonomy of its members in order to experience a great deal of cohesion. Family members feel close to one another, but the family doesn't develop clear boundaries around each person's identity. As a result, privacy and independent thinking are discouraged. A **disengaged system**, on the other hand, promotes independence at the risk of not developing a sense of family loyalty. The boundaries around individual subsystems are too rigid, and in the extreme case, members are unable to provide each other with social support. It is important to remember that these boundaries may be true of the family as a whole or that individual subsystems in the family may be enmeshed or disengaged.

Coordination of Subsystems In one sense, family life isn't much different from life in the corporate world. This is especially true of a large or extended family. Just as businesses are organized around teams of individual employees with different skills trying to coordinate their efforts to produce a product, so a family unit is organized into subsystems of individuals whose efforts must be coordinated in order to produce its products (reasonable facsimiles of persons, values, chores, and so on). Later in this chapter we'll look at the typical communication patterns of the various family subsystems. For now, it is important to realize that these subsystems do overlap and have to be coordinated. The husband–wife dyad cannot act in isolation. Whatever they do as husband and wife will also influence their roles in the parent–child subsystems they are a part of. A prime example of this is reflected in the tension many parents feel about both spouses working and being away from their children. While the parents may be convinced that they need the money, they may be equally concerned about how the children will handle (and interpret) being left alone or with a sitter. Careful

explanation may be necessary in order to enable these subsystems to adapt to the change without damaging the more permanent family relationship.

The Functions of the Family

The structured relationships that emerge through repeated episodes of communication do so for a number of reasons. When we examine the reasons for these communication patterns, we are really asking what their function or purpose is within the family unit. Communication within the family works in two very broad ways. *Internal* functions keep the system running and serve the individuals who make up the family unit. *External* functions or services are provided to the larger society. We shall look at each of these in turn.

Internal Functions
Families provide such basic necessities as shelter, warmth, and care. In addition, the family may also fulfill the following psychosocial functions: socialization, intellectual development, recreation, and emotional support.

Providing Care The human infant is one of the most helpless creatures on the face of the earth. Unable to provide for himself, he exists in an extended state of dependence on adults. Thus the most basic needs such as food, shelter, clothing, and caretaking become the first function that the family fulfills. This function has the status of moral, if not legal, obligation in most societies. In the United States, the courts may take a child away from his parents if he is not adequately cared for.

Socialization Beyond simple provisions, the family is also one of the primary teachers of what it means to be human, male or female, moral or immoral, polite or impolite, and a

Family Space: "We Shape Our Buildings and They Shape Us"

Winston Churchill reportedly said, "We shape our buildings and then they shape us." No doubt the design of corporate offices influences many business decisions that eventually affect our lives, but nowhere is the influence of the built environment more direct than in the home. Social scientists have documented the effects of overcrowded homes, the lack of privacy, the aesthetic design of rooms, lighting, decor, and many other features of the environment on human perception and behavior. Given what we know about the mutual influence of people and their environment, it's surprising that we don't exercise more control in shaping the homes that shape us.

Architects and builders design our homes, interior fashion designers and furniture makers create the products that fill them, and television and magazine editors, writers, and advertisers influence how we arrange and decorate the abode. How much of a role do we play in this process? Most of us exercise little control beyond choosing an available house, in the best location, at the right price. Have we really shaped the home that will shape us, or has someone else—a "professional"—done this for us? Do our homes (or apartments, or dormitory rooms) really fit us or are we forced to fit them?

The relationship between family interaction patterns and home design has been studied by Suzanne and Henry Lennard, who identified three types of fit: isomorphic, complementary, and nonfit.

Isomorphic fit occurs when a family's lifestyle and its environment match perfectly. The term *isomorphic* is derived from the roots *iso*, meaning "equal, homogeneous," and *morphic*, which means "having to do with shape." Take a family with very private and individual members, who need clear boundaries and their own territorial space. If they live in a large house with separate bedrooms, different activity centers, a library for studying, and a basement to get away to, then they have enough room to reinforce their separate interests.

Complementary fit refers to a counterbalance between specific aspects of the family lifestyle and the home environment. Kathleen Galvin and Bernard Brommel provide an example of a blended family with four teenagers who represent this type of fit. Before the two families merged, the teenagers had their own separate rooms and frequently withdrew when any tension arose. When the parents married, they rented a small apartment with fewer bedrooms. They did this in order to force the teenagers to interact more with each other and create a greater sense of "connectedness" as a new family. They tried to use a complementary home design to counteract a potential problem in family interaction.

host of other social graces. As children we learn what sort of behavior is deemed appropriate for boys and girls as a result of the sexual stereotypes provided by our family. The results of socialization are so ingrained that by the time we are near adulthood, many of our patterns of thought and behavior seem "natural" to us and hard to change. A child who is socialized to be patriotic may have a hard time understanding how anyone could not show respect for our national symbols. We have a friend whose mother required her children to stand at attention every time they heard the national anthem, regardless of whether they

The degree of "fit" between a family's lifestyle and the environment in which it is housed may determine how well the family gets along. (Millard Sheets, *Tenement Flats*, c. 1934)

A *nonfit* situation exists when the family and its environment are at odds. A family that lives a rough-and-tumble lifestyle would not fit well in a house with small rooms, expensive formal furnishings, and no storage space for all of its sports gear.

In addition to the basic design of the home space, the artifacts we use to fill that space may or may not "fit" with our preferred lifestyle. Media influences such as "Lifestyles of the Rich and Famous" and *Architectural Digest* may lead us to decorate

our homes as status symbols rather than comfortable places to live. Canadian architect Witold Rybczynski has written a penetrating book that addresses this question of what we want from our homes (see reference below). Maybe it's time we rethink the spaces that shape our lives before they bend us out of shape.

ADDITIONAL READINGS

Galvin, Kathleen, and Bernard Brommel. *Family Communication: Cohesion and Change.* Glenview, Ill.: Scott, Foresman, 1982. Especially the chapter on "Family Ecology."

Lennard, Suzanne, and Henry Lennard. "Architecture: Effect of Territory, Boundary, and Orientation on Family Functioning." *Family Process* 16 (1977): 49–66.

Mehrabian, Albert. *Public Places and Private Spaces.* New York: Basic Books, 1978.

Rybczynski, Witold. *Home: A Short History of an Idea.* New York: Viking Press, 1986.

were at a parade or watching a baseball game on TV. Many of us have been socialized in similar ways.

Intellectual Development Many parents spend a great deal of time, money, and anxiety to make sure that their children have ample

opportunity and rewards for academic achievement. The learning environment is loaded with educational toys, magazines, and special cable TV selections. Communication often takes the form of reciting the ABCs, counting, or responding to a battery of questions: "What's your name? How do you spell it? Where do

Assisting in intellectual development is one of the many functions that family life serves.

you live? What's your phone number?" Kindergarten is preceded by educational day care, and so on. At the other extreme, many parents neglect intellectual development, hoping the schools will do the job later on. Or they openly reject it, saying things like "I hope my child doesn't grow up to be smart. Who needs it?"

Recreation   Play is one of the major forms of childhood activity. Every family has its own repertoire of family games and traditions. Not every family plays together, but they can find ways to just "do nothing" together, which is essentially what the recreation function is all about.

Emotional Support   Probably the most important of the internal functions is the ability of the family to provide a sense of belonging—love, affection, kinship, companionship, acceptance, and resolve. This is especially important in terms of individual self-esteem, in which the strength drawn from the family serves as a springboard for confidence in dealing with the external world.

A number of social critics have lamented the fact that many of the functions once provided primarily by the family are now being taken over by the larger society (child care, schools, nursing homes, and so on). Christopher Lasch argues that, as a result, we expect

The family of Vietnam War POW Lt. Col. Robert L. Stirm runs to greet him on his return in 1973. Emotional support is a function that family members provide for each other, even when separation prevents actual communication. (Sal Veder)

the family to be primarily a refuge of emotional support.[11] Such an overemphasis on any one function may be asking too much of the system.

External Functions

The family serves the culture as much as it serves its individual members, in two primary ways: passing cultural values to its younger members and accommodating cultural change.

Transmission The family is the first and perhaps the most important transmitter of cultural values from generation to generation. Parents relay the cultural myths and guidelines they learned when they were young by reading the same stories, legends, and fairy tales to their children. They perform the same function when they reinforce the values their children glean from television fare. Many people overestimate

the influence of television programs on young children and underestimate the parents' ability to influence how children interpret what they see and hear. Parents play a vital role in this process. The attitudes and values that children hold are directly related to those of their parents, at least early in life and usually for much longer.

Straw polls taken in fourth-grade classrooms invariably show that children vote for the same presidential candidates as their parents. Parents are the ultimate authorities from a child's perspective, and the ultimate message from parents to children is how to belong to their own social circles and the larger culture. Every culture teaches its young to be patriots, to value their own way of life in comparison to other cultures. In our own culture, this means that parents must pass on values such as liberty,

The Ikai and the Van Noppen families join together to celebrate the marriage of Julie Ikai and Marc Van Noppen. Julie is a Japanese American; her father has come from Japan with Julie's stepmother and two half-brothers for the wedding. Julie's real mother also appears in this extended family portrait.

the pursuit of happiness, and, usually, material wealth, democratic rule, religious freedom, individualism, expansion of our horizons, and so on.

Accommodation   In addition to the passing on of unchanging cultural values, the family also encourages its members to adapt to many of the changes that any society goes through. Our own culture has undergone major social changes in the last 25 years. The role of women has been redefined, civil rights have been granted, or at least promised, to many minorities, and battles for freedom of sexual preference rage on. But these "changes" become real only when major social institutions such as the family, the church, and the corporation begin to accommodate them. In the family, old rules about what is "women's work" or which toys and games boys and girls should play with are gradually replaced. Now is a good time to assess how your own family has or has not adapted to some of these major cultural changes.

On a more mundane level, families ensure cultural change by competing with other families in the pursuit of a more elaborate lifestyle. "Keeping up with the Joneses" is an American middle-class tradition. American technology creates computers and video recorders; American families accommodate by purchasing them and making changes in daily routines and lifestyles so that they get their money's worth. Eventually, these superficial changes may result in changes in one or more family structures. The child who masters a computer language may be consulted more frequently and earn a more prominent position in the family's decision-making hierarchy.

THE EVOLVING FAMILY: CALIBRATING CHANGE

Families are not static social units. From the time two people decide to marry or start a family, they can expect change to play a major role in their affairs. Some of these changes are highly predictable, others are not. The successful family will be the one that learns to manage the typical stresses and strains of family life. The chances of being successful can be increased by understanding the dynamics of change and by developing some useful coping strategies.

The Dynamics of Change in the Family

The sources of change in family life are many. Among the most predictable changes are those associated with the family life cycle and stressful contact with outsiders. In addition, there are unpredictable crises such as illness or death, divorce or desertion. Each of these events may cause either a temporary or long-term upheaval in family structures, rules, and the boundaries drawn among family subsystems.

The Family Life Cycle

Over the years, researchers have pieced together the typical stages of the family life cycle. These stages represent the most likely sequence of events in family life. Most scholars would agree with the following seven **life cycle stages** adapted from the work of David Olson and Hamilton McCubbin.[12]

- Stage 1: Young married couples without children
- Stage 2: Families with preschoolers
- Stage 3: Families with school-age children
- Stage 4: Families with adolescents
- Stage 5: Launching families—sending young adults into the world
- Stage 6: The empty nest—life after the children
- Stage 7: Retirement years

While each of these stages is highly predictable (assuming a couple does have children), the degree of stress and strain will vary from family to family. The more a young couple anticipates how their life may change with the birth of a first child, the easier the transition may be. Many people now make elaborate plans for retirement; others wait until they get the gold watch before concerning themselves with the inevitable changes. Knowing what's ahead may not make for completely smooth sailing, but it does help one to prepare psychologically for impending changes. Talking about such changes in advance helps a family to negotiate and coordinate the future, rather than react to events as they happen.

Stressful Contact with Outside Sources

Just as the family life cycle produces change from within the family unit, so may other factors impose change from the outside. Every family member belongs to numerous groups and social institutions, all of which may produce stress that is brought home. The most obvious of these institutions are the school and the workplace. When a parent loses a job or a child is sent home from school for disciplinary reasons, the effect reverberates throughout the family system. Even more subtle stresses such as a bad day at the office may precipitate an argument between the spouses, which may be overheard by a child, who thinks it is her fault that her parents argue. Likewise, an entire family may experience stress from a neighborhood that disapproves of their barking dog or the "junkyard" appearance of their property.

Illness or Death of a Family Member

Every family has to anticipate the developmental changes inherent in the family life cycle as well as the impact of everyday contact with the outside world. But other crises such as death, major illness, or handicap are not so predictable. In one sense, these crisis events are inevitable; every family knows it will suffer loss in some form. But few families can prepare themselves *in advance* for such crises. There is a strong taboo in our society against talking about death. Perhaps it is a tribute to the power of the verbal code. We are afraid of the "magical" aspect of language, that words let loose may somehow escape our control.

Our unpreparedness combined with the emotional pain make the family system especially vulnerable during such crises. In addition, the physical loss or diminished capacity of a family member means that the system must change—someone else must function in the roles formerly played by that person. This is rarely an easy adjustment. The loss of a spouse may require that the remaining spouse get a new job, be both mother and father to the children (or, if the children are older, the spouse may become dependent on them), or may force the oldest child to take over household and baby-sitting chores, and so on. Some members of the family may resent anyone who tries to fill the shoes of another ("You're not my mother—you can't replace her!"). In some cases, the cohesiveness of the family may suffer, especially if the deceased member was the primary source of affection. In other cases, a slightly disengaged family may strengthen its bonds as everyone pulls together to offer reassurance and keep the system functioning.

Divorce or Separation of Family Members

Another major crisis in family life involves the deterioration, temporary or more permanent, of the relationship between one or more family members. Although the term *divorce* is usually reserved for the termination of a spousal relationship, it could just as easily be applied to any relationship within the family. Two older brothers who have not spoken to each other in years, a runaway child, a son or daughter who marries just to get away from home—all represent a breaking of the ties that bind. In each case, the crisis requires a readjustment in the family system. Most divorces, especially those involving children, are essentially a matter of redefining relationships rather than a total termination. The husband and wife who terminate their marriage usually both retain their roles as parents. This means that they maintain some kind of relationship with each other, even if it is indirect contact where the children serve as the channel for communication.

Is there a predictable pattern that families follow in dealing with unexpected losses such as death or divorce? According to a number of scholars, there is. Kathleen Galvin and Bernard Brommel have synthesized the work of these scholars into four basic **crisis stages**.[13]

- Stage 1: Shock resulting in numbness or disbelief, denial

- Stage 2: Recoil stage resulting in anger, confusion, blaming, guilt, and bargaining
- Stage 3: Depression
- Stage 4: Reorganization resulting in acceptance and recovery

These stages are normal, perhaps even necessary, for a successful adaptation to changed circumstances. At each stage, communication is crucial, if only for family members to express the emotion of denial, anger, and depression. Obviously, they can express these feelings to one another, but it may also help if their social network of friends and acquaintances lends a supportive ear. Well-meaning friends may avoid the family in their time of grief or distress, cutting off valuable assistance. What should you say? The best evidence suggests that a simple expression of sympathy and a willingness to listen are the best responses. Knowledge of the typical stages the family is going through should help you to understand (and not judge) what you hear.

Strategies for Coping With Change

Since nothing is as permanent as change, it is wise to start developing strategies your family can use in managing its own life cycle as well as handling unexpected events.

Anticipating Change

Everyone develops a basic philosophy or outlook on life. Some people expect their lives to be "settled" by the time they are 25 or 30. They expect to develop a routine and live that way "ever after." Others are frightened by such prospects. While we do not advocate a chaotic lifestyle with no goals, expectations, or ritualistic patterns, we do suggest that you come to terms with the fact that just when you think you've got it all together, a major change is

One of the most basic functions of the family is taking care of its young, which helps to establish a basis for trust.

probably right around the corner. One way to improve your forecasting ability is to read extensively about individual and family life cycles. These changes happen to most families, and it is unlikely that yours will be the exception.

Encouraging Family Cohesiveness

Families that develop and maintain at least a moderate amount of cohesiveness are more likely to survive stressful times than those that become too disengaged. When members lose touch with one another, providing emotional support in crisis situations becomes more difficult. Most families probably think of themselves as having strong bonds simply because they are family. Clichés like "blood is thicker than water" and "family comes first" reinforce the cultural stereotype of what it means to be a family. Yet a family needs to exhibit *observable* signs of cohesiveness—interdependent behavior patterns—that it can call on in time of need. Look for evidence of cohesion in your family's everyday interaction. What family rituals seem important to all or most members? What activities will members sacrifice if a family emergency arises? If some family members are away at college or live in another city, how regular are the phone calls or letters? These kinds of interdependent actions are probably the best indicators of cohesiveness.

Adaptability

Family interaction can easily get into a rut, following routine patterns of decision-making, assignment of chores, times and places to talk, and so on. When a family encounters stress or the loss of a member, some of these routines may actually become dysfunctional. A family that has always emphasized "logical thought" in its decision making may be unable to think clearly in an emotional crisis. Logic may not even be the best course of action in such situations. To be adaptable means that a family system has *alternative* ways to handle even the most routine problems.

How can you encourage adaptability? One way is to force the family to deal with minor changes on occasion. Successful management of small problems can increase coping power in the face of larger ones. Another simple activity is to ask family members to think of new solutions to typical problems, even while "the

old way" is still working. In business, these are called contingency plans, and it is considered a cardinal sin not to have any.

Social Networks

The old adage "No man is an island" could be applied to families as well. A family may be quite self-sufficient in good times and may have tremendous inner resolve during tough times, but it never hurts to have the support of neighbors, church members, or other "friends of the family." In troubled times, nothing may seem very stable within the family unit, and that's when a stable social network (of which the entire family is a member) can serve as a safety net. Members of this network can provide a perspective that is often missing in a time of stress.

FAMILY COMMUNICATION PATTERNS

Without adequate communication, family structures would fall apart, internal and external functions would be impaired, the continuity of culture would be disrupted, and the idea of "family" would evolve into a useless social concept. In this section we want to direct our attention to many of the communication patterns that keep families functioning, as well as some that threaten to tear at the fabric of family life. Some of these patterns are characteristic of the family as a whole; others are typical of subsystems within the family unit.

Interaction Patterns in the Family As a Whole

Family systems interact in ways that make their life together more than the sum of the individual members. Two broad categories of interaction will be considered: the creation of specific rules to guide family communication and the development of more general family themes and identities.

Family Communication Rules

For a family to function adequately, the behavior of its members must be at least partially coordinated. This coordination can be achieved through the establishment and enforcement of family rules. You may recall that in Chapter 7 we introduced two types of communication rules: regulative and constitutive. You will find that family life is full of both types.

Regulative Rules   These rules serve as guides for *action*. Regulative rules describe what kinds of actions define one as a member of the family. From an individual or a family perspective, these rules may be seen as *obligatory, prohibited, appropriate,* or *irrelevant.* As you read the following examples, think about the regulative rules that operate in your own family.

An *obligatory* rule is one that is usually verbalized as "you must" or "we have to." Some obligatory rules are blatant: "As long as you live under this roof, you will keep your room clean"; "Always be on time. Nothing is worse than being late." Others are the result of subtle, often nonverbal, example and reinforcement. "From the time we were very young, we always hugged and kissed each other before bedtime. No one said you had to, but Mom got this hurt-puppy look on her face if you forgot."

Most children probably think the world is populated with rules for what you "can't" or "shouldn't" do. "Don't raise your voice to me—or your father!" "Don't you dare go out of this house looking like that!" These rules generally describe behavior that may be OK for members of other families, but not this particular family. Occasionally, a rule statement may be a combination of obligation and *prohibition*: "I want you to be honest with me—but you don't have to tell me everything you do!"

A wide variety of family rules can be described as simply *appropriate*. These rules don't carry the force of an obligation but are deemed "good" behavior for a family member. Being friendly, polite to strangers, and sharing toys with a brother or sister might be considered appropriate actions. Any time a behavior is met with a response like "That was a good thing you did. I'm very proud of you," it probably reflects a rule or guide for appropriate communication.

Finally, some regulative rules are *irrelevant* as far as family membership is concerned. Those actions that a person performs that neither embarrass other family members nor evoke a response of pride can be considered irrelevant. For some families, a child's participation in extracurricular activities at school might be thought of as simply filling time; for another family it might be an obligation.

Constitutive Rules   While regulative rules guide action, constitutive rules determine meaning. For some families, a given behavior or communication pattern may have positive connotations, while others view the same pattern as negative. The following statements are examples of family members offering *interpretations* of behavior: "Helping your brother with his chores means that you care." "Talking to strangers is dangerous." "Going to X-rated movies is a sin." "A real man stands up for himself." Constitutive rules may have implicit regulative rules associated with them. When a person says, "Making snide remarks is a sign of disrespect," he or she is probably implying that you shouldn't make snide remarks to people. But that may not always be the case. If someone is acting stuffy, you may follow the regulative rule "A stuffed shirt deserves no respect."

Think for a moment about the constitutive rules that distinguish your family. Are there actions that your family interprets differently than most? What regulative rules are associated with them? Make a list of the rules in your family that are well known by everyone, which ones are unwritten, and which ones cause the most misunderstanding or conflict. Are there some things you can't talk about as a family? Are there other things that, while taboo in most families, are discussed openly in your own?

Family Themes and Identities

The family communication rules we just looked at apply to specific behaviors and instances. When we look at the overall pattern of family rules, we are likely to discover some general themes that influence the specific rules we follow. **Family themes** are recurring attitudes, beliefs, or outlooks on life shared by the entire family. Many families thrive on competition, subscribe to a particular set of religious beliefs, or view "togetherness" as the key to a happy life. Some families are anxious; they worry about everything. The Smith family has an overall outlook that "life is a gamble; take a risk." This family theme influences many of their everyday rules. They have fewer prohibitive rules than most families, and they always make themselves available for new experiences.

When family themes are prominent and the family unit is cohesive, a **family identity** emerges. Just as each individual develops a self-image, so members of the family share a group image, a sense of who they are as a unit. When you hear family members describe themselves as "fun-loving," "high achievers," or "responsible citizens," they are putting into words the constructs or images that govern their behavior as a group. We know an extended family that has labeled themselves as "sojourners" because none of them stays in one place very long. One member moved his family three times in one

One way that many families identify themselves is by designing a family crest. Draw an image inside this blank escutcheon to represent your family.

year. Another has moved from New England to the Southwest and back five times in six years. Most family members start getting "itchy" after two years in the same place.

How would you describe your own family's identity? What images come to mind? What themes or communication rules are associated with the family identity?

Interaction Patterns in Family Subsystems

Every family consists of one or more subsystems. In this section, we will describe several different family dyads, including the husband–wife, the parent–child, and the sibling subsystem.

The Husband–Wife Subsystem

The first subsystem in a family is the husband–wife relationship. Prior to the birth of the first child, this relationship is the focus of family life. Studies indicate that the quality of communication between the spouses is the single best predictor of satisfaction with the marriage.[14] How much satisfaction they experience depends, in part, on the type of marital relationship they negotiate and how they handle recurring issues such as control, togetherness and freedom, and expression of affection. Mary Anne Fitzpatrick and her colleagues have studied how congruent couples are in their relational definitions along three conceptual dimensions: autonomy–interdependence, conventional–nonconventional ideology, and conflict engagement–conflict avoidance. As a result, four very different types of couples have emerged from these studies: traditionals, separates, independents, and separate traditionals.[15]

Traditional couples are highly interdependent, share conventional views of marriage and family life, and engage in conflict on a fairly regular basis. They are also very expressive in their communication styles, and sharing information is a high priority with them. **Separates**, on the other hand, tend to be more autonomous—they give each other more room, they aren't as expressive, and while they hold fairly conservative views on marriage, they don't feel as strongly about their views as traditionals. In addition, they tend to avoid conflicts as much as possible. They deal with conflict situations by taking on complementary roles—one person decides what to do, the other follows. The **independent couple** differs from the others in that they subscribe to more nonconventional values and views about relationships. They are not as autonomous as

separates, but are only moderately interdependent. They are very expressive emotionally and do not avoid conflict with one another. In fact, independents have the highest levels of self-disclosure observed among all couple types. Fitzpatrick reports that 60 percent of the couples she has studied fall into one of the first three types. The remaining 40 percent are "mixed types," which means that the couple disagree in their definition of the relationship or in their views about marriage. The **separate/traditional couple** is the most distinct of these hybrid types. They have the most conventional sex roles of all types, self-disclose very little, ask fewer questions, and yet score consistently high on all ratings of marital satisfaction. One study reported that wives in this type of relationship have a more accurate understanding of their husbands than in any other type.[16] Of the four types, traditionals and separate/traditionals seem to be the most satisfied with their marriage, while independents and separates report the least satisfaction.

Regardless of the type of relationship, research indicates that satisfaction with the marriage tends to level off over time, and especially after the birth of the first child. The decline in satisfaction is usually compensated for by the satisfaction derived from the new role as a parent.[17] Research also shows a marked increase in traditional values and sex-role stereotyping once children arrive on the scene.[18] Thus it is possible that the transition to parenthood may lead to changes in the spouses' definition of their relationship. Another potentially detrimental change with the advent of parenthood is that a couple begins to spend more time in parental roles and less time with each other. Family therapists often advise spouses to check their talk when they are finally alone to make sure that, even then, they don't talk about the children. Ask yourself what rules you think a family should establish to increase the likelihood that the parents will have at least

BOX 10.2

Childhood in the 18th Century: What Shapes the Family That Shapes Us?

Figure 1
William Hogarth, *A Harlot's Progress, Scene I*

William Hogarth, artist and political satirist in early 18th-century London, is said to have produced "the most significant single body of hard facts about English manners of his age." His drawings, published in the popular broadsheets of London, were well known. At the time, London was a collection of merging villages, not yet the industrial city it would become in the 19th century. Hogarth's sympathies were with the oppressed lower classes, beleaguered servants, and innocent children being corrupted by the city. His satire was directed at the whole social structure (customs, laws, government and church officials) that failed to protect the children who were sent from the countryside to find work. He saw the family, and especially the child, as victims of a corrupt society—one he hoped the moral commentaries in his drawings would help reform. According to art historian David Kunzle, "Hogarth's perception of the child was as an essentially parentless creature in a society which reneged upon parental responsibility within both the private nuclear family and the public family formed by social institutions." A good deal of his work as an artist was devoted to criticizing a society that allowed such things to happen.

One of Hogarth's most important ventures was a series of five drawings, produced in 1730, known as *A Harlot's Progress*. The first and last of these drawings accompany this box, depicting Hogarth's view of the treatment of the family and its members by the very social institutions cre-

some "alone time" as a couple. How could this be conveyed to small children so that they don't feel abandoned or left out?

The Parent–Child Subsystem
The function of the parent–child subsystem is one of mutual socialization. An infant needs to be cared for, offered emotional support, and have appropriate behavior shaped through an imaginative blend of example and discipline. There is no question that the messages parents send a child influence the development of the child's personality and moral code. What parents struggle with is trying to determine precisely which communication patterns will lead to the desired outcomes.

Figure 2
William Hogarth, *A Harlot's Progress, Scene V*

ated to support the people. In the first plate (Fig. 1) we see an innocent young country girl, Kate Hackabout, arriving in London to stay with her cousin Tom and find work as a servant. But there is no family to meet her or protect her from the procuress (foreground) who seeks out and lures young women into prostitution. Note the other young girls in the wagon (background), who are under the watchful eye of a minister, seemingly protected from harm. The inadequacy of the church is seen, however, as the minister offers no assistance to the young Kate. Meanwhile, a variety of lecherous characters abounds (note the man in the doorway, hand in his pocket, believed to symbolize a Colonel Charteris, who was on trial for rape at the time of this drawing).

In the intervening scenes, Kate "progresses" from the role of servant girl to that of a prostitute, is arrested and sent to a women's prison, where she receives inadequate care. In the final plate, she has died a premature death, leaving an illegitimate child (center, in front of the coffin). The young child, alone and ignored by the "mourners," is no doubt doomed to a miserable life himself.

What Hogarth has shown us in these remarkable renderings is the role of larger social forces (whether corrupt or not) in shaping family life at a given point in history. We might do well to look at our current social structures (patterns of work, the legal system, government intervention, therapy professions, and so on) and contemplate how they shape roles and communication patterns within the various forms of the family as we know them today.

Source: *David Kunzle, "William Hogarth: The Ravaged Child in the Corrupt City," in* Changing Images of the Family, *ed. Virginia Tufte and Barbara Myerhoff (New Haven: Yale University Press, 1979), pp. 99–140.*

Experts differ widely in their specific advice to parents, and even a sampling of different views would be beyond the scope of this book. What does seem to be generally agreed upon is the fact that affection and support messages are the first priority of parenting, with control and discipline a close second. Research suggests that to gain the compliance of a child, a basic bond of *affection* must be established first. **Support messages** from parents such as praising, approving, encouraging, and showing affection are linked to higher levels of self-esteem in children and greater conformity to authority.[19] Desmond Morris has suggested that all children under two years of age need basic care and unconditional love; when they

Transmission of culture: A Japanese grandmother teaches a teenager the tea ceremony.

reach age two, restrictions and discipline should begin.[20]

The forms of discipline available to parents are not much different from the compliance-gaining strategies introduced in Chapter 9. In the parent–child literature they are referred to as **control messages**: coercion, induction, and love withdrawal. Extreme use of physical coercion tends to make children feel rejected by their parents and leads to aggression, dependency, and less internalization of moral standards. *Induction* refers to the strategy of reasoning with a child about his or her behavior ("You can't play with the train because you might break it"). The outcomes of using

induction are not very well known, because research studies have not taken into account the child's ability to *understand* the reasons used by parents. Sometimes parents withhold affection as a means of disciplining a child. This strategy is often effective in gaining short-term compliance, but the long-term effects on the parent–child relationship remain unknown.

The Sibling Subsystem

Sibling relationships are perhaps the most interesting relationships in a family. When siblings are young and close in age, they are a primary source of imagination and ingenuity. Twins frequently create their own private languages, and other siblings are almost as imaginative. An older sibling may socialize a younger brother or sister almost as much as her parents. Mix in a little sibling rivalry and you have relationships as rich as any other.

Siblings are peers and thus have a more egalitarian relationship with each other than either does with his parents. Since they can be more assertive with each other, siblings usually are. Their interaction is characterized by physical aggression and other forms of antisocial behavior. As children get older, they do mature and engage in more social behavior, cooperating to play games and so on. Cooperation increases more between same-sex siblings than it does between brothers and sisters, due no doubt to emerging sex-typed identities. Younger children tend to imitate each other a lot, but this also decreases more between opposite-sex siblings as they grow older.

Several other age- and sex-related tendencies have been borne out by research: younger children tend to like and revere their older siblings, and their liking is not reciprocated to the same degree; older brothers and younger sisters tend to have the most conflict-ridden relationships, while the older sister–younger brother relationship usually has the least conflict.[21]

IMPROVING COMPETENCE IN FAMILY COMMUNICATION

Throughout this chapter we have identified some of the structures, functions, and communication patterns that typically emerge in American families. Knowledge of these patterns is certainly a good first step in improving your ability to function effectively as a member of your family. But your family is bound to be different in some ways from the "norms" described here. Thus it is essential that you develop the ability to recognize and describe the patterns of interaction that your family actually follows. This task may take a considerable amount of your time, but it will be worth it. You might keep a journal in which you write down the communication behavior you observe in all of the subsystems of your family as well as those times when you are all together. Try to abstract the communication rules and family themes present in the observations you have recorded. Try to predict the evolution of your family system by imagining how things might change at the next step in the family life cycle or in the event an unexpected crisis occurred. Once you have described "the way things are" in your own family, you can begin to explore other alternatives. Ask friends how they handle similar situations in their families. Next time you read a novel or watch a film, pay attention to scenes involving families. What rules, themes, or identities do they project? What we are suggesting here is not an easy assignment. But it may well be the best way to improve your knowledge and ability to help create or revitalize your own family.

REVIEW TERMS

The following is a list of major concepts introduced in this chapter. The page number where the concept is first mentioned is listed in parentheses.

family (235)
subsystems (235)
family structure (235)
family functions (235)
evolution (235)
power (236)
positional structure (236)
person-oriented structure (236)
decision-making structure (236)
task leader (236)

SUGGESTED READINGS

Fitzpatrick, Mary Anne, and Diane Badzinski. "All in the Family: Interpersonal Communication in Kin Relationships." In *Handbook of Interpersonal Communication*. Edited by Mark Knapp and Gerald R. Miller. Beverly Hills, Calif.: Sage Publications, 1985. An up-to-date overview of theory and research on communication within the family structure.

Minuchin, Salvador. *Families and Family Therapy*. Cambridge, Mass.: Harvard University Press, 1974. This book is written for practicing family therapists but makes for enlightening reading by anyone interested in the family. Based on systems theory, it demonstrates family interaction patterns by exploring transcripts of some of Minuchin's own therapy sessions.

Satir, Virginia. *Peoplemaking*. Palo Alto, Calif.: Science and Behavior Books, 1972. A book that truly blends theory about families with practical, engaging activities that any family can use to better understand itself. It is written in a lively style and intended as a workbook for families interested in changing some of their rules and family structures.

PROCESS TO PERFORMANCE

TOPICS FOR DISCUSSION

1. As a class, offer your own perceptions of the "ideal" family. How do your versions differ from the one described on pages 233–34? Is there any harm in the fact that real families rarely live up to the ideal?

2. Discuss the appropriateness as well as the benefits and negative consequences of allowing children to be influential in the family decision-making structure. Is it better, for instance, that children "be seen and not heard," or for them to be treated as small adults with somewhat equal input and negotiating power? What other issues are at stake here?

3. How can families balance the tensions of enmeshment and disengagement as discussed on page 242? How do members of your own family signal when they need to be alone or in the company of others? Is it possible to designate "alone time" or "together time" for different family subsystems and the whole family? Discuss the value or harmful consequences of separate vacations for family members.

4. Another way to enhance discussion about family life is to identify the ways that families achieve each of the functions listed on pages 243–48. Discuss positive and negative communication patterns associated with each function.

5. As mentioned in the text, some critics believe that too many family functions have

been taken over by other social institutions. Schools have the major responsibility for intellectual development and even socialization. Day-care personnel or baby-sitters feed, clothe, and play with our children. This leaves the family with the primary function of giving emotional support. What are the risks of having the family "specialize" in only one or two functions? Does it place too much of an emotional burden on family members, especially when other activities and functions become "foreign" to the family?

6. Starting with the descriptions of couple types on pages 255–56, try to logically deduce the type of family (open, closed, or random; enmeshed or disengaged) that each couple type is most likely to produce. Is this a viable way to predict the evolution of a family? Why or why not?

OBSERVATION GUIDES

1. Write a brief paper describing the *evolution* of your own family. Start as far back as possible, relying on interviews with older members of your family (grandparents, great-aunts and uncles, and so on). Try to determine which family themes have survived the generations and which ones have characterized each successive generation.

2. Observe different television families—single-parent, extended, nuclear, and blended families (those created by adoption or remarriage). Look for common threads. Which commonalities are essential to the concept of "family" and which ones are just currently fashionable?

3. In the same vein as exercise 2, choose a fictitious television or film family and study several episodes of family interaction. Identify the family themes, regulative and constitutive rules, and other recurring communication patterns in evidence in the family and its subsystems. Compare the fictitious family with your own and other families you have known. Which themes, rules, boundaries, or patterns are unrealistic? Are TV families similar to or different from real ones? What expectations do TV families engender in real ones? Are there any dangers in the depictions of families on television?

CLASSROOM EXERCISES

1. **a.** Divide the class into several groups, varying in size from two to six. Each group will be a family unit for the duration of one week. Either the group or the instructor can decide who will play the roles of mother, father, oldest child, and so on. You may want to assign different ages to each of the children.

b. Once roles are determined, the "parents" should meet to discuss the values and rules that they want to use as guides to raising their children. At the same time, the siblings may meet and develop their own personas for the week.

c. Next, each "family" meets as a group to plan two or three outings for the coming week. These may include trips to the park, shopping excursions, a family dinner. Plans should be tailored to fit the ages of the children. Childless couples will, of course, plan their own events. These outings should be planned *and carried out* during the week.

d. Parents should make the "rules" for the week clear to each of the children. Some parents may insist that a child phone one or both of them for "permission" to go out at night, for example. (The instructor may wish to set some ground rules to prevent abuse. For instance, role playing might be limited to specific hours of the school day.) In the spirit of the exercise, family members should reluctantly follow some of the rules they don't like and, on occasion, try to see what they can get away with.

e. Each family member should keep a journal of thoughts, feelings, and observations of communication in the family. A short paper might be required in which family structures, functions, identity, rules, decision-making style, and so on are evaluated and commented on. A class discussion at the end of the week should be enlightening.

2. Divide the class into seven groups. Each group is responsible for researching one of the stages in the family life cycle and making a ten-minute report to the rest of the class. Research could focus on identifying (a) the major issues in each stage; (b) typical communication patterns; and (c) the most common family problems. Groups can use skits, role plays, and other audiovisual means for depicting family communication in each stage.

CHAPTER ELEVEN

In intimate relationships, we do not always need a reason to be together.
(John Singer Sargent, *Paul Helleu Sketching with His Wife*, 1889)

INTIMATE RELATIONSHIPS: CREATING DYADIC IDENTITIES

A YOUNG MAN APPROACHED the instructor of his interpersonal communication class and revealed the following dilemma:

I've dated the same woman several times, and it seems like we've got a pretty good thing going. I mean, we talk about things pretty openly and we get along really well. But last week she stumped me. We were talking along and she said something about what a "goofy relationship" we have and then she laughed pretty hard. I asked her what she meant, and she said, "Oh, nothing, really; sometimes we just strike me as being funny together." For the life of me, I don't get it. If we really have such a good relationship, then I guess she's just joking and I should take it in stride. But maybe she's trying to tell me something. Maybe the so-called joke is her way of telling me she's not so hot on this relationship anymore. Should I believe what she says or what I think she means? I sure wish I knew.[1]

This young man's experience is not unique. At one time or another, most of us have been in a similar situation. We have faced those awkward moments in a relationship where we're not sure which carries more weight: the messages being exchanged at the moment or

the definition of the relationship we thought we had prior to that exchange. As students of communication, we realize that relationships are constantly being defined and redefined through the communication process. We know that in the beginning of a relationship most of the messages we exchange are based on cultural scripts or limited knowledge of the other's social status and group memberships. To get to know someone on a personal level is a more complicated process.

In this chapter we want to explore how we move relationships away from the public level and toward the more personal. We'll begin by defining intimacy and its two major forms: friendships and romantic couples. Next we'll look at two ways these relationships can be created: through conscious planning and rational awareness of relational messages or through a slower, less conscious process of creating interdependence and other conditions for intimacy. Then we'll investigate the various ways people are attracted to one another over time, culminating in a review of the typical stages of development, maintenance, and decay in friendships and then in romantic relationships. Finally, we'll suggest some ways to manage intimate relationships more effectively.

HOW ARE INTIMATE RELATIONSHIPS FORMED?

Intimate relationships normally begin just like any other social relationship–governed by rules and conventions of politeness, the adoption by each person of a culturally provided face and line, and so on. But at a certain point these impersonal roles and rules are abandoned and replaced by a new, more personalized system of interaction. How does this happen? What are two people moving toward when they begin to create a private interpersonal relationship? Let's turn our attention to how private relationships develop.

Defining Private Bonds

In Chapter 2, we outlined how private bonds tend to differ from public ones in our culture (summarized in Table 2.1). It might help to think about each of the dimensions mentioned as *criteria* by which we judge a relationship to be more or less intimate. For instance, we said that private relations tend to place a greater emphasis on *who* the persons involved are (irreplaceable criterion), structuring their everyday lives around shared activities (interdependence criterion), sharing more unique information about themselves (particularistic criterion), negotiating unique rules to guide their relationship rather than following social norms (individualistic rules criterion), allowing emotion and affection to play an important role in their interaction (sentimentality criterion), and finally, deriving more rewards from the relationship itself as opposed to what the relationship can do for each person individually (intrinsic reward criterion).

We do not believe that every intimate relationship will fulfill all of these criteria or that the criteria represent some sort of "ideal" of intimacy. But we do conceptualize intimacy as exhibiting more of these criteria, more frequently, than public relationships do. For instance, people who work together on tasks that are highly interdependent, such as a members of a surgical team, may actually spend more hours in a day together than each spends with significant others. However, they probably wouldn't classify their work relationships as intimate unless they also exhibited several of the other criteria mentioned above. Adversarial relationships (see Box 11.1, pp. 268–69) fulfill most, but not all, of the six criteria, qualifying them as a form of intimate relationship. Thus relationships we think of as private or intimate generally share most of these six criteria. We can define **intimacy** as a unique bond created by two people through some combination of highly interdependent actions, individualized rules, and personal disclosures, and viewed by both parties as relatively affectionate, intrinsically rewarding, and irreplaceable.

A central feature of all relationships is that they are not static. Thus an intimate relationship may be more or less interdependent or sentimental or individualistic from day to day, or even from moment to moment. We might even say that intimate relations are created and "re-created" by repetition of familiar episodes with consistent roles and rules, or that they are renegotiated and changed through the introduction of new episodes or modified roles and rules. Thus two friends constantly rebuild their relationship by engaging in favorite episodes such as "going to the movies," "cross-country skiing," or "exchanging recipes" with each other. A married couple may reaffirm their intimacy through regular episodes of "recounting the day's events" and "talking about future plans." Or they may increase their intimacy by adding some new episode such as "camping in the woods" to their repertoire. Or they may shift the basis of their intimacy. They may become more *autonomous* (he takes cooking classes and a separate vacation; she joins a fitness club and starts "bowling with the girls") and compensate by increasing the amount of self-disclosure with one another.

From these examples we should realize that an intimate relationship isn't something we make and then put on a shelf to look at and admire. Relationships are a lot like driving the same way to work or school every day. We know there are other routes, but we continue to follow the familiar path. In the same way, we keep "rebuilding" the same relationship day in and day out by engaging in the same familiar episodes. Intimate relationships, then, only seem "stable" to us because we repeatedly glue together the familiar parts (interacts, episodes, and so on) or replace them with new ones that are similar in some way. And frequently they aren't very stable at all, as events signal changes on some or all six of the dimensions of intimacy.

Our culture teaches us to distinguish some types of intimate relations from others. We don't tend to think of lovers, best friends, and 20-year marriage partners in the same way. We'll focus on the two most common in our own culture: friendships and romantic couples.

Friendships and Romantic Relationships

On the surface, the differences between friendships and romantic relationships seem obvious. Rules for sexual behavior mark the distinction for some people. For others, mutual expressions of passionate love indicate romance, whereas friendship is based on strong liking or companionship. Others think of romance as short-lived, giving way to friendship if the relationship is to last. Try your own hand at defining the difference between friends and lovers. It's not as easy as you might think.

There probably are other, more subtle differences such as our expectations about where each type of relationship should fall on the six dimensions we've mentioned (how much sentiment should be expressed, how much and what type of interdependence is allowed, and so on). For instance, some theorists argue that behavioral interdependence among friends is normally voluntary; they don't usually make demands on each other's time without asking first.[2] In a marriage, such interdependence may be expected and even taken for granted. Thus while both types of relationships may be considered intimate ones, they tend to differ in one major respect. As relations develop over time, friendships tend to retain their voluntary nature, while romantic relationships show a tendency to build obligations and commitments into their bond.

Even within the same type of intimate relationship, such as marriages, we know that people work out their relationships in vastly different ways. For instance, any one intimate relationship might be characterized as highly irreplaceable, interdependent, and sentimental; moderately individualistic and intrinsic; but not especially particularistic. In such a relationship, neither person may be able to conceive of living with anyone else, even if one partner died. They may do almost everything together, from working in the same office to attending the same social events to going to bed at the same time. They may be very expressive in their affection for one another.

Or they may have both grown up in a subculture that dictated most of the rules for how partners are to relate to one another, and thus developed only a few rules that are truly unique to their own relationship. They may also have been taught to marry "the right kind of person" for reasons of social status or economic security, and so they derive as many extrinsic rewards from the relationship as they do intrinsic ones. And finally, they may enjoy talking about topics that many of us would

BOX 11.1

Adversarial Relations: The Intimate Enemy

Sherlock Holmes has his Moriarty, Krystle Carrington has her Alexis Colby. Wile E. Coyote peeks out from behind a large rock, waiting anxiously for the familiar "beep-beep" of his archenemy, Road Runner. Bugs Bunny plots one more time how to harvest the prize carrot in Elmer Fudd's garden. We hear Archie Bunker's verbal blasts at Meathead, and we can see that J. R. Ewing is setting up Cliff Barnes for yet another multimillion-dollar scam. Adversarial relationships such as these are very common, yet we seldom acknowledge how intimate they are. Most of us have someone we consider to be the bane of our existence—the punk in junior high school who always knocked your books off your desk, the office gossip who wants you to work someplace else, an in-law, perhaps, or even a very close friendship that resembles a love–hate relationship.

An adversary is perhaps best described as a formidable opponent, and the relationship as one tinged with animosity. Intimacy often develops in such relationships because of the need to know how the opponent thinks and is likely to act. We often use the analogy of chess or the game of "cat and mouse" to describe the moves and countermoves typical of adversaries trying to get the better of each other. It is not uncommon for archenemies to participate in a relationship so profound that each one's identity becomes shaped and bound by it. In Victor Hugo's classic *Les Misérables*, Police Inspector Javert spends the majority of his life in a single-minded pursuit of his enemy, an escaped convict named Jean Valjean. Javert is a principled man of law and order who follows Valjean like a bloodhound. Valjean rejects his life of crime, but cannot convince the skeptical Javert. Several years of searching, including numerous arrests and subsequent escapes, cements the bond between the two rivals. The reader may even wonder if Javert hasn't subconsciously allowed Valjean to escape, so the pursuit may continue and the relationship remain a vital one. In the end, it is their relationship that dominates. Javert cannot bring himself to deny Valjean his freedom.

Another common adversarial relationship in a democracy such as ours is that of the journalist and the politician. William Rivers points out the degree of interdependence between the two. The journalist has little to

consider "impersonal," such as world and civic events, the weather, and what's on television, so much so that they spend little time talking about and revealing private attitudes and feelings. And they may be very satisfied with their relationship.

Historical Influences in Defining Intimacy

We have defined intimacy as a flexible concept, fluctuating along several dimensions of behavior and meaning. We have done so because we think the meaning of intimacy changes from culture to culture, family to family, and from time to time within cultures and families. Let's look at the influence of family and cultural messages on how we define our own intimate relationships.

Family Messages

In the last chapter we discussed some of the types of long-term relationships that couples develop. Such relationships are often influenced by family interaction patterns learned earlier in life. Thus each of us may bring into a relation-

write about without the politician who speaks or acts (or fails to act when expected to). For their part, politicians often use the press to further their own ambitions because the government has no communication system of its own. But the common bond goes even deeper. As Rivers notes:

It is one of the central ironies of democratic life that the politician and the political journalist have so much in common. They are both generalists who must comprehend the overarching issues in an age of specialization. They are committed to serving the people—who regard both politics and journalism with an edge of mistrust. . . . They make their mistakes in public. Above, all, politician and journalist depend upon each other.

In fact, the adversarial relationship is crucial to the practice of democracy. Rivers identified the biggest problem in these relationships as the tendency for journalist and politician to become "sweethearts"—to become too trusting of each other. When this happens, the news reporter may find it easier to accept the information that is handed out than to question and challenge it. For democracy to flourish, adversarial relations must be maintained.

This need for adversaries may be true in other areas of our lives as well. Put yourself in the place of Wile E. Coyote and try to imagine life without Road Runner.

Source: *William Rivers,* The Adversaries: Politics and the Press *(Boston: Beacon Press, 1970), p. 2.*

---

ship quite different impressions of what intimacy means. Perhaps you can recall verbal or nonverbal messages you heard as a child that suggested to you what "ideal" relationships were like. These differing perceptions of intimacy no doubt influence how we come to define any current relationships.

Recent Cultural Messages

Likewise, our views of what intimate relationships should be like can be influenced by changing cultural messages. In a review of popular magazines from the 1950s to the early 1970s, Virginia Kidd chronicled a major shift in perceptions of and advice given about interpersonal relationships.[3] The 1950s and early 1960s vision of relationships was described by Kidd as a single standard of self-sacrifice and avoidance of conflict (Vision I). Every effort was made to keep your partner happy. This view eventually gave way to a second vision in the late 1960s, one in which self-sacrifice was replaced by self-fulfillment and conflict avoidance replaced by a norm of open expression of feelings, friendly or hostile (Vision II). Table 11.1 identifies some of the

TABLE 11.1

A comparison of interpersonal ideologies in two eras

Vision I 1950s–early 1960s	Vision II mid 1960s–early 1970s
SINGLE STANDARD is the norm for relational behavior, defined in terms of appropriate male–female behavior.	CHANGE is the norm for relational behavior; model marriage is a myth.
Relational meanings are PRECONCEIVED.	Relational meanings are FLEXIBLE, negotiable.
Deviation from norms is akin to EMOTIONAL PROBLEMS.	Deviation from norms can be seen as CREATIVITY, a way to negotiate new types of relationships.
Competence is creating an image resembling the cultural IDEAL.	Competence is OPENNESS; we can talk it out, work out a UNIQUE relationship.
Major prescriptions for communication	
SELF-SACRIFICE—make others happy.	BE YOURSELF—express your own feelings.
AVOID CONFLICT or causing others discomfort; conflict is negative.	COMMUNICATE. Failure to communicate is negative; "Suffering is not the worst thing in life . . . indifference is."
TOGETHERNESS. Simply being with each other is most important; "You won't even *want* a night out alone."	AUTONOMY. Togetherness is important as long as it doesn't interfere too much with own freedom.

Adapted from Virginia Kidd, "Happily Ever After and Other Relationship Styles: Advice on Interpersonal Relations in Popular Magazines, 1951–1973," *Quarterly Journal of Speech* 61 (1975): 31–39.

major differences in these two visions. Perhaps you can think of more recent cultural messages that suggest ways the dominant vision of intimate relationships is being modified or changed again.

Distant Cultural Messages

In order to fully understand how differently intimate relationships can be defined, it is instructive to look at our culture's more distant past. Perhaps the most interesting study of intimate relations past is Howard Gadlin's analysis of how the concept of intimacy has changed over the last 300 years in American middle-class, opposite-sex relationships.[4] Gadlin based his research on personal diaries and advice books from different periods of American life as well as on the views of various historians. He points out that prior to the industrial revolution in this country, intimate relations were characterized by close proximity (parents and children often shared the same bedroom) and a formality that we would today describe as impersonal. Part of the reason for this was that the world of work and the world of home were largely inseparable. A family grew its own food and exchanged any goods it produced at home for those few items members couldn't make. Personal life was not private; rather, individuals were under the constant surveillance of the entire community in which they lived. Perhaps the only way people could maintain any sense of separate identity was to reserve their innermost feelings and keep others at arm's length. While these definitions of intimacy don't necessarily influence our views today, they should indicate to us that current views may change as economic and cultural conditions change.

The Creation of Intimate Relations

Some researchers believe that intimate relationships develop because, like the Marines, people are constantly looking for a few good ones. The process is portrayed like shopping for a good pair of shoes. You keep trying pairs on until you find one that fits. This approach assumes that people are highly cognizant of their own behavior and the implications of their interactions with others. Other social scientists point out that intimate relations often seem to "just happen" and can't be predicted very well in advance. The conventional wisdom here is that you "just never know" when love is going to hit you. Furthermore, many relationships develop slowly, almost imperceptibly, mixing elements of both the personal and impersonal. Both views are probably true at times, since communication patterns and their meanings are often seen better in retrospect.[5]

Planning for Intimacy
Some analyses of how intimate relations develop attribute a lot of strategic planning to the partners involved. Initial interactions are described as "auditions for friendship," and interactants are thought to be consciously evaluating each other's behavior in light of how well the other matches some "ideal partner." In this view, most of the communication between two newly-mets is in the form of testing the other's credentials for intimacy: "Are you my type?" "Do you measure up to my standards?" "Here, take this test. Let's see if you can pass it."

But how frequently or to what extent do we actually test the intimacy potential of a new relationship? Certainly there are times when we take stock of our lives and may realize that our intimate relations are few and far between. First semester, freshman year may be one of those times. We meet hundreds of new people, only a few of whom will become close friends. We may be very conscious of how we select them and they select us. Dating is another example of the kind of situation in which we may be highly aware of the potential of a relationship. We are taught to use the dating game as a means for finding the right person; it is not usually seen as an end in itself, an activity to be enjoyed outright. The cultural messages we receive may encourage us to be more aware of the process. In our culture, the number of self-help books on achieving intimacy suggest that it is a prized possession. We may start to look at relationships as "commodities"—products to be purchased. If we adopt this view, we may indeed pay more attention to our shopping habits, making sure that we're good consumers of relationships.

In summary, there do seem to be occasions when we are highly aware of the intimacy potential of a new relationship. We may even plan encounters in advance, hoping that the relationship will move in the direction of intimacy. But there is no indication that we are always so conscious of where a relationship is going. In fact, many relationships survive for years on a relatively impersonal basis before they develop toward intimacy.

Conditions for Intimacy

Intimate relationships are not always planned; proposals are not always rehearsed. There is not always a pursuer and a pursued. But neither does an intimate relationship spring itself on the parties in full-fledged form. The development of such a relationship is part of the communication process. But for one reason or another, the partners involved have not perceived (or have ignored) the intimacy potential in the messages and activities they have shared. Researchers point to a number of factors that may be combined and either gradually or suddenly make us aware of a relationship's potential for intimacy.

One of these factors, **physical proximity**, simply increases the likelihood that two people will communicate more frequently with each other. This factor alone seldom leads to intimacy, unless there are few other people available for interaction. More often, proximity sets the stage for other factors to interact. Perhaps one of the most common and often overlooked sources that lays the groundwork for possible intimacy is the frequency of **shared episodes**. An episode is shared when two people engage in an activity that neither could do alone. Thus when two people work closely together, or go mountain-climbing together, or engage in any shared activity repeatedly, they increase their interdependence. At first, partners develop behavioral interdependence. All they invest in each other is an exchange of coordinated behaviors. Harriet Braiker and Harold Kelley point out that the normal pattern of development in close relationships is a movement from (1) behavioral interdependence to (2) the creation of rules and norms for joint action to (3) interdependence in personal attitudes and characteristics.[6] This suggests that establishing behavioral synchrony, while it does not in any way guarantee intimacy, certainly paves the way for future development should it be desired or encouraged. Earlier we mentioned that dating is usually seen as a precursor to a more serious relationship, although it could be viewed as an end in itself. Parents and teenagers often view the process differently. A teenager, seeing the date as just an activity, tells her parents not to worry, "it's nothing serious." The parent, perhaps intuitively recognizing the potential of such behavioral interdependence, admonishes, "Don't go out with anyone you wouldn't want to marry."

Other situational factors can influence movement toward intimacy. Times, places, and dates can affect how we feel and create what Mark Knapp calls a "state of **intimacy readiness**." Valentine's Day, spring fever, and the senior year of high school or college all qualify as intimacy producers.[7] Likewise, finding yourself in a situation that is normally defined as intimate may induce feelings of intimacy. You go to a dance with several friends and acquaintances; as the evening wears on, most of your friends drift off, leaving you alone in the company of the only other person in your party—one who happens to make an attractive partner. Fate strikes again—with consequences no one could have predicted. In these circumstances it doesn't matter so much who the partner is—what matters is that there is a partner. The relationship may be off and running before you've even had a chance to assess it.

Romantic feelings are another situational factor that influences movement toward intimacy, perhaps the most common factor in our culture. Most of us require that "falling in love" feeling before we legitimize a relationship as intimate. In their analysis of romantic love, Warren Shibles and Charles Zastrow identify three primary components: (1) an event that brings two people together, such as a date; (2) positive self-talk, an inner dialogue in which you convince yourself that the other is attractive; and (3) an emotional response or feeling of arousal (increased heart rate, nervous excitement, and so on).[8]

Interestingly, the absence of one component changes the nature of the feeling. Arousal and attraction without the event lead to romantic fantasies; the event and arousal without the attraction produce avoidance; the event and attraction but no arousal suggest friendship but not love, and so on. The most fascinating component, however, is the emotional response. A number of studies have demonstrated that any emotion, including love, consists of two things: physiological arousal and a cognitive label, such as love, hate, fear. The cognitive labels are produced by cultural and social definitions of the situation.[9] In one study, three groups of men experienced different levels of arousal before viewing videotapes of women they were told they would get to meet. Those who had higher levels of arousal were *more* attracted to beautiful women and *more* repulsed by less attractive women than those men who had been exposed to lower levels of arousal.[10]

Regardless of the type of intimate bond or our level of awareness about how it was created, researchers have long known that intimate relations rarely get off the ground without some form of attraction. People who find each other attractive communicate more frequently, giving their relationship the opportunity to develop in a more personal direction.

INTERPERSONAL ATTRACTION: OPENING THE DOOR

We may "like" a lot of people, that is, develop a positive impression of them through self-talk, without ever pursuing a more personal relationship with them. In some cases this may be "liking from afar" (without any interaction to speak of); in other cases, we may continue to interact with a person on a cultural or sociological level. Richard Sennett has referred to this type of interaction as **civility** or "an activity

which protects people from each other and yet allows them to enjoy each other's company."[11] We are likely to be attracted to a lot of people in this way. Many of the same factors that attract people to form civil, impersonal relations also lay the groundwork for more personal relationships should both partners desire to pursue one. In fact, one theory of attraction suggests that we begin almost immediately to evaluate others as potential friends or romantic partners. From the entire pool of people we meet, we begin a process of "filtering out" those who have little potential and taking a closer look at those who show promise.

Duck's Filtering Theory of Attraction

Steven Duck's filtering theory of attraction explains when and how we use the verbal and nonverbal cues of others to determine their attractiveness as a relational partner. He suggests that people use a distinct and sequentially ordered set of criteria to evaluate each other's attractiveness.[12] We assess the attractiveness of a new acquaintance and of people we have known for some time differently. Attraction is determined by different criteria as a relationship moves in a more personal direction. These criteria act as filters, sifting out those people who are not likely to fit in one of our social circles. According to Duck, the sequence of filters goes something like this:

Sociological or Incidental Cues
The first criterion of attraction is that people must have an opportunity to observe each other. Thus such factors as the proximity of homes or work sites, the frequency of interaction, and the expectation of future encounters encourage the development of attraction.

Other Pre-Interaction Cues
Once we know that we're likely to meet a person again, we begin to scrutinize his or her

behavior from afar. Physical cues such as height, weight, beauty, clothing, and other surrounding artifacts become useful as a basis for attraction. These cues may be used to infer the person's social status, income, and lifestyle. Perceptions of how similar or different we are may be inferred, but they are limited in scope. We may, however, use this information to determine whether we want to initiate a conversation and what topics of conversation might be appropriate.

Interaction Cues
Much more information becomes available to us once interaction begins. The topics of conversation we both enjoy, how long each person talks, smoothness of turn taking, as well as duration of eye contact and interaction distance may all be cues that help us determine liking. Some behaviors of the other may turn us off immediately, while others may take several interactions to evaluate. According to

Duck, the more we interact, the less important the sociological and pre-interaction cues will become as a basis for attraction.

Cognitive Cues
Eventually interaction behaviors enable us to form impressions of the other's attitudes, beliefs, and personality. Once these are formed, attraction is more likely to be based on assessments of these cognitive characteristics than on group memberships, clothing, or specific behaviors.

Interpersonal Magnets: Factors That Pull Us Together and Push Us Apart

The filtering process we have just described tells us how people assess attractiveness in a very general way. A lot of research has been conducted on more specific factors that draw people together and create attraction or repulsion between them. This research finds that people are often attracted to each other for one or more of the following reasons: perceptions of physical beauty, important similarities, reciprocated liking, complementary needs, and anticipated costs or rewards. We will look briefly at what this research suggests about the interpersonal dance of approach–avoidance.

Physical Beauty
As filtering theory suggests, physical beauty is often the most important basis for attraction *initially*. In Chapter 6 we talked about physical appearance as a nonverbal code. We also noted that most cultures identify prototypes of male and female beauty, which influence our perceptions of physical attractiveness. This suggests that we would most likely pursue relationships with those people we consider the most physically attractive. However, several research studies support a slightly different view, called the **matching hypothesis**. According to this research, the decision to interact and pursue a

more personal relationship is often based on the perception that we are relative "equals" in terms of physical attractiveness.[13] Many people assume they "don't have a chance" with someone they think is prettier or more handsome than themselves. As a result, we often evaluate the attractiveness of both self and other to see if we "match up."

Similarity

How many times have you heard it said that "birds of a feather flock together" or that two people are "kindred spirits"? Common sense tells us that people are attracted to each other because they have key similarities: they like the same food, the same politics, and the same kind of people. They share many of the same personality traits. Most of the research that has tested the similarity hypothesis finds some measure of support for it.[14] Even so, a clear understanding of the relationship between similarity and attraction has been elusive. For all the ways that two people can be similar there are just as many, if not more, differences between them. Too much similarity may be unhealthy in the long run, since it may result in boredom or failure to perceive enough alternative courses of action. Initially, the most important thing may simply be the perception that there are enough significant similarities to prolong interaction, enough topics of interest to talk about. In some cases, the basis for attraction may be a single commonality that ties together a lot of dissimilarities. For instance, two people may find that they both like to argue and, fortunately, they disagree on most everything else.

It is also possible that initial similarities may be misleading. Two people may have a common belief that they should "help others less fortunate," but fundamentally different reasons for that belief. One's belief is based on the fear that "God will punish me if I don't help others"; the other believes that "helping others

is the ultimate form of humanity." Thomas Lickona has argued that similarity in cognitive and moral development—not *what* a person thinks, but how he or she *reasons*—may be the most important type of similarity in the maintenance of long-term, intimate relationships.[15]

Reciprocal Liking

We are often attracted to another person for the simple reason that he or she has demonstrated an interest or shown liking for us first. Several studies confirm that expressed liking will usually be reciprocated.[16] If you think about it, it's only natural to like those who like us. After all, if someone is capable of recognizing what a wonderful person I am and enjoys *my* company, she must be a half-decent person herself. Likewise, the person whose face registers disgust when he sees me enter the room is likely to elicit the same response from me.

Some research shows that expressed liking may often be enough to offset initial perceptions of dissimilarity. Benjamin Broome found college students to be more attracted to foreign students who were quoted as saying Americans were easy to get along with, well-informed, and interesting to talk to.[17] In this case the expressed "liking" was for Americans in general; it wasn't even directed at the target.

While the reciprocal-liking hypothesis may seem natural, it doesn't always hold up. Under some conditions, we tend not to respond positively to those who show liking for us. The basic premise of the reciprocal-liking hypothesis is that each person likes himself. If, however, a person has a negative self-image, he may have a hard time convincing himself that others really do like him and may view expressions of liking as polite insincerity. This may be called the Groucho Marx syndrome ("I wouldn't join a club that would have me for a member"). Such a person thinks there must be something *wrong* with someone who would like him. Also, the expression of liking must be situationally appropriate. If there is any indication that the behavior of the other is patronizing or manipulative in some way, we may not reciprocate.[18]

Complementary Needs

According to psychologist William Schutz, each of us has differing degrees of three basic interpersonal needs: inclusion, control, and affection.[19] As a relationship develops, the degree to which one person's needs match or complement the other's may make them more or less attractive to each other.

The **need for inclusion** refers to how strongly we desire to be in the presence of other people. Obviously there are times when each of us wants to be alone, but some people may have a greater need for privacy. Schutz described such a person as an *undersocial*. Likewise, an *oversocial* person is one who seems to constantly need people around. This need takes two forms: (1) the need to include others in your own activities—a reaching out to others, and (2) the need to be included in activities initiated by others—as when others invite you to join their group or club. For a pair's inclusion needs to be complementary, they must be fairly similar.

The second interpersonal need, the **need for control**, refers to a characteristic desire to control the behavior of others or have others control our behavior. The person who likes to control others is called an *autocrat*; someone who prefers to let others decide is labeled an *abdicrat*. Control needs are complementary when one person likes to take charge and the other doesn't mind or actually prefers that someone else be in control. Since most people prefer to have some degree of control in their relationships, control needs often have to be worked out through negotiation.

Finally, people may differ in their **need for affection**. This refers to the degree to which an individual feels she must express affection or closeness to others or have others express affection for her. This differs from inclusion needs in that we may like to have a lot of people around us, but feel no particular motivation to get very close to them Or we may not care for the company of a lot of people, but want to be very close to those few we do include in our social circle. Obviously, when two people's needs for affection differ greatly, they won't be able to fulfill those needs for each other. As a result, attraction may wane when such needs go unfulfilled over a long period of time.

Costs and Rewards

According to one perspective on attraction, people exchange resources as they interact. These resources are often referred to as **relational currencies** and may be *economic* in nature (money, goods, services, and so on) or more or less *intimate* (time, friendship, love, and so on).[20] The outcome of any exchange of resources between two people can be viewed in terms of losses and gains. According to exchange theory, as interpersonal communication takes place, the ratio of costs to rewards derived by each person is a good predictor of how attracted each person will be to the relationship. One of the difficulties in testing this hypothesis has been identifying what communication behaviors and episodes are most rewarding or costly to a particular individual *prior* to interaction. It is still possible, of course, that people do base their attraction for one another on this kind of analysis, at least some of the time.

Other Sources of Attraction

It is unlikely that researchers will ever identify all of the sources of attraction that bring people together. Attraction may be based on important qualities of conversation itself (above and beyond what it suggests about underlying similarities, complementary needs, and so on). We can only speculate that such factors as humor or witty repartee, nonverbal behavior reminiscent of a previous relationship, and a host of other idiosyncrasies may be frequent bases for attraction. It may be a good idea to try to identify the things that you find most attractive about the content and manner of *talk* experienced in the various relationships you have already established.

Remember that the factors we have isolated as leading to attraction aren't as static as they may sound. Interaction affects our perceptions of similarity, complementarity, costs and rewards, and so on. We create these factors *in talk*. We cannot overemphasize this fact. Two people may have similar needs, but unless they make each other aware of their similarities, there is no basis for attraction. Self-perception theory (see Chapter 4) suggests that we may communicate with others in such a way that we later determine we *must* like them. Some research confirms that this frequently happens when people disclose personal information to relative strangers.[21]

As we interact with people, we may discover a number of ways we are attracted to one another that could serve as a basis for developing a more personal relationship. Next we turn our attention to how relationship development typically takes place.

THE CLOSER THE BETTER: REVEALING SELF TO OTHER

As the filtering theory of attraction suggests, being attracted to someone initially doesn't automatically move the relationship toward intimacy. Even though a person meets all the criteria for being an attractive "casual acquaintance" or "conversational partner," there may be little evidence that he or she would be "a good friend" or "romantic partner." For relationships to move in the direction of intimacy, qualitatively different communication patterns must be initiated and repeated. Researchers studying these changes in communication generally refer to the development as occurring in stages. In this section we will describe the typical stages of relational development, first for friendships and then for romantic couples, paying close attention to the communication patterns that typify each stage. Table 11.2 (p. 278) offers a comparison between the stages of development for friends and the stages typical of romantic relationships.

Stages of Development in Friendship

The study of friendship has been sorely neglected by social scientists. Romantic relations seem to have garnered most of the attention. Nonetheless, interest in how friendships take shape is increasing. One of the most comprehensive models of friendship development has been proposed by William Rawlins.[22] A typical friendship progresses through the following six stages.

Role-limited Interaction

Friendships start out like any other relationship. Initial interactions are characterized by the adoption of social roles and rules such as those described in Chapter 4. We have described these as public interactions governed by the rules of civility. Although some friendships may be forged quickly as the result of participation in an unusual set of circumstances (for example, life-threatening situations, being isolated from others), these are the exceptions.

Friendly Relations

As we indicated earlier, role interactions can be carried out in a number of ways. An adviser–advisee or employer–employee relationship may be characterized by businesslike attention to detail or may include overtones of positive sentiment. In completing a loan application, there is no *necessity* that banker and client

TABLE 11.2

A comparison of two models of relationship development

Friendship development (Rawlins)	Stage	Romantic development (Knapp)
Role-limited interaction	1	Initiating
Friendly relations	2	Experimenting
Moves toward friendship	3	Intensifying
Nascent friendship	4	Integrating
Stabilized friendship	5	Bonding
Waning friendship	6	Differentiating
—	7	Circumscribing
—	8	Stagnating
—	9	Avoiding
—	10	Terminating

Adapted from William K. Rawlins, "Friendship As a Communicative Achievement: A Theory and an Interpretive Analysis of Verbal Reports," unpublished dissertation, Temple University, 1981, and from Mark L. Knapp, *Interpersonal Communication and Human Relationships* (Boston: Allyn & Bacon, 1984).

exchange humorous anecdotes or friendly chit-chat. In many such situations, the friendly behavior pattern is to be enjoyed in its own right; it is not necessarily an invitation to furthering friendship. Nonetheless, friendly relations do establish the groundwork for a potential friendship to be built.

Moves Toward Friendship

When people interact in roles, their behavior is dictated by cultural rules and their reason for being together is "obligated" to a large extent. We would consider it rude and outrageous if a loan officer suddenly complained of being tired and cut short our banking transaction. Yet it is this very obligation of role playing that is a barrier to friendship and other intimate relations. Rawlins suggests that one of the fundamental defining elements of friendship is its voluntary nature. Friends may, with much greater success than the loan officer, complain of tiredness and be released from an ongoing activity. In the moves-toward-friendship stage, invitations to engage in episodes that are less role-bound are extended and voluntarily accepted. Many of these activities may be short in duration so neither party feels obligated to continue the interaction. Third parties may be included to avoid undue strain in these tentative explorations. Other activities may proceed in a kind of open-ended time frame. Since participation is voluntary, either party may decide when he or she wants to conclude the episode; neither party has a right to place demands on the other's time. "Going to a movie with several others" is a good example of a short-term third-party episode. The possibility of extending the evening at a favorite watering hole typifies the open-ended time frame.

Qualitative changes also occur in the content of interactions during this stage. Rawlins' research indicates that people begin creating "jointly constructed views" of the world during this phase. Talk may initially focus on similarities in attitudes and values, and gradually change to explorations of differences in opinions. When consensus results in the altering of viewpoints held prior to interaction, a jointly constructed view emerges.

Nascent Friendship

Once moves toward friendship become repetitive, a pair may begin to think of themselves as "becoming friends." Friendship is crystallized in this stage. Significant changes in communciation take place. Role interactions that once characterized the relationship are now seen as inappropriate. Rawlins refers to this as the development of "negative norms"—forms of communication that are now out of bounds. Even though the voluntary nature of friendship remains a constant feature, emerging friends often *choose* to participate in a wider range of activities and topics of conversation.

Stabilized Friendship

The establishment of friendship is rarely celebrated in our culture. There are few, if any, bonding rituals such as "becoming blood brothers." As a result, the bonds of friendship are often very fragile. Verbal legitimacy may be obtained by calling each other "friend," but the meaning of the term is weakened by overuse. Casual acquaintances often call one another friends, in spite of the fact that they know very little about one another. Immigrants to this country often have difficulty adjusting to how loosely we use the term. "I'm having *20 friends* over for a party—why don't you join us?" is a

Friendship is often characterized by voluntarily spending time together and enjoying highly relaxed forms of nonverbal communication.

real contradiction in terms for many non-natives.[23]

How, then, do we know when a relationship has become a stable friendship? Most writers emphasize the importance of developing trust. Obviously trust doesn't just materialize at a single stage of relational development. The process unfolds slowly, involving two related types of behavior. **Trusting behavior** refers to any behavior that increases one person's vulnerability to another. Anyone who voluntarily enters a dangerous situation with another person, or reveals very personal information to another, is engaging in trusting behavior. Police officers routinely place themselves in the trust of their partners. **Trustworthy behavior** is a response to trusting behavior that protects the vulnerability of the other. A friend who lets a secret slip out to a third party has failed to exhibit trustworthy behavior. The development of trust is a delicate process and takes considerable time as friends expose their vulnerabilities one by one, often with extreme caution.

Waning Friendship

Like any relationship, a friendship does not maintain itself. It requires effort on each person's part to keep in touch and to explore new activities and interests. Friendships may begin to wane as a result of neglect, lack of support from significant others, major violations of trust, deviance from important relational norms, competing demands on time, and a host of other possible factors. In terms of communication patterns, a waning friendship may be revealed by a growing increase in restraint where candor once existed, autonomy where togetherness was once the rule. When this is undesirable, we should probably be concerned, but avoid overreacting. Most friendships will go through periods like this. We all have friends who seem to disappear— no cards, no letters, no phone calls—only to resurface months later, fill us in on all the news, and go on as though there had been no interruption.

Many of the stages and communication patterns in friendship development are similar to those encountered in relations we define here as romantic couples—dating partners, spouses, long-term live-in partners. In fact, many couples describe themselves as "best friends" in addition to being romantically involved. Yet there are essential differences in the way romantic relationships develop and the communication patterns that constitute that development. We will look at these relationships next.

Stages of Development in Romantic Coupling

Romantic relationships progress in many of the same ways that friendships do, and the same issues of trust, candor–restraint and autonomy–togetherness have to be worked out. Since we have already discussed much of this, our review of the stages of development for romantic pairs will be somewhat brief. We'll try to point out the major differences between relationships that are moving along a friendship trajectory as opposed to those on the romantic path.

Although many models of the development of romantic intimacy are available, we will use one of the more popular ones, developed by Mark Knapp.[24] Five stages depict what Knapp calls "the process of coming together." Later we will look at the process of coming apart.

Initiating

This stage is similar to the "role-limited interaction" stage of friendship. Communication at this point largely consists of greetings and other types of contact required by the situation. The first day on a new job or the first day of a new semester present us with numerous opportunities to initiate relationships. Communication is extremely stylized to allow people to interact with little knowledge of one another. Initial filters of attraction may be applied and judgments of communication competence made.

Experimenting

If a relationship survives the initial contact, the pair may continue to use standard formulas of interaction to engage in "small talk." Some writers have even set the formulas down. One of them stresses six steps: (1) look for and respond to approachability cues; (2) search the situation for topics; (3) make transitions from one topic to another; (4) give and use free information—answer the other's question and then add a little more information so the other has more options for what to ask next; (5) ask specific rather than broad questions—to keep the conversation from being an exchange of generalities; and (6) take turns frequently.[25] This kind of patterned yet somewhat flexible talk enables a person to present a desired self-image, form initial impressions of the other, and isolate similarities for further exploration. A norm of politeness rules these interactions.

Intensifying

Most relationships don't move beyond initiating and experimenting. As in friendship, intimates-to-be make overtures to each other that signal a new intensity to their interactions. Knapp identifies a number of changes in verbal communication patterns: forms of address become more informal, increased use of the pronouns "we" and "us," the creation of private codes and verbal shortcuts, and so on. The prelude to a romantic relationship may be the request for and acceptance of a second date, since it signals willingness to intensify.

Relationships often intensify as a result of appropriate **self-disclosure**, when one person reveals information about the self that the other is unlikely to find out by any other means. Disclosures may differ in terms of amount, degree of personalness, and the positive or negative nature of the information revealed. Some rules of thumb for appropriate disclosure include that it be: (1) part of an ongoing relationship—which means self-disclosure too early in a relationship can be damaging; (2) relevant to the episode or topic of conversation;

(3) dealt out in small doses, beginning with fairly safe, non-intimate revelations; and (4) reciprocated—which is an indication that the other finds your disclosure to be appropriate. Although self-disclosures may begin at any stage of interaction, they are most likely to be perceived positively beginning with the intensifying stage.

In contrast to friendships, shared episodes are often labeled as "dates" and are typically imbued with perceptions of physical attraction and palpitations of the heart. As common as such feelings are reported to be, they are not necessary for continued relational development. Many romantic relationships actually develop as friendships, altering their trajectory much later. Likewise, many relationships initiated on a romantic basis are quickly realigned as "just friends," or, more likely, are terminated as one or both persons "falls out of infatuation."

Integrating

At this stage, romantic couples begin to organize their everyday lives around each other. Interdependence becomes more and more visible to others. As with friendship, jointly constructed views of the world emerge, plans are made with the other in mind, and social circles begin to overlap. In fact, one study of romantic relationships demonstrated just how important communication with the other's social network is. Malcolm Parks and Mara Adelman interviewed 172 college students, asking how frequently they talked to their dating partner's family and friends, and how much those people supported the relationship. Interviews three months later showed that those who were more involved with their dating partner's social network were more likely to still be dating. In addition, they also felt that they had a better understanding of their partner's behavior, attitudes, and feelings.[26] Integrating may occur in a number of other ways. Some people make

During the integrating and bonding stages, friends and lovers signal the nature of their relationship to the world, often through nonverbal means. (Pablo Picasso, *The Lovers*, 1923)

small purchases together that become common property. Others may change some of their habits so they can spend more time together. A divorced mother invites a potential stepfather to have dinner with her and her children. Perhaps you can identify other ways that integration takes place in terms of episodes or personality.

Integrating the lives of two separate individuals is no easy task. The process is fraught with difficulties, and most relationships must endure a lot of conflict to survive this far. Many people find their differences are too significant to encourage further development. As a result,

they terminate the relationship or reestablish a greater degree of independence and lessen the intensity of their involvement. For those who forge ahead, the role of interpersonal conflict is crucial. Social scientists are gradually learning the significance of conflict in the development of close relationships. Avoiding conflict may prevent people from discovering potentially rewarding aspects of a relationship. Overreacting to conflict or mishandling it can make continuing the relationship painful. Successful management of conflict often leads to greater understanding and commitment to a relationship. We will have much more to say about managing conflict in Chapter 13. For now we wish to emphasize that closeness in a relationship, successful integration, requires skillful management of disagreements.

Bonding

Once two people's lives have become intertwined to their mutual satisfaction, private commitments are often formalized. The bonding stage is really one that "institutionalizes" the relationship. A marriage ceremony, buying a house together, or making some other public commitment cements the bond. Now the relationship has a public image. Our repertoire of social masks and self-images must now be expanded to include this important relational image. The effect may be to give each individual new strength to pursue self-goals or to begin to suffocate the self, depending on how the relationship is worked out from this point.

Although the typical intimate relationship in our culture reaches the bonding stage by integrating two "selves" through reciprocated self-disclosures, this is not an absolute necessity. Close bonds are frequently created among members of sports teams, youth gangs, musical groups, and groups supporting some cause. These group members may feel bonded out of a sense of brotherhood or sisterhood, as opposed to knowing very much about one another's personal feelings or psychological profiles. Some unique professional dyads such as ice-skating duos, dancers, and trapeze artists develop a kind of intimacy based more on complex behavioral interdependence than on knowledge of the psyche. Yet we would be hard pressed to classify these relationships as simply based on sociological or cultural knowledge of each other.

Although relationships don't stop developing at this point, there is often a "honeymoon" period in which the emotional bond between two individuals seems to carry the day. This period rarely lasts very long, but let's hope it will last long enough for us to introduce the next section of the chapter.

TWO CLOSE FOR COMFORT: MAINTAINING IDENTITY IN INTIMATE RELATIONSHIPS

Once the bonds of friendship or romance are viewed as a long-term involvement, a new issue comes into play. Partners must negotiate how each can reestablish a sense of identity and more clearly define the boundaries between the self and the relationship to promote harmony.

Balancing Self-Identity and Relational-Identity

When two people form a close relationship, they give much of themselves to it. Accommodations are made by both parties so that the new relationship can fit into their already busy lives. Other relationships may suffer from lack of attention, as may some personal pursuits. Obviously, what's given up is replaced by much that is new, exciting, and promises to offer future rewards. At the same time, the bonding process can frequently lead to a feeling of being engulfed by the relationship. Intimates, espe-

cially those who live together, spend many of their nonworking hours in close physical proximity. And for those who subscribe to the "openness in communication" school of thought, the psychological intimacy can be overwhelming. The self-identity can get lost in the shuffle.

How do people deal with the problem of investing themselves in an important relationship while maintaining a strong sense of self? This is probably the major issue in managing close relationships. Some people react by becoming virtually self-less, contributing most of their energy to the relationship. Others place the emphasis on self-growth, maintaining close relationships so long as they don't stifle that growth.

Most of us, however, must learn to creatively manage the tension between self-identity and relational-identity. William Rawlins characterizes this tension in friendship as one of learning how to balance (1) the need to be expressive versus the need to be protective and (2) the need for autonomy versus the need for togetherness.[27] We think these two tensions are at the heart of long-term romantic relationships as well.

The Expressive–Protective Dialectic

When two people learn to trust each other, they're usually more willing to disclose both positive and negative personal information. The focus on trust reveals what Rawlins calls the *dialectic of expressiveness and protectiveness*. Friends share a desire to be expressive, to reveal personal thoughts and feelings. At the same time, however, too much openness may reveal areas of vulnerability. This leads to a need to be protective of each other's weaknesses. Protectiveness works in two ways. First, there is a need to protect the self. Each of us has vulnerabilities or old wounds we don't like to open. A relationship that extols the virtues of total openness may put undue stress on us.

BOX 11.2

"Go Away a Little Closer!": Why Men and Women Don't See Eye to Eye on Intimacy

Men and women view intimate relationships differently. In spite of major cultural changes in male–female relations, basic differences remain. In her book *Intimate Strangers*, Lillian Rubin examines them and offers a compelling theory to explain why men and women react differently to intimacy.

One of the most obvious differences is the way males and females regard verbal expressions of intimate feelings. One young woman interviewed by Rubin explained it this way: "I'm always doing my bla-bla-bla number, you know, keeping things moving and alive around here. But he's the original Mr. Shutmouth most of the time."

Her husband's response: "She tells me all the time we can't really be close if we're not talking to each other. It's hard for me to understand what she means. Doesn't she know that it feels close to me just to be in the same room with her?"

Are these reactions typical? Do most men and women have such a hard time agreeing on what it means to be intimate?

According to Rubin, men and women have a difficult time *understanding* one another, not because they don't try, but because they have developed fundamentally different personalities and ways of looking at relationships. In contrast to explanations that focus almost exclusively on culture *or* biology *or* psychology, Rubin argues for a complex blend of cultural fact, psychological development in childhood, and the reinforcement of social institutions.

Rubin's theory begins with a single cultural fact: Women are the primary caretakers of both male and female infants. As a result, the first true identification or relationship we develop is with a female. Rubin argues that this fact has such a great impact on our development as males and females that it will influence our relations with the opposite sex throughout adulthood. How does this single fact exert so much influence? It affects two primary personality developments in childhood: the crystallization of gender identity and the development of ego boundaries, or a sense of personal identity.

For girls, the development of a gender identity is quite easy. Since they are anatomically similar to their mothers and have already established such a deep emotional bond to the mother, they have little difficulty identifying themselves as female. This fact does, however, make it more difficult for a girl to establish firm ego boundaries. It is harder for mother and daughter to draw the line where one person ends and the other begins. According to Rubin, this helps explain why adult women value emotional relationships so much, yet often fear a loss of self when a relationship gets too close.

For boys, the process is almost the reverse. The process of identifying who they are, estab-

---

Second, we must be sensitive to similar vulnerabilities in our close friends. This means learning not to pry into certain areas.

Candor and restraint are both necessary to maintain a stable relationship. In fact, Rawlins argues, friends have to negotiate "necessary conditions for closedness." This tension is experienced on a topic-by-topic basis as friends and lovers decide which issues are ripe for candid disclosure and which are best handled with restraint.

The Autonomy–Togetherness Dialectic
This issue isn't limited to friendships, but it is an especially sensitive issue since the bond of friendship is such a voluntary one. Friends must

lishing a gender identity, is an emotional crisis. Until the time he must identify himself as a boy, his father has most likely been a distant, shadowy figure in his life. To identify with the father means he must renounce the most important, most emotionally meaningful relationship he has ever experienced—the bond of identification with his mother. Drawing on recent developments in psychoanalytic theory, Rubin shows how the separation from the relationship with the mother influences the development of the boy's ego boundaries:

To protect against the pain wrought by this radical shift in his internal world, he builds a set of defenses that, in many important ways, will serve him, for good or ill, for the rest of his life. This is the beginning of the development of ego boundaries that are fixed and firm—barriers that rigidly separate self from other, that circumscribe not only his relationships with others but his connection to his inner emotional life as well.

As a result of this traumatic process, the young boy represses his early identification with his mother. Emotions are sent reeling underground, hidden by a variety of fears and defenses. In the future, when a female asks him to tell her his feelings, he can only look at her in amazement, wondering what she means. Or at best, he can call upon a few surface emotions to tell her about.

What are the implications of Rubin's theory for communication in intimate, opposite-sex relationship? If males and females have been raised according to our typical cultural pattern, and if Rubin is right about the developmental processes, then creating mutually satisfying definitions of intimacy will be a struggle. It means both partners must be sensitive to the other's way of defining what kind of verbal or nonverbal episodes count as expressions of closeness. And it means that many of our reactions when the other gets too close are unconscious and will change very slowly and painfully. Just when it looks like we're going to make it, we'll probably fall back into the old ruts. Rubin suggests that we'll have to become "people in process," trying to change historic ways of being and relating. As a culture, we will have to change many of our institutionalized roles and ways of parenting, so that the next generation of children are not as limited in the ways they can relate to one another.

Source: *Lillian B. Rubin,* Intimate Strangers: Men and Women Together *(New York: Harper & Row, 1983). Excerpts from pages 56, 75, 77, copyright © 1983 by Lillian B. Rubin, are reprinted by permission of Harper & Row, Publishers, Inc.*

be careful not to assume that the other will automatically participate in any given activity. They cannot always take each other's time for granted. However, it's awkward to repeatedly ask each other about activities that we do together on a routine basis. The ability to balance this tension is the hallmark of good friendships. This tension also exists within romantic relationships. In fact, it may be more crucial because the amount of time spent together is usually much greater. Each partner in a relationship should realize that the more time they spend together, the greater the need for freedom is likely to become. And since no two people are alike, one partner may reach that threshold quicker than the other.

The success of long-term relationships often depends on how well a couple works out basic relational dilemmas, such as autonomy or togetherness.

These relational issues, themes, boundaries, and patterns are worked out by couples in much the same way that families work them out (see Chapter 10). In fact, our family of origin may contribute a great deal to what we see as the possible ways to work out these tensions.

Working Out Dialectic Tensions

One way to balance these tensions is to provide each other with occasional periods of time alone. Many mistakenly assume that being apart during the workday constitutes being alone, when it usually means being with a lot of other people. Some people develop individual hobbies or read to create alone-time. Partners need to negotiate and respect such times.

A lot of couples balance candor–restraint tensions, almost unconsciously, by mismanaging interpersonal perceptions. They buffer themselves by occasionally using ambiguous or tangential communication. For example, couples often talk around the edges of an issue they disagree on. They may phrase their views in such a way that the other can interpret some agreement, if he wants to. As long as the issue isn't crucial to their everyday interaction, they can engage in restraint.

In an insightful review of research, Allan Sillars and Michael Scott identified several perceptual biases that develop and are reinforced in intimate relationships.[28] Specifically, they found that intimate couples tend to (1) perceive their own relational communication (such as instigating conflict) as more positive than their partner does; (2) overestimate the similarity between their own and their partner's attitudes; (3) differ in their perceptions of who makes important family or relational decisions; and (4) describe relational problems in general rather than specific terms (for example, referring to each other's general traits rather than focusing on specific behaviors). This frequently leads intimates to blame each other for conflicts and to attribute their partner's behavior to personality traits, their own behavior to situational factors.

Sillars and Scott offer some interesting explanations for these perceptual biases. For one, they argue that *familiarity* increases our confidence that we understand our partner's feelings and attitudes. This confidence, based initially on self-disclosures and efforts to understand, may soon expand to areas that haven't been so thoroughly investigated. Thus we only *think* we understand each other. "Mind reading," often referred to as a cardinal sin in interpersonal relating, may actually serve an important function from time to time.

Emotional involvement is also a leading candidate for perceptual bias, according to Sillars and Scott. Intimates are at once each other's "most knowledgeable *and* least objective observer.[29] Overall, positive sentiment for one's partner may bias interpretation of messages in the direction of **assimilation**, or greater presumed agreement than actually exists. On the other hand, during periods of stress or conflict, messages may be interpreted on the basis of **contrast**, or greater presumed disagreement. Likewise, research indicates that when people experience emotional stress, their abilities to process information decline and they rely on more simplistic, stereotypical ways of thinking. Obviously, this can lead to perceptual biases.

When these tensions are not adequately balanced, the process of relational decay begins

to run its course. Next we turn our attention to the stages that characterize this process. As we describe these stages of "coming apart," remember that they aren't irreversible. Relationships are frequently rebuilt after short periods of decay. Naturally, rebuilding becomes more difficult when deterioration is the result of long periods of neglect or extremely painful conflicts and violations of trust.

Stages of Relationship Dissolution

Mark Knapp's model of relational change includes five stages of deterioration: (1) differentiating, (2) circumscribing, (3) stagnating, (4) avoiding, and (5) terminating. We will look at each one briefly.

Differentiating

When relational partners begin to remind each other that they are separate individuals and that they have other concerns besides their relationship, they have begun the process of differentiating. Often episodes of differentiating are triggered by seemingly innocuous events. A close friend, we'll call her Mary Ann Marker, described receiving a piece of junk mail shortly after her marriage to a man named Jones. A letter was addressed to "Mary A. Jones." At first she didn't recognize who the letter was meant for. When reality sank in, she said, it almost destroyed her identity. She didn't know who she was. She promptly informed her husband that she wanted to keep her maiden name. The emergence of two-career families, with the necessity of dealing with competing time constraints and goals, has made this stage more commonplace than it might have once been. This stage may be more accurately referred to as a stage of relational maintenance, since most intimate relationships cannot avoid periods of differentiating. Many couples may engage in a repetitive cycle of breaking up and making up, as they move from bonding to differentiating back to integration and bonding, and so on.

Circumscribing

Deterioration becomes more serious when couples begin to restrict their communication with each other on a regular basis. This may occur as a result of major violations of trust or increasing uncertainty about the quality of the relationship. Sally Planalp and James Honeycutt studied events such as deception, changes in personality or values, competing relationships or extramarital affairs, and betraying a confidence—all events that increased uncertainty about the relationship. Over one-quarter of the relationships ended as a direct result of such an event. Another one-third felt that their relationship was never as close after the event took place.[30] Knapp indicates that conversations in this phase are shorter in duration, limited to "safe" topics for fear of touching a raw nerve, and almost totally devoid of any new self-disclosures. The only time a couple seems happy is when they're putting up a front for their friends.

Stagnating

At this point in a relationship, both have developed such an expectation of unpleasant and unproductive talk that they feel there is little to be said. Relationships that are based primarily on extrinsic rewards may continue for many years at this stage. For most others, this stage is just a long and winding road on the way to termination.

Avoiding

When the unpleasantness of stagnation becomes unbearable, intimates begin rearranging their lives to avoid the necessity of face-to-face interaction. Separate bedrooms, working different shifts, and trial separations are examples of the behavior characteristic of this stage. The pain of interaction simply isn't worth it anymore.

Terminating

The final stage of interaction prior to physically and psychologically leaving a relationship consists primarily of talk that prepares each person for the impending termination. Often situational factors are responsible for the death of a relationship, as when one party has to move to another city or a college senior has to leave friends behind. Even under these conditions, people frequently disassociate themselves from their friends a few weeks before the move is made. Presumably, this makes the actual termination easier. Talk may take the form of emphasizing the benefits of the future ("It's off to the real world. Several interviews. Things are looking great!") or denouncing the past ("I'm getting out of this stinkhole. Four years—what a waste!").

Many organizations schedule "exit interviews" when their employees leave the company, in hopes of finding out why they quit and what can be done to prevent others from following the same course. This wise practice has not yet become routine in interpersonal relationships. Perhaps a few valuable lessons could be learned if we adopted such a policy.

IMPROVING OUR ABILITY TO MANAGE INTIMATE RELATIONSHIPS

Communication competence in intimate relationships is much more complex than interacting with strangers, casual acquaintances, or coworkers. As we have seen in this chapter, intimate relationships must be built, managed, and sometimes dissolved. This means that being competent in intimate relations may frequently require us to shift gears as a relation-

I wish that Stanley and I could like each other ~~when~~ when we are together - But we don't.

Patty Brann

The statement under the photograph—written by the woman pictured—aptly describes the situation.

ship moves in, out, and around the various stages we have depicted. Some of us may be very good at initiating relationships and maneuvering our way through the early stages of intimacy, only to discover that negotiating long-term arrangements seems to elude us. Others may have a frightful time getting started but are at their best when managing a committed relationship. And while many of us may repeatedly experience the deterioration and termination of intimate relationships, probably only a few have discovered ways to communicate effectively during such breakups so that we learn from our mistakes and failures.

We have suggested in this chapter that intimate relationships are the joint creations of two people who bring many similarities and differences in background, perceptions of what intimate relationships should be like, and rules for what messages mean at different points in the development of such a relationship. While the advice for managing specific differences may be less than you would like, chances are that any such advice would be outdated before you had the opportunity to internalize and use it. Rather than offer you cookbook approaches to serving up a good relationship, we suggest that you focus on developing a thorough understanding of the two major concepts of this book: the process of communication and the process of relationship development. You already know a great deal about both of these concepts. Now it is up to you to apply these concepts to the particular experiences of your own life.

You can start by reflecting on your own relationships with close friends, family, and those you are romantically involved with. Ask yourself some of the following questions:

- In what ways are your close relationships similar to or different from one another? What patterns of communication or problems keep cropping up, relationship after relationship?

- What are your own beliefs about what intimate relations should be like? Are you sure your various partners share those beliefs? Does it make any difference if they don't?

- Which of the explanations for interpersonal attraction best explains how each of your relationships was initiated? Did the bases for attraction change as the filtering theory suggests or not? How have you negotiated interpersonal needs? What relational currencies do you exchange?

- Have your relationships developed as the models of friendship and intimate coupling suggest? For yourself, what communication behaviors count as movement from one stage to the next? Do you think your partners would be likely to agree with you?

- How do you and your partners handle the tensions of expressiveness–protectiveness and autonomy–togetherness? Are your perceptions on these issues similar or different?

- Which of the perceptual biases in intimate relations seem to characterize your own ways of relating? Are these biases functional (do they promote harmony) or dysfunctional (do they create major problems)?

- How do you react when it becomes obvious to you that a relationship is experiencing the differentiating or circumscribing stage? Do you think your reaction is the best way of handling the situation?

- How do you react to the termination of an intimate relationship? Does the idea of an "exit interview" make any sense to you? What do you think the results would be?

These are only a few of the questions that we hope this chapter has raised regarding the development, management, and termination of intimate relationships. We believe that greater knowledge of how your own intimate relationships work is the major step toward managing them more effectively. Communicating this knowledge to one another may help immensely or it may actually promote more disharmony. The decision to do so should be based on what you think the long-term impact of that communication will be. The short-term effects can be misleading. Being candid may be painful in the short term but crucial to long-term satisfaction. On the other hand, some issues may require restraint, both short term and perhaps even in the long run. Knowing *when* to communicate about these issues is as much a part of the art of intimate communication as knowing *how* to talk about them.

REVIEW TERMS

The following is a list of major concepts introduced in this chapter. The page number where the concept is first mentioned is listed in parentheses.

intimacy (266)
physical proximity (272)
shared episodes (272)
intimacy readiness (272)
romantic feelings (272)
civility (273)
filtering theory (273)
physical beauty (274)
matching hypothesis (274)
similarity (275)
reciprocal liking (275)
complementary needs (276)
need for inclusion (276)
need for control (276)
need for affection (276)
relational currencies (276)
trusting behavior (279)
trustworthy behavior (280)
self-disclosure (281)
expressive–protective dialectic (283)
autonomy–togetherness dialectic (284)
assimilation (287)
contrast (287)

SUGGESTED READINGS

Levinger, George, and Harold Raush, eds. *Close Relationships: Perspectives on the Meaning of Intimacy.* Amherst: University of Massachusetts Press, 1977. Eight essays on different aspects of intimate relationships. Topics include a comparison of friendship and marriage, commitment, using attribution theory to explain distortions in intimate relations, and Howard Gadlin's analysis of the changes in perceptions of intimacy over the last 300 years in middle-class American culture.

Rubin, Lillian B. *Intimate Strangers: Men and Women Together.* New York: Harper & Row, 1983. This intriguing book is a compilation of case study interviews conducted by the author. Using a combination of cultural factors and psychoanalytic theory, Rubin offers a fascinating explanation for why male–female relationships are difficult to manage. Differing male and female perceptions of intimacy are explored in detail. Box 11.2 is based on this book.

PROCESS TO PERFORMANCE

TOPICS FOR DISCUSSION

1.   Use any of the questions raised on page 290 as a prompt for class discussion. Explore the risks as well as the benefits of talking about these issues with an intimate partner.

2.   Discuss the intimate relationships that you most admire. These may range from parents' to friends' to relationships depicted in novels or films. Of course, be sure to evaluate the "reality" of any fictional relationships you discuss.

3.   To what extent do you think people plan for intimacy or just respond to conditions for intimacy? Do you find yourself using initial interactions as auditions for friendship? If so, what do you look for? What tests or experiments do you use to discover intimacy potential? What risks are involved?

4.   Is involvement in a friendship as voluntary as Rawlins suggests? If so, are voluntary activities a major distinction between friendships and romantic relationships? What other differences in communication distinguish friends from intimate couples?

5.   When are people most likely to be in what Knapp calls a state of intimacy readiness?

6.   How can we best resolve the contrary notions that "birds of a feather flock together" and "opposites attract"?

7.   What sources of attraction, other than those mentioned in the chapter, can you identify? Using filtering theory as a guide, when do you think each of the sources of attraction you've identified plus those in the chapter are most salient?

OBSERVATION GUIDES

1.   Choose a close friend or romantic partner and enlist his or her cooperation in observing your communication together. Tape record or write out in dialogue form some of your conversations. If you write them down, do so as soon as possible after the conversation occurs, making sure you both agree about the substance of the conversation. Try to record the language used as accurately as possible. When you have recorded two or three conversations, analyze

them in order to determine (1) what stage the relationship appears to be in, identifying specific communication behaviors as support, and (2) what communication behaviors tend to maintain the relationship in that stage or encourage further development or differentiation.

2. Keep a journal for one week and record examples of how you handle the two dialectic tensions (expressiveness versus protectiveness, autonomy versus togetherness) in each of several important and intimate relationships. Review these entries at the end of the week and ask yourself whether you handled them successfully. Write down some things you could have said or done to improve your management of these two tensions.

CLASSROOM EXERCISES

1. Bring to class as many examples of cultural messages about attraction and ideal images of intimate relationships as you can find. These can include magazine and television advertisements, personal advice columns or talk shows, music videos or lyrics. In small groups, take some of these examples and rewrite or revise them to fit Vision I of Virginia Kidd's relational ideals (Table 11.1).

What other visions are possible? Create ads or responses to advice-column questions that would reflect these different visions. Talk about ways to evaluate and respond to cultural messages.

2. Your instructor will give you a copy of William Schutz's FIRO-B scale to complete before coming to class. This scale measures the interpersonal needs for control, inclusion, and affection. In class, your instructor will create several dyads, some pairing people with very different scores on the different needs, others who are similar on one need or another. Role-play the situations below assuming that you and your partner have an intimate relationship:

a. deciding whether to establish separate or joint checking accounts;

b. establishing rules for when and how often nights out with the "guys" or "girls" will be allowed;

c. what forms of public displays of affection you should engage in.

You may think of other situations as well. Then discuss as a class the impact of interpersonal needs, complementarity, similarity, and the negotiation of differences in needs.

CHAPTER TWELVE

Customer relations are often impersonal and sometimes unfeeling. Note the bureaucrats hiding behind rules and regulations in this eerie evocation of modern organizational life. (George Tooker, *Government Bureau*, 1956)

IMPERSONAL RELATIONSHIPS: COMMUNICATING WITH COLLEAGUES AND OTHER STRANGERS

LET'S DO LUNCH" can be dangerous. At least it was for Peter G. Peterson, Lewis Glucksman, and Wall Street's oldest continuing investment banking partnership, Lehman Brothers Kuhn Loeb. The story that follows, condensed from a *New York Times Magazine* article by Ken Auletta, demonstrates the severe consequences when executives fail to maintain civil relations and resort to ineffective means of communication.[1]

Peterson and Glucksman were co–chief executive officers at Lehman Brothers, Peterson having elevated Glucksman to be his peer only a few weeks prior to the disastrous luncheon. Peterson was proud of the fact that he had made an executive out of the rough-edged Glucksman.

Their differences were notable. Peterson was Ivy League, knew the Washington elite, and had been a successful executive with several other companies. He knew how to move among the upper crust. Glucksman, on the other hand, had worked his way up the corporate ladder over 21 years with the firm. He put in long hours and was a visible manager of the everyday affairs of the company. He took care of the inside; Peterson dealt with the outside clientele. Glucksman had come from a lower-middle-class family and resented what he thought was Peterson's snobbish, condescending attitude.

At the heart of their problem was a shared dislike for each other's role in the company. Glucksman was a "trader," Peterson a "banker." In the investment business, a trader buys and sells securities and must think fast and make firm decisions. A banker enjoys the luxury of a more relaxed, longer-term view of the business, advising clients, setting up mergers, and so on. Bankers refer to "lowly traders," while traders think of bankers as "haughty." Neither is very fond of the other, but both are needed for the business to function.

Things came to a head at a luncheon where Peterson was asked to make a presentation. Peterson arranged for Glucksman to be invited also. But at the luncheon, Peterson was seated at the head of the table, next to the host. Glucksman was relegated to an inconspicuous side seat, which made him irate. Further irritated by what he considered to be a name-dropping presentation, Glucksman began making noisy distractions with his silverware and the movement of his chair. To make matters worse, Peterson tried to include Glucksman in the presentation, and Glucksman responded by talking for several minutes, angering Peterson.

Glucksman reportedly left the luncheon in a rage, determined to oust Peterson. He was successful because of his support from company insiders. But ten months later, the company was faltering so badly that it had to be sold. The fall of Lehman Brothers was complete.

Why would two extremely capable executives let the friction between them ruin their company? Why couldn't they come to terms with their differences and respect each other's efforts? How often does this kind of problem lurk behind the mergers, failures, and losses of companies we read about every day? We hope that your own professional pursuits do not come to such bitter ends. And while we can't promise to provide you with infallible means of communication, we do think that this chapter will help you understand the world of public, or impersonal, communication a little better. Here you will find research and suggestions on communicating in everyday social transactions, in professional dyads, in small work groups, and across the organizational chart.

INTERPERSONAL COMMUNICATION IN PUBLIC SITUATIONS

In Chapter 2 we argued against the developmental view of interpersonal communication because it limits the kinds of relationships we should be concerned with. This view encourages us to focus exclusively on more intimate relationships, where psychological-level rules are used to interpret and react to message exchanges. As we said earlier, only a handful of our relationships can be considered friendships or intimate relations. We simply don't have the time or the need to develop every relationship into an intimate one. This means that *most* of our relationships remain in the impersonal, public sector of social interaction. To better understand how public interpersonal situations

work, let's consider who participates in them and what criteria might exist for successful impersonal interactions.

Participants in Public Interactions

The list of public relationships includes all your casual acquaintances, the neighbors with the picket fence, those crazy coworkers at the factory, your egotistic supervisor, representatives of your friendly federal, state, and local governments, your barber or hair-care professional, the clerks who sell you shoes, clothing, groceries, and lottery tickets; your doctor, dentist, and lawyer, as well as the dozens of total strangers you encounter every day. Now, you may feel that your interactions with these people are inconsequential and not worth the time it takes to read this chapter. We doubt that you really feel that way and encourage you to think about some of the basic considerations in any public interpersonal situation.

Criteria for Managing Public Interactions

To make public situations work, people invent standardized ways to interact without feeling too uncertain, investing too much of their private selves in the transaction, or disrupting the social order of things. We have identified the following criteria that seem to govern public interactions: (1) the interaction should involve appropriate roles and scripts; (2) interactants should be respectful of one another; (3) interactions should enable both participants to achieve their practical goals; and (4) interactions should allow some room for the expressive behavior of individuals.

Enacting Roles and Scripts
Becoming personally familiar with every sales clerk, stockboy, or cashier we encounter would be impracticable and inefficient. To save time,

Showing respect for one another has been the hallmark of civil relations in cultures the world over. (Paul Klee, *Two Men Meet, Each Believing the Other to Be of Higher Rank*, 1903)

protect our privacy, and make social interaction more predictable, members of our culture have worked out scripts and roles for most conceivable public interactions. A script, as defined in Chapter 3, is a highly predictable sequence of behaviors or events; it tells us what should happen next in a given situation. Roles (discussed in Chapter 4) define the expectations each person has of the other; they tell us who should perform each part of the script. A cashier would be baffled if you offered to pay for a shirt you had not yet picked out (because you messed up the sequencing of the script). Likewise, you cannot ask the sales clerk to "try the shirt on and see if it fits" (because that's not part of the sales clerk's role). Any interaction is more difficult when you don't know the roles or the lines of action, but public interactions are virtually impossible without them.

Showing and Deserving Respect

Even though our private lives are shielded from those we interact with in public encounters, we are still people and not simply automatons. In fact, the hallmark of social interaction is the giving and receiving of respect. Rom Harre, a noted social psychologist, argues that "the deepest human motive is to seek the respect of others."[2] Role interactions can become dehumanizing for one or both persons involved, but they need not. Very few social roles are designed to belittle those who play them. The problem usually arises because people don't understand the complementary nature of social roles—for example, no one can properly be identified as a doctor without having patients. Likewise, role interactions may go bad when a culture develops a misguided sense of individualism. According to some, our culture is

The Moulin Rouge, a Parisian dance hall and cabaret, was immortalized by the French artist Toulouse-Lautrec in over thirty paintings. Note how the artist was able to capture the diversity of the clientele: How does interpersonal communication change when we move into public contexts? (Henri de Toulouse-Lautrec, *At the Moulin Rouge*)

experiencing a trend toward narcissism—a kind of self-interest that devalues any relationship that doesn't help a person get in touch with the private, personal self.[3] When this happens, a large portion of the social world (strangers and casual acquaintances) become unimportant to us, unless we can quickly transform them into intimates. The result is a lack of respect for the vast majority of people we come into contact with.

When social roles are properly valued, respect is achieved by the use of some subtle social mechanisms. Erving Goffman has identi-

fied two such mechanisms that help people maintain **deference** or respect: avoidance rituals and presentational rituals. He has also shown that in order to be worthy of the respect of others, a person must show proper demeanor.[4]

Avoidance Rituals People show respect by purposely allowing one another the right to privacy. This means maintaining the cultural norms for appropriate personal distance as discussed in Chapter 6. You may have experienced discomfort when an overeager salesperson greets you at the door and hovers too closely, even though you protest, "I'm just looking, thanks." Another avoidance ritual is the use of formal titles and surnames rather than first names, a sign of respect that many fear is disappearing from the American sense of etiquette. Younger people seem to prefer the informality of first names and associate the use of formal address with snobbery or aloofness. Older Americans, on the other hand, are often offended at such familiarity. Can you think of other ways that people avoid trespassing on each other's privacy? Which ones do you think are most acceptable today?

Presentational Rituals Avoidance rituals show respect by identifying out-of-bounds role behavior. Presentational rituals, according to Goffman, show respect in a more positive vein. These rituals include salutations, compliments, providing minor services, and invitations to participate in group activities. Notice how each of these rituals shows respect in a typical morning at the office. Upon arrival at work, coworkers greet each other in a friendly manner, but they don't take a great deal of time to do so. "Good morning, Mr. Whitmore," "How are you, Ms. Pendergrass?" and so on. If one of them has been away on vacation, the greeting is usually much more expressive ("Well, what do you know! Look who's back from the tropics. Did you enjoy your vacation?") and a little longer in duration. This doesn't mean the parties are better friends; it is simply a matter of showing respect. To greet the returning vacationer in the same way as the associate you saw yesterday would be disrespectful, as though his or her absence was not recognized. Even when you dislike the other person, the show of respect simply maintains civility.

Throughout the day, colleagues may compliment each other on the way they are dressed, how they handled a client, or for the promptness in providing needed information. Or they may symbolize respect by providing small,

unrequested services such as pouring an extra cup of coffee or delivering an important piece of mail. Finally, respect can be shown by including everyone, even the office lowlife, in group activities. If a few people are stopping off for drinks after work, an invitation to anyone in earshot is an appropriate sign of respect. The invitee should be allowed to decline: It is the invitation, not the acceptance, that symbolizes respect.

Goffman notes that avoidance rituals and presentational rituals are in constant tension. To invite a colleague or acquaintance to join you is trespassing on his or her right to privacy. "A peculiar tension must be maintained, for these opposing requirements of conduct must somehow be held apart from one another and yet realized together in the same interaction: the gestures which carry an actor to a recipient must also signify that things will not be carried too far."[5] Thus the importance of offering invitations without expecting compliance, doing small rather than large favors (that might imply escalation of the relationship), and not overdoing the greeting ritual.

Demeanor To be civil means that you show respect toward others and behave in a manner deserving of respect. Every culture defines the qualities of a "decent" person a little differently, and cultures change over time. Goffman identifies the following characteristics of a properly "housebroken" human being: discretion and sincerity, modesty, sportsmanship, reasonable command of the language, control of body movements, control of emotions, appetite, and desires, and poise under pressure.[6] Perhaps you can add or delete items from this list to capture the state of proper demeanor people expect in today's world.

Priority Given to Practical Goals

People interact in public for one of two primary reasons: to accomplish some practical end such as the purchase of goods and services or simply to enjoy the company of others through role playing. Our top priority is often the practical. We go to the market to buy food and related items, not to visit with the personnel. This criterion may seem so obvious that it need not be mentioned, yet you have no doubt encountered people who have temporarily forgotten the purpose of a transaction. A customer who wants to return a defective product may get so annoyed at waiting in line that he barks at the clerk (whose ultimate goal is to provide customer satisfaction). In turn, the clerk reacts to the customer's rude behavior by saying, "I don't have to take this, sir. You can return your product when you get a new personality!" The customer storms away, shouting the equivalent of "I will never shop here again!" Only later do they both realize that they failed to achieve their practical goals.

Room for Expressive Behavior

The other primary reason for public interaction is often overlooked. We usually assume that practical goals are the major reason for interacting with people we don't know very well. But Richard Sennett suggests that for most of our history, people have reveled in the opportunity to "playact" in public.[7] **Playacting** simply means to try on new roles, to be someone you've never been before, to hide behind a mask and enjoy the company of strangers. Many public places exist where such behavior has a higher priority, but there are fewer now than in the past. People congregate and get "lost in the crowd" at concerts, sporting events, and large New Year's Eve parties. In these places, people can increase their repertoire of "identities" and can literally be anybody they want to be. We can still playact to a certain degree in groups of strangers, as when one stranger convinces another to join in an impromptu dance during Mardi Gras. Friends are more likely to engage in some scripted routine

from a favorite movie, and do it in front of a group of strangers as a form of entertainment. In short, some public interactions allow us the opportunity (at least) to be expressive, to enjoy life, to act the fool, and to give others some enjoyment by participating with us or playing the role of audience.

Now that we have seen some of the criteria that govern public interactions, we want to look more closely at interactions in the context of work. First, we'll describe patterns characteristic of professional dyads. Then we'll investigate the interpersonal communication processes in small work groups and large organizations.

INTERPERSONAL COMMUNICATION IN PROFESSIONAL DYADS

On average, people spend nearly one-third of their adult life at work. And over half of the jobs in the United States are now categorized as information-processing and/or providing services to the general public.[8] In these sectors of the labor market, communication has a very high priority. Surveys of corporate leaders reveal that the two skills most desired in new recruits are writing and speaking skills.[9] Also high on the list is the ability to deal with people on a one-to-one basis. The work situations in which people need to apply these skills vary a great deal, but we have grouped them into three broad categories: (1) interactions between supervisors and subordinates; (2) interactions between people in professional helping relationships; and (3) interactions between employees and the general public.

Communicating in the Supervisor– Subordinate Relationship

Most organizations rely on some type of formal hierarchy of authority, where some members

Some organizational role relations are clearly defined; others are more ambiguous. What do aspects such as posture, eye gaze, and territoriality suggest about the role relations in this painting? (Edward Hopper, *Office at Night*, 1940)

have legitimate rights over others. These rights include the assignment of work, supervision, and evaluation of job performance. Research indicates that supervisors spend roughly one-third to two-thirds of their time in direct communication with their subordinates, usually providing information about organizational policy and practices, the goals of the company, job instructions, rationales behind instructions, or feedback about performance. Subordinates, for their part, tend to provide

their superiors with information about themselves, job-related problems, tasks that need to be done, what they are currently working on, and information about policies and practices requested by the supervisor.[10]

Status Differences in Communication
The key attribute of the supervisor–subordinate relationship is that of status. Since supervisors have higher status by virtue of their position, they also seem to have "initiation

Work has become increasingly dependent on good communication skills to coordinate the division of labor.

rights." Supervisors are more free to start and stop discussions and to interrupt a subordinate; superiors can also choose to stand closer, touch casually, and use an informal mode of address; for a lower-status employee to reciprocate would be a sign of disrespect. In addition, superiors regularly expect subordinates to disclose information that makes them potentially vulnerable. For example, if you admit to your boss that you find it difficult to work with another employee, such information could be interpreted negatively and could affect your chances for a raise, promotion, or good evaluation. Given these problems, it is little wonder

that supervisors and subordinates often find themselves wary of one another.

Yet research also confirms that developing an effective relationship with your supervisor is one of the best predictors of job satisfaction.[11] How can you build a quality supervisor–subordinate relationship? Obviously, the supervisor is in the best position to set the tone for the relationship. He or she can make a concerted effort to avoid the negative effects of the status barrier. The subordinate can also do a lot by maintaining respect for those of higher status, without sacrificing personal integrity. As you read about the keys to effective supervision and directing communication upward, try to think of ways that status differences help or hinder communicative efforts.

Effective Supervisory Communication

In a comprehensive review of research on supervisor–subordinate communication, Frederic Jablin reports that more research has been focused on characteristics of effective versus ineffective supervisors than on any other topic.[12] The most complete list of characteristics related to effectiveness was provided by W. C. Redding.[13] He suggested that better supervisors:

- Are more "communication-minded"; they enjoy talking with subordinates.

- Are willing to listen and take appropriate action in response to employees' suggestions and complaints.

- Tend to "ask" or "persuade" employees more frequently than "telling" or "demanding" them to do things.

- Are sensitive to subordinates' feelings and ego-defense needs, careful to reprimand in private, and so on.

- Are more open in passing information along to subordinates, giving advance notice of changes, and explaining rationales behind policies and regulations.

There are problems with simple lists like the one above, however. A number of situational factors can influence effective leadership. Take the characteristic of being open with subordinates, for instance. As we shall see later, the "organizational culture" socializes its employees (supervisors and subordinates alike) to use particular communication styles and avoid others. A manager with an open style of communication may not last long in a "closed-mouth" organization. In addition, Jablin has shown that subordinates are more likely to respond to an open style when their supervisor is less involved in organizational politics.[14] Perhaps subordinates don't trust a superior who is likely to move on up the ladder as much as they do one who "stays home" and seems more loyal to his or her subordinates. Also, such politicking may actually increase the perceived status differences between superior and subordinate. Furthermore, the maturity level of an individual or group of subordinates can alter a supervisor's style. A supervisor is more likely to be successful by being demanding and less open with a group that demonstrates few work-related skills and a low motivation level. We will have more to say about that in our discussion of group leadership a little later in this chapter.

Directing Communication Upward

By now you know that interpersonal communication is a two-way street and that a supervisor cannot be successful alone. For their relationship to be a good one, both supervisor and subordinate must work hard to create and maintain it. What can you do as a subordinate to build a good working relationship? You can start by drawing some distinctions between *natural* role differences and *dysfunctional* role differences between yourself and your superior.

Natural and Dysfunctional Role Differences

Natural role differences arise from the fact that job descriptions differ. Supervisors have to be concerned about how policies and procedures affect their entire unit, not just one person. They're in a position of having to satisfy their superiors, other departments, perhaps even outside suppliers or customers. You aren't in that position and so your perspectives are likely to differ. This is good in many ways; it frees you from a lot of concerns and allows you to concentrate on your own responsibilities.

Dysfunctional role differences, on the other hand, are perceptual and behavioral differences that hinder productivity. Researchers call disagreements or misunderstandings about crucial organizational issues "semantic-information distance." Frequent disagreements about specific job duties and how much authority a supervisor has are not uncommon. These kinds of differences need to be discussed and settled, rather than allowed to drag on, slowing down productivity and souring the relationship. In addition, supervisors and subordinates both have a tendency to overestimate what the other knows or remembers about specific issues. As a result, acting on such assumptions can often lead to misunderstanding and trouble.

Upward Distortion   This strong tendency, which needs to be dealt with by every person in a position of reporting to a supervisor, is the tendency to distort information that is passed along to the superior. Studies show that this is most likely to occur when the news is negative or places the subordinate in a bad light. It is only human nature to present the best image possible, especially when the other person has a lot of influence over your future. Nobody wants to be the one to tell the boss that his new work procedure is a functional failure, that it takes more time and causes more mistakes than the old way. Research also suggests that subordinates who have advancement aspirations, who don't feel very secure in their jobs, or who don't trust their superiors are the most likely to distort information.[15]

This tendency can be overcome, however. Superiors often put less stock in positive messages received from subordinates and view negative reports as more accurate. In one study, supervisors stated that their most effective subordinates were also the ones most willing to report bad news.[16] Perhaps there is not so much truth to the old proverb about killing the messenger who bears bad tidings. Or perhaps

it is a good idea to test the waters first by reporting some very "minor" bad news.

Communicating in the Helping Professions

In times of emotional or physical stress, we often turn to friends for help. When the strain becomes too great or we become physically ill, professional help is needed. Our discussion of the helping professions is two-pronged. Some of you may be considering careers in one of these professions and want to know what message-sending and receiving skills will be most beneficial. For others, receiving the best professional care is an important concern. You are more interested in knowing what to expect and how to improve the care you receive through effective communication. There is a growing interest among communication scholars in investigating the communication patterns between professional helpers and their clients. We will look briefly at interactions in two general types of professional relationships: therapeutic and health-care dyads.

Client–Counselor Interactions

A formal therapeutic relationship exists any time an individual seeks out a professionally trained helper who is paid for his or her services. Psychiatrists, social workers, family therapists, the clergy, employment counselors, advice columnists, academic counselors, and parole officers make their living as professional helpers. On occasion, bartenders, prostitutes, teachers, and private detectives also find themselves in the position of offering advice or consoling a client. And, on a more informal basis, friends often provide each other with a therapeutic ear.

Carl Rogers, one of the pioneers in the study and practice of therapeutic communication, outlined three elements of communication

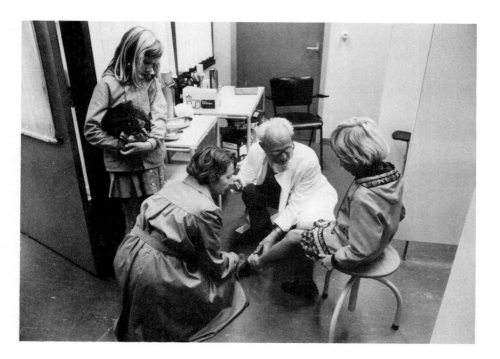

The medical interview, while highly scripted, can be imbued with a personal touch of warmth and concern.

that have become axiomatic in modern therapy: warmth, genuineness, and accurate empathy.[17] **Warmth** refers to messages that convey support and encouragement and create a positive environment for exploring problems and solutions. A therapist exhibits **genuineness** when she shows that her concern for the client is uppermost in mind. Equally important is **accurate empathy**, the ability to listen and understand the feelings and emotions expressed by the client.

Loyd Pettegrew and Richard Thomas conducted a study comparing clients' perceptions of the communicator styles used by their therapists with other people's perceptions of an untrained friend or acquaintance they had turned to for help. They found that friends and therapists alike whose behavior was perceived as friendly, attentive, relaxed, impression-leaving, and presented a good communicator image created the most positive therapeutic climate.[18] "Informal helpers" were seen as more friendly and genuine, but also as more dominating and contentious than their professional counterparts. The formal therapists were, however, viewed as more attentive and relaxed. Pettegrew and Thomas explained these findings by noting the differing expectations that people have of friends versus therapists. "Perhaps the client implicitly knows that the therapist's interest in him is of a professional nature and is, therefore, less concerned with the therapist providing friendly cues."[19]

Friends can be more dominating and argumentative because "the helpee holds a greater latitude of acceptable behavior for the informal helper, while assertive or argumentative behavior from formal helpers might jeopardize their professional relationship with the client."[20]

The strongest similarity between effective informal and formal therapists was their ability to accurately empathize—to understand the feelings and emotions of the helpee.

Communication in the Health Care Professions

Relatively speaking, only a small percentage of Americans turn to professional therapists to improve their mental health. But when our physical health is at stake, we rarely hesitate to seek out members of the medical profession. In this context, we are likely to interact with doctors, dentists, nurses, technicians, receptionists, medical records personnel, hospital administrators, and a host of others. Most of the research to date has focused on interactions of primary-care doctors and nurses with their patients. Those are the types of interactions we will focus on as well.

Communication between health care providers and patients is usually aimed at one of four primary goals: (1) diagnosis; (2) counseling patients about appropriate treatment; (3) gaining the cooperation of the patient in subscribing to recommended treatment; and (4) educating the patient about the nature of an illness, its causes, symptoms, and so on.[21] As this list indicates, the communication between these specialists and their patients is largely one-sided. Several studies confirm that doctors talk more than patients, ask nearly twice as many questions, and give more commands.[22]

Consumer advocates argue that this trend needs to be tempered. They suggest that patients should ask questions and insist on explanations for treatments they don't understand.[23] Several factors, however, discourage this kind of frank communication on the part of the patient. First of all, physicians are accorded such high status and viewed as so highly credible that patients feel unqualified to question or dispute them. Furthermore, many professionals and patients alike assume that the technical language of medicine is beyond the comprehension of the patient. Little effort is made to bridge the gap. Finally, the medical interview is highly scripted (opening greeting, reasons for visit, symptoms/physical examination, diagnosis, treatment/medication/testing, appointment for next visit), and scripted interactions are highly resistant to change, because people assume "that's the way it is."[24]

Knowing that these patterns exist, health care professionals and patients are mutually responsible for altering them when they prove unsatisfactory. Doctors and nurses should be sensitive to the reluctance of patients to question or ask for further explanation. And patients must overcome the passive nature of their role, remembering that doctors are primarily advisers, not dictators.

Communicating with Strangers: Customer Relations

Another common interaction is the one that takes place between customers and clerks. These roles are sometimes called "boundary-spanning" roles because the individuals who fill them interact primarily with people who are not members of the work organization. Typical roles include sales representatives, purchasing agents, public relations personnel, real estate agents, table servers, delivery persons, postal clerks, bank tellers, financial advisers, and so on.

In some ways, these relations are more difficult to manage because the status distinctions are not so clear-cut. Supervisors and subordinates know who the ultimate authority is, and professionals are expected to know more than those who seek their help. But the customer–clerk relationship has not been so neatly defined. Some customers view the role of a clerk as essentially a "servant," and many businesses instruct their personnel to "put the customer first." Other people recognize the relationship as one of mutual dependency and grant customer and clerk fairly equal status. Still other customers place themselves in a submissive role to the salesperson ("When you get the time, could you please show me the Nikon 35mm camera? I would really appreciate it. Thank you ever so much. No, that's OK, I'll wait.").

In spite of these differing assumptions about the nature of customer relations, there are some general guidelines. Perhaps the most important thing for a salesperson to remember is that different customers respond to different approaches. Just as in other contexts, people have learned different rules for appropriate or preferred interaction with sales representatives. When shopping, some like to browse and don't want to be "bothered" by salespeople—and they give off unmistakable nonverbal cues: lack of eye contact, turning away from approaching salespeople, and so on. Other people desire special attention and will wait for the clerk to approach them, demonstrate merchandise, or offer advice. Asking questions about their preferences is a subtle way to find out whether advice is desired or not. A clerk must always be sensitive to the customer's nonverbals—they will tell you if your rules are not their rules.

Most customers will respond to simple, courteous behavior and a pleasant but not overly friendly manner. In positions where repeat business is important, a clerk should find out the customer's name and remember to use the appropriate form of address (Mr., Ms., Dr., and so on). Many salespeople go out of their way to provide regular customers with a little extra attention, such as a card or phone call in advance of a sales promotion. That little extra often results in customer loyalty.

INTERPERSONAL COMMUNICATION IN GROUPS AND ORGANIZATIONS

In addition to the dyadic situations we've discussed, an employee must learn to communicate effectively with small groups of coworkers and find ways to plug into more specialized communication channels that flow throughout the organization. Let's begin by investigating the communication patterns of small work groups.

Interpersonal Relationships in Small Groups

Small groups exist in organizations for many reasons. Many groups are formally created as permanent functioning bodies within the organization: departments, committees, and work groups within departments are examples. The tasks of these groups may include decision making, problem solving, information sharing, or performing integrated work routines. On occasion temporary (ad hoc) groups are organized to produce new policies, redesign procedures, or smooth out problems between organizational units. Alongside these formal groups, employees form their own informal groups for sharing information and establishing acceptable work norms.

Regardless of the type of group, many of the dynamics of group interaction will be the same. Every group will evolve specialized roles for its members, norms and sanctions to govern

Smile Wars: The Emotional Price of Friendly Relations

"A smile is free. It doesn't cost you anything." Or so we've been led to believe. We routinely expect a big smile from anyone, particularly a female, who is supposed to provide us with friendly service. Even Miss Manners concurs, "Your doctor and your lawyer, if they but knew it, are as obligated to be pleasant to you as your waitress and your automobile mechanic."

But the constant smile of your friendly service personnel isn't free. It is emotional labor, defined by sociologist Arlie Russell Hochschild as "the silent work of evoking and suppressing feeling—in ourselves and in others." The result is emotional stress or burnout on the job. Smiling is hard work, and the obligation to smile has produced a silent war between service personnel and the customers they serve. Who suffers the most? Anyone who must have face-to-face contact with the general public during most of a six- or eight-hour shift. High on the list are sales clerks, hairdressers, nurses, teachers, social workers, and the nation's 70,000 airline flight attendants.

Hochschild was one of the first to bring the "smile wars" phenomenon to the public's attention. Her 1983 *Mother Jones* magazine article chronicled the training process and battle-weary saga of one flight attendant. The job's primary burden is the result of advertising that depicts (and

therefore promises) the airline flight to be awash in comfort, always on time, with each passenger getting personal attention from a genuinely friendly flight attendant. According to Hochschild, this creates expectations

---

group interaction, and some forms of social cohesion to keep the group together. Of all the roles in group interaction, the leadership role has gained the most attention from laypersons and experts alike.

Leadership and Dyadic Linkage

In most organizations, the leadership role in a task or decision-making group will be formally assigned. As a leader, you will be expected to motivate, direct, evaluate, correct, and work with the group in an efficient manner while ensuring high-quality production. What makes for effective leadership? For years researchers thought that leadership could be predicted by identifying the **personality traits** of leaders. They hoped to discover the consistent "stuff" of leadership: intelligence, charisma, sociability, and so on. But the correlation between personality and leadership has proved elusive. After more than 750 studies, the attempt to construct a profile of leader characteristics has been largely written off, and researchers have turned to other approaches.[25]

The assessment of **leadership style** is another way researchers have tried to determine effective leadership. Where the trait approach emphasized internal characteristics, the style approach profiled behavior. Three major styles were identified: autocratic, democratic, and laissez-faire. The leader who dominates, tells

that simply cannot be met, especially when flights are so crowded that attendants cannot serve breakfast once, let alone offer refills of coffee. When the harried flight attendant fails to smile, the TV commercial image lights up in the passenger's mind. "Where's my service with a smile?" he or she may think or even verbalize. "The smile in the ad makes the passenger view ordinary nonsmiling as facial loafing," says Hochschild.

An element of sexism is involved. When the request for a smile is verbalized, it is usually demanded *by* a male passenger and always demanded *of* a female flight attendant. Male attendants are fewer in number and are not required to be as pleasant.

The training of flight attendants leaves little room for doubt about the obligation to smile and to constantly suppress other, less pleasant feelings. Would-be attendants are often told to think of the cabin as the living room in their own home, and to treat passengers as guests. But the most often repeated advice was to smile, smile, smile, smile, smile. "Really lay it on," said one pilot. "Smile."

We all want friendly service. It is the cornerstone of repeat business. People should enjoy their jobs or find work elsewhere, right? Yes, but there is another problem here. Hochschild draws a distinction between *surface acting* and *deep acting* on the job. If the demand were simply to put on a friendly act, we could surface-act our way through our workday, reserving our private feelings because they are not demanded of us. But in a culture that emphasizes "being real" and an industry that sells job service as genuine feeling, it is hard to live with the idea that you are putting on an act. The only alternative is deep-acting. To do that, we must "evoke in ourselves the feelings we need in order to seem to feel the right feeling for the job." The distinction between the person and the job description becomes blurred, producing confusion and emotional stress.

The physical work of smiling is at least equivalent to standing on your feet all day, but the emotional toll is probably much higher. Think about that the next time you start to demand a smile or refuse to buy a product because the smile didn't seem genuine enough.

Source: *Arlie Russell Hochschild, "Smile Wars: Counting the Casualties of Emotional Labor,"* Mother Jones, *December 1983, pp. 35–40.*

others what to do, and uses strong rewards or punishments exemplifies the **autocratic style**. Research shows this style to be very efficient; such leaders are often respected, but not necessarily well liked, by their subordinates. It is not surprising that in our society the **democratic style** of leadership is the most popular with workers. A democratic leader seeks input from workers, believing that their participation in the work process will be a primary motivating force. As a result, this style is more time-consuming than the autocratic. And, in spite of its good press, the democratic style doesn't work in every situation. It assumes that workers want to participate and have essentially the same goals as management. The **laissez-faire style** is sometimes called the "hands off" approach to leadership. The leader allows capable workers to use their own judgment and to call upon him or her only when they need advice or a second opinion.

All three styles have one thing in common. It is usually assumed that, like personality, a leader adopts a single style and lives or dies by it. This may often be true, since we can become remarkable creatures of habit. However, evidence is mounting that the most successful leaders are those who can adapt their communication style to different situations and to different people.

Situational approaches to leadership emphasize the need to be flexible and to look at a

Communication in the workplace is sometimes restricted to nonverbal forms due to environmental restraints (noise, physical separation, and the like). Yet strong relationships are often developed by workers in situations similar to that pictured. (Jacob Lawrence, *Builders No. 1*, 1970)

variety of factors before determining the most effective communication strategies. Some of these factors include the *nature of the task* (how simple or complex it is), the *maturity level* of the work group (their ability and willingness to do the job), the leader's *legitimate power* (how much he has), and *leader–member relations* (how much the group likes and respects the leader).

One of the most interesting situational approaches takes on the conventional business wisdom that leaders should treat all of their subordinates in the same manner to avoid giving the impression of "playing favorites" or treating some employees unfairly. However, research conducted under the rubric of **dyadic linkage theory** calls this view into question. The dyadic linkage model of leadership suggests that every dyadic relationship is unique in some ways, and that effective leaders adapt their style to fit the person. This means that, as a leader, you might use a more autocratic style with those subordinates who respond well to direction, prodding, or an occasional kick in the pants. Likewise, you would be prudent to give more latitude to highly competent, go-it-on-their-own employees, and to use a more participatory, equal-status style with workers who perform the most critical functions in your unit.

In short, leadership requires sensitivity to followers' needs and a rather flexible package of communication options. Think about your most recent work experience. Imagine yourself as the leader of that group. How would you adapt your leadership style to each individual member? What would you do to motivate each one?

Membership and Identity

As important as leadership is, one should never forget to cultivate good group relations with coworkers. Work units are the heart and soul of most organizations. When a unit doesn't function well, the effect usually ripples throughout the organization. There are several aspects of group communication that you should become aware of and use to improve or maintain group relations. This includes the development of complementary roles, effective group norms, and a cohesive group identity.

Group Role Repertory Experts agree that for a group to work well together, members must take on different roles and reinforce each other for role performances. Most also agree on five specific roles that are most essential: task leader, social leader, information provider, tension releaser, and devil's advocate. These roles were discussed at length in Chapter 10; refer to that chapter for descriptions of each role. The important thing to remember here is that in playing group roles, members need to achieve a delicate balance of complementarity and duplication. In other words, group interaction is most effective when the role each person plays complements rather than competes with the roles of other group members. For instance, when Gibson provides the group with infor-

mation about projected sales figures (information provider), Gerber questions the validity of the figures (devil's advocate). In turn, Gibson provides additional information about how the figures were arrived at. Their actions are complementary because together they have increased the group's confidence that the information they have is accurate; they have advanced the group toward its goal. Sometimes, role behavior is not complementary. When an argument gets out of hand, Gibson breaks the tension with a joke. If Gerber follows with another joke, his behavior is competing with Gibson's, not complementing it (unless, of course, the first joke failed to ease the tension successfully).

Role specialization can be taken too far, however. Group members need to be able to play a variety of roles to cover for a group member who is absent or not up to par on a given day. It might be helpful to think of group members as having primary and secondary roles. Primary roles are the ones they play most frequently, secondary roles are the ones they are capable of performing when the regular performer cannot. It takes time for roles to develop in a new group, so you should expect competition for leadership and other key roles to take place until members find their niche. Roles that are not assigned formally will develop as a result of the positive or negative feedback the group provides to each member's communicative efforts.

Group Norms Group roles refer to behavioral expectations the group has for specific individuals. Group norms, on the other hand, are expectations the group has of *all* its members. Without norms, a group has no identity, no way of distinguishing itself from all the other work groups in the organization. And it has no way of governing the behavior of the whole group. A group can develop norms for high or low productivity, or members may establish a pattern of pulling practical jokes on one another.

Communication is the key to establishing good group norms and maintaining them or changing outdated ones. Effective groups tend to talk to one another about the standards they follow, and reinforce each other for performing well. The job satisfaction of individual workers has been traced to their working with colleagues who express positive attitudes about their jobs.[26] Most groups have key members, sometimes known as "opinion leaders," who are the most influential in changing the norms. A good leader will seek these people out when he or she wants to change the internal standards of a work group.

Group Cohesion   While roles and norms are necessary for effective group functioning, cohesiveness makes group life enjoyable and fulfilling. It provides members with a more complete sense of group identity and a sense of belonging. Simply defined, **cohesion** refers to the degree to which group members like one another and want to remain in the group. There are a number of factors that relate to cohesion: the expression of similarities in attitude, beliefs, and values; using group-related pronouns such as *we, us,* and *ours* instead of *yours* and *mine*; the development of trust; inside jokes, unusual rituals, traditions, or stories; surviving difficult times together, and so on. When a group begins to exhibit this kind of behavior, it is becoming more cohesive.

As much as cohesiveness is valued, experts point out the pitfalls of becoming *too* cohesive. When a group becomes too tight-knit, there is a tendency to try and maintain group relations at all costs. The result is a phenomenon known as **groupthink**: Critical thinking is sacrificed in order to promote group agreement.[27] Group members begin to think of themselves as incapable of making mistakes. Instead of mak-

ing decisions based on careful analysis of the facts and the alternative courses of action, they become sloppy and overconfident. They end up making bad decisions or defective products. Because of this tendency, experts recommend that groups be cautious about letting loyalty to the group become too important.

To promote effective group relations, it is healthy to develop communication patterns that reflect complementary roles, clear-cut norms, and a moderate degree of cohesiveness. Think about the groups you've worked with in the past. What were the roles, norms, and forms of cohesion of the most successful ones?

In addition to good relations between supervisors and subordinates and among work groups, it is also important to become adept at managing organization-wide communication channels. We will explore these channels next.

Interpersonal Communication in the Organization

In order to communicate effectively in an organization, you need to develop communication skills that will aid you in dealing with larger groups of people. Your perceptual abilities will also be in demand, as you will need to figure out which messages and which sources are important. We think you need to be aware of the socialization processes in organizations, communication networks such as "the grapevine" and how they function, as well as a short list of specific communication skills you will want to master.

Communication and Socialization

When a new employee joins an organization, two socializing processes are set in motion: The organization tries to indoctrinate the new recruit; the new recruit tries to "learn the ropes" and "make her mark" on the organization.

Uniform dress is one way to build identification among members of small groups or organizations. What are some other verbal or nonverbal ways that we shape group cohesion and identity?

From the organization's perspective, the new employee must be taught how to be a "good employee," and so is given written materials, canned presentations, and informal insights about the beliefs, values, and behaviors expected of her. While some of this socializing is through formal training and company publications, most of it comes from coworkers and supervisors. But the process is not an automatic one. As D. C. Feldman reports, a certain degree of trust and friendliness has to develop before the "regulars" will share vital information with a new recruit: "until incumbent employees felt they could trust recruits, they withheld information about supervisors' preferences and personalities, making the recruits less competent in the eyes of the supervisors."[28]

Typically, new recruits are fresh from college or an intensive training period and are eager to show what they have learned. It is infinitely wiser, however, to remain a student for a while—learning from coworkers, conforming to standards you may not really like, and earning their trust. This kind of compliant behavior will open the doors to "inside information" which, according to Fredric Jablin, "helps the new employee decode and interpret the scripts and schemas that prevail in the organization."[29] Then, once you're accepted as one of the group, you can begin making your mark.

Communication Networks

Having learned the ropes in your immediate work unit, it's time to venture out into the larger organization and tap into the flow of information that regulates movement up, down, in, and around the corporation. There

BOX 12.2

Business Etiquette: The Fine Art of Managing Relationships at Work

As a social concern, etiquette seems to go in and out of fashion. There have been times in our history when etiquette was admired, other times when it was merely tolerated, and still other times when it has been viewed as the sole property of snobs. But in the conservative world of business, etiquette has always survived. There have always been right and wrong ways to behave in job interviews, to eat your food during business luncheons, to manage an office romance, and to deal tactfully with your boss, coworkers, and secretaries. Some of the rules have changed over the years, but the fact that there are generally-agreed-upon rules has not changed.

Most experts on office etiquette argue that what constitutes "good manners" differs somewhat from company to company. But the difference is more a matter of degree than of kind. For instance, *not* to introduce two of your business associates who are unacquainted with one another is universally considered impolite. Furthermore, it is generally the rule that you should present a subordinate *to* a superior, and a female *to* a male (if they are peers). In other words, you should mention the superior's name first, as in "Ms. Smith, I would like to introduce you to Mr. Porter, one of our new sales associates." In a less formal office, first names would replace titles and surnames. In other companies, first names may be considered quite inappropriate. The best advice is to listen carefully to the way regulars interact with each other to discover the particular rules of that corporate culture.

A number of guidebooks on business etiquette have been published recently and are listed below for further reading. The range of topics is considerable, from what to wear to work to how to pronounce foreign items on a menu to successful ways of handling difficult situations. For example, Marjabelle Stewart and Marian Faux in *Executive Etiquette* argue that there is an etiquette for complaining to a boss about the poor work of a colleague. Assuming that efforts to work the problem out with the colleague have already failed, Stewart and Faux quote one em-

are actually many different kinds of communication networks in large organizations, most of them formed informally by people with a need for information that isn't available through regular, formal channels. Some networks, like the grapevine, have been named and are recognized by almost everyone. Others are almost invisible, and even the members of the network may not realize it exists. An informal network exists whenever members who do not formally report to each other exchange information on a somewhat regular basis. They may talk about almost any informational topic. An "innovation" network, for instance, might include people who share an interest in technology or "ideas" even though they are located in a variety of units and talk only when they happen to run into each other. When network members do talk, they may be able to use many of the innovations in their own department. Often they find out about new product lines and other techniques months before they are reported in company newsletters and internal memos.

ployee who was able to verbalize the rules: "You can't ever go in and bad-mouth a colleague. You really can't gossip, either. You mostly have to go in and describe the work situation to the boss—often without using names—and hope he gets the message."

The best advice, therefore, is to suggest another way of getting the work done, rather than to complain about the specific person. This avoids the back-stabbing approach, keeps office relations civil, and usually alerts the executive to take necessary action.

Etiquette books do offer useful insights because they are usually culled from years of experience or lots of interviews with people who have years of experience. But they are no substitute for a genuine desire to be gracious and a perceptive ear tuned in to the particular circumstances and climate of your office.

ADDITIONAL READINGS

Baldrige, Letitia. *Letitia Baldrige's Complete Guide to Executive Manners.* New York: Rawson Associates, 1985.

Martin, Judith. *Miss Manners' Guide to Excruciatingly Correct Behavior.* New York: Atheneum, 1982.

Stewart, Marjabelle Young, and Marian Faux. *Executive Etiquette.* New York: St. Martin's Press, 1979.

The **grapevine** is perhaps the most interesting and certainly the most researched of the networks. People are curious about the action behind the scenes and often talk about what they know or have heard in the hallways, beside the water cooler, or over coffee. Many people rely on the information gleaned from the grapevine to increase their own understanding of the organization, predict future changes, and consolidate their own power by being in the know. People who fail to tune in to the grapevine are often likely to be the subject of rumors. Research verifies that most people have a negative image of the grapevine, but would rather have possibly misleading information than no information at all.[30]

The most interesting findings, however, are those that dispute popular opinion about the grapevine. Contrary to what most people think, the grapevine is amazingly accurate. One study estimates that nearly 80 percent of the information acquired through the grapevine is basically accurate.[31] Several studies have found that information passed via the grapevine was

Organizational communication does not have to take place in stuffy old offices. Imagine trying to keep this bunch in tune.

distorted less than most messages passed through formal channels.[32] Astute managers know the value of the grapevine and frequently use it to spread information that their people need to know but that is too sensitive to be commented on publicly.

In organizations, information is power, and the lack of it can weaken your position in the company. We recommend that you view the grapevine as a viable channel of communication, always taking what you hear with a grain of salt. Try to cultivate other informal networks as well; you never know when such contacts will pay off. In addition, you'll be the

kind of informed employee who can be a true asset to the organization.

Useful Communication Skills

Knowledge of how interpersonal communication works is invaluable in any organization, as are the skills that you develop based on that knowledge. But there are also some more specific skills that you should include in your arsenal. While a full discussion of these skills is beyond the scope of this textbook, we encourage you to take additional coursework in public speaking, business and technical writing, and interviewing. Public speaking skills will enable

Some social critics argue that we have fewer opportunities for public forums where interpersonal communication can take place between relative strangers. When was the last time you hung around the polling place to chat with members of your community? (George Caleb Bingham, *The County Election*, 1851–52)

you to make strong, organized presentations to clients, key executives, coworkers, and the general public. Writing skills have diminished drastically over the last few years, and employers value anyone who can craft clear memos, formal reports, speeches, and so on. And finally, knowledge about conducting interviews will serve you well beyond the recruiting process. You may be called upon to conduct informational, appraisal, counseling, sales, or exit interviews. Each one requires a different approach to be successful. At the end of this chapter, we list additional sources you can turn to for help in these areas.

TOWARD COMPETENCE: MANAGING IMPERSONAL RELATIONSHIPS

To be a well-rounded communicator, you must manage public, impersonal relationships just as well as you do intimate ones. In this chapter we have described the major criteria that shape public encounters. These criteria can serve as general guidelines when other, more specific information is not available. For work situations such as supervisor-and-subordinate, customer relations, work group interaction, and networking, research indicates many of the expectations and communication patterns you will encounter. While the information presented here will help you a great deal, it is up to you to develop your own ways of finding out what is appropriate and possible in any given organizational culture. Organizations differ as much as national cultures do. Communication that is effective in one company may fail in another. For that reason, we suggest that you view yourself as an anthropologist, an immigrant, an alien, a stranger in a strange land whenever you join a new organization. Learn the rules that people follow, ask questions about their rituals, games, and pastimes. Determine who the key people are and what channels of communication they rely on. Try to view even the most familiar episodes of work and social life with a new eye, developing what one of our professors used to call "uncommon sense," so you will know as much about the strangers you meet as you now know about your best friends.

REVIEW TERMS

The following is a list of major concepts introduced in this chapter. The page number where the concept is first mentioned is listed in parentheses.

deference (298)
avoidance rituals (298)
presentational rituals (299)
demeanor (299)
playacting (300)
natural role differences (303)
dysfunctional role differences (303)
upward distortion (304)
warmth (305)
genuineness (305)

accurate empathy (305)
personality traits (308)
leadership style (308)
autocratic style (309)
democratic style (309)
laissez-faire style (309)
situational approaches (309)
dyadic linkage theory (310)
cohesion (312)
groupthink (312)
grapevine (315)

SUGGESTED READINGS

Deal, Terrance, and Alan Kennedy. *Corporate Cultures: The Rites and Rituals of Corporate Life.* Reading, Mass.: Addison-Wesley, 1982. An almost anthropological guide to "reading" behavior in the organization. This very enjoyable book shows you all the things to look and listen for when you enter the corporate world: the importance of rituals and stories, the major role players in the communication network, and the heroes who embody the company's real goals and values.

Goffman, Erving. *Interaction Ritual: Essays on Face-to-Face Behavior.* Garden City, N. Y.: Anchor Books, 1967. An in-depth look at the social mechanisms of public life. Essays on face-work, deference and demeanor, embarrassment, and much more. A fascinating look at how we conduct everyday life.

Martin, Judith. *Miss Manners' Guide to Excruciatingly Correct Behavior.* New York: Warner Books, 1979. A very humorous, but nonetheless excruciatingly correct, discussion of "proper" public communication. This book and Miss Manners' newspaper columns have gone a long way to restoring the perception that it's OK to be mannerly.

PROCESS TO PERFORMANCE

TOPICS FOR DISCUSSION

1. Discuss the four criteria suggested at the beginning of this chapter for managing public interactions. Are these the only or even the best criteria? What criteria would you add or delete from the list? Do your classmates agree? Discuss any differences of opinion.

2. Review the definition of playacting on page 300. Identify as many ways as you can that strangers playact in public. Do you think that playacting is healthy, damaging, or simply a waste of time? Ask several classmates to react to the claim that "most people today don't know how to interact with strangers, so they just ignore them."

3. Why do you think that upward distortion happens in organizations? Under what circumstances do you think a subordinate should keep quiet, disguise the bad news a bit, or be open and up-front about it?

4. What advice would you give doctors about conducting the medical interview with a patient? Keep in mind these three essentials: efficient use of time, accurate information processing, and patient satisfaction.

5. How important are status differences in the work and social world? When should status barriers be maintained, broken down, or built up? Why?

6. Research indicates that the grapevine is the least trusted but most utilized communi-cation network in most organizations. What do you think should be done, if anything, to change the influence of the grapevine on campus or at work?

OBSERVATION GUIDES

1. Visit a public square, park, or business area where impersonal transactions are likely to take place. Record examples of avoidance rituals and presentational rituals. Note what happens when one person oversteps the boundaries, such as being too polite or too personal. Also, try to label any other rituals or behaviors that you think make impersonal interactions more or less effective.

2. Observe a wide range of customer–clerk interactions. On the sales floor, record the communication patterns on the sale of big-ticket items such as furniture or automobiles as well as small purchases like shoes, grocer-ies, or health foods. In addition, hang around the customer service desk, where you can overhear people returning merchandise. Take notes following each observation, writing down message patterns. Then rate the results of the transaction as: (a) very effective, (b) OK, (c) somewhat problematic, or (d) not effective at all. Summarize what you have observed, noting which patterns of commu-nication are most or least effective. Then compare your observations with the sugges-tions on page 307 in this chapter.

3. Every college campus is an organization. From your perspective as a student, try to identify as many different informal communication networks as you can. Who are the *key* members of the grapevine? Who are the most influential decision makers? Who is tapped into the off-campus network? Which faculty seem to be most "connected" on your campus, and so on? What influence do these networks have on the goings-on at your campus? You can conduct similar observations at work.

CLASSROOM EXERCISES

1. Your instructor will assign everyone a role in a fictitious manufacturing organization. (Instructors, see directions for "Hi-Fli, Inc." in the Instructor's Guide to Farace, Monge, and Russell's *Communicating and Organizing*, available from Addison-Wesley.) For two or three class periods, the class will role-play an actual organization going about its everyday work routines. Students should observe their own communication with supervisors, coworkers, messengers, top management, and so on, and write down observations during assigned "coffee breaks." After the exercise is completed, discuss the communication patterns observed: status differences, upward distortion, leadership styles, and so on.

2. Rent a videocassette or film version of one or more movies that include work settings and scenes as a major part of the storyline. Films such as *9 to 5*, *Network*, and *Games Mother Never Taught You* are good examples. Choose several interesting segments to show in class. Small groups of students may be assigned to analyze different segments. The analysis should reflect research and theory presented in this chapter. For instance, a group could analyze the nature of supervisor–subordinate communication as portrayed in the film clip. Another group might choose to discuss the decision-making style and roles being played in a business meeting, and so on. Each group should organize its analysis for a 15-minute presentation to the class.

3. Each student thinks of the best and worst supervisor–subordinate relationship he or she has been involved in. These relationships may have taken place at work, in a volunteer agency, or in a classroom work group—anywhere a clear leader was established. As a class, compile two lists. The first one should include the characteristics of the most and least effective *supervisor* known. The second list should include characteristics of the most and least effective *relationships* observed. Be careful to distinguish characteristics attributed to the supervisor from those attributed to the relationships. Once you have completed the two lists, discuss which is the most instructive. Is it better to think in terms of personal traits or relational attributions? Why?

4. Divide the class into groups of three and assign one person to play the role of therapist, help seeker, and observer. Then role-play the following informal therapeutic relationships. In each situation, the "therapist" should try to enact the three essential traits recommended by Carl Rogers: warmth, genuineness, and accurate empathy. The "observer" should record the verbal or nonverbal messages that communicate (or fail to communicate) the three characteristics.

Situation # 1:

THERAPIST: *Bartender*
HELP SEEKER: *Regular patron at bar, an independent accountant*
SITUATION: *Patron reveals a problem relating to a potential client in the basket-weaving mail-order business. He wants the account but cannot find a single topic of conversation on which to conduct small talk. He asks the bartender for advice.*

Situation # 2:

THERAPIST: *Best friend*
HELP SEEKER: *East Coast young urban professional (yuppie)*
SITUATION: *Yuppie tells friend about a job offer on the West Coast. She really wants the job but can't seem to convince her boyfriend that there will be opportunities for him. He likes his current job and friends, but she thinks the move will do them good—if he gives it half a chance. She asks her best friend for advice.*

Situation # 3:

THERAPIST: *Attorney*
HELP SEEKER: *A recent widow, 45 years of age, one child*
SITUATION: *The young widow consults her attorney. She is trying to put her life back together but cannot decide whether to sell the house and move into an apartment or keep the house and rent out rooms. She is on the verge of tears as she thinks about the changes ahead of her.*

When finished role-playing, the observer should report what he or she saw, and all three students discuss how to improve informal therapeutic interactions. When, for instance, is a problem beyond informal help? How can you tell someone he or she needs to seek professional help?

CHAPTER THIRTEEN

(Roy Lichtenstein, *Forget It! Forget Me!*, 1962)

REPAIRING RELATIONSHIPS: CONFLICT MANAGEMENT AND LISTENING

RELATIONSHIPS DON'T ALWAYS turn out the way we want. They are often plagued by misunderstandings and arguments. In *Annie Hall*, Woody Allen tries to explain why most of us keep trying despite all the problems. He tells the story of a man who goes to a psychiatrist because his brother imagines himself to be a chicken. When the psychiatrist asks him why he doesn't turn his brother in, the man replies, "I would, but I need the eggs." Allen goes on to say: "Well, I guess that's pretty much how I feel about relationships. You know, they're totally irrational and crazy and absurd . . . but, uh, I guess we keep goin' through it because . . . most of us need the eggs."[1]

In this chapter we consider what can be done when relationships run aground. In particular we look at how misunderstandings and conflicts can be effectively contained and managed. We begin by examining some social mechanisms that help prevent relational problems. Next we consider how relational disagreements escalate into full-scale conflicts. Finally, we discuss communication skills that allow us to manage and even to benefit from conflict.

In the last section we focus on one of the most crucial of all conflict-reduction mechanisms, that of listening. Although we've left a formal discussion of this aspect of communica-

tion for last, we don't want you to think listening is unimportant. In fact, we've implicitly discussed it in almost every chapter. Because listening is an essential but often overlooked part of communicative competence, we end with a consideration of what listening is and how it can be improved.

PREVENTING CONFLICT: THE FUNCTION OF APOLOGIES AND ACCOUNTS

Disagreements have a way of escalating. A "harmless" joke can lead to shouts, tears, and packed bags. A cross look can cause days of misunderstanding. Without realizing it, we often offend others. Luckily, there are simple ways to keep everyday offenses under control. In this section we'll look at how apologies, justifications, excuses, and disclaimers help people keep their relationships on an even keel.

Repairing Offenses: Apologies

Most competent communicators try their best to respect each other's face and line. Try as we may, however, from time to time we put our foot in our mouth. When this happens, there are socially recognized routines to help repair the damage. One of the most effective is the ritual of apology. Apologies are so commonplace you may not have thought much about them. But as we shall see, they are powerful ways of repairing relationships.

Erving Goffman divides apologies into four obligatory "moves."[2] The first move is called the **challenge**. It is made when the target of an offense calls attention to the offense. Assume, for example, someone cuts in front of you while you're standing in line. You can ignore this annoying behavior, or you can say something like "Excuse me. I was here first. Please get in line." The challenge lets you confront the offense directly; you don't have to sit there feeling uncomfortable.

The next move is up to the offender. Although a challenge may be ignored or disputed, it will usually be met with an **offering**. The offering may consist of an account ("I'm late for a test. Do you mind?"), some form of self-castigation ("Sorry. I was being rude."), or an offer of compensation ("When we're done, let me buy you a cup of coffee to make it up to you."). In the offering, the offender acknowledges guilt and tries to make amends.

In the third move, the target decides whether to refuse or accept the offering. Sometimes an additional offering may be requested ("Just saying you're sorry isn't enough. I'm tired of your rudeness."). Generally, however, the target will be anxious to accept the other's apology. **Acceptance** may be given grudgingly ("Well, it really is annoying, but since you're late, go ahead.") or wholeheartedly ("Oh, that's OK. No problem.").

In the final step, the offender shows gratitude by expressing **thanks**. A simple verbal response like "Glad you're not mad" or a smile and nod may close the ritual. Once thanks has been given, interactants have repaired their relationship.

The moves in this simple communication ritual do a lot of relational work. Consider how relieved you feel when someone you care for apologizes to you, or how difficult it is to apologize when you're in the wrong. The verbal formula "I'm sorry" carries a lot of emotional weight and excuses a multitude of sins. Note also that the ritual is transactional: both parties must play their parts to set things back on course.

Accounting for Actions: Excuses and Justifications

Offerings don't always take the form of apologies; often they consist of accounts. **Accounting** is an attempt to redefine an offense to make it seem normal and appropriate. There are two ways to account for an action: to make the consequences of an offense appear less negative, or to minimize responsibility for those consequences. The first type of account is known as a justification; the second as an excuse.[3]

An individual who admits responsibility for an action but denies that it was wrong is offering a **justification**.[4] Telling a buddy who's had too much to drink that you're taking his car keys "for his own good" is a justification, as is explaining to a naughty child "I'm doing this to teach you a lesson." Of course, a justification's success depends on whether it is believed and accepted. Some justifications are inadequate. While standing someone up because of an emergency is justified, failing to show because you "had something better to do" is unacceptable.

In an **excuse**, the person admits that an act was unfortunate but denies responsibility for it. An excuse may be based either on a physical disability (drugs, alcohol, physical illness, or exhaustion) or on a psychological causes ("such as uncontrollable emotions, coercion by others, hypnosis, brainwashing, somnambulism, insanity, or mental illness").[5] Have you ever used

The peace treaty is a symbolic agreement to repair international conflict. Relationships must also develop symbolic ways of overcoming interpersonal stress.

any of these kinds of excuses to get yourself out of a jam? A lot of people have.

Think back to our discussion of attribution theory in Chapter 3. Excuses are really ways of persuading others to make favorable attributions about us. When a student explains that her paper is late because she has a temperature of 104, she wants her teacher to realize that circumstances rather than inherent irresponsibility are to blame. She hopes for a situational rather than a dispositional attribution.

When people are convinced that an offense was justified or excusable, they're likely to forgive and forget. Excuses and justifications help both parties reduce stress and minimize

conflict. They are therefore powerful repair mechanisms.

Avoiding Blame: Disclaimers

While excuses and justifications are ways of realigning actions after the fact, there are also ways of accounting for actions before the fact. When we know an action may cause conflict, we often try to ward off criticism in advance. A **disclaimer** is a way of making sure an action is not challenged.

John Hewitt and Randall Stokes have described five kinds of disclaimers: hedging, credentialing, sin licensing, cognitive disclaimers, and appeals for suspension of judgment.[6] Table 13.1 gives examples of these kinds of accounts. All are ways of saying, "I know I am about to give offense, but there are special reasons you should understand and forgive me." By accepting the disclaimer, the target agrees not to challenge what follows.

Every culture establishes ways of diminishing conflict. In modern middle-class America, apologies and simple verbal formulas like disclaimers, excuses, and justifications are approved ways. In Chapter 1, we discussed the ritual of insulting the meat, a very different cultural response to the threat of conflict. Box 13.1 (p. 328) discusses still another social pattern that may help to contain conflict. These rituals are very different from one another, yet each appears to address the same problem: how to stop conflict before it escalates. Perhaps you have experienced other cultural patterns that fulfill the same function.

WHEN CONFLICT ESCALATES: MANAGING SERIOUS DISAGREEMENTS

While rituals and routines like those we've just discussed are ways of warding off conflict, they aren't always successful. There are times when conflicts and misunderstandings threaten to destroy the fabric of the relationship. A popular belief holds that any conflict can be solved through communication, but this is simply not the case. Communication can't magically erase basic differences in values, goals, and expectations. If used realistically and skillfully, communication can solve relational problems. If not, it can make conflicts worse rather than better.

In general, conflict occurs whenever goals are blocked. **Intrapersonal conflict** occurs when a single individual is torn between two incompatible desires or needs. **Interpersonal conflict** occurs whenever the goals or actions of two people are incompatible: that is, whenever they cannot negotiate a mutually satisfactory outcome.[7] Both forms of conflict can produce stress. While most of our attention in this chapter will be on interpersonal conflict, intrapersonal conflict can affect relationships because it can cause irrational behavior. Box 13.2 (pp. 330–31) examines some of the ways people react to and protect themselves from this kind of conflict.

Positive Aspects of Interpersonal Conflict

Interpersonal conflicts can make us feel angry and abused; over time they can destroy relationships. This doesn't mean, however, that conflict is bad per se. Well-managed conflict should be welcomed rather than avoided. For several reasons, conflict can be healthy for a relationship.

1. *Conflict means interdependence*. After all, conflict is a sign that two people are involved in each other's lives. If people were entirely autonomous, they could not experience conflict. The fact that people fight means that they still care.[8] While repeated conflict may be a sign of danger, it means a relationship has not yet entered the stagnation stage. When conflicts are successfully managed and resolved, the aftermath is often an increase in cohesion. Many couples feel closer as a result of the conflict process.

2. *Conflict signals a need for change*. While change can be frightening because it disrupts familiar patterns, it can also be healthy. Remember, without the ability to adapt, a system will eventually run down. It is important to see conflict as an opportunity to become more adaptable and creative. A productive conflict

TABLE 13.1

Five types of disclaimers

Hedging	The actor lets the target know he or she is open to correction if what is said turns out to be in error.
	"This is just off the top of my head, so I may be wrong" "I'm no expert . . ."
Credentialing	The actor indicates special qualifications for getting away with something that would be considered offensive when done by others.
	"My record shows I'm not prejudiced, but . . ." "Some of my best friends are . . ."
Sin license	The actor lets the target know that he or she is about to break normal social rules but that there are good reasons for doing so under present circumstances.
	"I know this cake has 10,000 calories, but since it's my birthday . . ." "I realize I'm bending the rules here . . ."
Cognitive disclaimer	The actor tries to convince the target that while a behavior may appear strange or foolish, it actually makes sense.
	"This may seem crazy, but I'm absolutely sure that . . ." "Don't think I'm weird or anything . . ."
Appeals for suspension of judgment	The actor asks the target to wait before reacting negatively.
	"Hear me out about this." "Now, don't get angry before I finish."

For further explanation and discussion, see John P. Hewitt and Randall Stokes, "Disclaimers," *American Sociological Review* 40 (1975): 1–11.

allows participants to find new ways of relating to one another.

3. *Conflict allows problem diagnosis.* Many people tend to deny rather than to acknowledge problems. Overt conflict can provide information about mutual needs and expectations. It can let a couple know what they must do in order to stay together. It also acts as a safety valve. Regular conflicts keep problems from building up. A relationship in which no conflict ever occurs is unnatural. Its members may be engaging in unrealistic denial.

Mismanaged Conflict

One of the reasons we fear conflict is that most of the time we manage it very badly. Let's look at some of the things we all do that make conflict destructive rather than productive.

One way to mismanage conflict is to try to escape it. Individuals or couples undergoing intense conflict may sometimes experience "a mental paralysis which leads to no action at all."[9] They ignore the problem, appearing uninterested and unconcerned, although they are really experiencing intense emotion. The

BOX 13.1

If You Can't Stand the Shame, Don't Play the Game: Playing the Dozens as a Conflict-Reducing Ritual

"Sounding" or "playing the dozens" is a game of verbal insults played in black urban communities. Before a group of onlookers, opponents direct rapid-fire insults, often obscene, toward one another's relatives, commenting on their age, beauty, wealth, and the like. "Your mother so skinny she ice-skate on a razor blade" and "Your mother wear high-heeled sneakers to church" are examples of some of the milder sounds. (For more obscene examples, consult the sources below.) One of the goals of the game is to think of new and creative insults that top those of the previous player. At their best, sounds can be clever and even poetic. Players must be quick-witted and highly verbal.

There have been many explanations for this ritual. Some have seen it as displaced aggression resulting from social and economic pressures, while others have viewed it as a working through of Oedipal impulses. Still others argue that, whatever other functions it performs, it teaches safe ways of resolving conflict in daily interaction.

Thurmon Garner believes that people learn important lessons about conflict by playing this game. They learn to confront conflict by talking rather than fighting, to keep cool in tense situations, and to keep their wits about them.

As we have seen, one way to deal with conflict is to repress or minimize it. Another way, illustrated here, is to dramatize it by bringing it out in the open. Hostilities are revealed and expressed, but in an indirect and ritualized form, giving the community a nonviolent forum for conflict.

Participants also benefit personally, learning inventiveness, assertiveness, and poise. They can gain a personal sense of power, since successful players are highly regarded in the community. They also learn not to lose their temper and to "hang in" when the going gets tough. Participants learn to remain composed, calmly taking whatever failures fall their way. Finally, because contestants must play off one another, following the flow of the game, they learn to coordinate their thoughts and actions. Thus competition and cooperation are mixed together in a ritual that benefits both the individual and the community.

Source: *Thurmon Garner, "Playing the Dozens: Folklore As Strategies for Living,"* Quarterly Journal of Speech *69 (1983): 47–57.*

ADDITIONAL READINGS

Abrahams, Roger D. *Deep Down in the Jungle*. Chicago: Aldine, 1970, pp. 35–54.

Dollard, John. "The Dozens: Dialect of Insults." *American Imago* 1 (1939): 3–25.

Labov, William. "Rules for Ritual Insults." In *Studies in Social Interaction*, edited by David Sudnow. New York: Free Press, 1972.

Conflict and competition are often ritualized and contained in sport and entertainment. (George Bellows, *Preliminaries to the Big Bout*, 1916)

ultimate outcome may be literal escape. The couple walks away from each other, allowing the relationship to dissolve. While it may be inevitable that a relationship will end, escape doesn't give it a chance.

The opposite way of mismanaging conflict is by being too aggressive. Instead of ignoring the problem, the couple fights. While fighting isn't necessarily a bad thing, there are destructive ways to fight. George Bach and Peter Wyden discuss several of these.[10] One way to ensure that a fight will be harmful is to time it badly. Try not to begin a fight as your mate walks through the door after a busy day or

right before dinner guests are scheduled to arrive. People should be prepared to deal with conflict; adequate time should be set aside for the process.

Fights should also be kept up to date. If a fight is continually postponed, it may get out of control when it does occur. Failing to confront things as they crop up is known as **gunnysacking**. It's as though you stuck all of your grievances and hurt feelings into an old gunnysack, which gets heavier and heavier until it finally bursts.

Gunnysacking can lead to another unfair tactic, **kitchen-sinking**. In a kitchen-sink fight,

BOX 13.2

What, Me Worry? Ways of Hiding from Intrapersonal Stress

From time to time we all experience internal conflict and stress. When we cannot cope, we use defense mechanisms, behavior patterns that deny or disguise conflict-producing impulses. Defense mechanisms help us avoid pain, but because they are distortions, they diminish our ability to communicate effectively. Here are some of the most common ways to hide conflict.

Identification. One way to deal with the fear we feel toward an outside agent is to identify with that agent. We get rid of anxiety by becoming one with the enemy. Psychologist Bruno Bettelheim, who was a concentration camp prisoner in World War II, noted that prisoners would often take on the goals, values, and even the appearance of their SS guards as a self-protective device. A less tragic example can be found in teaching assistants who identify with tough senior professors by becoming harsh and demanding with their own students.

Displacement. When an impulse cannot be carried out on one object, we may direct it to another. Shouting at the boss is forbidden; shouting at one's spouse or kids may seem a less dangerous way to express emotions. Erotic impulses may also be displaced from an inappropriate love object to someone more available. Sexual drives may also be directed to creative or intellectual activities. By throwing ourselves into our work, we channel dangerous drives into socially acceptable pathways. This form of displacement is called **sublimation**.

Reaction formation. Sometimes an impulse is transformed into its opposite. A child who is hostile toward a parent may turn the hostility into excessive love and attachment. A man who is afraid of women or fears that he is sexually inadequate may become preoccupied with sex, becoming a Don Juan.

Projection. In projection we deny that we are the cause of an unacceptable thought or desire; instead, we see it as originating in others. Instead of acknowledging that we feel hate, we may believe others hate us. Sometimes we project onto an entire group. Minorities, for example, are often thought to embody all every possible argument (everything but the kitchen sink) is thrown in. Mary and Janet, two neighbors, may start arguing because Janet hit Mary's garbage cans while backing out of her driveway. In the course of the fight, however, they will use any weapon they can lay their hands on. Janet may call Mary a troublemaker, and Mary may counter by calling Janet selfish and reckless. Janet will then up the stakes by asking Mary why she is so particular about consideration, given the behavior of her children. Mary may respond by insulting Janet's husband. And so on. Before long, the original topic has been forgotten. The goal now is to draw as much blood as possible.

Another unfair tactic mentioned by Bach and Wyden is labeling, or **stereotyping**. If Janet were to say to Mary, "Of course you're inconsiderate. New Yorkers always are," she would be guilty of stereotyping. It is clear that this kind of typification will only make things worse.

Is there a middle ground between ignoring and aggressively fighting? How about compro-

of the unpleasant characteristics the majority group denies in itself.

Repression and **denial.** Sometimes an impulse is so conflict-producing that we refuse to recognize it in any way. Repression is the blocking of internal impulses; the person who refuses to experience any sexual feelings is repressing them. Denial is a failure to recognize external threats. The student about to flunk out of school who says "I'm doing fine" is denying reality.

Regression. A final way to deal with conflict is to regress, that is, to return to an earlier, less demanding state of maturation. When things in the adult world get to be too much, we may act childishly. The otherwise responsible woman may use a little-girl voice and manner when she's scared. The adult male may act like an immature teenager when he's embarrassed. If things get too bad, we may even climb into bed and pull the covers over our heads.

Defense mechanisms are not necessarily bad. They are what the name implies, ways of protecting and defending the self. When, however, they keep us from dealing constructively with a conflict, they do more harm than good.

Source: *Richard S. Lazarus,* Patterns of Adjustment and Human Effectiveness *(New York: McGraw-Hill, 1969).*

ADDITIONAL READINGS

Freud, Anna. *The Ego and the Mechanisms of Defense*. New York: International Universities Press, 1946.

La Planche, J., and J. B. Pontalis, *The Language of Psycho-Analysis*. London: Hogarth, 1980.

Sandler, Joseph, with Anna Freud. *The Analysis of Defense: The Ego and the Mechanisms of Defense Revisited*. New York: International Universities Press, 1985.

mise? Most people believe compromise is a positive way to deal with conflict. Surprisingly, writers on communication often warn against compromising, or at least compromising too soon. They feel that in premature compromise, both parties have to give up part of what they want and both end up unsatisfied. Often it's better to look for a new solution that satisfies both parties. Of course, if it's impossible to find a satisfactory solution, then compromise can be helpful. But it should be used as a last, not a first, resort.

Dealing Effectively with Conflict

If conflict is so easy to mismanage, what can we do to make it work for us? There are a number of ways of improving our ability to handle conflict. The first is to diagnose our current conflict style and decide whether it is helping or hindering us. The second is to learn how to express our feelings openly and honestly without suppressing them. The third involves learning some mechanisms for containing conflict.

Conflict is inevitable in social groups. Its frequency, however, is often a matter of norms; conflict was an expected part of life in the old West.
(Frederic Remington, *The Quarrel*, c. 1895–1902)

Diagnosing Your Conflict Style

Most of us have preferred ways of responding to conflict. Some get belligerent; others prefer to take abuse rather than fight. Once these conflict styles become habitual, they're hard to change. Most communication experts believe that we should match our style to the situation. There is a time and a place to be assertive, just as there is a time and a place to be passive.

In order to have a rewarding relationship, people must do two things: accomplish their personal goals while maintaining good rela-

tions. One way to define conflict styles is to consider these two goals.[11] Figure 13.1 shows how this works.

Let's begin with the lower right-hand quadrant of Figure 13.1. In this quadrant we place people whose primary concern is with achieving personal goals, even at the expense of a relationship. They try to overpower their opponents by using an aggressive, confrontational style. For these people, conflicts are competitive games; they may even enjoy fights—as long as they win. David Johnson

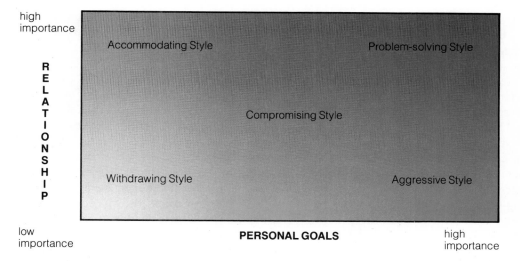

FIGURE 13.1

Conflict styles

compares each conflict style to a different animal.[12] He describes those who use the aggressive style as sharks.

Moving clockwise, we come to the lower left-hand corner. Individuals who fit here try to avoid conflict. For them, nothing is worth the hassle of a fight. When faced with disagreement, they withdraw, both physically and psychologically. According to Johnson, they are like turtles.

In the upper left-hand quadrant we find an accommodating style. Concern for relationship is high, while need to achieve personal goals is low. People who fit this quadrant try to smooth over all disagreements. If you are always the one who gives in just to keep the peace, you probably fill the role of accommodator. Johnson would describe you as a teddy bear. Teddy bears could benefit from becoming more assertive.

In the middle of Figure 13.1 are those who have a moderate concern for personal goals and for the relationship. These individuals often try to cut a deal, to negotiate a compromise. Johnson compares them to foxes.

Finally, in the top right-hand quadrant we have individuals who are committed both to personal goals and to relationships. They seek solutions in which everyone will benefit. Raymond and Mark Ross describe their style this way: "It is an enlightened style based on the assumptions that conflicts are natural in the human experience; conflicts are amenable to rational, cooperative problem solving; and a sensitive openness is the necessary first step."[13] Johnson likens people who use this style to owls.

Which style is the best? It all depends. While the problem-solving style is the most idealistic choice, it takes a lot of skill and effort and may not be right in all situations. There are times when each style should be used. For example, when a goal is more important than a relationship, an aggressive style may be called for. When buying a used car, it is not particularly important to forge a close relationship with the salesperson, but it is important to get a good buy. Here, the shark will do better than the teddy bear.

In some cases, neither the relationship nor getting your way is very important. This is when it makes sense to withdraw. If a very large man wearing black leather and chains wants to park his motorcycle in the spot you've been eyeing, why not park somewhere else? Unless you have something to prove, avoidance may be the better part of valor.

When the relationship is important, a more accommodating style is called for. If you and a close neighbor are pooling your money to buy a wedding gift for a friend and you disagree on what to buy, you may decide it is better to give in. If you really don't care a lot about the gift and you do care about your neighbor, accommodating may be best.

If, on the other hand, your emotional involvement and your needs are moderate, then try to compromise. Perhaps you are involved in business negotiations with someone. You want to maintain a reasonably good business relationship, but you also want to do well for yourself. Negotiating the best overall compromise is the strategy called for here.

Finally, when a lot is at stake, it's a good idea to take time to work things out using a problem-solving strategy. Serious marital disagreements, for example, need this kind of response. Forcing, avoiding, accommodating, or compromising won't work here.

The point is that you should develop the ability to enact all of these styles. Think about it. Are you pretty flexible, or do you find yourself "specializing" in one of these styles? If

so, try practicing until you can communicate effectively in more than one of these ways.

Effective Feedback

While it is important to approach conflict rationally and calmly, it is also important to express one's feelings clearly and directly. A key part of managing conflict involves honest feedback. In Chapter 2 we discussed feedback as information that allows a system to correct its behavior. Without feedback, it's impossible for people to coordinate their behaviors; with feedback they can adapt to each other. Misunderstandings will be inevitable unless feedback is used frequently and effectively.

While lists of rules for communication effectiveness sometimes make communicating seem a lot simpler than it actually is, there are some rules most authors agree will improve sending skills.[14]

1. *Own your own message.* Let's say you are extremely annoyed with your mate over his or her failure to cut the grass. Instead of working in the yard as promised, your partner has settled down in front of the TV to watch roller derby. Which of the following is the best way to bring up your feelings? Should you say, "You know, it doesn't really bother me, but the neighbors are beginning to complain. Everyone on the block thinks the grass is too high"? Or should you say, "I'm angry. You promised to cut the grass, but you haven't done it"?

If you're the one who is angry, it is dishonest to attribute the anger to someone else. Besides, telling someone that "everyone" agrees that he or she is inadequate leaves that person defensive and helpless.

2. *Don't apologize for your feelings.* If you keep apologizing, you put all the blame on yourself. Would you take the following comment seriously? "I'm sorry, I hate to bring this up, and I

Couples may be connected by complex emotional ties. Edward Albee, in his play *Who's Afraid of Virginia Woolf?*, examined the ebb and flow of conflict as it both defines and threatens to destroy a relationship.

probably have no right to feel this way, but it kind of bothers me when you talk like that."

3. *Make your messages specific and behavioral.* Your partner needs to know exactly what is upsetting you. Of the following two statements, which is best? "I think you've got a really rotten attitude" or "You just interrupted me. It makes me angry because I feel that you aren't interested in hearing what I have to say." Most experts in communication believe the second gives more information and is therefore more helpful. Changing one's entire attitude is a pretty tall order. Being careful not to interrupt is a much easier task. Often people simply don't realize they've been doing something offensive; they are more than happy to change when they get specific feedback.

4. *Make sure your verbal and nonverbal messages match.* If you try to appear calm and controlled while telling someone how angry you are, you are sending a mixed message. Similarly, if you use sarcasms to express your feelings, you disconfirm your partner. "I just love it when you do that" said in a sarcastic and biting tone is confusing and ineffective feedback.

5. *Avoid evaluating and interpreting your partner.* What can someone do in response to a statement like "You are just about the most egotistical, narcissistic person I've ever met"? Very little, except to feel inadequate and insulted. Instead of describing a behavior, you have attacked a person.

Conflict Containment

When conflict gets too large, it gets out of control. One way to keep conflict at manageable levels has already been discussed. That is to deal with conflict as soon as it arises. Another method is **fractionating**, breaking up a conflict into small, easily managed units. Trying to change everything overnight isn't the answer. Working on one small thing at a time is.[15]

Let's say you're in one of those momentary states when everything looks bad. You hate your entire life. Try to fractionate your feelings. If you find out that you dislike your job, you hate your neighborhood, and you're not thrilled with your social life, work on these problems one at a time. If you and your boss aren't getting along, sit down and try to list your dissatisfactions in simple, behavioral terms. Now you have an idea of where to begin. Through a process of negotiation you may be able to reach agreement about how to resolve your conflict.

One technique that may help you fractionate is **negative inquiry**.[16] Let's say your boss tells you he's unhappy with your performance. Instead of becoming defensive, try asking for as much information as possible. Say something like, "Could you tell me exactly what I'm doing that is below standard?" After he responds, go one step further: "Is there anything else you can think of? Are there other things I could do to improve?" You show your willingness to improve and gather useful information at the same time. Few bosses will be angry with an employee with a definite desire to learn.

It's also important to plan your approach to conflict and to analyze each conflict after the fact. Conflicts are usually stressful, and we know that under stress our thinking becomes very simplistic and stereotypical. That's why you should evaluate conflict strategies when your thinking is clearest.

LISTENING TO IMPROVE RELATIONSHIPS

Perhaps the best way to prevent and manage conflicts is to be a sensitive listener. Many conflicts arise because people thought they heard an insult that just wasn't there. Have you ever had the experience of arguing for an hour only to find out that you and your partner were in agreement all along? Careful, nondefensive listening would have solved the disagreement before it started.

In other cases, conflicts are based on real disagreements. Here listening won't prevent the problem, but it can help solve it. By showing the respect and regard for the other implicit in careful listening, you signal a desire to reach agreement. After all, how can a successful resolution be reached if you don't attend to the issue?

Listening is therefore integral to conflict, as it is to all aspects of communication. When we listen, we don't merely receive stimuli, we actively process and respond to them. In doing so we're changed by the meanings that have been created. Although it is common to separate communication into two parts, sending and receiving, this distinction is artificial. In actuality, we send and receive simultaneously.

If listening is hard to isolate, why do we end this book with a section on listening? We do so because too often people equate communication with message sending. By focusing on message reception and response, we stress the point that the essence of communication is the creation of meaning and that communication can occur during silence as well as during talk.

Types of Listening

Listening has many definitions. One of the most complete is offered by Charles Petrie: "the composite process by which oral language communicated by some source is received, critically and purposefully attended to, recognized, and interpreted (or comprehended) in terms of past experiences and future expectancies."[17] We would like to widen Petrie's definition a bit by suggesting that the stimuli involved in listening may be internal as well as external. We can listen to ourselves as well as to others. We also believe that listening should not be equated with hearing. Many of the communications we assign meaning to are visual. We receive information from all our senses. We listen to more than the spoken word.

Most books on listening emphasize that it has many purposes.[18] Sometimes we listen simply to discriminate between stimuli. For example, we struggle to identify a scary sound heard in the middle of the night; we listen carefully to determine whether our guests are coming "today" or "Tuesday"; we try to decide whether our boss's smile is sincere or feigned. This kind of listening is called **discriminatory listening** and is basic to all other forms of listening. We succeed in this kind of listening by recognizing a stimulus.

Sometimes we listen for the sheer pleasure of the activity. For example, we listen to our favorite records or tapes; we hear and see a stage production of a new play; we watch a classic movie and appreciate the director's cinematic skill. In all these cases we are engaging in **appreciative listening**. Here we succeed if we experience the stimulus in desired ways.

Much of the listening we do involves receiving and remembering new information. For example, we listen as our accountant explains what the new tax laws will mean; we concentrate as a child tells us what he wants for his birthday; we watch and listen as a friend directs us to her home. In these situations, we are involved in **comprehensive listening**. We try our best to understand a speaker's meaning as accurately as possible. We succeed if we can accurately re-create the intended meaning and hold it in memory.

We also listen to make judgments. For example, when we see a commercial, we listen to determine whether to buy the product; when we hear a politician talk, we must decide whether we support her views; when a friend asks to borrow more money, we try to evaluate our chances of being repaid. Here we are involved in **evaluative listening**. We go beyond comprehension; we make judgments about the intentions and competence of a source and about the completeness of the information. Here we do not succeed by simply understanding the appeal; success involves making sound decisions about it.

Finally, we listen to help others. When a child cries uncontrollably, we try to comfort and calm him; when a friend's most important relationship breaks up, we lend an understanding ear; when an acquaintance needs to talk out a decision, we help uncover options. In these cases we are taking part in **empathic listening**. Here our goal is to help someone else. We succeed when they are better able to understand or cope with a problem.

Each of these kinds of listening involves different skills. There is a great deal more to listening than simply recording passively a message as intended. Listening is a creative and complex process involving cognitive, emotional, and behavioral responses.

Empathic Listening

While all types of listening are important, the one most closely related to resolving relational problems is empathic, or therapeutic, listening. Empathic listening is the ability to listen with sensitivity and concern. It is especially important when emotions are involved.

The first and most important rule for empathic listening is to *respect the other's point of view.* People have to want to listen; they have to care about what the other person thinks and feels. A lot of relational problems occur because people are so preoccupied with their own ideas and emotions that they don't take the time to ask themselves what their partners are thinking or feeling.

In addition, most people are quick to dismiss what others say if it differs from what they believe. They tend to close down the perceptual process when encountering something they disagree with. It is essential to explore another's point of view rather than avoid it.

Most people spend more time in preparing their answers than in listening to others' statements. This leads to the second rule: *Make sure you fully understand what the other has said before responding.* How many times have you interrupted someone before he or she was done in order to make an objection or correction? If you're like most people, quite often. What happens as a result is that you may think you disagree when you don't. Interruptions rob you of information and serve to disconfirm others.

Once you think you understand what someone else is saying, you should *check your understanding by using paraphrasing.* To **paraphrase** is to state in your own words what you think the other person means. Paraphrasing isn't a matter of repeating what has just been said. Instead, you should describe your understanding of the comment in your own way. If a friend says to you, "I hate my physics class. Everyone is smarter than me. I know I'm going to fail. I don't know why you hang around with a dummy like me, anyway," check to make sure you understand what your friend is really trying to say. A paraphrase might go something like this, "Let me see if I understand. You're having trouble in class and it's making you doubt your competence. You're afraid I'll think you're dumb if you do badly."

Most people's first instinct is to comfort rather than to paraphrase. "Nonsense. You'll do fine. Don't worry" is a good response only if your friend is not serious. If she is really upset, such a response dismisses her fears, saying in effect, "You have no right to feel the way you do." A paraphrase allows you to make sure you know what is bothering her. It also shows that you are willing to listen. And it sets the stage for the two of you to explore the problem and work on it together. Of course, if you're not used to it, paraphrasing can seem odd. Try to vary the opening line of a paraphrase. It sounds trite and awkward to start off every statement with "What I think I hear you saying is . . ."

Finally, when you paraphrase, *make sure you express relational as well as content meaning.* In many interactions, feelings are more important than words. If your partner mentions, "You know, you forgot my birthday, not that it's that important, really," but you see signs that he is hurt by your forgetfulness, you should check out this feeling. "You're disappointed because you think I'm neglecting you" is a more accurate paraphrase than "I forgot your birthday, but you don't care." Some people have difficulty expressing their feelings overtly, so they hint instead. A good listener will try to read between the lines and will help others say what they really mean.

There are undoubtedly many other rules that can help improve listening. The important thing is to be aware that it is very easy to listen badly; listening is something all of us could improve. If you remember to check yourself, you'll find it fairly easy to avoid conflicts based on misunderstanding.

LISTENING AND THE COMPETENT COMMUNICATOR

Listening is an active, not a passive, process. To answer a simple question during conversation, we must attend to complex collections of verbal and nonverbal stimuli, re-create them mentally, decode them and search for their meaning and implications, add our own thoughts and emotions, and decide on a response. At the same time, we must filter out competing stimuli and control the signals we are giving off. Communication takes effort and commitment.

Too often, we are unwilling to invest energy in the communication process. We let our own thoughts and needs take precedence over others' messages; we drift off during conversations, only pretending to attend. Or we fail to notice relevant stimuli. We hear content but overlook relational messages. We listen to sounds, but we don't see what's happening. Sometimes during decoding we forget that words and actions have multiple meanings. We assume we understand what others intend when we don't. And even when we comprehend a message pretty much as intended, we may be too lazy to add anything to it. The goal of conversation is not simply to exchange meaning; it is to create something new.

The competent communicator avoids all of these pitfalls; first, by recognizing them and second, by actively developing the kinds of communication skills we have discussed throughout this text. If you'll recall, in Chapter 1 we presented a model of communicative competence. We said that the competent communicator exhibits interpretive, goal, role, and message competence. These kinds of competence are involved whenever meaning is created; they are as much a part of listening as they are of speaking.

To listen, communicators must have interpretive competence. They must be able to label, organize, and interpret verbal and nonverbal stimuli. They must possess a large and varied collection of schemata and constructs; they must make appropriate and useful attributions about themselves, the episodes they encounter, and those they interact with.

Competent communicators must also have message competence. They must recognize the verbal and nonverbal meanings implied by words and actions. They must be sensitive to the range of nonverbal cues that signal meaning. They must be familiar with their language, avoiding semantic pitfalls. They must also be pragmatically skilled, taking into account the importance of context in determining intended meanings.

Goal competence is also necessary. Competent listeners can decipher others' goals and relate communicative content to their own needs. They don't accept messages uncritically. They know their implications.

Finally, listeners must show role competence. People don't become invisible during listening. They are still communicating, still fulfilling expectations and adapting to others. Competent communicators know this. They try to understand what their partners want and need. They listen empathically by taking on the role of the other. Together, communicators negotiate speaking and listening roles.

Communication is complex. It isn't easy to communicate effectively. Communication takes knowledge, skill, and practice. But the results are worth all the effort. For communication is what allows us to connect and create. And after all, most of us need the eggs.

REVIEW TERMS

The following is a list of major concepts introduced in this chapter. The page number where the concept is first mentioned is listed in parentheses.

challenge (324)
offering (324)
acceptance (324)
thanks (324)
accounting (324)
justification (324)
excuse (324)
disclaimer (325)
intrapersonal conflict (326)
interpersonal conflict (326)
gunnysacking (329)
kitchen-sinking (329)
stereotyping (330)
fractionating (336)
negative inquiry (336)
discriminatory listening (337)
appreciative listening (337)
comprehensive listening (337)
evaluative listening (337)
empathic listening (337)
paraphrasing (338)

SUGGESTED READINGS

Adler, Ronald B. *Confidence in Communication: A Guide to Assertive and Social Skills.* New York: Holt, Rinehart and Winston, 1977. A complete guide to improving assertiveness.

Filley, Alan C. *Interpersonal Conflict Resolution.* Glenview, Ill.: Scott, Foresman, 1975. Easy to read, this brief book shows how to take a problem-solving approach to conflict. Good small group and organizational examples are included.

Frost, Joyce Hocker, and William W. Wilmot. *Interpersonal Conflict.* Dubuque, Iowa: William C. Brown, 1978. A good basic introduction to the subject, particularly strong on strategies and tactics for confronting conflict.

Wolff, Florence I., and others. *Perceptive Listening.* New York: Holt, Rinehart and Winston, 1983. A good discussion of all types of listening, with helpful hints for improving listening competence.

PROCESS TO PERFORMANCE

TOPICS FOR DISCUSSION

1. How do you respond when someone asks you to do something you don't want to? Do you use excuses and justifications, or do you simply refuse the request? What would you say in each of the following situations?
a. Someone you don't want to go out with calls and asks you out. You don't want to hurt his or her feelings, but this person is definitely not your type. You don't actually have any other plans, however. What would you say?
b. You told some friends that one of these days you'd help them clean out their basement. Now it's a beautiful sunny Saturday morning and your friends call and ask you to help. The thought of being in a dusty basement is not very appealing, especially since you've planned to drive out to the country for a picnic. What do you say?
c. You'd promised to pick your roommate up after work. Just as you were about to leave, however, a person you've been dying to get to know asks you for a ride downtown. You know it'll make you late, but this is your big chance, so you say yes. Now it's two hours later and you know your roommate will be steamed. What do you say?

2. Some authors feel that using disclaimers makes a speaker seem weak and unsure. Others believe they are a sign of politeness. This is significant, since there is some evidence that women use more disclaimers than do men. What do you think? Are women brought up to be more polite than men? Are

disclaimers a sign of uncertainty? Should women, especially in business, try to speak more forcefully and less tentatively?

3. Think of the last example of rudeness you encountered. Describe the behavior. How did it make you feel? What attributions did you make about the person who was rude? Discuss the kinds of behaviors you consider to be rude.

4. We all use defense mechanisms such as those described in Box 13.2 from time to time. Can you give examples of some of the ways you defend yourself? If that's too personal, describe some of the defense mechanisms you have observed in others. How do these ways of protecting the self affect interaction?

5. Popular wisdom has it that conflict is good for relationships. Do you agree? Think of some of the ways conflict can help relationships, using personal examples if you have been helped by conflict. Is conflict always good for a relationship?

6. In this chapter we list some rules for giving feedback effectively. Try to think of four or five additional rules.

7. This chapter lists some ineffective ways of fighting. Can you think of other things people do that will guarantee a fight will turn out badly?

8. Make up at least five rules for fighting effectively. Do you think you and a partner could abide by these kinds of rules? How could you ensure that they were followed?

9. The responsibility for communication must be shared between speakers and listeners. What can a speaker do to help his or her listeners?

10. College lectures call for good listening skills. Think of some rules for getting the most out of lectures. What should the student listen for? How can listening be improved?

OBSERVATION GUIDE

1. Analyze the last major fight you had with someone. What caused it? What did you do that was productive? What did you do that was destructive? How could the conflict have been improved?

2. What is your personal conflict style? Locate yourself on the conflict grid. Why do you think you've developed the style you have and how do you think it affects your relationships? What could you do to improve it? Try to make some changes and observe what happens. How do others react to you? How do you feel about yourself?

3. Think back to a recent interaction. Describe and analyze your listening behavior. What kinds of listening were involved? List all the things you listened to during the interaction, including competing stimuli. What factors interfered with listening? What factors enhanced it?

EXERCISES

1. There's something wrong with each of the following feedback statements. Working with a partner, try to identify what it is and

then correct it. (To do so, you may have to add some details.)

a. I hate to say anything, but everyone in the group is mad at you. You never do your share and that puts everyone in a jam.

b. Your behavior is so typical. Instead of discussing things rationally, you cry and seem to think I'll give in. Women!

c. I'm sick and tired of your attitude.

d. You know perfectly well what's wrong. I shouldn't have to tell you. If you loved me, you'd know.

e. I understand you have to protect your precious male ego, but I'm not going to put up with your thoughtlessness anymore.

f. I'm mad because you always treat me as though I were a child. When? Well, always.

g. (make up several more examples of poor feedback and correct them)

2. Work in groups of three. Using the role-plays below as guides, practice giving feedback and paraphrasing. Read the first story. One of you will be character A, the other character B, and the third the observer. Act out your roles, being sure to follow rules for effective feedback and empathic listening. The observer should stop the action each time a feedback rule is violated and should check to make sure that paraphrases sound natural and actually capture intended meanings. If a paraphrase is incomplete or unnatural, the observer will ask you to try again. Once you have worked through the first role play, switch roles and go on to the next.

a. A is the departmental secretary. She types for ten faculty members, all of whom give her work whenever the mood strikes. B's tests are hard to read and usually needed in a rush. A resents it when B hands her a test in the afternoon and says he needs it by 9 the next morning, especially since B is not particularly polite about it. A feels she has other things to do and doesn't see why she should put aside that work just to help B. However, she is somewhat intimidated by B.

B is a senior professor who does a lot of publishing and consulting. B doesn't have the time to make tests up days in advance and is frustrated by the comparative inefficiency of the support services at the university. B feels an efficient secretary could easily type a 20-item test in an hour and can't understand what the problem is. He gets particularly frustrated when he sees the secretary spending time on the phone, talking to and advising students, and gossiping with junior faculty. As far as he can see, her job is to type, not to be a social director and counselor.

b. A is a parent and B is a 14-year-old. B is quite bright and has been put forward a year in school. Consequently, most of B's friends are 16 and have learner's permits. The trouble occurs when B's friends want her to go out with them. A does not want his daughter to drive around with 16-year-olds. He knows that the older kids get reckless sometimes and he's afraid that B doesn't have the maturity to know what to do in a dangerous situation, for example, if one of the kids decides to drink and drive. A has offered to drive B and her friends to the movies or to drop off B and pick her up afterward. A feels that B shouldn't be given the privileges of a 16-year-old; after all, B is still only 14.

B of course thinks the situation is unfair. It is totally embarrassing to have parents drive one around. B has the social insecurities of most teenagers and feels that she'll never be popular if she is treated like a child. B feels her parents' objections are completely unreasonable. Her friends aren't the kind who will drive too fast or be irresponsible. Lately B has taken to going out without telling her parents.

c. A and B moved in together recently. At first everything was great, but now A is beginning to feel trapped. B wants them to do everything together. A feels guilty for wanting time off to go out drinking with his friends. When he does stay out late, he feels he owes B an explanation. B never says anything, she just looks hurt, which only makes A more uncomfortable. When A takes B with him, it's even more awkward. None of the other guys has to drag someone with them all the time; A feels like he can't have any fun, and the guys put a lot of pressure on him.

B is miserable. She feels that moving in is a commitment, kind of like being married. She is perfectly happy to spend all her time with A, and she can't understand why he isn't happy with her. The fact that he wants to be away from her hurts. She wonders if he picks up other girls when he's out with the guys. She knows the guys pressure each other to do some pretty obnoxious things. She resents his nights out, yet she doesn't want to be a nag. She has no idea what to do.

REFERENCES

CHAPTER ONE

1. Carl Sagan, ed., *Communication with Extraterrestrial Intelligence (CETI)* (Cambridge, Mass.: MIT Press, 1973), p. 344. This book is a transcript of a conference held in 1971 at Byurakan Astrophysical Observatory, Yerevan, USSR. While it is technically difficult, the chapters "Message Contents" and "The Consequences of Contact" are easy to follow and very illuminating.

2. See. for example, Cyril Ponnamperuma and A. G. W. Cameron, *Interstellar Communication: Scientific Perspectives* (Boston: Houghton Mifflin, 1974). For a more popular discussion, see Carl Sagan, *The Cosmic Connection: An Extraterrestrial Perspective* (Garden City, N.Y.: Anchor Press, Doubleday, 1973).

3. Sagan, *Cosmic Connection*, p. 42.

4. For an excellent history of the study of communication, see Nancy Harper, *Human Communication Theory: The History of a Paradigm* (Rochelle Park, N.J.: Hayden, 1979).

5. Frank E. X. Dance and Carl E. Larson, *Speech Communication: Concepts and Behavior* (New York: Holt, Rinehart and Winston, 1972).

6. S. S. Stevens, "A Definition of Communication," *The Journal of the Acoustical Society of America* 22 (1950): 689–90. Quoted in Frank E. X. Dance and Carl E. Larson, *The Functions of Human Communication* (New York: Holt, Rinehart and Winston, 1976), p. 25.

7. Dean Barnlund, *Interpersonal Communication: Survey and Studies* (Boston: Houghton Mifflin, 1968), p. 6. Quoted in Dance and Larson, *Functions*, p. 25.

8. John T. Masterson, Steven A. Beebe, and Norman H. Watson, *Speech Communication: Theory and Practice* (New York: Holt, Rinehart and Winston, 1983), p. 5.

9. Bernard Berelson and Gary A. Steiner, *Human Behavior: An Inventory of Scientific Findings* (New York: Harcourt Brace Jovanovich, 1964), p. 527. Quoted in Dance and Larson, *Functions*, p. 24.

10. Sarah Trenholm, *Human Communication Theory* (Englewood Cliffs, N.J.: Prentice-Hall, 1986), pp. 4–5.

11. Aldous Huxley, "Words and Their Meanings," in *The Importance of Language*, ed. Max Black (Englewood Cliffs, N.J.: Prentice-Hall, 1962), pp. 4–5.

12. Joost A. M. Meerloo, "Contributions of Psychiatry to the Study of Human Communication," in *Human Communication Theory: Original Essays*, ed. Frank E. X. Dance (New York: Holt, Rinehart and Winston, 1967), p. 132.

13. *Ibid.*

14. Clifford Geertz, "Deep Play: Notes on the Balinese Cockfight," in *Myth, Symbol and Culture*, ed. Clifford Geertz (New York: W. W. Norton, 1971), p. 7.

15. John C. Condon, "When People Talk with People," in *Messages: A Reader in Human Communication*, 3rd ed., ed. Sanford B. Weinberg (New York: Random House, 1980), p. 58.

16. Erving Goffman, "On Face-Work," in *Interaction Ritual*, ed. Erving Goffman (Garden City, N.Y.: Anchor Books, 1967).

17. *Ibid.*, p. 10.

18. Donald J. Cegala, "Interaction Involvement: A Cognitive Dimension of Communicative Competence," *Communication Education* 30 (1981): 109–21; Brian H. Spitzberg and Michael L. Hecht, "A Component Model of Relational Competence," *Human Communication Research* 10 (1984): 575–99; John M. Weimann, "Explication and Test of a Model of Communicative Competence," *Human Communication Research* 3 (1977): 195–213; David R.

Brandt, "On Linking Social Performance with Social Competence: Some Relations Between Communicative Style and Attribution of Interpersonal Attractiveness and Effectiveness," *Human Communication Research* 5 (1979): 233–27.

19. Dell H. Hymes, "On Communicative Competence," in *Sociolinguistics*, eds. J. B. Pride and Janet Holmes (Harmondsworth, England: Penguin, 1972), pp. 269–93; Ruth Ann Clark and Jesse G. Delia, "Topoi and Rhetorical Competence," *The Quarterly Journal of Speech* 65 (1979): 187–206.

20. Stephen W. Littlejohn and David M. Jabush, "Communication Competence: Model and Application," *Journal of Applied Communication Research* 10 (1982): 29–37; Brian H. Spitzberg, "Communication Competence as Knowledge, Skill, and Impression," *Communication Education* 32 (1983): 323–29.

21. Clark and Delia, "Topoi."

22. James C. McCroskey, "Communication Competence and Performance: A Research and Pedagogical Perspective," *Communication Education* 31 (1982): 1–7.

CHAPTER TWO

1. The situational approach is fairly standard in our field and can be found in most introductory communication texts. An especially well-developed discussion can be found in David L. Swanson and Jesse G. Delia, "The Nature of Human Communication," *Modules in Speech Communication* (Chicago: Science Research Associates, 1976).

2. For a discussion of the form of "inner speech," see Lev Semenovich Vygotsky, *Thought and Language*, ed. and trans. Eugenia Hanfmann and Gertrude Vakar (Cambridge, Mass.: MIT Press, 1962). An interesting source for a discussion of the elliptical and condensed quality of intrapersonal communication is Sigmund Freud, *The Interpretation of Dreams*, ed. and trans. James Strachey (New York: Avon Books, 1965).

3. William W. Wilmot, *Dyadic Communication*, 2nd ed. (Reading, Mass.: Addison-Wesley, 1979), p. 19.

4. For an interesting discussion of organizational culture, see Ernest G. Bormann, "Symbolic Convergence: Organizational Communication and Culture," in *Communication and Organizations: An Interpretive Approach*, eds. Linda L. Putnam and Michael E. Pacanowsky (Beverly Hills, Calif.: Sage Publications, 1983).

5. Robert Cathcart and Gary Gumpert, "Mediated Interpersonal Communication: Toward a New Typology," *Quarterly Journal of Speech* 69 (1983): 268.

6. Sarah Trenholm, *Human Communication Theory* (Englewood Cliffs, N.J.: Prentice-Hall, 1986), pp. 17–18.

7. Gerald R. Miller, "The Current Status of Theory and Research in Interpersonal Communication," *Human Communication Research* 4 (1978): 164–78.

8. Arthur P. Bochner, "The Functions of Human Communication in Interpersonal Bonding," in *Handbook of Rhetorical and Communication Theory*, eds. Carroll C. Arnold and John Waite Bowers (Boston: Allyn and Bacon, 1984), p. 550.

9. Gerald R. Miller and Mark Steinberg, *Between People: A New Analysis of Interpersonal Communication* (Chicago: Science Research Associates, 1975). See also chapters 1 and 4 in Cassandra L. Book and others, *Human Communication: Principles, Contexts, and Skills* (New York: St. Martin's Press, 1980).

10. Shelley Duvall and Robert A. Wicklund, *A Theory of Objective Self-Awareness.* (New York: Academic Press, 1972).

11. Wilmot, *Dyadic Communication*, pp. 9–10.

12. For an overview of general systems theory as related to communication, see the following: B. Aubrey Fisher, "A View from System Theory," in *Human Communication Theory: Comparative Essays*, ed. Frank E. X. Dance (New York: Harper & Row, 1982). B. Aubrey Fisher, *Perspectives on Human Communication* (New York: Macmillan, 1978), especially the chapter on the pragmatic perspective; George A. Borden, *Human Communication Systems* (Boston: American Press, 1985).

13. In his book on small groups, B. Aubrey Fisher presents an excellent discussion of feedback: *Small Group Decision Making: Communication and the Group Process*, 2nd ed. (New York: McGraw-Hill, 1980).

14. For two additional discussions of interpersonal trajectories, see Jesse G. Delia, "Some Tentative Thoughts Concerning the Study of Interpersonal Relationships and Their Development," *Western Journal of Speech Communication* 44 (1980): 93–96; Steve Duck, "Social and Personal Relationships," in *Handbook of Interpersonal Communication*, eds. Mark L. Knapp and Gerald R. Miller (Beverly Hills, Calif.: Sage Publications, 1985).

15. Bochner, "Interpersonal Bonding," p. 547.

16. William K. Rawlins, "Openness As Problematic in Ongoing Friendships: Two Conversational Dilemmas," *Communication Monographs* 50 (1983): 1–13, and "Negotiating Close Friendship: The Dialectic of Conjunctive Freedoms," *Human Communication Research* 9 (1983): 255–66.

17. The tendency of our culture to desire intimacy in all relationships has been discussed by a number of historians and social critics. See, for example, Howard Gadlin, "Private Lives and Public Order: A Critical View of the History of Intimate Relations in the United States," in *Close Relationships: Perspectives on the Meaning of Intimacy,* eds. George Levinger and Harold L. Raush (Amherst: University of Massachusetts Press, 1977), pp. 33–72; Christopher Lasch, *The Culture of Narcissism* (New York: W. W. Norton, 1978); Robert N. Bellah and others, *Habits of the Heart: Individualism and Commitment in American Life* (Berkeley and Los Angeles: University of California Press, 1985); Judith Martin, *Common Courtesy* (New York: Atheneum, 1985).

18. Judee K. Burgoon, "Privacy and Communication," in *Communication Yearbook 6,* ed. Michael Burgoon (Beverly Hills, Calif.: Sage Publications, 1982), p. 225.

19. *Ibid.*

20. Our discussion of relational competence is loosely adapted from the work of Linda Harris. In explaining her model, however, we have omitted its theoretical grounding in CMM theory. For a fuller understanding of her model, see Linda Harris, "Communication Competence: An Argument for a Systemic View," unpublished paper, Department of Communication Studies, University of Massachusetts, 1979.

CHAPTER THREE

1. Ellen J. Langer, "Rethinking the Role of Thought in Social Interaction," in *New Directions in Attribution Research 2,* ed. John H. Harvey, William J. Ickes, and Robert F. Kidd (New York: John Wiley & Sons, 1978), pp. 35–58.

2. Charles Berger and William Douglas, "Thought and Talk: 'Excuse Me, But Have I Been Talking to Myself?'" in *Human Communication Theory,* ed. Frank Dance (New York: Harper & Row, 1982), pp. 42–60.

3. Albert Hastorf, David Schneider, and Judith Polefka, *Person Perception* (Reading, Mass.: Addison-Wesley, 1970).

4. William W. Grings, "The Verbal Summator Technique and Abnormal Mental States," *Journal of Abnormal and Social Psychology* 37 (1942): 529–45.

5. See R. Hastie, "Schematic Principles in Human Memory," in *Social Cognition: The Ontario Symposium 1,* ed. E. Tory Higgins, C. Peter Herman, and Mark P. Zanna (Hillsdale, N.J.: Lawrence Erlbaum, 1981). See also S. E. Taylor and J. Crocker, "Schematic Basis of Information Processing," in *Social Cognition: The Ontario Symposium.*

6. Nancy Cantor and Walter Mischel, "Prototypes in Person Perception," in *Advances in Experimental Social Psychology 12,* ed. Leonard Berkowitz (New York: Academic Press, 1979).

7. George Kelly, *The Psychology of Personal Constructs* (New York: W. W. Norton, 1955).

8. Clark McCauley, Christopher L. Stitt, and Mary Segal, "Stereotyping: From Prejudice to Prediction," *Psychological Bulletin* 87 (1980): 195–208.

9. Robert Abelson, "Script Processing in Attitude Formation and Decision-Making," in *Cognition and Social Behavior,* ed. J. S. Carroll and J. N. Payne (Hillsdale, N.J.: Lawrence Erlbaum, 1976), pp. 33–45.

10. Stanley Deetz and Sheryl Stevenson, *Managing Interpersonal Communication* (New York: Harper & Row, 1986), p. 58.

11. William Ittelson, Karen Franck, and Timothy O'Hanlon, "The Nature of Environmental Experience," in *Experiencing the Environment,* ed. Seymour Wapner, Saul B. Cohen, and Bernard Kaplan (New York: Plenum Press, 1976), pp. 187–206.

12. Joseph Forgas, "Affective and Emotional Influences on Episode Representations," in *Social Cognition: Perspectives on Everyday Understanding,* ed. Joseph Forgas (London: Academic Press, 1981), pp. 165–80.

13. Michael Brenner, "Actors' Powers," in *The Analysis of Action: Recent Theoretical and Empirical Advances,* ed. M. von Cranach and Rom Harre (Cambridge: Cambridge University Press, 1982), pp. 213–30.

14. Steven Duck, "Interpersonal Communication in Developing Acquaintance," in *Explorations in Interpersonal Communication,* ed. Gerald R. Miller (Beverly Hills, Calif.: Sage Publications, 1976), pp. 127–47.

15. Seymour Rosenberg and Andrea Sedlak, "Structural Representations of Implicit Personality Theory," in *Advances in Experimental Social Psychology 6,* ed. Leonard Berkowitz (New York: Academic Press, 1972), pp. 235–297.

16. Harold H. Kelley, "The Warm–Cold Variable in First Impressions of Persons," *Journal of Personality* 18 (1950): 431–39.

17. Leonard Zunin, *Contact: The First Four Minutes* (Los Angeles: Nash, 1972).

18. Walter Crockett, "Cognitive Complexity and Impression Formation," in *Progress in Experimental Personality Research 2,* ed. Brendon A. Maher (New York: Academic Press, 1965), pp. 47–90. See also Jesse Delia, "Constructivism and the Study of Human Communication," *Quarterly Journal of Speech* 63 (1977): 68–83.

19. Jesse Delia, Ruth Ann Clark, and David Switzer, "Cognitive Complexity and Impression Formation in Informal Social Interaction," *Speech Monographs* 41 (1974): 299–308. See also Claudia Hale and Jesse Delia, "Cognitive Complexity and Social Perspective-Taking," *Communication Monographs* 43 (1976): 195–203.

20. Crockett, "Cognitive complexity and impression formation," p. 21.

21. Mark L. Snyder, "The Self-Monitoring of Expressive Behavior," *Journal of Personality and Social Psychology* 30 (1974): 526–37.

22. Mark L. Snyder, "Self-Monitoring Processes," in *Advances in Experimental Social Psychology 12*, ed. Leonard Berkowitz (New York: Academic Press, 1979), pp. 86–131.

23. Robert Carson, *Interaction Concepts of Personality* (Chicago: Aldine, 1969).

24. Harold H. Kelley, "Attribution Theory in Social Psychology," in *Nebraska Symposium on Motivation 15*, ed. David Levine (Lincoln, Neb.: University of Nebraska Press, 1967), pp. 192–240.

25. *Ibid.*

26. For a review, see Lee Ross, "The Intuitive Psychologist and His Shortcomings: Distortions in the Attribution Process," in *Advances in Experimental Social Psychology 10*, ed. Leonard Berkowitz (New York: Academic Press, 1977).

27. Edward E. Jones and D. McGillis, "Correspondent Inferences and the Attribution Cube: A Comparative Reappraisal," in *New Directions in Attribution Research 1*, ed. John H. Harvey, William J. Ickes, and Robert F. Kidd (Hillsdale, N.J.: Lawrence Erlbaum, 1976).

28. Bernadette Park and Myron Rothbart, "Perceptions of Out-Group Homogeneity and Levels of Social Categorization: Memory for the Subordinate Attributes of In-Group and Out-Group Members," *Journal of Personality and Social Psychology* 42 (1982): 1051–68.

CHAPTER FOUR

1. Peter L. Berger, *Invitation to Sociology: A Humanistic Perspective* (Garden City, N.Y.: Anchor Books, 1963), p. 66.

2. *Ibid.*, p. 78.

3. Ruth Benedict, *Patterns of Culture* (New York: Penguin Books, 1946), p. 2.

4. Theodore M. Newcomb, Ralph H. Turner, and Philip E. Converse, *Social Psychology: The Study of Human Interaction* (New York: Holt, Rinehart and Winston, 1965), p. 326.

5. George J. McCall and J. L. Simmons, *Identities and Interactions* (New York: Free Press, 1966), p. 67.

6. Charles Horton Cooley, "The Social Self: On the Meanings of I," in *The Self in Social Interactions, Vol. I: Classic and Contemporary Perspectives*, ed. Chad Gordon and Kenneth J. Gergen (New York: John Wiley, 1968), pp. 87–91.

7. Leon Festinger, "A Theory of Social Comparison Processes," *Human Relations* 2 (1954): 117–40.

8. Daryl J. Bem, "Self-Perception Theory," in *Advances in Experimental Social Psychology 6*, ed. Leonard Berkowitz (New York: Academic Press, 1972).

9. McCall and Simmons, p. 67.

10. Erving Goffman, "On Face-Work," in *Interaction Ritual* (Garden City, N.Y.: Anchor Books, 1967).

11. *Ibid.*, p. 226.

12. Erving Goffman, *The Presentation of Self in Everyday Life* (Garden City, N.Y.: Doubleday, 1959), p. 24.

13. Sarah Trenholm, *Human Communication Theory* (Englewood Cliffs, N.J.: Prentice-Hall, 1986), p. 105.

14. Erving Goffman, "Role Distance," in *Encounters: Two Studies in the Sociology of Interaction* (New York: Bobbs-Merrill, 1961), p. 108.

15. Goffman, *Presentation of Self*, pp. 212–28.

16. Morris Rosenberg, "Psychological Selectivity in Self-Esteem Formation," in *Attitude, Ego-Involvement, and Change*, ed. Carolyn W. Sherif and Muzafer Sherif (New York: John Wiley, 1967), pp. 26–50. Quoted in William Wilmot, *Dyadic Communication* (Reading, Mass.: Addison-Wesley, 1979).

17. W. Barnett Pearce, "The Coordinated Management of Meaning: A Rules-Based Theory of Interpersonal Communication," in *Explorations in Interpersonal Communication*, ed. Gerald R. Miller (Beverly Hills, Calif.: Sage Publications, 1976), pp. 17–35.

18. Gerry Philipsen, "Places for Speaking in Teamsterville," *Quarterly Journal of Speech* 62 (1976): 15–25.

CHAPTER FIVE

1. See, for example, John Kihlstrom and Nancy Cantor, "Mental Representations of the Self," in *Advances in Experimental Social Psychology 17*, ed. Leonard Berkowitz (Orlando, Fla.: Academic Press, 1984), pp. 1–47.

2. William J. McGuire and C. V. McGuire, "The Spontaneous Self-Concept As Affected by Personal Distinctiveness," in *Self-Concept: Advances in Theory and Research*, ed. Mervin D. Lynch, Ardyth A. Norem-

Hebeisen and Kenneth Gergen (New York: Ballinger, 1981).

3. William J. McGuire and Alice Padawer-Singer, "Trait Salience in the Spontaneous Self-Concept," *Journal of Personality and Social Psychology* 33 (1976): 743–54.

4. Harry Stack Sullivan, *The Interpersonal Theory of Psychiatry*, ed. Helen Swick Perry and Mary Ladd Gowel (New York: W. W. Norton, 1953), pp. 79–80.

5. Dennis R. Smith and L. Keith Williamson, *Interpersonal Communication: Roles, Rules, Strategies, and Games* (Dubuque, Iowa: William C. Brown, 1981), pp. 122–29.

6. William W. Wilmot, *Dyadic Communication: A Transactional Perspective* (Reading, Mass.: Addison-Wesley, 1975), pp. 44–45.

7. Anthony G. Greenwald, "The Totalitarian Ego: Fabrication and Revision of Personal History," *American Psychologist* 35 (1980): 603–18.

8. Daryl J. Bem, "Self-Perception Theory," in *Advances in Experimental Social Psychology 6*, ed. Leonard Berkowitz (New York: Academic Press, 1972), pp. 1–62.

9. Edward T. Hall, *Beyond Culture* (Garden City, N.Y.: Anchor Books, 1977), p. 231.

10. Hazel Markus, "Self-Schemata and Processing Information about the Self," *Journal of Personality and Social Psychology* 35 (1977): 63–78.

11. Hazel Markus, Marie Crane, Stan Bernstein, and Michael Siladi, "Self-Schemas and Gender," *Journal of Personality and Social Psychology* 42 (1982): 38–50.

12. Eric Berne, *Games People Play* (New York: Grove Press, 1964).

13. W. Barnett Pearce and Vernon E. Cronen, *Communication, Action and Meaning* (New York: Praeger, 1980), p. 136.

14. Steven Berglas and Edward E. Jones, "Drug Choice As an Externalization Strategy in Response to Noncontingent Success," *Journal of Personality and Social Psychology* 36 (1978): 405–17; also Edward E. Jones and Steven Berglas, "Control of Attributions about the Self through Self-Handicapping Strategies: The Appeal of Alcohol and the Role of Underachievement," *Personality and Social Psychology Bulletin* 4 (1978): 200–6.

15. Robert Norton, *Communicator Style: Theory, Applications, and Measures* (Beverly Hills, Calif.: Sage Publications, 1983), p. 58.

16. Donald Darnell and Wayne Brockriede, *Persons Communicating* (Englewood Cliffs, N.J.: Prentice-Hall, 1976), p. 176.

17. *Ibid.*, p. 178.

18. Roderick Hart and Don Burks, "Rhetorical Sensitivity and Social Interaction," *Speech Monographs* 39 (1972): 75–91.

19. Roderick Hart, Robert Carlson, and William Eadie, "Attitudes toward Communication and the Assessment of Rhetorical Sensitivity," *Communication Monographs* 47 (1980): 1–22.

20. James C. McCroskey, "Oral Communication Apprehension: A Summary of Recent Theory and Research," *Human Communication Research* 4 (1977): 78–96.

21. *Ibid.*, p. 79.

22. Michael J. Beatty and Ralph R. Behnke, "An Assimilation Theory Perspective of Communication Apprehension," *Human Communication Research* 6 (1980): 319–25.

23. Richard Lippa, "The Effect of Expressive Control on Expressive Consistency and on the Relation between Expressive Behavior and Personality," *Journal of Personality* 46 (1978): 438–61.

24. Snyder, pp. 96–97.

25. Richard Sennett, *The Fall of Public Man: On the Social Psychology of Capitalism* (New York: Random House, 1974).

26. Christopher Lasch, *The Culture of Narcissism* (New York: W. W. Norton, 1978), pp. 37–38.

27. See Linda M. Harris, "Communication Competence: Empirical Tests of a Systemic Model," Ph.D. dissertation, University of Massachusetts, 1979. See also Pearce and Cronen, pp. 197–212.

CHAPTER SIX

1. John Fowles, *Daniel Martin* (Boston: Little, Brown, 1977).

2. Judee Burgoon and Thomas Saine, *The Unspoken Dialogue: An Introduction to Nonverbal Communication* (Boston: Houghton Mifflin, 1978), pp. 6–10.

3. Desmond Morris, *Manwatching: A Field Guide to Human Behavior* (New York: Harry N. Abrams, 1977), pp. 86–91.

4. Paul Ekman and Wallace Friesen, *Unmasking the Face: A Guide to Recognizing Emotions From Facial Expressions* (Englewood Cliffs, N.J.: Prentice-Hall, 1975).

5. Albert Mehrabian, *Nonverbal Communication* (Chicago: Aldine-Atherton, 1972), p. 2.

6. Daphne E. Bugental, Jacques W. Kaswan, Leonore R. Love, and Michael N. Fox, "Child versus Adult Perception of Evaluative Messages in Verbal, Vocal, and Visual Channels," *Developmental Psychology* 2 (1970): 367–75.

7. Jeffrey G. Shapiro, "Responsivity to Facial and Linguistic Cues," *Journal of Communication* 18 (1968): 11–17; see also Leon Vande Creek and John T. Watkins, "Responses to Incongruent Verbal and Nonverbal Emotional Cues," *Journal of Communication* 22 (1972): 311–16.

8. Miles Patterson, *Nonverbal Behavior: A Functional Perspective* (New York: Springer-Verlag, 1983), p. 9.

9. Ashley Montagu and Floyd Matson, *The Human Connection* (New York: McGraw-Hill, 1979), p. 17.

10. Abraham Maslow and Norbett L. Mintz, "Effects of Esthetic Surroundings I: Initial Effects of Three Esthetic Conditions upon Perceiving 'Energy' and 'Well-Being' in Faces," *Journal of Psychology* 41 (1956): 247–54.

11. See, for example, Mark L. Knapp, *Nonverbal Communication in Human Interaction* (New York: Holt, Rinehart and Winston, 1978), pp. 83–113; Lawrence Rosenfeld and Jean Civikly, *With Words Unspoken: The Nonverbal Experience* (New York: Holt, Rinehart and Winston, 1976), pp. 161–85.

12. Steven Kaplan, Rachel Kaplan, and John S. Wendt, "Rated Preference and Complexity for Natural and Urban Visual Material," *Perception and Psychophysics* 12 (1972): 334–56.

13. Albert Mehrabian and James Russell, *An Approach to Environmental Psychology* (Cambridge, Mass.: M.I.T. Press, 1974).

14. Rosenfeld and Civikly, p. 147.

15. Stanford Lyman and Marvin Scott, "Territoriality: A Neglected Social Dimension," *Social Problems* 15 (1967): 235–49.

16. Edward T. Hall, *The Silent Language* (New York: Doubleday, 1959).

17. Edward T. Hall, *The Hidden Dimension* (Garden City, N.Y.: Doubleday, 1969), pp. 133–34.

18. Edward T. Hall, *Beyond Culture* (Garden City, N.Y.: Anchor Press, 1970).

19. For a summary of this research, see Burgoon and Saine, pp. 93–94.

20. James G. Martin, "Racial Ethnocentrism and Judgments of Beauty," *Journal of Social Psychology* 63 (1964): 59–63; A. H. Illife, "A Study of Preferences in Feminine Beauty," *British Journal of Psychology* 51 (1960): 267–73.

21. Elaine Walster, Vera Aronson, Darcy Abrahams, and Leon Rottman, "Importance of Physical Attractiveness in Dating Behavior," *Journal of Personality and Social Psychology* 4 (1966): 508–16.

22. James E. Maddux and Ronald W. Rogers, "Effects of Source Expertness, Physical Attractiveness, and Supporting Arguments on Persuasion: A Case of Brains over Beauty," *Journal of Personality and Social Psychology* 39 (1980): 235–44.

23. Morris, p. 282.

24. See, for example, L. Aiken, "Relationships of Dress to Selected Measures of Personality in Undergraduate Women," *Journal of Social Psychology* 59 (1963): 119–28; Lawrence Rosenfeld and Timothy G. Plax, "Clothing As Communication," *Journal of Communication* 27 (1977): 24–31; Mary B. Harris and Hortensia Baudin, "The Language of Altruism: The Effects of Language, Dress, and Ethnic Group," *Journal of Social Psychology* 91 (1973): 37–41.

25. Thomas F. Hoult, "Experimental Measurement of Clothing As a Factor in Some Social Ratings of Selected American Men," *American Sociological Review* 19 (1954): 324–28.

26. Adam Kendon, "Some Functions of Gaze-Direction in Social Interaction," *Acta Psychologica* 26 (1967): 22–63.

27. Ekman and Friesen, p. 40 and p. 52.

28. For a brief review, see D. R. Rutter, *Looking and Seeing: The Role of Visual Communication in Social Interaction* (Chichester, England: John Wiley, 1984), pp. 49–54.

29. P. C. Ellsworth, "The Meaningful Look," *Semiotica* 24 (1978): 15–20; Miles Patterson, "An Arousal Model of Interpersonal Intimacy," *Psychological Review* 83 (1976): 235–45.

30. Irenaus Eibl-Eibesfeldt, "Similarities and Differences Between Cultures in Expressive Movements," in *Nonverbal Communication*, ed. Robert Hinde (Cambridge: Cambridge University Press, 1972), pp. 297–312.

31. Michael Argyle, Mansur Lalljee, and Mark Cook, "The Effects of Visibility on Interaction in a Dyad," *Human Relations* 21 (1968): 3–17.

32. Clara Mayo and Marianne LeFrance, "Gaze Direction in Interracial Dyadic Communication," paper presented at the annual meeting of the Eastern Psychological Association, Washington, D.C., 1973. Cited in *Gender and Nonverbal Behavior*, ed. Clara Mayo and Nancy Henley (New York: Springer-Verlag, 1981).

33. Rutter.

34. *Ibid.*

35. Ekman and Friesen.

36. For a review of these studies, see Judith Hall, *Nonverbal Sex Differences: Communication Accuracy and Expressive Style* (Baltimore: Johns Hopkins University Press, 1984), pp. 59–84.

37. Paul Ekman and Wallace Friesen, "The Repertoire of Nonverbal Behavior: Categories, Origins, Usage, and Coding," *Semiotica* 1 (1969): 49–98.

38. Morris, pp. 50–51.

39. G. L. Trager, "Paralanguage: A First Approximation," *Studies in Linguistics* 13 (1958): 1–12.

40. David W. Addington, "The Relationship of Selected Vocal Characteristics to Personality Perception," *Speech Monographs* 35 (1968): 492–503.

41. James McCroskey, Carl E. Larson, and Mark Knapp, *An Introduction to Interpersonal Communication* (Englewood Cliffs, N.J.: Prentice-Hall, 1971), p. 117.

42. Susan Milmoe, Robert Rosenthal, Howard T. Blane, Morris E. Chafetz, and Irving Wolf, "The Doctor's Voice: Postdictor of Successful Referral of Alcoholic Patients," *Journal of Abnormal Psychology* 72 (1967): 78–84.

43. Ashley Montagu, *Touching: The Human Significance of the Skin* (New York: Columbia University Press, 1971).

44. Brenda Major, "Gender Patterns in Touching Behavior," in *Gender and Nonverbal Behavior*, pp. 15–37.

45. Richard Heslin, "Steps toward a Taxonomy of Touching," paper presented at the annual meeting of the Midwestern Psychological Association, Chicago, 1974.

46. Major, p. 33.

47. Nancy Henley, "Status and Sex: Some Touching Observations," *Bulletin of the Psychonomic Society* 2 (1973): 91–93.

48. Equilibrium theory was first introduced by Argyle and Dean and has been modified considerably by Miles Patterson. Patterson has renamed the modified theory a "sequential functional model." We have chosen to retain the term equilibrium theory for heuristic purposes. See Michael Argyle and Janet Dean, "Eye Contact, Distance and Affiliation," *Sociometry* 28 (1965): 289–304; Patterson, pp. 13–34.

CHAPTER SEVEN

1. Helen Keller, *The Story of My Life* (Garden City, N.Y.: Doubleday, 1905), p. 36.

2. Daniel J. Boorstin, *The Discoverers* (New York: Vintage Books, 1983), Book One: Time.

3. For a nice summary of the differences between verbal and nonverbal codes, see Judee K. Burgoon and Thomas Saine, *The Unspoken Dialogue: An Introduction to Nonverbal Communication* (Boston: Houghton Mifflin, 1978), pp. 18–20.

4. For an attempt at a structuralist breakdown of nonverbal behavior, see Ray L. Birdwhistell, *Introduction to Kinesics* (Louisville: University of Kentucky Press, 1952), and *Kinesics and Context* (Philadelphia: University of Pennsylvania Press, 1970); and for a critique of this attempt, see Allen T. Ditmann, "Review of *Kinesics in Context*," *Psychiatry* 34 (1971): 334–42.

5. Umberto Eco, *A Theory of Semiotics* (Bloomington: Indiana University Press, 1976), p. 7.

6. Our list is a composite made up of functions suggested by the following authors: Joost A. M. Meerloo, "Contributions of Psychiatry to the Study of Communication," in *Human Communication Theory: Original Essays*, ed. Frank E. X. Dance (New York: Holt, Rinehart and Winston, 1967), pp. 130–59; Roman Jakobson, "Closing Statement: Linguistics and Poetics," in *Style in Language*, ed. Thomas Sebeok (Cambridge, Mass.: M.I.T. Press, 1960), pp. 350–77; and Dell Hymes, "The Ethnography of Speaking," in *Readings in the Sociology of Language*, ed. Joshua Fishman (The Hague: Mouton, 1968), pp. 99–138.

7. Sigmund Freud, *Introductory Lectures on Psychoanalysis*, trans. & ed. James Strachey (New York: W. W. Norton, 1966), pp. 25–79.

8. For a full discussion of the relationship between language and uncertainty reduction, see Charles R. Berger and James J. Bradac, *Language and Social Knowledge: Uncertainty in Interpersonal Relations* (London: Edward Arnold, 1982).

9. Michael Stubbs, *Discourse Analysis: The Sociolinguistic Analysis of Natural Language* (Chicago: University of Chicago Press, 1983), pp. 48–49.

10. If you are not familiar with language structure, you may find Frederick Williams, *Language and Speech: Introductory Perspectives* (Englewood Cliffs, N.J.: Prentice-Hall, 1972), a useful introduction to the subject.

11. *Webster's Third New International Dictionary* (Springfield, Mass.: Merriam-Webster, 1981).

12. Dan I. Slobin, *Psycholinguistics* (Glenview, Ill.: Scott, Foresman, 1971), p. 96.

13. John R. Searle, *Speech Acts: An Essay in the Philosophy of Language* (Cambridge: Cambridge University Press, 1969).

14. CMM theory is one of the most popular of recent communication theories; there are many articles on the subject. We suggest you try W. Barnett Pearce, Vernon E. Cronen and Forrest Conklin, "On What to Look at When Analyzing Communication: A Hierarchical Model of Actors' Meanings," *Communication* 4 (1979): 195–220, and Vernon E. Cronen and W. Barnett Pearce, "Logical Force in Interpersonal Communication: A New Concept of the 'Necessity' in Social Behaviors," *Communication* 6 (1981): 5–67. For an overview and bibliography, see Vernon E. Cronen, W. Barnett Pearce, and Linda M. Harris, "The Coordinated Management of Meaning: A Theory of Communication," in *Human Communication Theory: Comparative Essays*, ed. Frank E. X. Dance (New York: Harper & Row, 1982), pp. 61–89.

15. Edward Sapir, *Selected Writings of Edward Sapir in Language, Culture and Personality* (Berkeley and Los Angeles: University of California, 1958), and Benjamin Lee Whorf, *Language, Thought and Reality* (Cambridge, Mass.: M.I.T. Press, 1966).

16. Sapir, p. 162.

17. Henry Allan Gleason, Jr., *An Introduction to Descriptive Linguistics*, rev. ed (New York: Holt, Rinehart and Winston, 1961), p. 4.

18. Slobin, p. 125.

19. Whorf, p. 240.

20. *Ibid.*, p. 243.

21. Basil Bernstein, ed., *Class, Codes and Control*, vol. 2 (London: Routledge and Kegan Paul, 1973).

22. The sample dialogue is taken from Raymond S. Ross and Mark G. Ross, *Relating and Interacting* (Englewood Cliffs, N.J.: Prentice-Hall, 1982), p. 93.

23. Two useful reviews of these studies can be found in chapters 2 and 3 of Barbara Westbrook Eakins and R. Gene Eakins, *Sex Differences in Human Communication* (Boston: Houghton Mifflin, 1978), and chapter 6 in Judy Cornelia Pearson, *Gender and Communication* (Dubuque, Iowa: William C. Brown, 1985).

24. Robin Lakoff, *Language and Women's Place* (New York: Harper & Row, 1975).

25. Eakins and Eakins, p. 48.

26. *Ibid.*, p. 49.

27. See, for example, Wendell Johnson, *People in Quandaries: The Semantics of Personal Adjustment* (New York: Harper & Row, 1946); S. I. Hayakawa, *Language in Thought and Action*, 4th ed. (New York: Harcourt Brace Jovanovich, 1978); J. Samuel Bois, *The Art of Awareness*, 2nd ed. (Dubuque, Iowa: William C. Brown, 1973); and John C. Condon, Jr., *Semantics and Communication*, 3rd ed. (New York: Macmillan, 1985).

CHAPTER EIGHT

1. Paul Watzlawick, Janet Beavin Bavelas, and Don D. Jackson, *Pragmatics of Human Communication* (New York: W. W. Norton, 1967), p. 52.

2. *Ibid.*, p. 51. See also Jurgen Ruesch and Gregory Bateson, *Communication: The Social Matrix of Psychiatry* (New York: W. W. Norton, 1951), pp. 179–81.

3. Watzlawick *et al.*, p. 52.

4. Stephen W. King and Kenneth K. Sereno, "Conversational Appropriateness As a Conversational Imperative," *Quarterly Journal of Speech* 70 (1984): 264–73.

5. Julia T. Wood, "Communication and Relational Culture: Bases for the Study of Human Relationships," *Communication Quarterly* 30 (1982): 75–83. See also Mary Anne Fitzpatrick and Patricia B. Best, "Dyadic Adjustment in Relational Types: Consensus, Cohesion, Affectional Expression and Satisfaction in Enduring Relationships," *Communication Monographs* 46 (1979): 167–78, and Gerald M. Phillips and Nancy J. Metzger, *Intimate Communication* (Boston: Allyn & Bacon, 1976).

6. Robert C. Carson, *Interaction Concepts of Personality* (Chicago: Aldine, 1969); see in particular chapter 6, "Contractual Arrangements in Interpersonal Relations."

7. *Ibid.*, p. 184.

8. See, for example, Gregory Bateson, "Culture Contact and Schismogenesis," *Man* 35 (1935): 178–83; William C. Schutz, *The Interpersonal Underworld* (Palo Alto, Calif.: Science & Behavior Books, 1966); Timothy Leary, *Interpersonal Diagnosis of Personality* (New York: Ronald Press, 1957). For a summary of early relational work, see Malcolm R. Parks, "Relational Communication: Theory and Research," *Human Communication Research* 3 (1977): 372–81.

9. Judee K. Burgoon and Jerold L. Hale, "The Fundamental Topoi of Relational Communication," *Communication Monographs* 51 (1984): 193–214.

10. Frank E. Millar and L. Edna Rogers, "A Relational Approach to Interpersonal Communication," in *Explorations in Interpersonal Communication*, ed. Gerald R. Miller (Beverly Hills, Calif.: Sage Publications, 1976).

11. B. Aubrey Fisher, *Small Group Decision Making*, 2nd ed. (New York: McGraw-Hill, 1980), p. 327.

12. Burgoon and Hale, p. 198.

13. *Ibid.*

14. For a general overview of some classic research on similarity and attraction, see Ellen Bersheid and Elaine Walster, *Interpersonal Attraction* (Reading, Mass.: Addison-Wesley, 1969). For a discussion of similarity as a device in developing relationships, see Steve Duck, "Interpersonal Communication in Developing Acquaintance," in *Explorations in Interpersonal Communication*. For experimental evidence of the effects of attitude similarity on attraction, see the work of Michael Sunnafrank; for example, "Attitude Similarity and Interpersonal Attraction in Communication Processes: In Pursuit of an Ephemeral Influence," *Communication Monographs* 50 (1983): 273–84.

15. Evelyn Sieburg, "Dysfunctional Communication and Interpersonal Responsiveness in Small Groups," unpublished dissertation, University of Denver, 1969. For a good summary of Sieburg's theory, see Frank E. X. Dance and Carl E. Larson, *Speech Communication: Concepts and Behavior* (New York: Holt, Rinehart and Winston, 1972), pp. 140–43.

16. Watzlawick, Bavelas, and Jackson. See Chapter 6 for a discussion of the "logic" of paradox.

17. Gregory Bateson, Don D. Jackson, Jay Haley, and John H. Weakland, "Toward a Theory of Schizophrenia," *Behavioral Science* 1 (1956): 251–64; Jay Haley, *Strategies of Psychotherapy* (New York: Grune and Stratton, 1963).

18. Lynda Rummel, Sarah Trenholm, Charles Goetzinger, and Charles Petrie, "Disconfirming (Double Bind) Effects of Incongruent Multichannel Messages," in *Interpersonal Communication: A Rhetorical Perspective*, eds. Ben Morse and Lyn Phelps. (Minneapolis: Burgess, 1980).

19. The Palo Alto group includes Gregory Bateson, John H. Weakland, Paul Watzlawick, Janet Beavin Bavelas, Don D. Jackson, and Jay Haley. To understand this approach, see the section on the pragmatic perspective in B. Aubrey Fisher, *Perspectives on Human Communication* (New York: Macmillan, 1978).

20. For an overview and model of interact sequences, see B. Aubrey Fisher and Leonard C. Hawes, "An Interact System Model: Generating a Grounded Theory of Small Groups," *Quarterly Journal of Speech* 57 (1971): 444–53.

21. See Watzlawick, Bavelas, and Jackson for the original example, pp. 54–59.

22. William W. Wilmot, *Dyadic Communication* (Reading, Mass.: Addison-Wesley, 1979).

23. *Ibid.*, p. 127.

24. Vernon E. Cronen, W. Barnett Pearce, and Lonna M. Snavely, "A Theory of Rule-Structure and Types of Episodes and a Study of Perceived Enmeshment in Undesired Repetitive Patterns ('URPs')," in *Communication Yearbook 3*, ed. Dan Nimmo (New Brunswick, N.J.: Transaction Books, 1979).

25. Wilmot, p. 128.

CHAPTER NINE

1. Saul V. Levine, "Radical Departures," *Psychology Today* 18 (8) (August 1984): 20–27.

2. *Ibid.* See also Rodney Stark and William Sims Bainbridge, *The Future of Religion: Secularization, Revival and Cult Formation* (Berkeley and Los Angeles: University of California Press, 1985).

3. For a thorough overview of all of the learning theories, see Frederick H. Kanfer and Jeanne S. Phillips, *Learning Foundations of Behavior Therapy* (New York: John Wiley, 1970).

4. The original source is I. P. Pavlov, *Conditioned Reflexes* (London: Oxford University Press, 1927).

5. See, for example, B. F. Skinner, *Science and Human Behavior* (New York: Macmillan, 1953).

6. Albert Bandura, *Social Learning Theory* (Englewood Cliffs, N.J.: Prentice-Hall, 1977).

7. Mary John Smith, *Persuasion and Human Action: A Review and Critique of Social Influence Theories* (Belmont, Calif.: Wadsworth, 1982), p. 202.

8. George Caspar Homans, *Social Behavior: Its Elementary Forms* (New York: Harcourt Brace Jovanovich, 1959), and John W. Thibaut and Harold H. Kelley, *The Social Psychology of Groups* (New York: John Wiley, 1959).

9. Good discussions of relational currencies are provided in Kenneth L. Villard and Leland J. Whipple, *Beginnings in Relational Communication* (New York: John Wiley, 1976), and Kathleen M. Galvin and Bernard J. Brommel, *Family Communication: Cohesion and Change* (Glenview, Ill.: Scott, Foresman, 1982).

10. For an overview of consistency theories, see Mary John Smith, *Persuasion and Human Action*, or Richard E. Petty and John T. Cacioppo, *Attitudes and Persuasion: Classic and Contemporary Approaches* (Dubuque, Iowa: William C. Brown, 1981).

11. Fritz Heider, *The Psychology of Interpersonal Relations* (New York: John Wiley, 1958).

12. Charles E. Osgood and Percy H. Tannenbaum, "The Principle of Congruity in the Prediction of Attitude Change," *Psychological Review* 62 (1955): 42–55; Percy H. Tannenbaum, "The Congruity Principle Revisited: Studies in the Reduction, Induction, and Generalization of Persuasion," in *Advances in Experimental Social Psychology*, vol. 3, ed. Leonard Berkowitz (New York: Academic Press, 1967).

13. Leon Festinger, *A Theory of Cognitive Dissonance* (Stanford, Calif.: Stanford University Press, 1957); Jack W. Brehm and Arthur R. Cohen, eds., *Explorations in Cognitive Dissonance* (New York: John Wiley, 1962); Robert A. Wicklund and Jack W. Brehm, *Perspectives on Cognitive Dissonance* (Hillsdale, N.J.: Lawrence Erlbaum, 1976).

14. Charles R. Berger and James J. Bradac, *Language and Social Knowledge: Uncertainty in Interpersonal Relations* (London: Edward Arnold, 1982); Charles R. Berger and Richard J. Calabrese, "Some Explorations in Initial Interaction and Beyond: Toward a Developmental Theory of Interpersonal Communication," *Human Communication Research* 1 (1975): 99–112.

15. Milton Rokeach, *Beliefs, Attitudes, and Values* (San Francisco: Jossey-Bass, 1972); *The Nature of Human Values* (New York: Free Press, 1973); and "Value Theory and Communication Research: Review and Commentary," in *Communication Yearbook 3*, ed. Dan Nimmo (New Brunswick, N.J.: Transaction Books, 1979).

16. Daniel Katz, "The Functional Approach to the Study of Attitudes," *Public Opinion Quarterly* 24 (1960): 163–204.

17. Aristotle, *Rhetoric*, trans. W. Rhys Roberts, and *Poetics*, trans. Ingram Bywater (New York: Modern Library, 1954), pp. 24–25. For more modern formulations of the notion of credibility, see Carl I. Hovland and W. A. Weiss, "The Influence of Source Credibility on Communicative Effectiveness," *Public Opinion Quarterly* 15 (1951): 635–50, and David K. Berlo, James B. Lemert, and Robert J. Mertz, "Dimensions for Evaluating the Acceptability of Message Sources," *Public Opinion Quarterly* 33 (1969): 563–76. For critiques of the credibility construct, see Gary Cronkhite and Jo Liska, "A Critique of Factor Analytic Approaches to the Study of Credibility," *Communication Monographs* 43 (June 1976): 91–107, and Gerald R. Miller and Michael Burgoon, "Persuasion Research: Review and Commentary," *Communication Yearbook 2*, ed. Brent D. Ruben (New Brunswick, N.J.: Transaction Books, 1978), pp. 29–47.

18. John R. French and Bertram Raven, "The Bases of Social Power," in *Studies in Social Power* (Ann Arbor: University of Michigan Press, 1959).

19. Edward E. Jones and Thane S. Pittman, "Toward a General Theory of Strategic Self-Presentation," in *Psychological Perspectives on the Self*, ed. Harry Suls (Hillsdale, N.J.: Lawrence Erlbaum, 1980).

20. Karen Tracy and others, "The Discourse of Requests: Assessment of a Compliance-Gaining Approach," *Human Communication Research* 10 (1984): 513–38.

21. Gerald R. Miller and others, "Compliance-Gaining Message Strategies: A Typology and Some Findings Concerning Effects of Situational Differences," *Communication Monographs* 44 (1977): 37–51; Michael E. Roloff and Edwin F. Barnicott, "The Situational Use of Pro- and Anti-Social Compliance-Gaining Strategies by High and Low Machiavellians," in *Communication Yearbook 2*, ed. Brent D. Ruben (New Brunswick, N.J.: Transaction Books, 1978), pp. 193–205.

22. Gerald Marwell and David R. Schmitt, "Dimensions of Compliance-Gaining Behavior: An Empirical Analysis," *Sociometry* 30 (1967): 350–64.

23. William J. Schenck-Hamlin, Richard L. Wiseman, and G. N. Georgacarakos, "A Model of Properties of Compliance-Gaining Strategies," *Communication Quarterly* 30 (1982): 92–100.

24. Michael J. Cody and Margaret L. McLaughlin, "Perceptions of Compliance-Gaining Situations: A Dimensional Analysis," *Communication Monographs* 47 (1980): 132–48; Michael J. Cody, M. L. Woelfel, & W. J. Jordan, "Dimensions of Compliance-Gaining Situations, *Human Communication Research* 9 (1983): 99–113.

25. Tracy and others, pp. 520–22.

26. *Ibid.*, pp. 533–34.

CHAPTER TEN

1. John Cheever, "Goodbye, My Brother," in *The Stories of John Cheever* (New York: Alfred A. Knopf, 1978), p. 3. Reprinted with permission.

2. See, for example, Salvador Minuchin, *Families and Family Therapy* (Cambridge, Mass.: Harvard University Press, 1974), pp. 50–51.

3. Virginia Satir, *Peoplemaking* (Palo Alto, Calif.: Science and Behavior Books, 1972).

4. Kathleen M. Galvin and Bernard J. Brommel, *Family Communication: Cohesion and Change* (Glenview, Ill.: Scott, Foresman, 1982), p. 4.

5. Ronald E. Cromwell and David Olson, eds., *Power in Families* (New York: Halstead Press, 1975), p. 5.

6. Basil Bernstein, *Class, Codes, and Control* (London: Routledge and Kegan Paul, 1971).

7. Ralph Turner, *Family Interaction* (New York: John Wiley, 1970), pp. 97–116.

8. Minuchin, p. 53.

9. David Kantor and William Lehr, *Inside the Family* (San Francisco: Jossey-Bass, 1976).

10. Minuchin, pp. 54–56.

11. Christopher Lasch, *Haven in a Heartless World* (New York: Basic Books, 1977).

12. David Olson and Hamilton McCubbin, *Families: What Makes Them Work* (Beverly Hills, Calif.: Sage Publications, 1983), pp. 30–34.

13. Galvin and Brommel, p. 234.

14. See John M. Gottman, *Marital Interaction: Experimental Investigations* (New York: Academic Press, 1979).

15. Mary Anne Fitzpatrick, "A Typological Approach to Marital Interaction: Recent Theory and Research," in *Advances in Experimental Social Psychology 18*, ed. Leonard Berkowitz (New York: Academic Press, 1984), pp. 1–47. See also Mary Anne Fitzpatrick and Diane M. Badzinski, "All in the Family: Interpersonal Communication in Kin Relationships," in *Handbook of Interpersonal Communication*, ed. Mark Knapp and Gerald R. Miller (Beverly Hills, Calif.: Sage Publications, 1985), pp. 687–736.

16. Fitzpatrick and Badzinski, p. 700.

17. B. Rollins and R. Galligan, "The Developing Child and Marital Satisfaction of Parents," in *Child Influences on Marital and Family Interaction: A Lifespan Perspective*, ed. Richard Lerner and Graham Spanier (New York: Academic Press, 1978), pp. 71–106.

18. Alice Rossi, "Transition to Parenthood," *Journal of Marriage and the Family* 30 (1968): 26–39.

19. See, for example, B. Rollins and D. Thomas, "Parental Support, Power, and Control Techniques in the Socialization of Children," in *Contemporary Theories About the Family*, ed. Wesley R. Burr, R. Hill, F. I.Nye and I. L. Reiss (New York: Free Press, 1979), vol. 1, pp. 317–64. See also S. Steinmetz, "Disciplinary Techniques and Their Relationship to Aggressiveness, Dependency, and Conscience," in *Contemporary Theories About the Family*, vol. 2, pp. 405–38.

20. Desmond Morris, *Intimate Behavior* (New York: Bantam Books, 1971), 252–54.

21. For a brief review of this research, see Fitzpatrick and Badzinski, pp. 713–17.

CHAPTER ELEVEN

1. The authors would like to thank Vernon Cronen for providing this example. We have paraphrased the account; any inaccuracies are our own.

2. See William K. Rawlins, "Friendship As a Communicative Achievement: A Theory and an Interpretive Analysis of Verbal Reports," Ph.D. dissertation, Temple University, 1981. See also, Kaspar D. Naegele, "Friendship and Acquaintances: An Exploration of Some Social Distinctions," *Harvard Educational Review* 28 (1958): 232–52.

3. Virginia Kidd, "Happily Ever After and Other Relationship Styles: Advice on Interpersonal Relations in Popular Magazines, 1951–1973," *Quarterly Journal of Speech* 61 (1975): 31–39.

4. Howard Gadlin, "Private Lives and Public Order: A Critical View of the History of Intimate Relations in the United States," in *Close Relationships: Perspectives on the Meaning of Intimacy*, ed. George Levinger and Harold Raush (Amherst: University of Massachusetts Press, 1977), pp. 33–72.

5. For models of relationship development that portray participants as making rational choices and being highly aware of the process, see Irwin Altman and Dallas Taylor, *Social Penetration: The Development of Interpersonal Relationships* (New York: Holt, Rinehart and Winston, 1973); Charles Berger and Richard Calabrese, "Some Explorations in Initial Interaction and Beyond: Toward a Developmental Theory of Interpersonal Communication," *Human Communication Research* 1 (1975): 99–112. For arguments that people are less conscious of these processes, see Charles Berger, "Self-Consciousness and the Adequacy of Theory and Research into Relationship Development," *Western Journal of Speech Communication* 44 (1980): 93–96; Jesse Delia, "Some Tentative Thoughts Concerning the Study of Interpersonal Relationships and Their Development," *Western Journal of Speech Communication* 44 (1980): 97–103.

6. Harriet Braiker and Harold Kelley, "Conflicts in the Development of Close Relationships," in *Social Exchange in Developing Relationships*, ed. Robert Burgess and Ted Huston (New York: Academic Press, 1979), pp. 136–68.

7. Mark L. Knapp, *Interpersonal Communication and Human Relationships* (Boston, Allyn & Bacon, 1984), p. 192.

8. Warren Shibles and Charles Zastrow, "Romantic Love vs. Rational Love," in *The Personal Problem Solver* (Englewood Cliffs, N.J.: Prentice-Hall), p. 21.

9. See Stanley Schacter and Jerome Singer, "Cognitive, Social, and Physiological Determinants of Emotional State," *Psychological Review* 69 (1962): 379–99; also Miles Patterson, "An Arousal Model of Interpersonal Intimacy," *Psychological Review* 83 (1976): 235–45.

10. Gregory L. White, Sanford Fishbein, and Jeffrey Rutstein, "Passionate Love and the Misattribution of Arousal," *Journal of Personality and Social Psychology* 41 (1981): 56–62.

11. Richard Sennett, *The Fall of Public Man* (New York: Random House, 1978).

12. Steven Duck, "Interpersonal Communication in Developing Acquaintance," in *Explorations in Interpersonal Communication*, ed. Gerald R. Miller (Beverly Hills, Calif.: Sage Publications, 1973), pp. 127–48.

13. Elaine Walster, Vera Aronson, Darcy Abrahams, and Leon Rottman, "Importance of Physical Attractiveness in Dating Behavior," *Journal of Personality and Social Psychology* 4 (1966): 508–16.

14. For a summary of this research, see William Griffitt, "Attitude Similarity and Attraction," in *Foundations of Interpersonal Attraction*, ed. Ted L. Huston (New York: Academic Press, 1974), pp. 285–308.

15. Thomas Lickona, "A Cognitive–Developmental Approach to Interpersonal Attraction," in *Foundation of Interpersonal Attraction*, pp. 31–59.

16. Charles Backman and Paul Secord, "The Effect of Perceived Liking on Interpersonal Attraction," *Human Relations* 12 (1959): 379–84; also Fritz Heider, *The Psychology of Interpersonal Relations* (New York: Wiley, 1958).

17. Benjamin J. Broome, "The Attraction Paradigm Revisited: Responses to Dissimilar Others," *Human Communication Research* 10 (1983): 137–52.

18. See David R. Mettee and Elliot Aronson, "Affective Reactions to Appraisal from Others," in *Foundations of Interpersonal Attraction*, pp. 235–83.

19. William C. Schutz, *FIRO: A Three-Dimensional Theory of Interpersonal Behavior* (New York: Holt, Rinehart and Winston, 1958).

20. Kenneth Villard and Leland Whipple, *Beginnings in Relational Communication* (New York: John Wiley, 1976); U. G. Foa, "Interpersonal and Economic Resources," *Science* 171 (1971): 345–51.

21. John Berg and Richard Archer, "The Disclosure–Liking Relationship: Effects of Self-Perception, Order of Disclosure, and Topical Similarity," *Human Communication Research* 10 (1983): 269–82.

22. Rawlins, "Friendship As a Communicative Achievement."

23. Margaret E. Gruhn, "German-American Language Patterns As Indicators of Cultural Communication Boundaries: A Cross-Cultural Analysis," paper presented at the Speech Communication convention, Denver, Colorado, November 1985.

24. Knapp, pp. 29–58.

25. Susan R. Glaser, *Toward Communication Competency: Developing Interpersonal Skills* (New York: Holt, Rinehart and Winston, 1980), pp. 105–19.

26. Malcolm R. Parks and Mara B. Adelman, "Communication Networks and the Development of Romantic Relationships: An Expansion of Uncertainty Reduction Theory," *Human Communication Research* 10 (1983): 55–80.

27. William K. Rawlins, "Openness as Problematic in Ongoing Friendship: Two Conversational Dilemmas," *Communication Monographs* 50 (1983): 1–13.

28. Alan L. Sillars and Michael D. Scott, "Interpersonal Perception between Intimates: An Integrative Review," *Human Communication Research* 10 (1983): 153–76.

29. *Ibid.*

30. Sally Planalp and James Honeycutt, "Events That Increase Uncertainty in Personal Relationships," *Human Communication Research* 11 (1985): 593–604.

CHAPTER TWELVE

1. Ken Auletta, "Power, Greed and Glory on Wall Street: The Fall of Lehman Brothers," *New York Times Magazine*, Feb. 17, 1985, pp. 29–43.

2. Rom Harre, *Social Being: A Theory for Social Psychology* (Totowa, N.J.: Littlefield, Adams, 1979), pp. 22–26.

3. For example, see Richard Sennett, *The Fall of Public Man* (New York: Random House, 1974); see also Christopher Lasch, *The Culture of Narcissism: American Life in an Age of Diminishing Expectations* (New York: Norton, 1979).

4. Erving Goffman, *Interaction Ritual: Essays on Face-to-Face Behavior* (Garden City, N.Y.: Anchor Books, 1967), pp. 47–95.

5. *Ibid.*, p. 76.

6. *Ibid.*, p. 79.

7. Sennett.

8. John Naisbitt, *Megatrends* (New York: Warner Books, 1982).

9. E. Foster et al., *A Market Study for the College of Business Administration, University of Minnesota, Twin Cities* (Minneapolis: College of Business Administration, University of Minnesota, November 1978).

10. Daniel Katz and Robert L. Kahn, *The Social Psychology of Organizations* (New York: John Wiley, 1966), pp. 239–45.

11. Gerald A. Goldhaber, *Organizational Communication* (Dubuque, Iowa: William C. Brown, 1983), p. 226.

12. Fredric M. Jablin, "Superior–Subordinate Communication: The State of the Art," *Psychological Bulletin* 86 (1979): 1208.

13. William C. Redding, *Communication within the Organization: An Interpretive Review of Theory and Research* (New York: Industrial Communication Council, 1972), p. 443.

14. Fredric M. Jablin, "An Exploratory Study of Subordinates' Perceptions of Supervisory Politics," *Communication Quarterly* 29 (1981): 269–75.

15. For a review, see P. D. Krivonos, "Distortion of Subordinate-to-Superior Communication," paper presented at the annual meeting of the International Communication Association, Portland, Oregon, 1976. See also Norman Maier, L. Richard Hoffman, and William Read, "Superior–Subordinate Communication: The Relative Effectiveness of Managers Who Held Their Subordinates' Positions," *Personal Psychology* 26 (1963): 1–11.

16. Cal Downs and C. Conrad, "Effective Subordinancy," *Journal of Business Communication* 19 (1982): 27–37.

17. Charles B. Truax and Robert R. Carkhuff, *Toward Effective Counseling and Psychotherapy* (Chicago: Aldine, 1967).

18. Loyd Pettegrew and Richard Thomas, "Communicator Style Differences in Formal vs. Informal Therapeutic Relationships," in *Communication Yearbook 2*, ed. Brent D. Ruben (New Brunswick, N.J.: Transaction Books, 1978), pp. 521–37.

19. *Ibid.*, p. 534.

20. *Ibid.*

21. Daniel Costello, "Health Communication Theory and Research: An Overview," in *Communication Yearbook 1*, ed. Brent D. Ruben (New Brunswick, N.J.: Transaction Books, 1977), pp. 557–67.

22. See, for example, Paul Arntson, David Droge, and Harry E. Fassl, "Pediatrician–Patient Communication: Final Report," in *Communication Yearbook 2*, pp. 505–22;

B. Freeman, V. Negrete, V. Davis, and M. Korsch, "Gaps in Doctor–Patient Communication: Doctor–Patient Interaction Analysis," *Pediatrician Research* 5 (1971): 298–311.

23. See "Professionals," *Buyer's Market*, vol. II, no. 3 (March 1986), ed. Luke W. Cole, p. 3.

24. Arntson, et al., p. 521.

25. For a review of trait research, see R. D. Mann, "A Review of the Relationship between Personality and Performance in Small Groups," *Psychological Bulletin* 56 (1959): 241–70.

26. Charles O'Reilly and David Caldwell, "Informational Influence As a Determinant of Task Characteristics and Job Satisfaction," *Journal of Applied Psychology* 64 (1979): 157–65.

27. Irving Janis, *Victims of Groupthink: A Psychological Study of Foreign Policy Decisions and Fiascos* (Boston: Houghton Mifflin, 1972).

28. Daniel C. Feldman, "The Multiple Socialization of Organization Members," *Academy of Management Review* 6 (1981): 309–18.

29. Fredric M. Jablin, "Task/Work Relationships: A Lifespan Perspective," in *Handbook of Interpersonal Communication*, eds. Mark Knapp and Gerald R. Miller (Beverly Hills, Calif.: Sage Publications, 1985), p. 633.

30. Julie Foehrenbach and Karen Rosenberg, "How Are We Doing?" *Journal of Communication Management* 12 (1982): 3–11.

31. Keith Davis, *Human Behavior at Work* (New York: McGraw-Hill, 1972), p. 280.

32. William Davis and J. Regis O'Connor, "Serial Transmission of Information: A Study of the Grapevine," *Journal of Applied Communication Research* 5 (1977): 61–72; Evan E. Rudolph, "Informal Human Communication Systems in a Large Organization," *Journal of Applied Communication Research* 1 (1973): 7–23; Eugene Walton, "How Effective Is the Grapevine?" *Personnel Journal* 38 (1961): 45–49.

CHAPTER THIRTEEN

1. Woody Allen, *Four Films of Woody Allen* (New York: Random House, 1982), p. 105.

2. Erving Goffman, "On Face-Work: An Analysis of Ritual Elements in Social Interaction," *Psychiatry* 18 (August 1955): 213–31.

3. For a general discussion of accounts, see Marvin B. Scott and Stanford M. Lyman, "Accounts," *American Sociological Review* 33 (1968): 46–62. See also James T. Tedeschi and Marc Riess, "Identities, the Phenomenal Self,

and Laboratory Research," in *Impression Management Theory and Social Psychological Research*, ed. James T. Tedeschi (New York: Academic Press, 1981).

4. Tedeschi and Riess, p. 7.

5. *Ibid.*

6. John P. Hewitt and Randall Stokes, "Disclaimers," *American Sociological Review* 40 (1975): 1–11.

7. Morton Deutsch, "Conflicts: Productive and Destructive," in *Conflict Resolution through Communication*, ed. Fred E. Jandt, pp. 155–97. (New York: Harper & Row, 1973), p. 156.

8. Joyce Hocker Frost and William W. Wilmot, *Interpersonal Conflict* (Dubuque, Iowa: William C. Brown, 1978), pp. 17–19.

9. Raymond S. Ross and Mark G. Ross, *Relating and Interacting* (Englewood Cliffs, N.J.: Prentice-Hall, 1982), p. 124.

10. George R. Bach and Peter Wyden, *The Intimate Enemy: How to Fight Fair in Love and Marriage* (New York: Avon Books, 1970).

11. For early formulations of the grid approach and a discussion of its use in the managerial context, see Robert R. Blake and Jane S. Mouton, *The Managerial Grid* (Houston: Gulf Publishing Co., 1964), p. 10, and Jay Hall, *Conflict Management Survey* (Woodlands, Texas: Teleometrics International, 1969). See also Ross and Ross, pp. 143–46, and David W. Johnson, *Reaching Out: Interpersonal Effectiveness and Self-Actualization*, 3rd ed. (Englewood Cliffs, N.J.: Prentice-Hall, 1986), pp. 207–10.

12. Johnson, pp. 207–10.

13. Ross and Ross, p. 145.

14. The rules for effective feedback we have listed are adapted from Johnson, pp. 81–83.

15. Frost and Wilmot, pp. 136–38. See also Roger Fisher, "Fractionating Conflict," in *Conflict Resolution: Contributions of the Behavioral Sciences*, ed. Clagett G. Smith (Notre Dame, Ind.: University of Notre Dame Press, 1971).

16. Frost and Wilmot, p. 138.

17. Charles Robert Petrie, Jr., "What Is Listening?" in *Listening: Readings*, ed. Sam Duker (New York: Scarecrow Press, 1966), p. 329.

18. See, for example, Andrew D. Wolvin and Carolyn Gwynn Coakley, *Listening* (Dubuque, Iowa: William C. Brown, 1985), and Florence I. Wolff, Nadine C. Marsnik, William S. Tracey, and Ralph G. Nichols, *Perceptive Listening* (New York: Holt, Rinehart and Winston, 1983).

SUBJECT INDEX

AUTHOR INDEX

ILLUSTRATION CREDITS

Page 1, The Saint Louis Art Museum, Gift of Mrs. Stratford Lee Morton (detail from *Friendship Quilt*, Baltimore, 1848)

Page 2, The Bettmann Archive (sixteenth-century woodcut)

Page 4, © Don Ivers/Jeroboam, Inc.

Page 7, Jim Harter, ed., *Animals: 1419 Copyright-free Illustrations of Mammals, Birds, Fish, Insects, etc.* New York: Dover, 1979

Page 8, © 1978 The Art Institute of Chicago, All rights reserved. Buckingham Fund, 1958.120 (Japanese, Guardian Figure, Kamakura period, 1185–1392, polychromed wood sculpture)

Page 9, National Gallery of Art, Washington, DC, Collection of Mr. and Mrs. Paul Mellon (*Breton Girls Dancing, Pont Aven* by Paul Gauguin)

Page 11, The Saint Louis Art Museum, Museum Purchase (*The Knitting Lesson* by Jean François Millet)

Page 17, Jim Harter, ed., *Animals: 1419 Copyright-free Illustrations of Mammals, Birds, Fish, Insects, etc.* New York: Dover, 1979

Page 22, The Phillips Collection, Washington, DC (*The Luncheon of the Boating Party* by Pierre Auguste Renoir)

Page 24, AP/Wide World Photos

Page 27, The Thomas Gilcrease Institute of American History and Art, Tulsa, Oklahoma (*Pueblo Green Corn Dance* by Fred Kabotie)

Page 29, © Alex Webb/Magnum Photos, Inc.

Page 33, Jim Kalett/Photo Researchers

Page 34, The Saint Louis Art Museum, Gift of Mrs. Stratford Lee Morton (*Friendship Quilt*, Baltimore, 1848)

Page 45, The Cleveland Museum of Art, Purchase, Leonard C. Hanna, Jr., Bequest (detail from limestone raised relief of king's scribe Amenhotep and wife Renut with three members of family, c. 1275 B.C., Egyptian)

Page 46, Bowles and Carver, *Catchpenny Prints, 163 Popular Engravings from the Eighteenth Century.* New York: Dover, 1970

Page 50, © Jesse Levine, Laguna Sales, San Jose, California

Page 52, Photo from an Italian film featuring Constance Dowling. Photo courtesy of Leland Moss

Page 53, Photo from the movie, *Duel in the Sun*

Page 55, © 1987 The Detroit Institute of Arts, Gift of C. W. Churchill in memory of his father (*Grandma's Hearthstone*, 1890, by John Haberle, American, 1856–1933, oil on canvas, 8 feet by 66 inches, accession no. 50.31)

Page 57, Jim M'Guinness and Bookbuilders West

Page 58, Collection of Whitney Museum of American Art. Purchase, with funds from the Richard and Dorothy Rodgers Fund (*'61 Pontiac*, 1968–69, by Robert Bechtle, oil on canvas, 60 by 84 inches, acq. no. 70.16)

Page 61, The Metropolitan Museum of Art, Bequest of Stephen C. Clark, 1960 (*The Card Players* by Paul Cezanne)

Page 63, From *Nine Nations of North America* by Joel Garreau. Copyright © 1981 by Joel Garreau. Reprinted by permission of Houghton Mifflin Company

Page 66, left, The Metropolitan Museum of Art, Gift of Howard Mansfield, 1936 (Ill. Book III) (Thin people from Japanese illustrated book: *Manja*, Vol. VIII, by Katsushiko Hokusai)

Page 66, right, The Metropolitan Museum of Art, Gift of Howard Mansfield, 1936 (Ill. Book III) (Fat people from Japanese illustrated book: *Manja*, Vol. VIII, by Katsushiko Hokusai)

Page 68, Leonard Freed/Magnum Photos, Inc.

Page 78, The Metropolitan Museum of Art, The Michael C. Rockefeller Memorial Collection, Gift of Nelson A. Rockefeller, 1972 (1978.412.323) (Belt Mask, Nigeria, Court of Benin)

Page 81, Albright-Knox Art Gallery, Buffalo, New York. Room of Contemporary Art Fund, 1941 (*Family at Supper* by Pablo Picasso)

Page 83, Jim Harter, ed. *Music, A Pictorial Archive of Woodcuts and Engravings*. New York: Dover, 1980

Page 85, Collection, The Museum of Modern Art, New York. Gift of Mrs. Simon Guggenheim (*Girl Before a Mirror* by Pablo Picasso)

Page 86, AP/Wide World Photos

Page 89, top, © Charles Harbutt, Archive Pictures, Inc.

Page 89, bottom, © Bill Ross, Woodfin Camp

Page 90, © Jill Freedman/Archive Pictures, Inc.

Page 93, Jim Harter, ed. *Women, A Pictorial Archive from Nineteenth-Century Sources*. New York: Dover, 1982

Page 98, top left, Mme. H. Lutjens Collection/Giraudon/Art Resource (*Portrait de L'artiste, 1888* by Vincent van Gogh)

Page 98, top right, © 1987 The Art Institute of Chicago. All rights reserved. Joseph Winterbotham Collection (*Self-Portrait* by Vincent van Gogh)

Page 98, bottom left, The Metropolitan Museum of Art, Bequest of Miss Adelaide Milton de Groot (1876–1967), 1967. (67.187.70a) *Self-Portrait with a Straw Hat* by Vincent van Gogh)

Page 98, bottom right, Louvre/Giraudon/Art Resource (*Self-Portrait* by Vincent van Gogh)

Page 101, Jim Harter, ed., *Animals: 1419 Copyright-free Illustrations of Mammals, Birds, Fish, Insects, etc.* New York: Dover, 1979

Page 102, Bowles and Carver, *Catchpenny Prints, 163 Popular Engravings from the Eighteenth Century*. New York: Dover, 1970

Page 105, The Metropolitan Museum of Art, Robert Lehman Collection, 1975 (*Self-Portrait at Age Twenty-two* by Albrecht Durer)

Page 107, © 1987 The Art Institute of Chicago, All rights reserved. Gift of Mr. and Mrs. Daniel Saidenberg, 1957.72 (*The Red Armchair* by Pablo Picasso, 1931, oil on canvas, 130.8 x 99 cm)

Page 114, Charles Mills Gayley, *The Classic Myths in English Literature and in Art*. New York: Blaisdell, 1939

Page 117, Jim Harter, ed., *Men, A Pictorial Archive from Nineteenth-Century Sources*. New York: Dover, 1980

Page 122, © 1987 The Detroit Institute of Arts, City of Detroit Purchase (*The Wedding Dance*, c. 1566, by Pieter Brueghel the Elder, Flemish, 1525/30–1569, oil on panel, 47 by 62 inches, accession no. 30.374)

Page 125, Carol Belanger Grafton, ed., *Humorous Victorian Spot Illustrations*. New York: Dover, 1985

Page 127, The Metropolitan Museum of Art, Rogers Fund, 1948 (Memy-Sabu and His Wife, c. 2420 B.C., Egyptian)

Page 129, Carol Belanger Grafton, ed., *Humorous Victorian Spot Illustrations*. New York: Dover, 1985

Page 131, center and top left, Jim Harter, ed. *Women, A Pictorial Archive from Nineteenth-Century Sources*. New York: Dover, 1982

Page 131, top center, top right, bottom center, and bottom right, Jim Harter, ed., *Men, A Pictorial Archive from Nineteenth-Century Sources*. New York: Dover, 1980

Page 137, Photos from P. Ekman and W. F. Friesen, *Pictures of Facial Affect*. Palo Alto, California: Consulting Psychologists Press, 1976. Copyright Paul Ekman

Page 139, Jim Harter, ed., *Men, A Pictorial Archive from Nineteenth-Century Sources*. New York: Dover, 1980

Page 141, The Vigeland Sculpture Park, Oslo, Norway (*Father, Mother, and Child* by Gustav Vigeland)

Page 143, The Metropolitan Museum of Art, Rogers Fund, 1960 (60.30) (*The Fortune Teller* by Georges de La Tour)

Page 146, AP/Wide World Photos

Page 154, The Cleveland Museum of Art, Purchase, Leonard C. Hanna, Jr., Bequest (limestone raised relief of king's scribe Amenhotep and wife Renut with three members of family, c. 1275 B.C., Egyptian)

Page 156, Jim Harter, ed., *Animals: 1419 Copyright-free Illustrations of Mammals, Birds, Fish, Insects, etc.* New York: Dover, 1979

Page 157, top, The Museum of Modern Art/Film Stills Archives

Page 157, bottom, Helen Keller, *The Story of My Life*. New York: Doubleday, 1954

Page 161, Bowles and Carver, *Catchpenny Prints, 163 Popular Engravings from the Eighteenth Century*, New York: Dover, 1970

Page 167, Carol Belanger Grafton, ed., *Humorous Victorian Spot Illustrations*. New York: Dover, 1985

Page 172, The Metropolitan Museum of Art, Gift of Robert E. Tod, 1929 (29.36) (detail of a court robe, late nineteenth century, Chinese)

Page 178, Orsay (Jeu de Paume)/Lauros-Giraudon/Art Resource (*La Famille Bellelli* by Edgar Degas)

Page 181, The Cleveland Museum of Art, Purchased from income J. H. Wade Fund (*Little Flower of Love* by Giovanni Battista Piazzetta)

Page 183, Harold H. Hart, *The Illustrator's Handbook*. New York: Hart, 1978

Page 186, Jim Harter, ed. *Women, A Pictorial Archive from Nineteenth-Century Sources*. New York: Dover, 1982

Page 187, © Estate of Grant Wood/V.A.G.A., New York/Cincinnati Art Museum, The Edwin and Virginia Irwin Memorial (1959.46) (*Daughters of Revolution* by Grant Wood)

Page 197, The Metropolitan Museum of Art, The Michael C. Rockefeller Memorial Collection, Gift of Nelson A. Rockefeller, 1968 and Purchase, Nelson A. Rockefeller Gift, 1967 (1978.412.1516) (Mixed media sculpture, nineteenth–twentieth century, Papua, New Guinea)

Page 202, National Gallery of Art, Washington, DC, Samuel H. Kress Collection (Central panel of triptych, *The Fall of Man*, workshop of Albrecht Altdorfer)

Page 215, Jim Harter, ed. *Women, A Pictorial Archive from Nineteenth-Century Sources*. New York: Dover, 1982

Page 219, The Saint Louis Art Museum, Museum Purchase (*The Country School* by Winslow Homer)

Page 221, Layton Art Collection, Milwaukee Art Museum (*The Sawdust Trail* by George Bellows)

Page 222, Jim Harter, ed., *Men, A Pictorial Archive from Nineteenth-Century Sources*. New York: Dover, 1980

Page 231, The Vigeland Sculpture Park, Oslo, Norway (detail of *Father, Mother, and Child* by Gustav Vigeland)

Page 232, National Gallery of Art, Washington, DC, Andrew W. Mellon Fund (*The Copley Family* by John Singleton Copley)

Page 235, Collection, The Museum of Modern Art, New York, Advisory Committee Fund (*The Family* by Marisol)

Page 242, Copyright Sylvia Johnson 1981/Woodfin Camp & Associates

Page 245, National Museum of American Art, Smithsonian Institution, Transfer from the U.S. Department of the Interior, National Park Service

Page 246, © Danny Lyon/Magnum Photos, Inc.

Page 247, AP/Wide World Photos

Page 248, © Lynne Jaeger Weinstein 1985/Woodfin Camp & Associates

Page 251, © Jane Scherr/Jeroboam, Inc.

Page 254, Jost Amman, *293 Renaissance Woodcuts for Artists and Illustrators*. New York: Dover, 1968

Pages 256 and 257, Sean Shesgreen, ed., *Engravings by Hogarth: 101 Prints*. New York: Dover, 1973

Page 258, © Michal Heron 1983/Woodfin Camp & Associates

Page 264, The Brooklyn Museum, Museum Collection Fund (*Paul Helleu Sketching with His Wife* by John Singer Sargent)

Page 269, Jost Amman, *293 Renaissance Woodcuts for Artists and Illustrators*. New York: Dover, 1968

Page 274, Harold H. Hart, *The Illustrator's Handbook*. New York: Hart, 1978

Page 279, © Eli Reed/Magnum Photos, Inc.

Page 282, National Gallery of Art, Washington, DC, Chester Dale Collection (*The Lovers* by Pablo Picasso)

Page 285, Carol Belanger Grafton, ed., *Humorous Victorian Spot Illustrations*. New York: Dover, 1985

Page 286, Ken Heyman

Page 289, Jim Goldberg/Archive Pictures, Inc.

Page 294, The Metropolitan Museum of Art, George A. Hearn Fund, 1956 (*Government Bureau* by George Tooker)

Page 297, Collection, The Museum of Modern Art, New York, Gift of Mme. Paul Klee (*Two Men Meet, Each Believing the Other to Be of Higher Rank* by Paul Klee)

Page 298, © 1987 The Art Institute of Chicago, All rights reserved. Helen Birch Bartlett Memorial Collection, 1928.610 (*At the Moulin Rouge* by Henri de Toulouse-Lautrec, 1892, oil on canvas, 123.0 x 141.0 cm)

Page 301, Collection Walker Art Center, Minneapolis, Gift of the T. B. Walker Foundation, Gilbert M. Walker Fund, 1948 (*Office at Night* by Edward Hopper)

Page 302, Jim Harter, ed., *Men, A Pictorial Archive from Nineteenth-Century Sources*. New York: Dover, 1980

Page 305, Copyright Herve Gloaguen/VIVA 1978/Woodfin Camp & Associates

Page 308, Jim Harter, ed. *Women, A Pictorial Archive from Nineteenth-Century Sources*. New York: Dover, 1982

Page 310, Henry Art Gallery, University of Washington, Gift of the Artist (*The Builders No. 1* by Jacob Lawrence)

Page 313, Jim Harter, ed., *Music, A Pictorial Archive of Woodcuts and Engravings*. New York: Dover, 1980

Page 315, Jim Harter, ed. *Men, A Pictorial Archive from Nineteenth-Century Sources*. New York: Dover, 1980

Page 316, Jim Harter, ed. *Music, A Pictorial Archive of Woodcuts and Engravings*. New York: Dover, 1980

Page 317, The Saint Louis Art Museum, Museum Purchase (*The County Election* by George Caleb Bingham)

Page 322, Rose Art Museum, Brandeis University, Gevirtz-Mnuchin Purchase Fund (*Forget It! Forget Me!* by Roy Lichtenstein)

Page 325, AP/Wide World Photos

Page 328, Leonard Freed/Magnum Photos, Inc.

Page 329, National Gallery of Art, Washington, DC, Andrew W. Mellon Fund (*Preliminaries to the Big Bout* by George Wesley Bellows)

Page 331, Jim Harter, ed., *Animals: 1419 Copyright-free Illustrations of Mammals, Birds, Fish, Insects, etc.* New York: Dover, 1979

Page 332, National Cowboy Hall of Fame Collection, Oklahoma City (*The Quarrel* by Frederic Remington)

Page 335, Photo: The Museum of Modern Art/Film Stills Archives. Courtesy of Warner Bros.